You Can Go Home Again

You Can Go Home Again

To my dear, dear
friends from Beacon,
forever grateful
for the prayers
Jim M[illegible]

James F. McGowan Jr.

Library of Congress Number:		2004195042
ISBN :·	Hardcover	1-4134-7921-9
	Softcover	1-4134-7920-0

This book was printed in the United States of America.

To order additional copies of this book, contact:
Xlibris Corporation
1-888-795-4274
www.Xlibris.com
Orders@Xlibris.com
23789

CONTENTS

For my Father
My peace is his peace

Foreward

A friend told me about a Disney cartoon character named Stanley who carries around this huge book, *Stanley's Book of Everything.* Well . . . welcome to "Jimmy's Book of Everything."

I've really tried and tried to shorten this up and to tone her down. Honest. You may find it hard to believe, but what you see here is about 60 pages shorter than the original. I've re-edited and re-edited, purged and purged, paid a couple of editors to help me do some more, I'd hoped a 'traditional' publisher would take me on so they could help with the chore—but alas it did not happen. "It's good, it's well written", these are some of the things I heard. One editor from New York even called it *wonderful.* But "memoir just does not sell" was always the final verdict. Thus the self-publishing folk called *Xlibris* and quite a bit of my own money to get this thing printed.

But this is not just memoir—it is memoir mainly in the form of a journal. And being a journal, written by a guy with a not-particularly organized way of thinking, there is very much a 'stream of consciousness-meandering-all over the place' feel to it. I beg you not be too put off by it. I beg you meander along with me, to perhaps put aside your linear, organized way of thinking and just join me on the wild ride the journey/journal became. Reading this and not being too taken back by the circuitous lack of cohesion might be good practice actually. For in the grasp of the non-linear commodity of spirituality or awareness or interconnectedness (or however you want to term it) is where we find the wherewithal, oomph or chutzpah to work through the linear '*day-after-day*'s of our lives.

So enjoy; if the journal gets too confusing or disconnected, skip or speed-read through. Bounce around; go back and forth, do whatever. There IS some pretty neat, revolutionary even, thought in here. There is even some closure by the end. Only some though—for in reality, among the wondrous myriad of things life presents, resolved dilemmas and permanently closed items are not among them. A resolved dilemma or an item closed gives birth to new items and new dilemmas. Hegel was right on with that one. The endless cycle of death and rebirth found in our physical world surely is mirrored in our human interactions. We keep flowing along—that's the constant.

One further note; I have changed my real last name as author of this book. A good friend named Pat F., a long term member (and server) in my local *Alcoholics Anonymous* area told me that in speaking so much about AA here, I would be in violation of some of their traditions if I were to use my real last name. SO in the interest of protecting my personal anonymity, and that of certain of my family and friends, my last name and those of certain others, are changed here. If anyone wants to find out my (or our) real name, there is an audit trail bigger than the Appalachian if they choose to bother. But bother they shouldn't, this is an everyman tale anyway.

A wonderful one-minute meditation by Anthony de Mello, an Eastern Indian Jesuit whose thought and philosophy you will find scads of in the ensuing pages, frames the matter perfectly.

AUTONOMY

> *The Master seemed quite impervious to what people thought of him. When the disciples asked how he had attained this stage of inner freedom, he laughed aloud and said, "Till I was twenty I did not care what people thought of me. After twenty I worried endlessly about what my neighbors thought. Then one day after fifty I suddenly saw that they hardly ever thought of me at all."*

Preface/Prelude

Postscript as Preface
October 16, 2003

On the night of the day I was so hurt and perturbed from all the rejection and indifference I was near ready to give up on the entire book project, I had a dream.

As surreal as it was in content, it *felt* that real. I was THERE.

I was in colonial times. The enemy was approaching, I had to stay behind for a spell but didn't have to stay as long as I did, but because I did, they arrived before I could get out. A person I knew who was kind of in with them but really on our side was on the advance of them coming into where I was. He just winked at me. Then I was outside. Marching up were all sorts of guys I at first thought were good guys, with blue American uniforms, but then I realized the uniforms were these blue/red hybrid things. The flag too was an indistinguishable mix. I thought if I panned out from the main column, I'd get by them. But I realized that would not work. Thinner columns of 'them' had panned out also. What I HAD to do was go tell George Washington something.

Next thing I was in the town and many of the guys were dressed up like baseball players—sort of. I knew I was in a different era. A good friend (that I know from the real world) was there. When I told him I was moving about no longer stuck in time, and that some girl that I'd seen in a dead-zonish-type vision was going to get shot, he said, "we've been waiting for you to join us. Now you know what I've been talking about". But when I told him of the girl who was going to get shot, he asked, "do you KNOW the girl?" When I said 'sort of', he said that was not good enough . . . . that my not knowing her meant it was fantasy and not real—particularly being that the girl was attractive.

Then I was awake. Wide. No lingering about half asleep. I got up immediately up to write down the dream.

Meaning? I turn to portions of the entry from six weeks ago that was supposed to close this book.

Labor Day
September 1, 2003

The 'sacred feminine'.

It's a cold rainy Labor Day here in Philly. This year, at a time when Mars is so very visible in the night sky, it landed exactly on September 1. Schools will start early. The summer draws to an abrupt close.

I spent most of my Labor Day weekend down in good old Ocean City, NJ. In a day and a half, I read all 450 pages of Dan Brown's fascinating The DaVinci Code. (Sure wish I could write something that page-turnable!)

Brown's hero and heroine search for the Holy Grail and its link to the sacred feminine we seem to have lost. I wonder if all of the Blessed Mother's recent visitations have anything to do with that lost sacre-fem. I think of the East Indian saint called Amma whose minstry involves literally hugging the tens of thousands who come to see her. I think of her powerful and moving talk of 'motherly love'.

In the epilogue of another wonderful book I read a while back, William Hallahan's The Day the American Revolution Began, we are told some historians suggest if the colonists had adopted a plan by a moderate Pennsylvanian named Galloway, that the American Revolution could have been avoided . . . that America could eventually have become a self-

governing part of the British Empire like Canada. Furthermore, they conjectured if there was no American Revolt, there need not have been a French one—and the turn of events that led to the 20th century's two world wars might have been avoided. But alas we cannot change history.

The DaVinci Code suggests something a lot of biblical scholars do—that the subjective process that kept some books in and many others out of the official Bible was hardly God-inspired . . . that Christendom became a male-dominant, aggressive institution far removed from the real message of Jesus. I agree with that appraisal like 100%. Again we can't change history.

Near 40 years ago, a saint of a man they called Pope John XXVIII, started the process of trying to right that far-too-old wrong. On January 24, 2001 in Assisi Italy, a congregation of leaders from most of the world's religions, including the Dali Lama and the head of the Muslim and Jewish churches, all accepted John Paul II's invitation to join together to pray for peace. A meeting, I feel, a step very much in that same literally, beatific, direction. As I think of the fall off in grace and progress from that meeting to last Holy Thursday's 'back to the past' encyclical that, among other things, reiterated the Church policy that Catholics cannot receive sacraments in other churches, I literally shudder.

In Brown's exactly current fictional account, a new liberal pope pulls the rug out from under the archconservative Opus Dei's of the Catholic world. The fact that Rome is stacking the deck with conservative cardinals insuring our next pope will be one in line with the prevailing hard line stance, makes 'the Code's proposition seem very much like wishful-thinking.

As the Pentecostals save, and the Muslim, Jewish and Catholic hard liners grow in power and influence, as we continue to rape and pillage our world and its people in a baccanalian orgy of self-gratification, I wonder exactly where we are headed. Are we straying even farther from the will of that Father Jesus spoke so frequently about? I think of another book, Diarmund O'Murchu's Quantum Theology which suggests that if we do not change our ways, it will take a newly evolved people to carry out God's plan—that within a hundred years or so, via violence or pollution we will have annhialted ourselves.

The AA 'rooms' will have a new influx of folk in the coming weeks. Happens every year. "After Labor Day, I'm gonna quit". I said it myself a lot of my years 'out there'. The few who grow to truly work the program our founders laid out for us, will chase that God's will thing, and will not only never drink or drug again, they will also know a peace hard to describe. They will reverse a trend of relapse and death that is currently running rampart in our fellowship.

They say it will be near 87 years before anyone will be able to see Mars the way we saw it this week. I wonder if enough of us follow our Destiny so that there still will be anyone around to watch.

The dream and the epilogue? Did the blue/red soldiers represent Galloway's moderate plan? Was it John Paul II and not George Washington to whom I had to get a message? Is he the one I *know*, who shortly is going to die? And is history, and his 'inner circle', drawing him away from the plan God, or Destiny, has for him?

I saw a headline the other day . . . *"Inner Circle" tightens as pope's health fades*. I think of the literary agent, the first one who declined an early raw edition of this book, who is also John Paul's agent. I think of the scene in the Francis of Assisi biography, *Brother Sun, Sister Moon*, where the pope has a change of heart, ignores his cardinals and embraces the poor and disheveled Francis. I think of my preposterous presumption. I think of this book and my desperate struggle to make it work. I think of how desperately I need help.

I think of a poem I wrote several years ago . . . a poem that, like yesterday's dream, came to me in the middle of the night . . . only days after the escape described below.

The will to go on . . . .

When tweaked by ev'ry prick and thorn
when the only love you know is lorn
when you're surely sure you can't go o-en
. . . . it is then you know that I'll be there . . . .

When winds in face and n'er in back
when all the rest seem'n mode-attack
when the will to go you simply lack
. . . . it is then you know that I'll be there . . .

And so you go when gut says no
tho you feel beneath a place called low
you go because somehow you know
. . . 'tis then fo sho . . . that I'll be there

* * *

On the first Monday of April 2000, in a typical *Day's Inn* room, I sat dejected and despairing. About 36 hours prior I had had near six months of continuous sobriety. For that long, I was on the right side in my ongoing struggle with my addiction. The day had been scheduled off so I could put the finishing touches on the new draft of a final capstone project that was all that stood in the way of a master's degree from the University of Pennsylvania. That degree and severance package I was to receive for the layoff I had been sort of promised, were to be my ticket to ride from the hospital finance job I'd had for over 17 years. I was going to live my dream, go to Ireland and write a book.

But on that bleak Monday evening, the capstone, the layoff and the future were in an orbit far away. The mother-lode of my ATM card sitting in my office drawer some 3-5 miles away was the only thing drawing me . . . it and the money it could supply so that the pipe sitting next to me could be refilled with the substance that was destroying my life. A miracle of sorts happened that night. My "please dear God, do not let me go get that card," prayer was answered. As I said that prayer though, the strangest thing happened—a flickering image of my great grandmother came to me. Somehow, some way, an image or a thought of my great grandmother, Sarah—a centerpiece of the family history capstone project and the book it was going to become—joined me in that desolate room. But there were certainly no great white light or any feeling of deliverance—there was no sense of triumph. In fact as I trudged out the room, I was even annoyed at the choice I had made. When one is on crack cocaine run, it rarely ends if there is any means to continue. But when I got into my car and headed north towards home and not south towards the card, the run was over. The rewrite of the capstone paper was begun the very next day. The original, with the anti-Joyce, anti-godless-intellectual rants that had been vociferously rejected by my primary reader, was scratched. The resultant paper was probably a better one anyway—one more in tune with the limited scope of the capstone. Six weeks to the day after I escaped the Day's Inn, I sat in a rainy, miserable Franklin Field with the other graduates. If there were five people older than myself sitting there, that was a lot—there certainly weren't ten.

About two months after the graduation ceremony, approximately 100 days in the warm sun of sobriety, marked the spot as I closed a very early morning journal entry with the notation "I am so confused, so confused!" The reigning confusion seemed to be about my future and the layoff package that had been withdrawn. And as I fretted with the idea of walking away from a safe secure job, again came the deadly siren call of my addiction. By that day's end I would be $600 poorer and would again be sitting alone with a dry pipe in a hotel room. I'd visit the insanity only one more time. And at mass on that August 15's, Feast of the Assumption, Mary's inclusion of "He will confuse the mind of the proud" in her *Magnificat* chant of "all the things the Lord will do," revealed the *real* source of my confusion. It seems the re-embrace of the faith of my youth, to which my recovery had led me, had also unfortunately brought with it a veil of pride . . . a different pride than the cock-sure strut of things and sexual conquests that mark our world and unfortunately also many of today's AA rooms, but one nonetheless. A week later I'd walk the steep hill at a Kentucky retreat house called Gethsemani. There, at the foot of a statue of Jesus kneeling on a rock, my brief "Lord take away the pride" prayer was answered to the extent that I have not had to get loaded since. My spiritual pride that was so difficult to discern, has been dislodged to at least that degree.

On the day I boarded the plane to go to Ireland the following February, my sobriety meter read exactly 6 months. (The job—*sans* the layoff package!—had been bid adieu to ten days prior.) It is still ticking. There is no reason it need ever be reset again. That very first night in Ireland I began the journal. That journal what was to supply the 'over there' info for the *From Whence They Came* chapter of the linear '1876 until the present' account of my family and me, became the bulk of the book. The fertility of the 47 days I spent in Ireland almost forced an account of this type on me. Foot and mouth disease struck while I was there. The ongoing controversy regarding the Irish Republic's president Mary McAleese receiving communion in an Irish Anglican Church raged. The bishop leading the assault on Mary (so to speak) was made a cardinal while I was there. In America another Columbine occurred; the stock market crashed, the "Celtic Tiger" feeling the heat. The Irish North/South peace process seemed stalled. Then I came home and kept the journal going for a while—the times and my life still seemed so rich. Life—rich or poor, full or empty, however, choogles along. Books end. The taming of this wild tale has gone on far longer and was far more difficult than I ever dreamed it would be. The time comes when the author has to simply get the book between the covers. That time has come.

As for my family, the people in that picture on the cover, although I did not end up writing specifically *their* history, it is very necessary to add that everything I write and did become, I lay humbly and gratefully at their reverent feet. (Perhaps their story is another book.) For it was in the safe cocoon of their faith and love, *both* devotional and experiential . . . that I came to be, and then, after my life sent me careening far and low, to be set free from the bonds of painful and deadly addictions. If you feel there is not enough of them in these pages, I apologize; likewise if you feel those depths to which I did traverse, dishonors their memory. But I hope that is not the case. I hope you can bask, with me, in the glow of my escape, of my freedom . . . . a freedom I truly believe I'd not have know, had I not been of their lineage.

So forward Christian soldiers (*and non-Christian civilians you too*—as I said in a poem one time.) Next we *march* through the century before I land in the loving lap of Erin, of Cavan, and of the very real first journey of the rest of my life . . .

Book I

Walk through a Century—
The Planting of the Seed

". . . and bring out the fatted calf here and kill it, and let us eat and be merry, for this my son was dead and is alive again . . . he was lost and is found."
Luke 15: 23-24

1904

Port Richmond
Philadelphia, Pa. USA

"For God's sake, where is Sadey?" From the passenger seat in the very crowded carriage, Peter, bellowed.

"She was just out back . . . I'll go get her." Owen, the eldest volunteered.

"She best not have dirtied up that beautiful dress she's wearing!" Sarah, her weary mother offered from the seat next to Peter.

An excited, *still* clean and polished little Sade, latched onto Owen's hand, soon came down the driveway. The family portrait picture trip was finally underway.

Sarah's mind drifted to another trip—one taken 28 years earlier—on a far more crowded and less gentile vehicle, the trip from Ireland to this wonderful yet so different new world called America. In 28 years they had made it in a very big way. Peter's successful masonry business had netted them this new big brick house on Monmouth St; the clothes she and her family wore were distinguished and proper. The abject poverty she (and he) had left behind, and that they'd known in their early days here, was history now. The brash little guy with the big moustache, in a sense had made good on his promise that he was going to achieve great things in the new land.

How many times now had she heard him tell the tale of how, the first time he'd seen her, he knew she would be his bride? First on the long-two-day trip from Cavan to Cove, then on the hellacious voyage across the great Atlantic . . . my how that little West Cavanite could spin a yarn! Though they officially parted company after landing, he going off to a waiting brother, she to the employ of Mrs. Sweeney, he never really stopped wooing her. And he was already doing quite well by the time, six years later, when she allowed him to put the ring on her finger.

Owen came only 15 months after. (Was amazing it took *that* long, the ferocity of his . . . well . . . .) Owen would do well taking over the role as patriarch. Charming, handsome, kind, steadfast—the right woman would smooth out the edges.

James came a year-and-a-half later—he was the kindest and the gentlest, even more so than the girls, but he was also somewhat timid and sickly—she wondered how he would handle the future. Two years later, Frank, brilliant and studious, with an already accomplished eye at the easy money. But he tended to fits of petulance and melancholy . . . if the world treated him badly, she hoped he could take it. Then little Benny, quiet and kind, but already a follower. And the two little ones Eddie and Pete—what mischievous hand fulls they were! And Eddie, even just past infancy—already a wheeler and dealer. Pete slower but every bit as ready to take the easier path.

All the boys really—one need only look to none of them taking on the hard labor trade of their father to find this frightening New World commitment to non-work. And after what we went through! Perhaps we made things too easy on them.

And the girls: Mame—named for Mary and rightfully so . . . her great capacity for kindness and charity already so apparent. That almost sad smile—perhaps in the way Mary's was told her heart would be pierced by what they would do to her son, Mame feels the stings of a world that seems to be growing colder. Then Anne also charitable, but smart, so very smart . . . and like the smart ones often are, too reluctant to bend. And Little Sadie—named for me, I guess that is also appropriate . . . what an independent spirit! She is an American, I suppose, in every sense of the word.

Then poor little Catherine. I should not have succumbed to the 'ferocity' that time . . . one-and-a-half years of life is far too short. But at least we got to know and love her. She rests in the bosom of God now, soon enough our time together will last forever.

But such forlorn musings are not for now. This is a happy occasion. How many Irish families can afford to have a professional portrait taken? In fine clothes and traveling in a fine carriage, no less. It is for us to put on only the happy face. Who knows where this picture will end up?

The picture ended up on a wall in Ellis Island and in the American Folk Part in Omagh, North Ireland . . . on the cover of the video and two different 1998 glossies about the Irish in America . . . in countless frames on many tables and walls from Philadelphia to the West Cavan spot in Ireland that Peter left behind.

Owen, my grandfather, is in the far right corner. He would be called 'the Chief'. His brother Frank is next to him. (His grand daughter, my cousin Maureen, was the one the one who took the photo to the to ethnic history institute called the Balche. They made it available to the world.) Brother Jim is next over. Bennie stands on the end. At the bottom, like two little bookends, are Eddie on the left, and Peter on the right.

The girls: Ann on the left of center, Mary on the right. Sade sits at the bottom. Mom and dad, Peter and Sarah, honored always, sit in the middle.

1927

Port Richmond
October 25

"I hope you are proud of me grandmom. I was steadfast today. The tears I kept to a minimum. Dad tried so very hard, but he was so shaken. Grandpop was a mess. My tears I feel more now. 'In the silence of your room', Jesus once told his disciples is where they should go to pray . . . perhaps it is that way for me. For if ever anything was a prayer, it is this. My world will be so much emptier without you. Be with me, granny, please. Continue to guide me and enlighten me . . . let me continue to be amused by the memories. NOW I can tell you I know you fixed the board when I got good enough to beat you at checkers!

It is an awkward time to lose you. I am as good a student as any at Nativity—you should be very proud. But next year it is on to high school—on to high school and out of Richmond, give me your strength and wisdom that I may carry on."

James the second son of Owen, and my father, offered this prayer on the day they buried his grandmother. The family was still physically close that windy October day—that Peter had bequeathed $1,000 to each of his married children if they laid roots within a mile of the Monmouth Street home had taken care of that. Yet a large piece of the heart of the clan was removed from their mortal world. But Sarah had fought the good fight, all of her progeny were imbued with ideal of love of God and neighbor . . . and of the indelible connection the two involved. Like a flame that never extinguishes, her light would carry on to many a generation.

1935

Center City Philadelphia
November

"Aunt Irene? How are things up there in Brooklyn? I miss you very much. Well actually I hate to be making this call, but it's cold down here in dad's little apartment, there's no food in the refrigerator, and I'm not sure if me and Jady can make it through another winter like this. Last year was very tough."

My mother, Florence Rivers, a freshman that year in *Hallahan Catholic High School for Girls*, was the one making the call. Her sister Jady was two years older. Her dad wasn't there. He wasn't there a lot. Aunt Irene was their mother's sister who took my mom in each summer. Another aunt took Jady. Having lost their bed-ridden mother to tuberculosis at least 5 years previous, and with a dangerously negligent father their only adult authority, my mom and her sister's lot was a scary one. Before long a very distant aunt and Cork, Ireland native by the name of Ellen O'Driscoll-Connelly-Caldavala, who was running a boarding home in West Philadelphia, became the ward and guardian of young Florence and Jady. "Aunt Nell" had hardly had an easy life herself—the real love of her life, a tall handsome Irishman named Connelly had been killed while working on the railroad—and with no unions or pension or disability to speak of in those 'robber baron' days of America, she was given nothing to raise her two children. But as was the way in 1930's America, people made further sacrifices to do what needed to be done. By whatever means possible, two more seats were set at the dinner table each night for the two young ladies from downtown. Alas much more than food and lodging was given them, for the first time a female presence took a sustained part in their rearing. And what a presence it was! Real live Irish, wit, wisdom, and 'no shoes on the table'—type superstition became very much a part of who, at least, my mom, would become. It was probably from her Aunt Nell, where my mom learned to spin a positive yarn regardless of the situation around her.

For certain though, my maternal grandmom, likewise, surely had an effect on the life of her younger daughter. Laying in bed, wincing in pain, clutching her rosaries and speaking to her beloved St. Anthony is the major memory my mom had of her mom. Well mom apparently inherited the love of the rosary—*and* that devotion to St. Anthony. I have an older brother named Tony as living proof.

Promises made and vows spoken, however, mean less when factual circumstance prevents their being kept. Mom was able to make good on her promise to St Ant that if my dad made it home from WWII safe, to name her first-born son after him. Likewise if my family had not been from Philadelphia where all the way up to the late '60's, Catholic grade *and high* schools were free, my bon vivant 'starving artist' maternal grand dad would not have been able to make good on his deathbed promise to the elder Florence Rivers to send their two girls to Catholic school. And if they had never made it to Hallahan, my mom would not have become best friends with a statuesque brown-haired beauty from Port Richmond named Elizabeth Martin. If she'd not met her, she'd never have been introduced to the first cousin of Betty's boyfriend. Both the cousins were named Jim McGowan, and they were so close my Uncle Paul, who would eventually wed my dad's sister Natalie, once said, "I dated Nat for a year before I asked her why she had two brother's named Jim."

Prayers answered? Vows kept? As my mom called up to Brooklyn that day, the powder keg that was our world, would soon explode into a conflict they called World War II. It was a changed-forever world, but only around eight years later when a mysterious 'something' came to my dad during a mortar attack in North Africa. Seems during this attack, he jumped into a foxhole, perfect cover for anything but a hit directly on his back. The instinctive feeling to get up and move to the less secure cover behind a rock, provided him a vantage point to see a poor comrade literally jump into his grave, as the improbable direct hit became reality. "I wore out that statue praying for your father during the war," mom once told me regards the St Anthony statue in the basement church of St. John's right down in the heart of Philly's center city. I wonder how much influence St Tony, specifically had on my dad's thought-process that life-saving moment.

The twists of fate, the tick tocks of time that mark our destinies.

1940

December 24
Port Richmond
Philadelphia, Pa

"Jesus Christ, Jimmy! Are you trying to kill me here!" Natalie screeched as she tottered on the ladder, Christmas ball in hand. The ensuing hug of her older brother Jim was one for the record books.

"But you said you weren't coming back for Christmas!"

"Nat you've never known loneliness like being in a room at a Y in New York City as the holidays swirled all around you. I had to come home."

But it was more than that. The loneliness was a huge part of it . . . but the bigger part was my father knew the time had come to mend the fence with his dad. The last letter, the 'I'm sorry too, son' one, had torn him apart. There in the glorious hills of Graymoor, under the care of the firm but saintly Fr. St John the Baptist, he'd fired the first blast of apology dialogue at the wall of resentment and silence that had grown between them. As he'd said his prayers and done his chores, and wandered about the hills, Fr. John's advice haunted him. 'What was it that Jesus had said? 'If you come to make an offering at the temple but have a feud to resolve with your neighbor, leave the offering, make your amend, then come back to the temple'. The right or wrong part was not the issue. Finally he knew that. His dad was in pain . . . six years later mom's death still plagued him. The petulant 'did you ever think what it would have been like if I had died and not mom?' from the letter in September, was a dead giveaway. 'The Chief" had big bulging chinks in his armor.

And the extra beers down at Byrne's Tavern neither fixed the chinks nor took away the pain. A man lost without his woman, just like his grandpa had been . . . I wonder if that is why Fr St John told him a vocation was not for him . . . . maybe, he thought, I'm more like dad than I'd like to admit. "But there sure as hell ain't no Natalie in *my* life! Heck there ain't even a job!"

Owen McGowan, my grandfather, died on October 30, 1941. He and my father had 10 months ro cement their amend. The only time my mother, who had met my father not long after he'd come home from New York, would see Owen would be in his coffin.

1959

December 22
Resurrection of Our Lord School
Philadelphia, Pa

The wait seemed endless. The smell of wet, woolen jackets and bodies sweating inside them filled the school basement where we waited. I was not a 'bus' kid . . . I walked the approximate mile to and from school most days, but this day, because of a big snowstorm, we all had to wait to get transportation home. And we non-bus kids, who had no mom or dad at home with a car to get us, had to wait until the bus kids routes had been ran, until we got our rides home.

But I didn't mind at all. It was a snapshot memory of a time when the happiness seemed boundless. I was in second grade and actually kind of liked school. The allure of *new* had not yet worn off and sweet, kind, tall Sister Rita Damien was my teacher. My belief in Santa Claus was pretty much on the way out that afternoon—as soon as logic entered the Santa saga, the gig was pretty much up. A nudge from next door neighbor, Tommy Beaver, on the way to school one day, got the mental 'but how is he going to get from Europe and Mexico and everywhere to MY house in one night?' juices flowing, and thus 2nd grade was the last year even the hint of belief was still around. But the seep of the Santa legend did nothing to dim the euphoria I felt that day. Like a cooing babe nestled in his mother's arms, my belief in the Other Christmas Story—with the angels singing and the shepherds and wise men and sheep and cows et al paying homage to the little baby Jesus who was the Savior of the World—held me sweetly in place that snowy December afternoon. Times were still good then; a new Ford every two years, a week or two down the Jersey shore—God was being good to us, because we were being good to Him. Christmas morning was a hailstorm of ripped wrapping paper and opened boxes and 'wow look at this, and wow look at that'. I knew that scene was just a few days away as I waited for that bus home to the hot chocolate I also knew would be waiting. That Christmas was probably the whitest one I ever knew. We were as safe and secure as those little winter scene figurine things you shook up and the snow came falling.

Alas though, a decade was ending. The kindly bald guy they called Ike who used to golf a lot, seemed like the Santa Claus of a government that made it possible for us to live the life we led. I doubt at the time I even knew of segregation; the marches and the battle for equality had not yet begun. There were stories in the Sunday papers about Laos and the Far East, and maps with one country colored this and another colored that, but they really meant nothing to me. We did have our little air raid drills in school and such, but they seemed more like a break from the mundane class work, then preparation for something horrible that was going to happen. In our hearts we knew we really were safe. The sweet blind faith of youth had me under her wings.

1965

June 14
Connie Mack Stadium
Philadelphia, Pa.

It was a hot sultry night and my dad and me were there when an immensely talented African-American third baseman named Richie Allen ripped a grand slam over the giant scoreboard in right center field. The blast earned our beloved Phillies a split of the twi-night double header versus the real good San Francisco Giant team of Mays, McCovey and Cepada. Not many hitters, especially right-handed ones, cranked balls *over* that massive scoreboard—so we were there for a somewhat historic moment in Philadelphia Phillie baseball lore . . . . a lore that unfortunately is and was one of monumental futility. Indeed no team in any sport, in any game, in any league, has throughout history, lost as many games as the 'fightin Phils'. And as we sat there that night, only nine months had passed since the "Great Collapse" of 64. Allen was the "Rookie of the Year" for that team and he was one of the few players who did not completely choke during the awful ten game losing streak—a stretch that, in a sense, was a microcosm of their dubious history. Nearly every fan remembers . . . a 6.5 game lead that disintegrated in the last three weeks of the season . . . before or since I've never cried so much. I don't know how many strips of "already bought-never to be used" World Series tickets would cross my brow that fall.

By June the following year, the mirage that '64 team had been, was not yet completely exposed. The Phils were still somewhat in the hunt—about 5 games out of first. They'd fade by the end of the season, eventually drifting back to their usual spot as the bottom of the standings . . . where they'd remain until a late 70's renaissance, that in 1980, would finally net them their *only* world championship in near 125 years of existence.

But as Allen's moon shot disappeared into the North Philly night, the seeds of racial hatred and discontent that would three year later, turn many 'hoods just like this one into war zones, had already taken root in the Phillies clubhouse. A big burly white outfielder named Frank Thomas would either that summer or the next have a racial slur induced baseball bat swinging brawl with Allen. Another white/black clubhouse brawl, between a big black outfielder named Wes Covington and a bigger white catcher named Gus Triandos, was nowhere near as publicized as the Allen/Thomas one, but it happened—and all of it spoke volumes of the simmering discontent in the Phils clubhouse.

As I look back, that twi-nighter was probably the last time my dad, as my *dad,* took me to a ball game. For a different Diaspora was taking place in the McGovern household. It seemed mostly a financial one—my dad had lost his successful floor-covering salesman job and was bouncing from one poor-paying, time-consuming retail sales job to the next and thus there was no room in the family budget for ball games and all that went with them—but it was certainly more than that. The 'times' were indeed a changin. I had just graduated from grade school then, the hurt that I'd not been invited to any of the graduation 'make-out' parties, still no doubt simmering between my ears. The "Happy Days" at Reso were over—the perils of puberty shaking the gates of my safe little world. The changing attitudes regarding sex and morality would deluge me from the tube, the movies and the tales I'd hear from my fellows. It seemed my instincts and the world pulled me one way, my naiveté' and my religious upbringing, the other. Through jagged, incongruent seams the tear would ravel. It wound take many years and many tears until I would learn that the schism was a bogus one—that the sacred meld of heart and soul *and* body was not only possible, but that it was as natural as it was wholesome.

The all all-boys Catholic High School I'd go to that September had a near 3,000-member student body as big as I was small. I'd drift from my grade school crowd to one around the plays and the stage crew. I'd eschew the personal invite of the kind, warm priest who ran the plays, and stay on the crew (even though, then AND NOW, I had no clue how to wield a hammer or such!) I'd choose to not go join the school paper, even though I always liked to write. Gonna, coulda, shoulda—'twas very early on that cha-cha became the major dance step of my life. I'd skip the proms, because I was too afraid to ask anyone to be my date. What was the name of the friend of my buddy's date? Donnabella? She was waiting for my call even, but somehow it never came.

Gonna/Shoulda. At the end of my high school days, via this guy who knew that guy, who knew that guy, I'd drift to a new crowd . . . a fun, funny verbal crew that loved to drink beer.

1970

St Joseph's College
Philadelphia, Pa

"So you really think less of me because I still go to church?"

"Well yeah. But it's not just the going to church, it's the going because you have to. I mean do you ever get anything out of it?"

Mike had a point. It had been a long time since 'I got something out of it'. I just went because I was used to going. Plus it sure was no picnic lately getting up after a hall party or whatever and then going to Church on Sunday morning. That I was not forced a few times as I was sleeping off a real bad load was very cool indeed. Mom and dad are, I guess, letting me move on.

But there were other things. Reading Joyce's *Portrait of the Artist as a Young Man* last summer put a real floodlight on all the hypocrisy of ol' Mother Church. But I surely ain't no Joyce. I am moving towards being a 'fallaway' mainly because it is the path of least resistance. Hangovers are a lot more prevalent in my world than are philosophical stands. Apathy is a darn good way to deal with this crazy-ass world. Let others carry the anti-Nam banners . . . just pass me the joint or the beer, dear brother.

1978

West Chester, Pa

This was a jet-black blackout.

"Charl, ya ever get that feeling when you wake up and you got no idea where you are?"

Coming to on a coach on the other side of the room in this anonymous room, obviously going through the same, "Where am I," thing, Charl, the Gourmet, responded, "happens all the time. First thing I do is check to see if there are bars on the windows."

Were no bars, we were cool. The particulars of how we ended up in West Chester when we'd started out the night drinking down in West Philly, never really did get worked out. Turns out the room we were sleeping in was that of a brother of a friend. This bro of a friend, usually attracted babes pretty well, so that was probably the reason we headed up this way. But as was damn near ALWAYS the case, with the babes, we ended up not. And that glorious first piss! Being on the road here, was a very good thing the mattress didn't end up soaking up a purely liquid 'nocturnal emission'. God know that mattress at home has more soaking-induced 'turnovers' than the local bakery!

The blackouts are part of the deal really. Some are jet-black, like this one, with others there's hazy recollection. I get a lot more of them. The psychosis run seems pretty well over now—how did it shake out anyway? St Joe's was done in '73. In '74 I chucked the HUP job and headed down the shore. By September I was cooked. Nuthouse, shock-treatments, the whole bit. By summer I was back pretty well in the groove—back down the shore partying, cutting down on the medications. But by fall I was full-blown manic, getting arrested in downtown hotels trying to get in rooms I didn't pay for; applying for the head coaching job of the Eagles, etc. I relented to the heavy anti-psychotic 'cure' if they didn't make me go back to the shocks. Then the 'zombie' year of '76. But by now things are pretty cool. They weaned me down eventually to just Lithium . . . and I'm weaning me off of that. But it's time I got me a real job; and a nice little girlfriend somewhere sure wouldn't hurt . . . .

1991

January 25
Super Bowl Sunday
Frankford Section
Philadelphia

"What are you some kind of freak? That's a dude dressed up like a women sitting next to you, buddy."

I didn't know—or at least I don't think I did. I didn't even remember getting my car and picking this thing up. What I did remember was that jerk-off Scotty Norwood missing a field goal that would have made my $500 'over 39.5 total points' bet a winner and not a loser. So my big payoff week of $800 is now yet one more losing week. I'm now near $300 in the hole. One more week to the Credit Union to pay off the 'man'. But it wasn't just the missed field goal. Why didn't friggin Buffalo try to move the ball closer? Why did the goddamn Giants march all the way down the field, chewing up almost all the clock, to then settle for a lousy field goal? 20-19 they went ahead, they stayed ahead and I came up a point short. So what else is new?

"Because you live a block away, I'm gonna cut you a break. DO NOT move this car. Leave it right where it is. Little miss whatever-the-fuck-you-are, you come with me." For some reason the cop let me off. A drunkalizer would have gone through the roof. As drunk as I was (I was one cat who got his money's worth at 'all you can drink' Super Bowl parties), I could not have done anything with that hooker anyway. When I stopped caring or noticing that they might be dudes in dame's clothing, I don't remember.

A good goddamn thing I scheduled off for tomorrow. Some folk never work the day after Christmas. I never do the day after the Super Bowl. I may be in too many stupors for sure, but at least I ain't stu-pid.

1992

April 4
Atlantic City NJ

Leaving the reception I told the groom, my would-be sponsor who'd been sober quite a few years, "this is it Jack . . . tomorrow I stop drinking."

Tatinger's, The Irish Pub, then back to the casino. Black from one point in Tatinger's to a come-to in the Pub . . . talking to Swedish stewardesses if I remember. A tap of ATM at the casino, losing a few more dollars, a re-tap. a 'no funds available'. Luckily I had enough money left to cab back to the hotel on the White Horse Pike.

No funds available. As recently as Christmas time there had been over $6000 in there. I missed no paychecks during that period. There was a big car bill, there was losing to the 'book', but mostly the money went up in the smoke of a crack pipe. I don't even remember which of the hookers was the first to turn me on to it. But I sure knew where to find my 'steady'. She could always cop; she had a nice place to get high. She was kind of cute and sort of nice. How many hours and dollars had I spent in that shanty little apartment on top a store, under the El? There was no booze involved the Sunday night I'd gone right there from dinner at mom's house. I had graduated from the drink. It was the drug, the pipe that had me now. In that little cupa coffee I had 'in the rooms' a year-and-a-half ago (the first time Jack had tried to pass it on to me), they told me without an admission of powerlessness, I had no chance.

The pipe has taught me powerlessness.

The day after Jack's wedding, I walked into the rooms of AA. To this day, I have never walked out.

2000

It was on April 3rd of 2000 when I escaped that *Day's Inn* hotel room. 10 months later I landed in Ireland.

Book II

The Journal

Journal 1

Ireland

Part I *Cavan*

February 8, 2001
Day one (a retrospective)

Like an unborn babe clutching the insides of a mother's womb, I too lay in a fetal position, bundled in the plush warm comforter against the cold of the room and the house. For over an hour my mind had spun, but the cold and the 4:00 AM hour and the whatever it is that draws, and has, for almost ever now, drawn me from that which I know I should do, all conspired to keep me under the covers. But like the babe erupting though the birthing channel, the cover at last was chucked aside, and the first full day of my Ireland adventure was born.

The frigid home of the charming Ann O'Reilly, a co-worker of Concepta McGovern of the Cavan Genealogical Center, was where I lay bundled under those covers. The Center, Ann's house (and me) are in a tiny little town called Cavan Town. Ann had been kind enough to open her home to me as a boarder for a portion of my research and write visit to the land of my fore family. I'd been led to the e-mail address and incredible knowledge and efficiency of Concepta by the honorable Judge John Latrelle, Chief Justice of Carbon County Pennsylvania, and a cousin's father-in-law, who'd uncovered the Center in his relentless search for information about my family.

And this Concepta; many times in life we are disappointed when we finally meet a person we, have admired from afar or with whom our minimal contact has greatly heightened our expectations. My fears that this might happen with Concepta were unfounded. She was and is even more than I expected. Ann, Concepta and the center are located in Cavan Town, a goodly distance from the McGowan land up in Corlaugh in the western part of Cavan County. The parish Derryvilla where they reside is noted on only the most detailed local maps. My great grandfather Peter left that exact spot some 125 years ago. The Creeny Milltown spot where my great grandmother, Sarah Sheridan, had left the same year, is considerably closer. In both places members of the extended families still reside. Today, or the next, or the next, I will go and visit with both.

It is truly amazing what a nice shower, some real deep sleep and the warmth and kindness of folks you didn't know as recently as fourteen hours ago, can do to lift one's spirits. But the minor little annoyances that had marked my trip thus far burst upon me last night. As I unpacked the scads of stuff I decidedly did not need on this journey, with the torment, inconvenience and altering of plans that the lugging around of SO MUCH STUFF fresh in my head, the paramount and debilitating unmanageability of my life came over me in a fuselage of unexpected tears. Another bottom it seems. Far less deadly and dangerous than many or most of the others I have known but one deadly and dangerous enough to keep me from accomplishing the many wonderful dreams I just recently have made the commitment to spend the remainder of my life pursuing.

And so here I sit. Ann's perfectly functioning computer in the vacant room next to mine helps ease the sting of my laptop not working. (Either the result of a faulty electricity adapter or because of my careless jockeying of it on the plane last night.) The $200 worth of remaining gift certificates (from the $350 worth my co-workers at the job of eighteen years from which I walked three weeks ago, gave me as a going away gift), will tide me over until I come up with a way to access cash being that my particular PLUS ATM card does not seem to work.

The laptop and a bunch of the other unneeded stuff will be *shipped* back to America to ease the burden of my subsequent traveling. When I get home I will not even have to clean up the disgraceful, disorganized pig sty of a room I left behind, because I am sure my 82-year old mom and my sister Sally will have cleaned it for me. A happenstance that deservedly shames me and one that I must make sure does not happen again.

On a disc or a drive or a page somewhere, another poem I started but never finished, begins like this:

Resolves dissolve
way way way more oft
than they get done did

Certain resolves NEED to get 'did' though . . . . for they stand in the way of all that come behind them. The incredible wonder and peace and beauty of reentering the kingdom of God's love has, at many times in the past six months or so, staggered me with torrents of tears far different and warm and holy than the ones I shed last night. But in reality are they? For every Yin there needs to be a Yang, every high needs an accompanying low. The only high that *really* lasts is the boundless expanse of God's love. The glory of its coming back into my life, and of the real treasures that await all or any who likewise invite it back in, will be behind everything I write. All else is eyewash. And perhaps nothing requires more focus, discipline and organization than writing. And up to this point in my life, I have exhibited very few of these qualities. But in exactly the same way the *choice* for an alcoholic to not drink or drug when one is on the firing line, must be made whether it feels like God has anything to do with it or not—the *do*ing of things I am not used to doing, must get started. Eventually of course, in the realization that it was God, and *only* God, that allows an addict to NOT do what his body demands that he do, (or that allows an incessant procrastinator to get started when he seemingly can't) is the beginning of an entirely new way of living.

Last night as the clock struck midnight and as I made the discovery of this wonderful computer, I jotted down the following notes. It turns out it is it about a whole class of folk who've forgotten, or who never had or who have replaced that God with something else. It is a beginning.

---

12 midnight—Ireland time.

In Philly it's 7:00 PM. 7 PM Friday night. Getting ready time, getting primped and polished and propped time.

But here, midnight. The band plays down. I don't even know the 'closing' time. Out here in rural County Cavan, it's probably pretty soon; in Dublin it's surely at least two hours away. But in both spots, it's definitely the home stretch. For some the buzz is shifting to a load, the 'prowl' taking on a desperate air. For some the load's already set in, and the nonsense and bullshit is already happening; the scuffles, maybe a fight—usually over one or some of the 'prey'.

For others there is no panic. The pro's. For them now is the time to get more serious, to zero in. A lot of these will be successful, a lot probably not, but of the loads and the hanger's on and the rest, almost all will not. Perhaps one or two will 'fall in love' . . . . the object for most of the girls *and* the boys (and that which is *right now* in the front or back of the minds of most of those across the sea: 'getting ready')—and for some it may be the real deal, but for most, alas, it will not be.

We lonely souls oft do
encounter—and go bump in the night.

But as the newness erodes
Our respective emptiness implodes
What we thought we had had
. . . and the darkness returns

is how I put it in one poem. The progression and eventual disillusion of such temporary fixes I described like this in another:

and then comes the night in a club, in a
bar
and the one just appears who'n your eyes
he puts stars . . .
and you meet and you blend
and you meld and you mate . . .

And house you will play
in the blissfullest daze
and it seems to just be
that this real IS happy . . . .

But as time goes on by
and for this bliss you must try
and as it slips you oft sigh
and then it's gone and you cry

Be your part he or it she
matters not totally
but this mate who was all,
cuz the weight (or what'er)
he does fall . . . . and your life
slows to crawl . . .

Then the cringe, then the pout
the 'why me', the self-doubt
'it must be me that's in err
if that that *don't stay stirred . . .*

Poems—words on a page. Alone again on a Friday night in the back room of a little house in a tiny hamlet called Cavan Town.

I was all of the above in my many years in the bars—except of course for the 'pro'. And, as it would turn out, when I put down the drink, I was still the same in the AA rooms—where all the other types still primped and prowled and succeeded and failed.

I am still the same person I was all those years, in the twenty plus years I so-unsuccessfully trolled the bars and clubs, and the almost nine years I did the same in 'the rooms', but I do think differently. Alas, the after closing-time, drunk-induced, hadn't-scored, pained and lonely spins down into the abyss of prostitutes and crack cocaine that became even worse after the drinking had stopped (and I'd rang up some pretty significant "clean" time), have done the trick. The awareness of the absurdity of my way of life *and* recovery, at long last, did induce a '*na mas*' in my soul sincere enough for the only Power that had ever had any chance of reviving me to work His magic.

And now it's after 1:00 AM. Some of the more unrulies have no doubt involuntarily vacated the hot spots. I sho' 'nuff been there. The wake-up "how'd I get *here*" perusal, did, somewhere between 10 and 15 times, career-wise, reveal those bars on the windows. But back in the bars the pros are zeroing in. The shrieks of laughter of the smitten targets at the probably suggestive, but tried and usually very funny, repartee, at times, may be a bit false. Both he's *and* she's are veterans of these banal encounters.

But for most, the malaise of another unsuccessful Friday night is beginning to set in. 'Is *this* all there is?' indeed. The second of the poems mentioned above ended like this:

Perhaps we'll think of a time
when life had meaning and rhyme
(when coke cost a dime!)
And we lived and believed
and folks didn't 'ways deceive . . .

But these days of gone by
are by define all bye-bye
and the catch-er inda rye
catches not by 'n' by

and as the child has to leave
the safe cocoon of the womb
the sweet blind faith of the youth
gives way to the 'logical' truth

. . . and the myths of belief
seem as old as dead leafs
and we tread a 'new' path
with a far diffrent mast
of smart, sharp and fast

but when the fast gets too fast
and to the depths we are cast
we hope too long it won't last

and if our luck don't desert
there's not excruciate hurt
and with grim reap we don't flirt

but ev'n without these extremes
a dull empty sho seems
like a bottomless pit
and we think "why not quit
for all this crud I submit?"

And inside still's the cry
"it is here *where I lie*
the ess of all that you are
lies in here these four walls"

mayhaps on a cold winter night
we say with all of our might,
"God some peace, some non-pain!"
and we'll ask to receive
and with a chill—we'll believe . . . .

The poem is called "the Daily Grind."

Day 2

Cavan Town is a treasure. People are people. Though plenty of them, there is not as much red hair, or as many freckles as I'd anticipated. When the worker in the Dunne's supermarket stocking a shelf offered to go fetch me a little cart as my hands were way full, demonstrated the 'extra mile' attitude the people have here—and which is largely absent in America.

But on this rainy and overcast day, far more typical of the weather here than yesterday's warm and brilliant sunshine, I'm much impressed with the number of 'working class heroes' here in Ireland. Swarms of helpful employees crammed the aisles in Dunne's supermarket, most of them kids; they certainly can't make much. Ann, my landlady, it turns out is a civil servant. The Cavan Genealogical Research Center is a state-funded enterprise—one far bigger and broader in its scope of activities than I had imagined. The Government trained her and placed her in a job. Such real active care of the people, even as the costs of gasoline and phone service and such that makes even 'getting by' quite a struggle, seems to note a far more social and friendly atmosphere than the hard-core marketplace-driven prosperity of America. Things there are good now, but what about down the road?

10:30 PM end of day two

"I just wish God would take me . . . I wish he'd just give me the courage to end it all." The girl who said these words at the AA meeting tonight looked to be about eighteen or nineteen. In three days she goes back to court—and most likely back to jail. That she was so high she does not remember the robbery for which she is accused, is not a defense that will fly. The horrid six-year jail stay of the not-too-distant-past, now seems far closer than do the 90 days she'd managed to stay sober.

And after the meeting I said words to her about a Higher Power—the words not empty to me, but seemingly so to she. When she'd shared from the floor all I could think of was the one lost sheep the shepherd who will leave the other 99 to rescue. And on the way home, I regretted not offering to go to court with her. Mr. Fix-It at it again. And maybe I still will go, maybe when I return to that group that has many meetings, if she has chosen to "keep coming back," I'll offer to do so. Maybe it would be educational for me to see how the court system here works.

Maybe.

If anyone wants a ringside seat to the maudlin and the marginal of the human condition, to the stupefying maybe-ness of life, let him sit in an AA meeting in a little town on a rainy Saturday night.

Day 3 (Sunday)

Driving past the ruins of the Bawndoy workhouse, where 125 to 150 years ago the famine-stricken Irish were sent, not to work, but to be herded, to be fed sparingly if at all, and more often than not to simply die, Concepta was speaking of the July 12 Orange Day marches. During these marches that take place all throughout Northern Ireland, the Catholic streets are closed down and blocked off, and Catholics (the ones who cannot afford to 'holiday' out of there for the weekend—as vast numbers of them do) for their own safety, do not venture out of their homes or neighborhoods. She remarked bitterly how Mother England would never allow something like that to happen on her island, and how sad it was that young Protestant children were among those doing the marching and banging the drums.

The workhouses are a major part of the horror story of Ireland in the famine and post famine years. They were scattered all throughout the land. The starving legions who because of the potato drought could no longer pay their indentured servant rent to their English or Protestant Irish landlords, were sent to these, to be crammed together along with the rats and vermin, to suffer from scurvy and every and any other form of disease—and then often to die. Man and wife were separated; men in one house, women in the other. The children usually stayed with the mother. Families, singles, wed or unwed mothers who were literally found starving along the sides of the roads, were picked up and taken to these.

Then and now. 150 years . . . the bitterness and hate still remains. Like a chill up my spine, I remember some time ago an American reporter asking a nine or ten-year-old Belfast boy why he hated *them* so. I really do not remember if it was a Protestant talking about a Catholic or vica versa. "They're dirty, they're stupid, they can't be trusted . . . they're just awful people." How did it happen? Why is it *still* so much that way?

I wonder how my little cousins feel about all this. Are any of these animosities part of who they are? For the first time I met them today. Their home up in Derryvilla was the final stop on the grand tour of many of the reaches of West Cavan on which Concepta volunteered to take me. (Of course the woman coming to lock up the Church next to the graveyard, where we'd been lingering about, knew exactly where Sean-Tommy-Owen lived. Sean his name, Tommy his dad, Owen his granddad—honest, that's how they do it! The Owen of the Sean-Tommy-Owen chain was the younger brother, by some 17 years, of my great grandfather Peter.) And these little Irish faces of Sean's children, looked so much like the faces of many of my cousins back home. Theirs were of the light-skinned, slightly-freckled, somewhat elongated features variety I've seen so many of here. The dark-haired, dark-eyed other general type seem to have the more rounded features. (I am much more one of them.) But in the faces of all of the kids, on the streets, in the department stores, in the pews in mass this morning, but most certainly, here in the modest kitchen of my cousin Sean-Tommy-Owen, there was no hate, no animosity. What there was, was wonder, inquisitiveness, innocence, purity, honesty. Souls still uncorrupted, staring out into a world and at another face. Devoid of agenda, non-paralyzed by fear, uncontaminated by hate and greed and decadence. One person looking at another . . . . not Protestant, not Catholic, human. And when I look back at any and all of them, I long to catch *them* in the rye, to let them know that the cold and the cruel of the world, need never steal that innocence.

"A man must become like a little child . . . " , indeed. But as de Mello noted, "not to think like a child, but to be as open and honest and questioning as one."

So on the same day I finally meet some of my relatives, some of the logistic problems of my trip seem to be clearing up. After mass and a walk up the hill to the magnificent view found outside the convent of St. Claire's, an ATM machine back down in town was found that accepted my card. And then after the afternoon ride with Concepta, I figured out how to get the adapter to work so my laptop is back up and running. Like the river that makes its own bank as it flows along, my journey is taking care of itself.

1:15 AM

Call it jet lag, call it being on Philly time, call it what you will (drinking too much damn tea maybe!) . . . but when the sleep won't come as my head spins, up I must get and write. And the thoughts that spun just now were of Concepta.

Driving through the hills and towns and bypasses and bypassed bypasses, listening to her tell of the land and the history and of life, is not a small matter, not something to be taken lightly. Knowing her is a treasure; her choice to confide in me, an honor. When I told her she should read my current 'bible' of sorts, Anthony de Mello's *Awareness,* she said she really has no time to read. She has 4 grown boys and one 18-year old girl, still living at home. After a day of hard, honest, extremely efficient work at the genealogical center, she heads home and feeds them. She heads a lady's guild. When she takes time to pick up a book, she reads a few pages and falls asleep. But Concepta (so named because she was born on December 8th, the feast of the Immaculate Conception) does not need to read *Awareness*, she *is* awareness. The pale blue green eyes are smile and determination, reality and mirth. Her heart and soul is of Cavan, of the people, of living. As we neared the end of our ride we passed St Felim's geriatric hospital, the locale of the AA meeting I attended the last two nights. And when she told me it too was once a workhouse, and then after that a birthing hospital for the poor and forgotten unwed mothers, and of 'Bullie's Acre', the unmarked pit where the starved, diseased bodies of no one knows how many babies and mothers who did not make it, are buried, the passion she felt for these was not cloaked in sentimental pity. But in her *com*passion for them, lies the groundwork with which she goes about her day-to-day activities, doing what she can, in her own little way, to rid the world of the cancer lying behind such atrocities, a cancer still very much with us. Yet hers is a compassion born and bred of something deeper than concerned social activism or merely temporal idealism. Like the roots providing a tree with the life source of its strength and beauty, Concepta's very real, yet humbly understated concern for all of mankind, is grounded in an undying belief in the only Source that ever could, would, or will be able to sustain real universal brotherhood. And when in a jocular aside to my dear landlady Ann, she says, "maybe you should know more about that church schedule", she is not ashamed to denote where she goes to tap that Source. I feel very fortunate that I'll be able to see much more of Concepta in my time here.

Day 4

I went back to the AA meeting at St. Felim's tonight. The young girl who was talking suicide two nights ago was there. I offered to go to court with her, but court is not up here, but down in Dublin. I asked how she was getting down there and she said a friend was taking here, and then she blew out of the meeting. My anticipated prospective "Judge, I'm from America and I'll teach her the steps" grandstander will, thus, not be played.

She was very high, told me she's been taking pills for days. If she goes in front of the judge as bleary-eyed as she was tonight, she probably has no chance of getting off. And if convicted felons here are immediately interned, I'll probably never see her again. Maybe she'll get sober in jail, probably she won't—she does not seem to believe there is any way out. Without the second step, "came to believe that a Power greater than ourselves can restore us to sanity", there is little chance of recovery via those twelve steps. I *will* pray for her—this here is a prayer.

Another member of this group (for anonymity sake, I'll not mention his name), joined me on a bench in the center of town this afternoon. I asked him about the Orange Day parades and he painted a less gruesome picture. "It's getting better, We have to learn to respect other people's tradition."

Perhaps this member's 12-step schooling, of how deadly the holding onto of resentments can be, has served to soften his stance. He told me of a cousin of his from up in Omagh who was blown up by a bomb set off by a kid he played with as a child, and how his family has grown to forgive the boy. To forgive like that seems impossible for one who holds no belief in a power Greater than himself.

But even as I withhold my friend's name as I speak of his wise prudent counsel, (he drove me home from the meeting tonight), I am troubled at how my writing so much about AA would put me in blatant violation of the tradition that at the level of press and radio, we must always remain anonymous. But to tell my tale and to leave out AA, seems impossible. Nothing has been more a part of how I got from there to here than my entry into the fellowship and active study and practicing of those steps in all my affairs. The friend who told me way back nine years ago that AA "is a sneaky way to get back to the ten commandments," had it only half right. It is also a practical *utilitarian* way to get back to them.

And as I think of this poor young girl, whose fate is now in the hands of a judge, the seemingly obvious cliché, "you can't stop drinking, drinking," comes to mind. But if one really studies and practices the program, one realizes that is the attitude that must adopted in all or any activities. And for me lying night after night up here, words and ideas pulsating through my brain, I am fully aware of the necessity to just get up and start putting them down.

And as the cognition of the horrible mess of a room back in Philadelphia I left behind, and the even more horrible messes I chose not to clean up before I left my job some three weeks ago, the baggage of continued not doing what I knew I should have been doing, is a weight I am forced to carry with me.

But AA and the steps also offer a way out of such weighty misgivings. After listing and sharing all the resentments, misdeeds, etc with God and another human being, eventually as best and as thoroughly as we can, we make amends for them. And as I sit here on an island where amends on both sides are still so desperately needed, where a peace accord signed on the day we Christians commemorate our Savior's open invitation to take our burdens to Him on the cross, seems to have bogged down in name-calling accusations and posturing, I view a place where some 12-step-type spirituality could really help.

So I speak of the steps, of my recovery. Perhaps the Oxford Group (out of which AA grew), and their agenda of really changing the world that I find very much there in the pages of AA's Big Book, has become a part of me. As I sit among these people I love and am of so much, I wonder how much of the neurosis and psychosis that is almost as much a part of the Irish legacy as is their wit and wisdom and reverence *and* drinking, can be laid at the "we don't air our dirty laundry" closed—mouths? Perhaps in the same way the British envoy who helped lay the groundwork for South Africa's historical peace accord, suggested in today's paper that a new paradigm in the peace process be adopted, that clinging to strictures of the Good Friday accord is hopelessly bogging things down, we 12-steppers should take our world-changing message out of the closet. As a new century dawns, perhaps we should look back more closely at our founders. These were, in fact, so rooted in that Oxford Group's attempt to get back to the first century Christianity "change the world" message, that they'd found so carefully laid out in the Bible's Book of James, that one of the early names considered for the AA fellowship was "the James Group".

But no that is decidedly not the route where the AA of today is headed. In many of the rooms where I go, if one speaks of the steps and the Big Book, he is mockingly labeled a "Big Book thumper". In many of these rooms today the prevailing message is "don't drink and go to meetings." The closing *Our Father* is leaving a lot of meetings. I recall being at an AA convention in Manhattan several years back and there was a big brouhaha about singing *Amazing Grace* to close out the event because it was *too religious.* On a day where on one side of the newspaper a scientist who was part of the massive break though genome project proudly stated "it is a great day to be a human," and on the other was the story of two early post-teen girls plunging off a road to their birthday celebration drunk-driving deaths, seeing how this era's "let's leave God out of this" attitude hath even made it's way into the fellowship that saved my life, I literally cringe.

The first century after Christ—when there were no Catholics or Protestants, surely not Muslims; how and why and where did the message of He who died on that cross get so garbled? Have we deemed it fiction, or merely no longer pertinent?

And so as the birds outside chirp, and a truck pulls up out back, I realize that it is now a new day. The bolded **DAY 5** reminds me that I should be getting a little more sleep.

Day 5

Pat Bennett, the next door neighbor, was doing some minor cement patching on the outside wall as I walked up just now. Amidst the very cordial pleasantries we shared, he told me of a McGowan who had a pub up in Glengevlin (in West Cavan—the real home of my ancestors), who, when a group of Yanks stopped in during July or August and asked for ice for their drinks told them "this is the wrong time of year to get ice up around here."

I just now got off the phone with my cousin from up in Corlaugh who told me she would come and 'collect' me at the town bus station tomorrow night at 5:00 PM.

I'm going to call Dympna Sheridan, (the wife of my cousin on my great grandmother's side) back and see if Friday would be okay with for that particular *me* collection.

There is an AA convention in Donegal March 2-4 that I'm pretty sure I'm going to attend. I'll take the bus ride up to Omagh to see the recreated village of Irish American history, next week.

At the library the gent who always seems to be there using the Internet, told me to check the microfilm back issues of the Anglo-Celt newspaper to see if I can find a mention of my great-grandfather's 1928 return here. Once on the computer, I got a nice reply to the e-mail I sent last week to a Protestant Irish girl from Belfast I met last summer while she was working in the Ocean City NJ *Bed and Breakfast* for the wife of my friend and first AA sponsor, Jack. Unfortunately she will be in England for all of my stay—a real shame I told her and it truly is.

The growing sense that this journey is taking me and not I, it, is among the most lovely and serene I've ever known. Lovely is like the only word they use over here for good, nice, cool or great. And they have every reason to use it with the confounding frequency they do.

12:15 AM

Looking at the sky from outside my new AA friend's home in the country tonight, it was so clear you could actually see the dust-like arrangements around the bigger stars that I believe are galaxies. And when I mentioned this, my buddy spoke of a friend of his from AA who, like himself, was a "slipper and slider" (the term used over here for frequent relapsers). The guy was a very successful photographer who loved astronomy and the stars. My buddy had shot a video of the friend and the friend's son on the same night he'd brought out his real top-of-the-line telescope to look at those stars. He watched the video just recently for the first time since the guy died of an overdose later last summer. When they say alcoholism and addiction are deadly diseases, they are not joking.

For the first time in a long time, I went to meetings four straight nights here. (I was the speaker twice—*fer sherr* one of the reasons for my newfound enthusiasm!) We drove to tonight's meeting with a gentleman who's been sober for 30 years now. On occasion, he'll go on 'holiday' to a Rehab and spend the entire day going over the Big Book with the patients. His 'share' after mine was probably more lengthy, and was a HELLUVA lot more meaningful. I'm getting to better understand the people here though. At Saturday night's meeting I understood about a quarter of what the people said, tonight it was more like three-quarters. But on the way home this genuine article AA guru, told us that when he had been 22 years sober, he was destitute and near on the streets. Not drinking, but stark raving out of control He knew the Big Book, the 'program', the whole deal, but he didn't live it—it had not penetrated his heart. I know the feeling. And then eight years ago, in a little unheated skid row-type room, before going to bed, he genuinely and humbly asked God to help him. The next morning he woke up and just knew he had to go help others. This bright, shining, confident success of a man with whom I had the pleasure to take a 20 minute drive to and from a meeting tonight, has been doing that pretty much every day ever since.

"When I was hungry, you gave me to eat . . . ."

We AA's have the wonderful gift of power*less*ness. We know, left to our own devices, we are doomed. That so many of us die or live lives of misery and confusion after being introduced to the program, because we never really find and/or ally our will with the Power that can save, sustain, and bring us to dizzying heights of serenity and happiness, is a crime unimaginable. People like George who dedicate their lives helping others to access that Power are the real heroes of AA.

When George dropped me off, for the first time since I've been in Ireland, I took a late night rosary walk. It was a Tuesday night, the same night a group of us meet in the dining room of my good friend Mike the Monk's for our rosary prayer group. At this weekly gathering of we "Brothers and daughters of Carmel" there are donuts galore, decaf coffee and wonderful fellowship. Almost all of us are in AA. Mike the monk is so named because he spent time in the 50's at the Trappist monastery in Kentucky called Gethsemani—a place made famous because Thomas Merton lived there. It *is* the 7th story mountain of the 1940 best seller autobiographical book of that name. Mike was searching for his life then, but he was still drinking. Almost 20 years later, the twelve steps of recovery would bring him back to his faith in a different and sober way.

These rosary walks for the last year or so, are something I do four to five times a week back in my nice peaceful neighborhood in Northeast Philadelphia. I can get quite emotional during these walks, usually when I think of my life in relation to the mystery I am contemplating, or of my father's simple "say a Hail Mary for me will ya Jim?" request that I heard throughout his lifetime. But many times it happens when I am on that third one of three "faith, hope and charity" introductory Hail Mary's. Tonight on a night when the stars were so plentiful and seemed to be lying so low that they surrounded me, the heaving chest and the teary eyes came one Hail Mary sooner; the *hope* seemed to me as close and as real as the frost I breathed as I walked.

3:30 AM

Recently I received an e-mail from a Japanese spiritual writer named Hiroyuki Nishigaki telling me some morning, "I will hear the sound of a thousand birds chirping before dawn". He was writing in response to the following excerpted essay I had sent him.

Qigong, God's Love and Recovery

Saturday June 3, 2000 *6:00 AM*

I woke up this morning to the sound of chirping birds. There is something about waking to that sound and feeling connected with nature and with peace and contentment . . .

Until eight years ago, the vast majority of my Saturday mornings were spent "coming to" and not waking up; groggy, hung over, miserable and repentant, after another Friday night of alcoholic drinking. Chirping birds were a major annoyance. Occasionally I'd find myself in a jail cell or gutter or on a park bench. But despite the fact that I drank like that, because I'd kept a job and owned a house and such, I had convinced myself I did not have a problem. My drifting into another addiction, smoking crack cocaine, scared me into the recovery rooms of Alcoholics Anonymous. There I was introduced to the spiritual solution to my drinking/addiction problem the 12 steps are all about.

The first three of those 12 steps are about admitting powerlessness, and believing that a Power greater than oneself can provide a solution and then deciding to turn our will over to that Power. The 4th through 9th are about the finding and pruning and making amends for those objectionable aspects of a personality that led to the alcoholic drinking to begin with. Ten through twelve are basically maintenance/growth steps, about immediate admission and amending of day-to-day wrongdoing, expanding the prayer and meditation part of our lives, and then taking the message to fellow sufferers. I specifically thought (and think) of qigong as actively doing the meditation part of that 11th step. The step reads:

Sought through prayer and meditation to improve our conscious contact with God, praying only for knowledge of His Will for us and the power to carry it out.

And it fits perfectly. The qi provides the power . . . and if I adhere to the qigong insistence that I be virtuous, in that area at least, I am doing God's will. But as I look back over these eight years, and view the many and debilitating relapses back to the crack cocaine part of my addiction, my deficiencies in the doing ALL of God's will for me, have become apparent. It has been a long grueling, yet in-the-end, enlightening and miraculous process.

The latest of these miracles happened less than one month ago in this very room after a brief early evening nap and the awakening to the bells from the church up the street, (along with the bird chirping). The thought of getting high was pretty strong before that exactly one-hour 6:00 to 7:00 PM nap. After the nap, the thought was gone and it has not returned. And the feeling I felt upon that awakening, from a whole hour of having wrapped myself up in a fetal position, was one of being loved . . . was of being cuddled up in the arms of the Universe or God. And the thought that went through my head when I awoke, was what Dr Yan Xin says in the (practicing instruction) tape about fitting our will with the will of all.

. . . . well just a moment ago, as I lay in that strange netherland between sleep and wake, the chirping of a few (not a thousand!) pre-dawn birds awakened me. And so I tackle the difficult task of bringing my Yan Xin Qigong practice into my tale. My reluctance is about not wanting to sound like I am too far *out there*. But to leave it out would be doing a gross injustice to a fellowship and practice that has been instrumental in my progress.

As for the particulars of what Qigong is, or more specifically what Yan Xin Qigong is, I can only scratch the surface. But I do know that it is not a religion. It is an ancient Chinese practice that is all about the cultivation and utilization of qi (or energy). It has a written history of 3,000 years and a spoken one of 7,000. Dr Yan Xin, for whom Yan Xin Qigong is named, is 52-year-old man who is a renowned Qigong master who has been practicing traditional qigong since he was four. He is licensed as a doctor in both Western and Eastern medicine. The stories of energy transfer kind of things he does, and of near-miraculous cures are wild and pretty well documented. He has been honored as a "sage of out time" by none other than President George Bush—the first one, and has been recognized officially by the governments of Canada and the state of New York. He has also been closely associated with officials of the government of the People's Republic of China.

Considering today's anti-religious climate, perhaps the non-religious aspect of qigong is its most attractive feature. Practitioners, religious or otherwise, draw on this external qi, to improve themselves and the world around them. My fellow practitioners are probably right and I am probably wrong when they tell me my "the qi is the grace of God" interpretation is nonsense, but I hang my hat on what Dr Yan Xin, himself, said on the topic.

"Therefore someone who believes in a religion and at the same time is a Qigong practitioner will discover that all the time, there is an image larger than human existing in all the places. This is what "God is in your heart and "God is with you" means. One should not only be able to see but feel this image. Then the more miraculous effects in your chosen religion will be revealed to you.

In two months it will be two years that I have been practicing and I bask in the glow of the way that **has happened** for me. Never in my life have I come close to sticking with any kind of meditative practice that long. So as I sit here tonight, quite sure the only YXQ practitioner in Cavan Ireland, the advertised benefit of requiring less sleep is the most obvious one I've received on this trip. Four or five hours sleep, and a brief afternoon nap are sustaining me fine. A big 7-8 hour crash I'm sure is due soon. When it gets here, it gets here.

Day 6

Moving day . . . the last entry that will be made on the sturdy old Compaq computer in Ann's back room. (The stay here was only temporary—until I could land in a real *Bed and Breakfast* in town.) But I will miss this spot only a fraction of how I will miss Ann. This home, this room, that ridiculously cluttered bedroom (that I have to get to and clean up now!) but mostly in the teas and the chats and the many meals Ann prepared for me—I was placed in the perfect warm, homey, loving place to begin this journey. The pittance of a fee I was charged to stay here, if multiplied by a hundred, would not be payment enough to my dear friend Ann for all that I owe her.

———

11:30 PM (or as the clock in my new room reads 23:30)

I am moved into a B & B room as tiny as any room ever could be. I had tea with my new landlady, Angela and her friend Avril before I went out this afternoon and they are lovely lovely people. I am far closer to the center of town now, and although this room is very small, it will be perfect.

My cousin Maura and her husband Jim just dropped me off after I spent the most lovely evening dining and chatting with them. They are two of the most informed, intelligent and charming people I have ever met. It seems Jim used to teach at the Kilnacrott Abbey where I attended the AA meeting last night . . . and where I'm looking to maybe stay for a few days in a week or so. (Among the many really neat things about Ireland is that people not only do not seem to mind your dropping their name, they seem to like it; so next trip to Kilnacrott, drop Jim's I will!) It was less than two years ago when Maura's parents, Tommy Owen and Mary Alice died. Both were in their nineties and as is often the case with the McGowan clan, Maura told me her mom is the one I would have loved talking to—that she, the in-law, was the one who remembered the best.

In a book called *The Way to Love*, Anthony de Mello writes, ...

" . . . . Remember a time when you felt like you had power, you were the boss and people looked up to you; or when you were popular. And contrast that with the feeling of intimacy, companionship—the times you thoroughly enjoyed yourself in the company of a friend or with a group in which there was fun and laughter.

Having done this, attempt to understand the true nature of worldly feelings, namely the feeling of self-promotion, self-glorification. They are not natural, they were invented by your society and your culture to make you productive and to make you comfortable. These feelings do not produce the nourishment or happiness that is produced when one contemplates Nature or enjoys the company of one's friends or one's work."

Jim and Maura McGowan Hannigan gave me a heaping portion of nourishment and happiness tonight. The voluminous portions of these I have received these last six days, defies comprehension. I cannot believe I've been here less than one week.

Day 7 (Thursday—end of week one}
February 14, 2001

The first gray day since Sunday. Three consecutive days of sunshine in February in Ireland is unheard of. I feel very blessed. ("Pet days" is what Concepta told me these unseasonably warm days are called.)

One of my all-time favorite movies is called *Local Hero,* a tale of a hotshot young executive who is sent by a huge oil conglomerate to literally buy a small town in Scotland because they'd discovered oil off its shore.

In the movie's final scene, the young hot shot is seen looking out off his balcony in his luxurious high-rise apartment in Houston, the sounds of sirens and horns piercing the night. And back in the Scottish town, which of course ended up not being bought, but does end up being fallen in love with by the hot shot . . . . in the town's single red phone booth (a spot where there were many hilarious scenes of almost the entire town coming up with pence for, and hanging around, as the hotshot would call back home) you see and hear ringing as the night becomes dawn.

And that is how I feel right now. All I want to do is call Jim and Maura. That it ends up they are just seven miles away, and not the near 30 miles to Corlaugh, and that Jim drives their last remaining at home child here into Cavan town each day for school, is a real blessing. The last daughter is Assumpta; you guessed it, born August 15, the feast of the Assumption. I feel relieved that I have many more weeks here. I'll be in touch with them soon. In a bit I'll call to arrange an exchange of reading materials—me-to-they my *Awareness* "bible", and they to me a eulogy Jim wrote about a beloved teacher, and the piece on the more ancient history of our family that Maura wrote.

So on this the day after St. Valentine's day and thinking about *Local Hero,* I'm reminded of a lovely girl back in the states with whom I saw the movie for the first time, and who affectionately used to call it *our* movie. And as I sit here on the other side of a great ocean from her, feeling genuinely happy that she recently married, I am aware enough to know she was not the one for me, simply because she did not end up being the one for me. As I approach the almost nine-year anniversary of one of my friend's "you oughta get married" solution to my drinking and drugging problem (the first friend I'd told about my coke addiction), I realize and accept that that was not the correct solution. That without the subsequent leaps and stumbles and falls, the decisions and actions that brought me right here and now to this exact place, were the right ones, not because they were righteous ones but because they were *the* ones. And the further awareness is with me right now that at any time any person anywhere has the capability and the grace to look at himself, to review his path, both recent and distant, and to do the next right thing, or even more exactly, the next thing rightly, regardless, even especially regardless, as to whether he is in the midst of a string of things done wrong stretching back as far as he remember. Then he too can rejoin the endless perfect flow of the Way or of God's will.

As again I think of the eyes of the children here, and recall the words of my cousin-in-law Jim last night about the difference in between the attitude or demeanor of a city boy and a country boy, and as the natural cry of the lovely 6-week old grand daughter of Angela whom I met minutes ago, sounds in my room here, I take heart in the unshaken belief that any person, country or urban, if he really stretches his memory back far enough, upon him will burst, and maybe not even burst, more likely just trickle, like a tear out the corner of an eye, if not the exact memory, at least the *feeling* of a time when the love was pure and innocent. When, before the clamors of *getting and getting* clouded the horizon, he knew what it meant to be really loved. But as always, because it is a part of my past, I drift back to the using partners and their kids. And I go back to a night, when on a subsequent run to get us some more, the glossed-with-wet-eyes of a mother who realized her son hanging 'round the porch of our denizen of smoke, was headed way same. And even as I am being drawn in by the gravitational pull of the love and the charm of this magical Isle, I know that to *that* mother, those mothers, to they and their children, is the 'to whence' to which, I eventually must go.

Day 8
February 15

In the three or four months before I left Philadelphia, I had the extraordinary fortune to meet a gentleman named Joe Malone. Joe hailed from Port Richmond and lived on the same street on which my dad grew up. But my connection to Mr. Malone had another element to it. My AA sponsor, Jamie, who ironically lives 4 doors away from the big Port Richmond house on Monmouth Street my great grandfather Peter had built, has a brother who was married to one of Joe's daughters, and fathered three children by her. Joe was fighting cancer the whole time I knew him. He finally died about two weeks before I left for here.

On the afternoon of his in-Church wake that took place the same day as the evening funeral mass, because I'd locked the keys of my car inside it before going inside the Church, my sponsor's sister, whom I'd met at the Church-wake, had been kind enough to drive me to the Philadelphia riverside spot where her brother worked and that was a mile or so down the road from the church. And then Jamie had been even kinder enough to allow me to borrow his car so I could drive make the 15-20 minute drive home to get my spare key.

Once home however, I was delayed by a call from a new AA friend who was drunk and was laying the "what's the use of living" rap on me. By the time I got the car back down to the Port Richmond dockside, Jamie was quite annoyed. My explanation held little water. "He was drunk, you were talking to the bottle." He was right . . . he was almost always right *and* right on in his advice to me as my AA sponsor. Through the confounding string of relapses that had taken place in the preceding two years, his advice had been pretty much the same, "Give the place you work an honest eight hours, and stop judging people, particularly the ones in the meetings, and the obsession to get loaded will be removed." He'd heard enough of my mantra "that job does not fulfill me". He knew of my penchant to spend far too many of my paid working hours e-mailing my little homilies, almost literally all over the world. He'd seen me in the meetings and had heard me talk down the messages of members with viewpoints different than mine. He knew I was doing specifically wrong a lot of the time, and how harmful that doing was. I did too actually, but I simply could not stop. The pride was still too strong.

So my sponsor had had to dash in and out of the pre-mass wake, because I'd taken so long to get his car back. Mass is not Jamie's thing these days, and in my still prideful, "have returned to the flock" way, I was sure that is why he seems agitated a lot. At least now I'm not so sure.

I did make the funeral mass, though, and on the day after, on the afternoon of his somewhat private burial (announced in the Church but not written in the death notice), as the skies cleared up from a miserable rainy morning and what must have been a really messy graveyard scene, I wrote the following account. Not until eight days later, on the day I actually left town, did I finally get around to mailing it to members of his family.

January 30, 2001

Time passing. Hours become days, days become weeks . . . months . . . years . . . a lifetime. The moment we spend as walking, breathing human beings is terminate. Only that we really know. In the same way the dark gray misery of this morning's rain blossomed into the bright blue beautiful sky of the afternoon, nature will eventually reclaim the skins and bones we rent for a spell. Moments ago, rain hats, umbrellas—now the drinking in of the brilliant sunshine. The heavens have opened up you might say. Last Thursday, January 25, in the Year of Our Lord, 2001, they opened up and welcomed Home their loyal and humble servant, Joseph Vincent Malone.

I only got to meet him four or five times, but that was enough. Enough to get to know him. Enough to know that I'd been blessed to have been a friend to a very special man.

The first meeting, that was supposed to have been just a stop-in and say hello, lasted well more than an hour. He was healthiest then. Time and cancer had designs on his body . . . it was in his brain, in his lungs, everywhere. The other meetings maybe a half-hour, 45 minutes. The last time was right after Christmas and was only for about 20 minutes. And the only evidence of the gradual decline were the flickering eyelids the last couple of visits—the medication kicking in. I don't know if the pain was bad or constant, but I never saw him wince or cringe. Showing the pain was not his style.

One of nine born in the row house at 2602 E Ann St, he also fathered nine. And he became a widower almost immediately after the last was born. For the 38 years after that, he apparently continued to be everything a man a, a father, a grandfather and a great grandfather was supposed to be. As a worker for his beloved Nativity parish, the time and effort he extended were boundless. The charming 17-page "Over Home" piece he wrote about the family and his life, and that he was kind enough to share with me, reveals a story as warm and wholesome and moving as anything I've ever seen.

And now as I think back I wish I'd listened more, I wish I hadn't been so damned adamant about sharing my plans and dreams and such. Here I was in the presence of a modern-day saint, a man whose life was as exemplary as any human being ceaselessly trying to do God's will as any I have ever known, and way too often I was the one doing the talking.

I'd been led to Joe because he grew up on the same block as my dad and I was told he was a wealth of information about Nativity and Port Richmond. And while he certainly was, and while he knew much about my dad and his family (and everything else!), it did not seem we talked all that much about them. We talked about everything, a changing world, God's plans for us . . . . and something my mom had said to me one time about my father, "your father was the least judgmental man I ever knew," echoed in my head, each time we talked. Joe was quite obviously a man who left the judging to God. He had other jobs to fill—and fill them, to the hilt, he did.

And so now the responses to my talking will necessarily be non-verbal. The chair in the corner of the room on Ann Street will be strangely vacant. But in the same way that a blind man's hearing and other senses are so much better tuned, now Joe has access to only my spiritual, non-physical side. And for all of us who knew him, the strength, faith and plain old holiness available to us via that connection, is something in which we should always revel.

At the remarkably beautiful mass, attended by two bishops and about eight other priests, his son Frank, a priest from Little Rock, Arkansas, during a stirring humorous and very upbeat eulogy, stressed "no regrets." How true. And of course there are memories, with their soothing and moving emotions. But memories too are terminate—individual points of consciousness squeezed in amongst the n'er ending, oft-involuntary procession of mindful apparitions we call thoughts. That which is not terminate though, is love. But love is not only everlasting, it is ever-fortifying. And for those of us who knew Joe, the selfless simple way he loved and treated all who ever knew him, like the warmth of the sunshine or the chill of the night, will always be a part of us. Into the very sinews of our being, in all we do and in all we meet, like the tongues of fire resting on the apostles' heads, that love can, should and must help to be our guiding force.

75 years ago, in that very same Nativity church, 13 clerics were among the throng attending the funeral of my great grandmother Sarah Sheridan McGowan. She was so beloved in the neighborhood that her funeral procession stretched all the way down to Monmouth Street—a full half-mile. She too was a tireless worker for the Nativity Church her husband Peter had helped to build. But it was not until one of Joe's grand daughters offered a passionate post-communion, violin rendition of 'Danny Boy', did the beauty and emotion of the endless, unbroken chain of faith and love represented by Sarah and Joe {and so many others}, who lived and breathed and tried so diligently to follow God's plan, engulf me. One need go no farther in the search for hope.

In eight days I will return to Ireland, I will walk the ground Sarah walked and then left 125 years ago. She never got to go back. And I will take with me the brief but beatific gift of having known Joe Malone. The real glory is that this is a gift I will have forever.

After Jamie's mom told me the family had scattered a bit since Joe died, I sent the piece to her. I'm sure the story will get to the right hands.

But meanwhile back on the 'old sod', yesterday's travels, mainly because no one was around to talk to, led me up to St Pat's Cathedral. As I approached, like cats out of a bag, a crew of nine or ten-year-old boys, were exploding out the door. I told the cute little redhead who'd told me it was choir practice that I too was in the choir as a kid, but he didn't seem interested.

As I sat alone in the back of the church, an older gentleman sauntered up to the organ. He turned out to be Fr. Terry Kerns, the priest whose picture I'd noticed in the church bulletin with an uncanny resemblance to Benny Hill. After some warming up, the tune he glided into was *Danny Boy.*

Later today, I will walk that ground that Sarah did.

The beauty of the quaint reverent church in the tiny little town called Milltown and where Sarah, as a child, used to pray, is marred by scaffolding on its South wall. When we went outside Hugh showed me the little slivers in the cement into which cold rain water must seep, that is probably the reason the paint inside will not dry properly. The cosmetic masonry project is, thus, threatening the foundation of this church.

Hugh knows these things because he is a fixer, a mechanic, a farmer. And when he showed me the scar from the major operation he'd had on his wrist less than two years ago, I realized how really life*style* threatening the ailment had been. A "cold wet pair of gloves" he'd surmised had been the cause for the deep infection that had locked his hand into the half-open/half closed fist he demonstrated. "Each day working at it, trying it open it, some days you'd only improve a fraction of an inch . . ." was the way he described the solitary physical therapy that followed the major three day's-worth of draining surgery that had removed the infection, but had not corrected the locked-in bone atrophy. "But eventually it started to open up, and when it did, the progress was really good," was how he described the light-end-the-tunnel process that netted him nearly 95% usage of the hand.

I don't know if I've ever seen a picture that did less justice to a face than did the one Judge Latrelle had e-mailed me of Hugh and his family. The face of this Hugh Sheridan, who less than a year ago, we never even knew was related to Sarah, had to somehow, somewhere, some way have shared blood with my father. It was especially in the eyes. The link to his grandfather James, half-brother to Sarah, and son of Bernard, had been made because of the Judge's digging, (with an large assist from a sorta cousin from Chicago whom I'd met via a McGowan/ Sheridan website) and the obvious painstaking efforts of Concepta's Genealogical Center research crew.

Thus it seems appropriate that the naming of my uncle Bern, who died the same 1988 year as my dad, and who was more responsible for the coming alive of the McGowan family history than anyone—in light of the fact that it was Dympna who remembered the ins and outs of the tree the judge had sent them; in the same way Mary Alice, the wife of Tommy Owen who died only last April, two months before Tommy made his two-month 'lost without her' march to his final resting place was the one who I was told remembered everything, and in the same way so many of the nester in-law McGowan moms, including, maybe even especially, *my* mother (about whom my dad's first cousin and best friend, my Uncle Jim once said, "if you want to find out about the McGowan's ask, Floss")—should have been named after Sarah's side.

We were in the graveyard behind that little Milltown Church when, with heaving chest and choked-up voice, I told Hugh and Dympna about the time a flickering image of Sarah had been part of the prayer that had helped me escape a hotel room in the midst of a deadly, dangerous situation. When I told them this, it was after we'd been to the ruins of the Drumlane Abbey not far from where Sarah had lived, still standing since the 13th century and next to which the sun and the mist collided on the surface of a lake that drifted round a tiny isle and into an almost mystical-in-the fog mountain range. Hugh told me there was a legend that the monks had built a tunnel under the water to this isle to escape Viking raiders. It was after Dympna's,"what's that swan there doing by itself?" and "well they sure won't do her much good over there, will they?" had wrapped Hugh's "well there's a flock across the road" response. And it was after they explained to me how swans keep the same one mate for life.

And it was before Hugh stopped to check on the glitched water pumping station shack for which, as one of the many hats in the area he wore, he was in charge of maintaining, and whose malfunction elicited call after call during my entire visit. And it was before Hugh had showed me his cows, and explained who the bull was and told me how through the gaps in the wooden floor planks the cow dung falls, and how it's then gathered by a big machine and then used to fertilize the ground on which the hay the cows eat, grows. And it was before he commented several times and told me to look at the way the cow who'd just given birth, stood guard over her calf. And it was before he explained how the one little dog outside, scuttering and playing and yelping at another little dog, had almost died of loneliness before the new friend had replaced their beloved collie who'd been hit and killed by a car. And it was before I'd taken a piece of rock from the rubble heap across the lane where they deposited the remains of the house in which Sarah had lived. And it was before one of the most delicious dinners I have ever eaten, and the dinner table teasing of young, tall and sort of embarrassed Paul about his new haircut. And it was before the never-for-one-second *un*perfect three hour by the fire chat with Hugh, Dympna, and their beautiful daughter Anita and her handsome witty and charming fiancée' John, who both live in the house, but not *together*, as they did for years in England. They will marry in August in the Milltown Churh and are building a house across the street. Dympna told me Anita is a bit of a rebel and was the one with probably a spirit most like Sarah's. She'd also told me Paul was more like her, to which Hugh had said, "Be Jees, but Paul is *quiet!*"

And at the firm, final handshake when Hugh, for the third time, offered to drive me the hour trip to Black Lion to see some people I'd been told would be helpful, I knew he meant it. And when Dympna, whose love and warmth and presence had been the amphitheater in which the entire perfect symphony of a day had played, kissed me good-bye and insisted that I should certainly come back, I knew she meant it too.

And when, after John had driven us expertly through the dense fog back to Cavan town and Anita gave me a good-bye hug that was firm and tight and fraught with nothing but good wholesome affection, I knew there has never been a time in my life when I felt that I am exactly where I should be, as much as I did right then.

Day 9

It will be cold in Cavan tonight. Very cold. Cavan cold. The temperature for the first time since I've been here will be seasonable Ireland winter weather. I am glad that there was response to the turning of the knob on the little radiator across the room. Tonight I will need the heat—no matter how tight I wrap myself in my covers and in myself—tonight I'll need help to stay warm.

As the cold at last descends, and as this string of 'pet' days seems to be drawing to a close, it seems too that the fairy tale of a journey this has been for me thus far, will now begin to get harder . . . that even as the connections and circle of people to whom I am being led grows almost by the minute, I sense this journey into the night and day of my soul, is now to become more arduous.

It is not only in the ever-expanding choices of things to do that getting to know so many more of the people here has effected, (although this is certainly a part of it), it is more about the letting go the past, even, maybe even especially, the very recent past this magnificent pilgrimage thus far represents. The clutter of grand (or lovely) is still clutter. To take in all this wonder and move on. To avoid the drifts into sentimental day-dream. And as I write words that try to keep clear of psycho-babble, as I try to accept the help being given me both temporal and not so . . . it begins to dawn on me that making any such distinction is, and always has been, a large part of the problem.

In a land and a world of monumental change, change perhaps more pronounced than at any single moment since the dawn of humanity, the glorious gray of *people* comes to me. But it does not burst upon my consciousness, rather it creeps upon and around me like last night's fog, not in the beatific bright of precise clarity, but rather in the obscure yet loving veil of human weakness.

People living, trying to get by, to make it through the night. Eyes, clear or not so . . . but eyes that look back . . . some seeming forever on the brink of tears. Others straight and steadfast, almost none because of the phony focus of philosophical assuredness or religious certainty. I find few Pharisees here.

And is there any place better than Cavan to make this perilous trek into the cloudy? Only in Cavan will you hear people say "down in Belfast and up in Dublin" and that is because the river Erin that flows through here goes south to north. Only in Cavan will you find the sprawling conglomerate of the Slieve Russell Hotel around the bend a piece from the ruins of the Bawnboy workhouse. Only in Cavan will you find Kilnacrott Abbey school, once a fine secondary school that took the students the haughtier St. Patrick's College would not, now a virtual ghost town since a horrific pedophilia scandal and an even more horrific cover-up, brought her to her knees.

Cavan. I wonder if it was cold the 1876 day Peter made that trek down the long long road from Derryvilla. I wonder how Sarah felt as she walked away from the Milltown home she would never see again. I wonder how much either of them took with them. Two people from whence my family came.

On that glorious Saturday last June when the largest conglomerate of their descendants since the first one 25 years ago, joined at the annual picnic—"looking down from heaven" seems so awfully remote; among us too ghostly; mere memories too fleeting. In groping for the *how*, it seems we miss the point. Exactly as it is with God, we do not *know*, we feel.

When I walk at night and say the rosary, as I ponder the Mary mysteries and the devotion my dad and my great grandmother had to her, my wrapping together of them is a human perceptual tool laughable in its shallowness. But it is a good thing to do because it is humbling . . . it is holy . . . it is an exercise in trying to better myself. And as magnificent as are the bursts of emotion that frequently accompany these walks, the *real* payoff is in the increase of my effectiveness. But it is not an effect of power . . . rather it is one of weakness . . . of humbling awe of that which I do NOT know. Through a weak membrane, stuff, like grace, flows more easily. With it, I can change the world . . . without it I am but a hollow gong.

* * *

I'd chosen the latter of the, "after you look at the lake, you can keep going straight and the looped street will take you back to the center of town. Orrr you can turn around and come back just the way you came," options that had been presented to me by Ann Winterborne Gaffney, the mother of the man who will marry my Sheridan cousin, Anita, next August. That is the way she phrases things; information followed by absurdity. "You can use the bathroom only if you close your eyes walking up the steps, the ironing board is there—no you don't have to do the ironing." She dots her sentences with rolled eyes, thrown back head, or quick spouts of laughter. Always laughter. She stands erect, making faces speaking in a strict perfect haughty tone imitating some vain person. When I asked how you raised 13 kids in that little house on top of the store where I found her, she chimed, "and guests!. Taking care of two geriatrics once at the same time, in different rooms and with different ailments, didn't know what to do with them!". Once when a family or whomever moved in, Eddie (her husband) said, "Woman I counted seven heads sticking out the covers of that bed, can't you *do* something!" "Of course I can dear, as soon as you knock out a wall." This morning she was a "if you're looking for someone to talk to, stop and see my mom" story. Tonight, an hour or so afternoon chat, dinner and more chatting, and being taught "one-two-three, one-two-three" dancing in a Pub, later; she is a friend forever.

An English Catholic, with a still very handsome English-looking face, her accent is wonderful but perfectly understandable. When her earthy, *very* earthy, husband Eddie came home from a day of work building houses, as she'd popped in and out minding their little store, (and his sister minding the store), stopping in and telling stories, moving a box of fancy dishes so my legs could fit under the table, "if I were a proper host, I'd have served you on these", Ann's job was done for a while. It was almost understood that Eddie would take me to see Jim McCabe, a local historian of sorts. When I asked Eddie on the way if he'd heard of a very old retired schoolteacher in town called "the Master" (to whom I'd been directed by my friend in town when I made some queries about Irish history) he told me, "the master would tell you to see Jim McCabe."

Jim greeted Eddie's "I've got a friend from America," with a warm "I should hope so I sure don't want to be looking just at the likes of you." Jim and Eddie both have "lived in" faces; old, creviced, crammed with character. Eddie's is round and that of a laborer; his eyes are constant devilish mirth. Jim's is thin, a scholar's face, serious, the laughter in them understated. Friends for God knows how long. The visit was cut short because Eddie had to buy lottery tickets. "We'll close down Bridge

Street for the party and I'll fly you back from America when I win," he told me later in the pub.

And in the pub, when I caught Ann referring to a place in Dublin as UP there, contradicting her earlier, "Dublin is south, so I call it down, Belfast is north so I call it up," statement, she sighed "Well if you keep getting it beat into your skull; a woman is not to think for herself!" When I said I'd never met anyone who thought for herself the way she did, she replied, "Yes, but the trick is to not let them *know* that you do!"

On the ride over to Jim's when I told Eddie my *Danny Boy* tale, he said, "Ann's been know to sing that one pretty well." Her goodbye rendition when I leave Cavan, which I know she'll not deny me, is already choking me up.

Day 10 (Sunday)

I awaken to thoughts of Eddie. Through the ever-present grin, "You'll put that in your book, will ya?" When it comes to words Eddie is a nester. But he knows, he listens, he understands. When we left Jim McCabe, he tells me exactly how to get back there because he knows I must go back there, and he knows I must go alone. And he realizes I paid no attention, so back in town, he told me any of the cabbies would take me.

Ann knows that he knows too. "You'll have to come back and meet Eddie." When he arrived, there was no "in the other room" discussion. He sat down and immediately broke bread with me. She'd passed me on to him because she knew he would know what to do next. Like the swans with an instinct true to themselves and to the earth, they know.

He wants me to write a little toast combining their 40th wedding anniversary and the marriage of their son John the third-born of 13 children, but the first one born in Cavan. (Sean Quinn, the multi millionaire and colossus of an entrepreneur who built his sprawling empire from what originally was a gravel pit, had to sweeten well the package that brought John back from a good job in England to his empire here in Cavan.) John—"Now we know why we never see him in Cavan town," Eddie'd remarked as they drove up to the lovely country home of Hugh and Dympna—is an absolute gem of a person. Eddie does not know yet that I can not write his speech because then it would be my speech. August 19 the wedding, "you'll have to come back" they said many times. What John and Anita and the huge Slieve Russell per head tab, even with an employee discount, will think of this invite, I do not know.

John and Anita "living in sin" whilst in England seems a label so inappropriate. Their commitment to each other is very real and not even close to the same stuff of many of the "here today, gone tomorrow" live-in relationships which pollute American society . . . and American AA rooms.

But when before I even met her, Dympna had told me "Anita is a bit of a rebel," I figured she probably practiced her faith no more. But hers and John's is a well thought-out choice, not the slothful "whatever" that characterizes the American fallaway. Their choice is bedded in the revulsion of the hypocrisy of mainly the cover-ups to the pedophilia scandals. In our frank discussion on the way back here through the fog, John spoke knowledgeably of the quagmire of the easy wealth and comfort the *Celtic Tiger* (the name given to the economic boom in Ireland) seems to be drawing many of his contemporaries toward. He is aware of the quicksand nearby. While he and Anita most certainly have not chucked the "Babe with the bath water", they do not choose to immerse themselves in water they find offensive, or rituals they find meaningless.

Maybe I was lucky because, not the rituals, but the very words of Jesus *had to* come through for me. There was a morning when I lay on my bed at home; a crack run had begun about ten hours earlier. A different hotel room and the means to continue were only a couple of blocks away. In three hours the banks would be open and my credit card could net me cash. Again the struggle to avoid going back. So I did what my friends in recovery had suggested, "put it off if even for a moment, you're only five minutes from success." And so instead of heading right back, I lay there and prayed, and even though the coke still had to be swirling through my brain, as best I could, I tried to silence myself and let peaceful thoughts come to me. And what came to me was to read that day's piece in the *Serenity for Everyday* book that breaks down the New Testament into 365 "related to the steps" segments—a book my sponsor had given me because he wanted to help, because he knew the spiritual solution had somehow eluded me. That day's reading happened to be the gospel story in Matthew when Jesus said, "take my yoke upon you, for yours is rough and cumbersome and mine is light and easy." The tears came immediately that morning; the day became a sober one; that time, many followed.

But all over the place even up here in Cavan there is a sense of the old going away, of the rituals and words of Jesus becoming passe', of the dangerous mist of greed and "hurry hurry, get ahead" headed this way. When Jim Hannigan, in that delightful Tipperary chime of his, apologized for making me wait in the car on the way out to his and Maura's lovely home the other night, his "part of the way up here, you stop and talk to someone you meet," he followed it up with, "but I'm afraid were losing that. We don't have time anymore." You hear it all over. And the place from whence it is drifting up, is of course Dublin. Dublin the stop at the end of my pilgrimage. I have this sense, certainly one too concrete a concept to depict this particular human condition, as are ALL concepts attempting to depict human interaction, and the sense is that like the river Erin there has been a shift in the current; that in the healing ecumenism 'tween North and South, surely still in its very early embryonic stage, but alive and growing nonetheless, maybe is represented the lamb's blood of protection from the Dublinesque (Americanesque in actuality) poison seeping on up. And it is perhaps here in Cavan, in the very earthy heartland of Ireland, where this beatific stand, like Myles the Slasher at the Bridge of Fineai, might begin to be made.

* * *

"Twice my arse!" Angela, my landlady, said to her friend Theresa who'd just stopped in, re my inaccurate count of how many times I'd had to be let in my room because I left the keys in there. "Yesterday morning he was lucky he was not in the raw." (Theresa had a deep smoker's kind of voice and a face all of which looks like laughter, very similar to that of my dad's deceased youngest sister, Natalie.) The latest 'forget' had been last night at 2:00 am. "You're lucky my daughter was here to let you in. If it was only me you'd have been out all night."

Angela. Until the Concepta–December 8, Assumpta–August 15, I'd never made the "angel"-Angela connection. I wonder how much a husband that died of a heart attack a long time ago has to do with the air of sadness frequently etched in that so kind, so connected, so knowledgeable a face.

Angela has two children and her daughter Regina has been here at the B & B more often than not. Regina and her two children, one six-weeks, gorgeous and just beginning to smile, the other two-and-a-half always running around without pants, are part of the charm of being here. When I told Angela of Anita and John and how I don't think they do church much, even though she no longer does, she said, "When they have kids they'll go to church again."

Angela, Angel-a . . . . when I just took down my weeks worth of dirty laundry that B&B landlady's just do not ever include in the deal, I was reminded of my sister Sally saying, "Oh don't worry about Jimmy. He'll have all kinds of mom taking care of him over there." "He can't even make a cup of tea!", dear Angela she said in that sooo-Cavan accent, the other day.

Angela, Angel-a, when I told her, the night before I met the Sheridans, the tale of Sarah's image and the escape from the hotel room clutches of my addiction, she said, "Why don't you make your great grandmother your patron saint?" How many people, I wonder, who go to church each and every week in their Sunday best, would say that and would *mean* it. And my doing exactly that at 7:30 Mass in St. Clare's lovely little chapel the morning of the Milltown trip, laid the groundwork, I suppose, for the glorious day that was to follow.

* * *

I just met with my cousin Maura who was dropping her daughter Aegean at the Cavan town bus station for the trip back to Dublin. (Aegean lives and goes to school in Dublin, but comes home most weekends.) I told Maura that I don't know if I'd ever seen anyone with eye color as close to the gray/green of my father as hers. But as I think of it, and of how much Hugh Sheridan's eyes also reminded me of my father, I realize hers are sharper and more determined than were my dad's . . . that dad's had a goodly portion of the Sheridan softness, almost a wetness, in his. And in my father's case, those eyes were mirrors of a soul beyond compare.

I wonder often about his Alzheimer's. When he came here to Ireland with a large group of the family in 1983, it was already apparently there. At the airport during a lengthy delay, after watching him drop out of a game because he couldn't remember the card suits, my uncle Jim Flynn said to my mom, "Floss I had no idea it was that bad. Jim used to be the best pinochle player in Port Richmond.". But something else happened on that trip, a day or so earlier the sight of the Book of Kells had filled dad with awe and wonder. Who knows, perhaps, among my dad's last real good conscious moments happened here in the land of his fore-family.

For you see my father really *was all that.* He was as smart as a whip, was far better than me at math and the like. My sister Mary Ellen, living in Cincinnati, seems to have gotten those genes the most. Mary Ellen and my other sister Sally, all of us, but especially, I guess the girls, seemed closest to him . . . . as it should be. It seems appropriate, I suppose, that Mary Ellen, being the older girl, was the first to get to the VA hospital when he died in August of '88. The picture from the family archives of the two of them in the back seat of a car on the day of her wedding, may be the single most attractive picture of any ever taken of my immediate family.

In that picture, she is in her virginal white, and dad in a tux and with a grin as big as the Cliffs of Mohar. My sister really *was* a virgin that day in 1971. By then she was already strange; by 1981 she'd have been a freak; by '91 an anachronism; by now a dinosaur. How did it happen? How could we, in *one generation*, take a belief and a way of life central to the very fiber of mankind up to that point, and turn it into something considered beyond laughable in its naiveté?

But many of those 17 years between Mary Ellen's wedding and my dad's death were hard and desperate ones for him. (Almost exactly 17; both events took place in August. It is amazing how many terminal events in my life took place in August. And now I am invited back in August for my Sheridan cousin's wedding.) And who can tell, maybe it was his Sheridan artistic side that made things so very rough on him.

For indeed he was an artist. He sang beautifully, could dance up a storm, but what he did best was write. It took me far too long to look at the letters he sent home from the war. It has taken me even far too much longer to look at more of them. The best, the one my mother refers to always, which describes the frozen hands of a priest offering up the host during a battlefield mass, is stuck in a box in the basement that I have refused to take the time to go through.

To get through that war, though, my father needed help. And when my brilliantly perceptive uncle, the same Jim Flynn, told me "you're father was the wrong one to be thrust into the fiercest longest fighting of the war," he was not commenting on my dad's courage, he was talking about his sensitivity. He was in the worst of it: North Africa, France, Germany. But in those letters, back and forth between he and my mother, I found from whence the help did come. *Almost every day*, my mother wrote him. Though not a match for his return notes in eloquence, they more than made up for it in the demonstrations of her undying faith in him. I don't remember in how many of the returns did he say, "My darling Florence, you cannot imagine how much I needed your note. I am amazed by your faith in me." My mom and dad fell in love in those letters, they became engaged in them . . . and the breathless, anticipation of the *first* night together comes across those pages with all the beauty and purity of a fresh snowfall on a countryside morning.

And by war's end this young man with a "naturally pessimistic bent" (as he'd called himself) was ready to be the head of our family. The marriage and that first night took place within a month (naturally!) The early struggling years were over by the time my recollection starts. But the happy days that the fifties were changed radically in the first half of the 60's—the first decade of the world as we know it today. He'd lose his successful wholesale floor covering sales job in the recession of 1962, and, the splendid American Dream life of two weeks down the shore and new car every other year, like wine turning to vinegar, would become, for us, the bitter drink of financial insecurity. Re-mortgages, loans; the words, "not making the draw", and "going in the hole", would become part of the muted and sad nighttime conversations between mom and pop.

As the "GD box" that he called our TV began it's steady siren call of consumerism, it represented, to the max, the beginning of the descent of the American culture into the mind-set where the only real sin was not having enough things. I wonder what it was like for him, downstairs alone, sipping the three or four ounces of beer each night, the twin terrors of getting the ends to meet, and even more so, the one of watching everything he ever believed in being chucked, like garbage out a window, tearing him apart. I wonder how much the forces of his own procrastination, his "not right this minute"s, were really about a deep never-that-I-heard mentioned sense that he could have done more, his art and his dreams drowning in a sea of responsibilities; this soulful, brilliant, kind man stuck in a schizoid quagmire of "want to but can't" and "how and why did it happen?" I wonder if this was the quicksand that seeped through his neurons and scattered his brain.

But then again my dad was about faith. That Jesus told us a man must become like a little child before he can enter the kingdom of heaven, and that my dad led a life trying very closely to follow the teachings of this Jesus, and that Alzheimer's patients become like little children—the 'death notice' that I once called his admission to the VA hospital was actually a release. His more complete participation in the Resurrection that had always been his (and that is offered to ALL people) did not become complete for him until the snares and tears of the world that were attached, (*not* necessarily, although he did not know that) to his particular skin and bones, finally had no more hold on him on that fateful day of August 22, 1988.

And now the moments of melancholia are fleeting, even disappearing. The "wish I had told him" longings in actuality are as silly and shortsighted as is thinking the most important thing about our relationship was what we *said* to each other. *And* if I fail to bask in the glow of all the righteous things that he was and which, because of the way he was, will be for*ever*more . . . if all the parts of him that really matter are not part and parcel of each and every thing I do or say for my remaining tenure on this lovely planet—then I deny both he and I our rightful portions. The monumental meaning of his life loses its import in exactly the degree that I fail to do that. The fruits of his piety, goodness, reverence and love cannot inspire and brighten and enlighten me, if I do not believe in them. Perhaps because of that, as much as for any other reason, in the warm wonderful glow of the "faith of my father", is where I now spend all my days.

Day 11

Cavan town is set up like a sort of semi-circle. The two main streets are Farnham and Main. Just past St Patrick's cathedral (I wonder if anybody ever did a head count of the St Patrick churches on this island!), Main Street loops down the rounded part of the circle and meets back up with Farnham on the way out of town. The traffic circle in the middle of town, where Farnham hooks, is new. The Cavanites seem to have a hard time figuring out the circle. Just this morning, because I'm never in a hurry anyway, I decided to head all the way down to Main Street (where most of the stores and people are) to do my heading up town. Being a pedestrian around that circle can be very scary!

Last night though, when I copped a ride home from the St. Felin's AA meeting the gent giving me the ride, went down Main Street—even though I'm up the hill, one block the other side of Farnham. And being that I'd intended to meditate ("And what do you *do* with this qigong?" "You just sorta breathe out and in" "Oh I do that already, otherwise I'd die") and write and chill a bit, because I had to pass their place, I decided to stop for just a second at Ann and Eddie's, which is on Bridge Street just below Farnham.

An hour later I was sitting by the fire in the *Eagle Saloon*, with two of their lovely friends Marge and Margaret. (THIS was Ann and Eddie's "home" bar. Now I know why the owner of *The Well,* round the corner, had made such a fuss over them the night before.) Both knew and loved Angela . . . something I hear over and over. Ann O'Reilly had not just hooked me up with an inexpensive place to stay, she'd placed me where she knew I needed to be. The "being taken care of" sense I've had since arriving in this town is amazing.

When I asked if they knew Theresa too, whom I'd met that previous morning, Margie (who looks like my Aunt Mary Whinney—although Margaret says she looks like Barbara Streisand, "except she's not a Jew,") it turns out is her sister. Her denoting that "Tees" is also the life of the party, filled out the 'Aunt Nat' similarity.

Tees, Phyllis (another friend), Angela, and Avril, the other boarder and me sat around the table this morning sipping tea. When I announced I was going to the bank, Tees offered to 'hold my package'. But today is Monday, it was to be a 'take care of biz' day for me. But the biz did not go well. When I stopped, Concepta was too busy to see me. My in-town AA friend would not confirm a ride to the AA meeting in Kilnacrott tomorrow night. But it was more than that. These things were the smoke and not the fire going on . . . a fire that needs constant fanning. The best thing that happened last night was when Margaret's very attractive younger daughter joined our talk at the *Eagle*. After I'd spoke of the fun and *neat*ness of doing what I'd always wanted to do and the believing that it IS God's will for me to be doing it, she sort of drifted away in thought. Probably thinking of a boyfriend, but maybe not. Maybe again. Maybe she thought this sounds different.

Something different. The memory hits me of the change of the look on the face of James Garner, playing AA co-founder Bob Smith, in the wonderful *My Name is Bill W* movie, when James Woods, playing Wilson said, "Hold on sir I'm here to help me, not to help you," the first time they'd met. Something different, something new. Smith who had been in the Oxford Group for years, was a devout, decent man but simply could not stop drinking. But when Wilson a fellow suffering from the same addiction brought him the message, he too did recover. (A movie for God's sake; how much blasted anonymity is there in that?) Wilson and Smith—two very American names, the founders of AA that brought the very pragmatic American "we got a problem, here is the solution" program to the world.

When I met my AA friend on the street, he returned to me the *12 Steps To A Deeper Faith* pamphlet I'd left in his car last week, he seemed not all that interested. "I am an alcoholic, I help other alcoholics." Well me too, bro, but look around ya' boy, you see anyone else suffering?

This pamphlet was written by a non-addicted priest, who, upon noticing the bright cheery alive spirituality of an AA member who had worked the program, had worked it too . . . only for him the first step substance he chose to admit powerlessness over, was his spiritual apathy. And it had changed his life. Can you think of any priest or person you know who suffers from that?

I think of two different priests I know—one AA, one not. The AA one was given permission to change a closed down Philly Catholic school into a 12-step spirituality center. But neighborhood protest clogged it down. As I left Philadelphia he was residing in my own upper middle class parish, taking his time to look for another place. This warm devout man, with whom over eight years ago, I shared my first fifth (sharing wrongs done) step, and whose humble beautiful little church two neighborhoods removed from my dad's *Nativity*, is the place where I came back to my faith, seems stuck.

The other priest; brilliant, Irish, an author, a devout man and a very good friend, but sad very sad. The weight of almost single handedly keeping alive a parish in the worst part of Philadelphia weighing him down, he too had no interest in the pamphlet, nor in the Aw*areness* book I gave him and almost begged him to read. "Wake up, put away your toys, drop your conditioning and attachments and know that you are happy," is essentially de Mello's message. I realize now I had not the right answer to the "what's so wrong about feeling sad?" query Father Mac had laid on me before I left for Ireland, and before he'd given me his blessing and before his remembering me in the delightful little 5:00 PM Mass he has each day in his sacristy. Now I do. You cannot be *happy* when you are sad.

I keep going back to those little rooms through which Ann Gaffney floats, one room to the next, back to cook or make tea, out in the store—I don't know how many times I've gone in there, refused food and ended up sitting behind a meal. Last night it was Eddie thrusting a sandwich into my hand. Everyone who comes in gets fed. Does she have loaves and fishes back there!? I was hungry and was given to eat. But it is not food mainly she gives me, she gives me the key to happiness. She lives, she laughs, she loves, she enjoys. And her first born son of Cavan who will wed the daughter of the grandson of Sarah's brother, brought her to me.

The clock strikes 21:24 (whatever the hell that is—almost 9:30.) I'm outta here; time to smell some roses.

* * *

Back at 23:22 almost midnight.

It was not until last night that I heard about our bombing of Iran . . . and today on CNN the 'battles of the day" included,

Serbia, and South Korea. Later as a diagram showed the stellar view of the insulated bubble that will mark the "we can get you, you can't get us" geometry of the USA's new defense system about whose coming a statesman had said, is not a question of if but only of when, I wonder how, if at all differently this system will change the dice we roll out of the Pax Americana we've imposed on the world.

Pax indeed. Somewhere I read or heard the number is around 40 for the number of armed conflicts raging at this time. This South Korean strike seems to be about GM offering to bail the auto manufacturer out *If* they will cut their workforce. I wonder if some marketing system could measure the relation of each clout of a club to the number of dollars that will make their way into a shareholder's pocket.

I just left Ann and Eddie, and her response of "he's trying to be", to Eddie's charming-yet-quirky sister Eileen's query "is he a holy man", sent me flying up here. I was supposed to meet Ann and Eddie at mass yesterday, but we missed each other. Just as well, I got some writing done. A Columban missionary had said mass, and I wish I'd have run into them long enough to hear Eddie say "look he brought his woman" about the little Filipino nun collecting the envelopes at the door on the way out. He seemed delighted to have turned the heads of a few of the ladies in town.

I have a friend, Gregory, at home, probably my best friend; and his father was pretty much Eddie. As a kid Gregory would leave for mass before mom and then double back and play pinochle with the dad and two of his buddies. (His dad Chuck's emphysema provided an excuse to not go.) I wonder though, my buddy's irreverence has more of an edge to it than did his dad's. I suppose spending a lot of your formative years pretty sure you're going to hell can leave pretty deep scars. I e-mailed Greg today and along with a movie trivia question, I told him he'd probably hate this book—but that in reality, if you stripped everything away, me'n'he believe pretty much the same thing. We're so different, yet so alike.

He was born seven days after me, he shares a birthday with Ben Franklin, I with Ray Bolger. (AND I know all the words to *If I Only Had a Brain* and I sing them too!)

Gregory loved *Awareness*, just finished it the second time. The first time he read it was after I'd brought it out to him as a peace offering a month after my not having been there for him when his older brother by one year died from of all things a bee sting, leaving a wife and six kids behind. He was pretty much in tears the night I finally went out to his house, "All I wanted was some contact from my friends." But I was busy . . . on retreat even . . . . then to Boston, then Long Island. Is "when I was lonely, you brought me comfort" among those things Jesus mentioned in the gospel about "the kingdom"? In that particular gospel, Jesus says that laundry list about reaching out to your neighbor twice, once for those who did, and then again for those who didn't. It always seemed kind of redundant to me, but it was probably because he wanted to really drive home how important that story was.

Gregory taught me a lot about my self-centeredness. Just recently, the exact words he had used about me stopped me from an intended salvo at my sister. (And as I think back of a finger-in-face to a *fellow* slipper'n'slider about "spitting in God's face, each time you drink", the cause of mine own very-next-day, slip was easy to find.)

I like to think I am like my father in many ways, but a lot more trying needs be done if I ever expect someone to call me non-judgmental. And I will tell you this; any spirituality that has no room for Chuck on the "in" side, sho 'nuff ain't for me. His, near-death opening-eyed, thumbs-up, to Gregory's "Bates says hi" (I am/was Bates—a nickname pinned to me in college, and one with which, I am afraid, stuck,) is among my favorite all-time memories.

And so this little "rush up here to write" turns out not at all what I'd intended. So be it. May Chuck and all the other, decent, kind and gentle *non*-practitioners, (in all the faiths for that matter—a pretty large net of folks I'd say!) rest in peace.

Day 12

The last two mornings I said the rosary after mass at St Claire's with the six or seven people who stick around each day. I figure I might as well. As "angelic" as Angela is, she is not an early riser. (Quite a few more people showed up today than yesterday. Gail whoever, whom I met both days on the way back up the hill after mass, was looking in a nouveau-type flower pot shop window, not liking what she saw; an "Orange lodge" is what I think she called it.)

But when they said all those after the rosary prayers that I never remember, I was reminded of this guy Billy who each week comes to Mike the monk's rosary group. I always kid him how he does know those prayers. He has over ten years sober and probably for 400 of the 520 or so weeks of that time, he's come to the rosary group. Billy is a really good guy; when my relapse parade began about 5 or 6 years ago, he was briefly my sponsor. He attends mostly 6:00 PM meetings, and is not much of a step or Big Book guy. I used to see him at the 4:30 "quick-as-a-flash-last-game-in-town" PM mass at Northeast Philly's St Bernard's Church. He lived with a real nice recovering woman for a while; they were a great couple. I was very disappointed when they broke up.

Near every week, though in the rosary group's post-coffee-break reading of the following week's gospel and little "how it fits us" comments, Billy's rap is pretty much the same. For whatever point of morality the gospel makes, Billy says, "I'd like to be there, but that just ain't me babe." God what wonderful faith! Like the publican in back of the church, "God be merciful to me a sinner."

I remember the Holy Saturday night, I guess it was two years ago now. Eight days earlier I'd bid goodbye to about six months sober time. I'd gotten through, or *almost* gotten through, a Holy Week where the addiction, like wolves howling at the door, was all about me. A Holy Thursday stop with my Jewish friend Mitch's dying mom, and her telling me how, at the last minute, Mitchell (as she always called him) her non-practicing son and not her son, the rabbi, had changed his mind, and had performed for her a Passover Seder, had, I thought, pulled me out of the fire. I woke up that Saturday morning fresh and ready to take on the world . . . I meditated, wrote some guidance—I might have even *exercised.*

But the resurrection was premature. By 11:00 PM that night, $300 was gone, and I was sitting in the back of a little adoration chapel crushed and confused. I was really there just to get warm, as I'd been out since early afternoon, and the shorts and tee shirt day had turned into a chilly night and to kill time until my sister and her friend would be asleep and not hear me coming in. They'd opened up their home to me 15 months earlier as refuge from my nice South Philly house, that had become *un*-nice and to where the "players" would come knocking. Minutes earlier as I'd seen the girl from round one of the two-ring circus of the day's relapse (the girl up the way had a better deal so I spent my last $100 there), heading up the Avenue to feed the beast I'd unleashed, the remorse and shame I felt, were perhaps the prayers I felt too ashamed to utter as I sat in the back of that chapel.

So there I was the next day on Easter Sunday two years ago, another day one of the rest of my life. Mom was away so we weren't doing Easter dinner, and I made my way down to my dad's Nativity parish for 12:00 mass—alone. But the family of my friend Nick from AA, who is not even Catholic, but whose wife and kids are, took me in for the day. It was three o'clock by the time we sat down to as big and delicious and sumptuous a breakfast I ever ate.

Again I was hungry and was given to eat.

Just yesterday, my good good friend Trentin Tom, the man who turned me on to a very valuable downtown Philly *University of the Arts* writing class last fall, and who is going back himself tomorrow night, e-mailed me and he was helping the a different Nick ("Nicky glasses" he calls him) who is just back thirty days sober again. My God the world can be a beautiful place! And another word will not be entered into this account until I go over to the Internet café and copy and paste Tom's beautiful *Bells of St Eustace* poem here.

I hear the Bells of Bishop Eustace School
peeling
And I recall when I was just a boy kneeling
Serving Mass for Fr. Lewis
Who always acted like he knew us
And who'd always say when we'd done
wrong
But, then he'd say we still belonged.

Too bad those days are all gone
Too bad those days are long gone.

I used to ride the night ray-deo
Up and down the bright glowing dial
And then I'd say a Confeteor Deo
As if I were on a self-imposed trial.

But, soon after Fr. Lewis leftus
We'd steal from the Friars' supply of Chivas
From the Rectory's private basement store
And the ray-deo rocked like never before
Yes the ray-deo rocked like never before.

Time went by and we flew away like geese
in a snowstorm looking for shelter.
And the seasons and years pulled us away
From each other, from God, helter skelter.

And there came a point at which to consider
Was I worse off with God? Was I better?

Now, in my room overlooking this school
I wish in my youth I'd not been a fool
But tried to follow the Golden Rule
Instead of acting like a one-eyed mule.

Still, I hear the Bishop's Bells
As the sound carries across the fields
And I can remember Fr. Lewis tell us
That God is merciful and all wounds heals.

So, please let the Bells of the Bishop rock on
For all of those who care to belong
Let them rock for the Sinner
Let them rock for the Saint
Let them rock for the winners
As well as who ain't.

Day 13

The light from the candle flickered sweetly on the soft, white, *very* big and *very* round face of one-year old Darrah. Though that young he knew enough to go 'phew phew' and point to the candles behind the head of Angela who held him . . . remembering, I suppose, last week's first birthday. He is a real "gurrier" Angela told me, which means a roughneck. Breen, a year older and his brother, and quieter and more timid, (not a guerrier), after a little prodding, helped blow out the candle (with a big surreptitious assist from Angela.) The two boys are Angela's grandchildren; her son Sean, who's crew fixed the shower next to my room, is their dad.

My across-the-sea nephew Thomas is a guerrier, and is now four going on five. We have a great picture of my sister Sally feeding him one time, the green from the whatever all over her sleeves, his hands wrapped round hers, pulling cause she wasn't shoving it in his mouth fast enough. A camera was not there for my favorite—when in his walker, a bottle clutched tightly in his mouth, he looked to be leading a calvary charge coming 'round the corner, chasing after his sister Kiera, two years older and my godchild.

Me'n'he are famous buddies: among his first legible utterances (a babysitter told my sister-in-law), was a garbled version of the fist pumping "the moose is on fire" chant that I had taught him. I'd also taught him and Kiera and their older sister Caitlin, a rythmic hand-slapping thing my dad had taught me as a child. (And which my sister Mary Ellen still thinks I do wrong. And somehow now, so does Caitlin!)

I guess Caitlin was nine, Kiera four, and Thomas two, in that fateful spring, summer and fall of 1997 when my addiction really had me. And Thomas' chubby fingered attempts to do the hand slap, and Kiera's bright happiness that could fill a world, and an "out of nowhere" unsolicited hug by Caitlin as I sat at the kitchen counter, are the representative specks of memory, that the oasis of love and safety, my long journey across town to dinners at my brother Tommy's house that year, represent for me.

I remember driving home, a near hour's drive, tears rolling down my cheeks, thinking I was too dirty and debased to have deserved that scene I'd just left. I *knew* I was not through with the acting out and that was the thought that really killed me.

Thomas and Kiera and me romped around the outside of the restaurant during the party that my family had for me a few days before I left for Ireland. The demon is gone now. And if not for the adhesive my wonderful family provided in those days when I was falling apart, I'm quite sure I would not be here right now.

*   *   *

Possibly the kindest, gentlest man in this Cavan Town, maybe in any town, is a chap by the name of Michael Smith. Nobody disagrees. If I had a pound for every time he's said to me "ah that's grand, Jim", I would have to worry about no more ATM tapping. (By the way, he told me last week to make sure to mention his name when I go to Kilnacrott.) He like lives in the library and today I was showing him a few e-mail tricks. He's a tad unusual, is bone-thin, wears gloves in and outside, and talks about having to go home and take a nap each day. Angela also told me that years ago, he'd gone to be a priest, but did not make the cut. She also told me about how a bad dose of a medication, fueled subsequent medication, etc. I wonder how much A has to do with B, and B has to do with C. I don't know why he didn't make the cut, but I will ask him. Michael is as devout a Catholic as can be . . . a regular at 10:00 mass at St Pat's. In a brief discussion re our current Pope, Mike, Tom, the librarian and me all agreed he is a very good man. Yet as I listen to the women in this town—women whose love and decency and kindness has overwhelmed me—their almost universal rejection of this positive assessment makes me wonder more about the Church in general, and the pope in particular. And when I read in *The Irish Independent* of the promotion of a cardinal named Ruini, with a *"reputation as the Vatican's conservative-minded eminence grise, with the power that stems from being constantly at the pontiff's side,"* and of the pass over of a Cardinal named Martini, whose call for a Third Vatican Council to *"address roles of women, priestly celibacy, contraception and abortion"*, who will now go trucking down to a *"life of study in Jerusalem"*, I wonder some more.

Seems to me an inverse route from the one Paul and the boys took.

Day 14 3:45 AM (end of week two)
February 21, 2001

The abrupt end to the notes above were because I'd misread that silly clock last night thinking the 19:19 meant 8:19 and not one hour earlier.

And it was very wrong of me to pay little attention to the words being spoken by the two Protestant clergymen at the in-town ecumenical meeting I'd rushed off to. (Although neither of these two blokes were exactly Billy Graham!) The only right thing I did at that meeting was to sit on the other side of the little old Protestant woman my dear cousin Maura had brought, and who, when Maura realized was sitting in a row by herself, suggested we move. I hadn't noticed as I was too busy rambling on. And maybe because of the silly joke or two I said to her during the meeting, when it was over, she was kind enough to let me get her cane that rested on the radiator beside me. The genuine smile at my "now you got the cane, so you'll be able" quip, (I doubt if 'ol Phyllis laughs out loud much—as if that quip deserved a gargantuan guffaw!) was about the thousandth times I've felt touched by God in this lovely little town called Cavan.

It's 4:27 AM now. (The clocks over here are right until noon.) Considering how troubled my mind was when I crawled under the covers last night, the sleep came pretty easy. My pre-hop in bed prayer was very brief.

Prayer. Yesterday morning's gospel was the one about the really nasty demon, the apostles couldn't remove, but that Jesus did. The words used were "with a demon like this, only prayer will remove it." (I think one of the other gospel writers says prayer and fasting—I like this version better, I have a rough time with fasting.)

4:27 here; 11:27 Philly—Tuesday night. Mike the monk and the crew are a few hours removed from the rosary gathering on the tiny street in Philly's Tacony section, a stone's throw, it turns out from the home in which I was born. Mike who's like the most Catholic guy in the world, says the gates of hell are closed during the meeting. Mike also sat across from me once when I had one day sober again, and said "Alright that's behind you. Time to move on." And he gave me a piece written by Padre Pio, a 20th century saint and stigmatic, that said something like "the worst thing we can do in the time of sorrow is to consider it a punishment from God, rather it is an opportunity to take it to Him on the cross."

Mike also talks about Jesus needing help with that cross, that he could have been looking 2,000 years down the road for someone to provide that help. He also always includes "intentions of the Holy Father" in his pre-rosary recitations of what we're praying for. Maybe we should all pray that this tired old man might choose his counsel a little more wisely.

I don't know if I've been asleep at the wheel lately or something, but up until the "back to the past—Salvation only through the risen Christ" encyclical written last August that I was told was inspired by his arch-conservative counselor Cardinal Ratzinger (August again), I'd thought JP2 had been on a pretty good roll. That "not part of the schedule" trudge up to place a paper in Jerusalem's Wailing Wall last Easter personally knocked my socks off. And then there was the May Day papal inspired, "end Third World debt" concert in Rome, with Amy Lennox, and Lou Reed of all people. "Maybe there IS hope for the world", was the subject I used when I e-mailed the notation about that concert to about a hundred people. The pope, in eurythem, walking the wild side—imagine! And maybe it was then that Ratzinger and the boys started getting scared. "May Day" end debt, maybe this was a bit too radical, "I mean we are a corporation here". Maybe that is when they decided to really load up his schedule so he couldn't think straight, so they could seep their own petrified poison into his brain.

Lots of maybes, lots of suppositions—many coming from one article in one paper with anti-Catholic leanings, on a rock of faith of an island called Ireland. Maybe we could have a PEOPLE'S vote. Some Sunday morning let the people decide if a new Vatican council should be held. Run that up that papal chimney and see how many people will smoke it. I'll bet quite a few. And maybe one of the first points of business could be to hold another council with people from other faiths. But in the same way Dostoyevsky's "Grand Inquisitor" told Jesus to hit the road, I doubt such an idea would go very far. After all a CARDINAL like Ratzinger is a lot closer to Jesus . . . than a people like maybe Michael Smith.

De Mello says there aren't bad people, there are only blind people. I was told Ratzinger was one of the main men behind Vatican II. Maybe he got scared. Maybe the Light of an open, honest, real brave new world blinded him. Of course he and the rest of the conservative cardinals surrounding the pope aren't bad men; they think what they are doing is right. But still waters not only run deep, they stagnate. They are men just like Peter and Paul were. Somehow, someway, though, the message of that Jesus guy that one knew intimately, and that the other got knocked off his horse by, got skewed—I think most of us can agree on that . . . . including, I would hope, these cardinals.

———

In a little bit, if I'm still awake, I'll stroll on over to St. Clare's. And I'll listen to the Word. Lots of days it's very pertinent. Yesterday this priest with a great Cavan brogue, in the prayer of the faithful, prayed for people who don't believe in God, which was very cool. For the second day in a row he skipped the kiss of peace handshake, which is very uncool. An island that gave us the wonder of the book of Kells, unfortunately also gave us those abominable tombs we call confessionals—Yin-Yang galore.

But the main thing this island probably gave to civilization is a whole lot of those things Jesus told us were so important, called prayers. Ruins of monasteries are all over the place. And if you remember the only formal prayer he actually taught us, he thought it important enough to mention " . . . as we forgive those who trespass against us." As painfully boring as that ecumenical thing was last night, it sure am a start. They have teens speaking next week; maybe it'll be better.

Later on I'll pop over to the library and give Michael Smith some more pointers on e-mail . . . maybe I'll ask him or maybe I won't about the priest thing. (I think I'm hanging around Ann Gaffney too much.) One thing for certain, I'll almost surely cash in a few more "aahhh you're a good man, Jim's". And maybe they'll be an e-mail from America from my friend Gregory. I sure hope so.

* * *

I did go to St Claire's at 7:30 . . . after about a one hour not ready-to-sleep-yet lie there. My head raced and, for some reason I was feeling none too happy. It is now 10:15 and the second I really woke up a few moments ago, I knew I was peaceful and contented. Very nice indeed.

DeMello says to drop all attachments. Bad AND good come and go. Now is real good. Tomorrow might not be so . . . so what. I think I'll go down and get some breakfast . . . . and I'll print out and show some people what I've written. I've yet to learn to drop my attachment to approval, but perhaps that time will come.

17:58 (5:58 PM Philly Time)

It didn't even take an entire day for the pendulum to swing. De Mello says we'll swing into action once we do the dropping of the attachments and conditioning. The walk around town with a hundred ideas in my head that now just ain't there. And the realization that now it's too late to go to the Sheridan's tonight and the this'n'that have me kind of troubled. I realize I've not called home for a week and that right now my mom is probably out for a spell.

Another mother sat downstairs this morning at Angela's breakfast table—a mother who just lost her 37-year old daughter to cancer. The daughter sounds like she was a very special person. She wants her ashes scattered in a field by her two children—one four & one six—and then to have a tree planted there. How exactly she ended up in Angela's lap I do not know, but with Angela and the other full-time boarder, Avril (from down in Kells) sitting and talking to her, I knew she was in good hands.

I offered some words about the important part of her daughter still being with her, and they might have helped a bit. Thank God she has a strong ox of a son who was also there to help look after her. The woman was from Wales and I guess her daughter and her son-in-law lived over here. It seems like the sort of family in which the son-in-law will make good on his promise to bring the kids across the channel frequently.

I guess the biggest difference between here and America is that almost all of the children I've run into here seem to have mothers and fathers. Especially in American AA rooms, the majority of the mothers are unwed.

One such single mother had very wet eyes Christmas a year ago. She was crying at the official death of a crack prostitute daughter who'd been flung out the window of a car like a used up candy wrapper, by two guys speeding down an Interstate. There was nary a blip in the paper, the evening news, whatever. I'm told it happens all the time—body bags being carried out of abandoned houses in Kensington or North Philly or wherever. Bullies Acre would be filled in a couple of weeks if you took the cumulative scraps of skins and bones of such from say Philly, New York and maybe Chicago. Throw in all the cities, big and little where addicts die forgotten in the night (or day—little difference for a junkie or crackhead, down freak, whatever), in America, the land of milk and plenty, and lots and lots of acres would be needed to hold the volume.

Crack, the pipe was my thing. Heroin—'dope' for short in the lingo—seems the most abrupt killer. Needles-in-arms heaps on bathroom floors in burnt out "abandominiums"—they even have a name for 'em. Crack can get you pronto, in a heart freezing flash, but usually it doesn't. I used to hold the hit in as long as possible. That I was so non-proficient a smoker probably saved my life. I was getting better at it though.

As I think about how much better that woman downstairs looked later on as Angela and Avril had held her hand so expertly, the main thing she had to go on was that her daughter had led a good decent life, and that it was cancer and not some crazy addiction that had snuffed it out. I too was a good decent person, but a painfully sick addicted one that August night in 1997 when my sister Mary Ellen came home and found my mom alone crying in the living room dark, "I know Jimmy's dead in that house down in South Philadelphia." The shivers up my spine as to what it would have done to her if she'd been right are pretty well gone now. One thing most everybody who makes it to the recovery rooms will agree on, somebody else's prayers got them there. Whenever I think, "what good is it to specifically pray for someone," I need only think about the solitary rosaries my mom said for me in that very same chair.

I just got off the phone with her and she was happy as a lark to hear from me. She spends a lot of time in that chair these days; the arthritis and clogged arteries and diabetes have slowed her down a ton. I've been trying to seamlessly get her into this story; Ann Gaffney (at whose little rooms behind the store, I just had another wonderful meal) keeps asking me about her. I guess she knows I need to go there . . . maybe all those other thoughts swirling around in my head, like the water stuck in the pipes Hugh Sheridan presides over, will come gushing through, once I ignite the sensor switch the description of my mom just might be.

Gushing out may be the word to describe my birth. When the time got near I came flying out with such impatient force, emergency surgery was required for the C-section delivery that damn near killed her. (All six of us kids were c-sections. Mom always says that's why we have such nice shaped heads.) It was so bad and damaging her pediatrician quit her when she chose not to have the tubes tied, a decision with which the Church would have had no problem. Folks really did consult the Church in those days on such matters, certainly my folks did. The next pediatrician said his predecessor was way off base, the danger was really minimal. And if you were to look at my younger brother Mark and the twins at the end, Tommy and Sally, you can well see my parents' choice for life was a good one.

Mom said I was real good baby, spoke very early (now there's a shocker!) but I had one major problem; I would not go to sleep. It's funny it is just very recently I can recall sitting at the top of those steps as my first memory. As I've heard mom say about 500 times, "you'd just sit there, you wouldn't come down. We'd put you back in bed and then look up ten minutes later and there you were." I wonder what I was thinking sitting there, I guess the "still want the party to go on" thing I've always had. (The image of Sarah in that hotel room, was a bit more concrete than this memory, but not much . . . definitely in that same "skirt the sub-conscious" mode.)

Of course I think about my mom and Sarah . . . without question the two women who influenced me more than any others. That to this point, no somewhat-permanent romantic interest has come along is not something I'm tickled about, but that attachment, here, now, while on this sojourn, is probably a good one to not have. Sarah and Florence, one from a time and an era gone by, and the other so much smack dab in the middle of this one it would make your head spin. A lot of time mom spends in that chair she is watching her beloved Philadelphia Seventy-Sixers (professional basketball team). Her boys she calls them. And I am not exaggerating when I say of the 82 regular season games, she watches probably at least 78 of them. Even the West Coast ones most of the time.

It was just last November when she stopped being the oldest person in our area to be collecting unemployment. At eighty she'd been laid off from the job on the information desk at the same University of Pa. Hospital where I worked. She now volunteers one half-day a week. And for those four hours is still probably the most hard-working and proficient person "on the desk" that she had gone to for 28 years prior.

I'm sure it is from her that I have this hunger for people. Her hunger is more like about love or interest, or if you want to get down to it, nosiness. "Oh here comes the questions . . ." you'll hear one of us say when mom, not all that discreetly, starts peppering any new person who comes around for info. One of the recent pryees is the new boyfriend of my niece Elizabeth. The guy is a prince, sent my mom his own birthday card last January 28. The guy is very smart, book smart, unlike the street smart, last boyfriend of Elizabeth's. I happened to overhear mom's response to Elizabeth's "What can I say grand mom, I guess I just like them smart," last Christmas day. Elizabeth roared when mom said "I guess opposites attract."

Elizabeth, my sister Mary Ellen's younger daughter is absolutely crazy about my mom. And her little spoken tribute at the 80th birthday BLAST we had for her granny in January of '99 helped add to an absolutely magnificent night. Another of the tribute's that night came from my cousin Jimmy, one of the nine children of her old Hallahan buddy, my Aunt Betty and my Uncle Jim. The tribute was a dynamite poem that ended with something like;

"And take a look at her folks
she's one in a million."

I'm pretty sure Jimmy's birthday is May 5th. Mom ain't pretty sure, she knows. Just like she knows the birthdays of Jimmy's eight siblings . . . as well as the birthdays of countless other members of the family. Not years, just the days. If I've heard her say, "I'm not good with years," once I've heard it a thousand times. Driving around I pepper her for info, Uncle Jim is right, ask Floss. She remembers . . . events, things said, the occasion even, but "I'm no good with years."

And that's just it, mom is not about the chronology of days that make up the history of a family or a world even, she is about the stuff that makes them worthwhile. A birthday is a held baby, a remember to send a card . . . in that flowing handwriting that looks like a Tipperary accent, the cards keep going out:

the sinews of meaning
that wrap our events
is where there is holy
is where there is love

That is what I mean about the McGowan women in-laws, Sarah, Mary Alice, Dympna, Floss. That which they wrap around we descenders of the holy tree *is* what it is all about. A line connecting them would not work. A web holding us together would be a lot closer. A firm but very gentle comfortable to be in web, though.

I tease mom a lot about the little mystery/romances she goes through one after the other. I say, "how bout you read a page or two of *Awareness* in between books". She's maybe read 10 of the pages. Her "I'll read it while you're away" promise I'm quite sure won't be kept. She's another one that doesn't have to.

De Mello tells us to drop our conditioning and attachments and we will realize we are happy . . . not get happy, realize it. Trying to *get* it, only produces frustration. I spent most of the last 36 or so of my 49 years on this planet frenetically trying to get it. I should have just looked at mom. She *lives* and is happy because she loves and cares about people, and they do so back. No complicated Yin/Yang philosophical distractions there.

23:29. Almost midnight. I wrote through the Sixer game (Wednesday night—they were probably playing.) I feel I might have done mom short. But I wrote what I wrote. And guess what? Mom wouldn't mind if dad got a better tribute. I remember the way she'd want us to watch *Father Knows Best* or *Leave it to Beaver* because the dad in those shows was not a buffoon like in *Make Room for Daddy* or in *Ozzie and Harriet*. Mom knew the proper pecking order of a real family. These days I often hear her sigh "Thank God I'm not raising a family in today's world.". Right on mom, what would you guide us to, *Spin City* or *Will and Grace*?

Day 15

I gave Angela a copy of de Mello's final meditations called *The Way to Love* yesterday and she did not like it one bit. But it lay open on the dining room table to the spot she'd left it because she is probably going to go back and pick it up again. Angela is a hero because she *thinks*. There are a lot of heroes over here in Ireland.

Yesterday turned out not so bad after all. I took Anne O'Reilly and Concepta out to lunch. Concepta is going to take me out to Black Lion on Saturday, I'm doing mass and I'll bet one monster of a breakfast over at Dympna and Hugh's on Sunday. Mentioning that to Angela my bed and *breakfast* maven last night, was probably not a good idea.

When I told Michael Smith yesterday, that I'm going to have a hard time leaving this town to go home, he said, "ahhhh Jim, you're home now lad."

* * *

I was going to take a break, but being that Angela did not make good on her "Okay then breakfast is a 8:00 sharp" promise/threat she made when I told her about the "not exactly an early riser" thing I put in here the other day, here I am.

I just came from mass and it just happened to be the feast of the Chair of St Peter the Apostle. And in Peter's first letter (he only wrote two) he says "Be the shepherds of the flock . . . not for sordid money. Never be a czar over any group . . ."

After watching a Vatican cardinal swearing in ceremony, yesterday (big news over here because the very conservative Archbishop Connell of Dublin was sworn in), the pomp and circumstance of the thing that would make a British royal ceremony look like a Saturday night caeli, I wonder about the czar part. The Church's corporate holdings versus the money part is too obvious to even go into.

But the very best thing I did this morning after I went into the sacristy and borrowed the Bible to get the quote I used above, was to go back in the Church and say the rosary with the ladies sitting there. And through three decades worth the rosary was empty as thoughts of the lyrical crap I'd come up here to key into this journal and *not* any prayers for any intention, entered into this head of mine. But then it stopped, I was all the way up to the "find him in the temple" 4th joyful mystery when I really prayed, that this holy brilliant Polish man we call John Paul II would have a change of heart. (Speaking of the 'find Him in the Temple' story, there might be one more argument that Jesus was not an only child. Do you really think Mary and Joseph were the kind of parents that would be so much into their *friends*, they'd lose track of their *only* child?) And what better way, time or place to be dedicating such a prayer to him than by saying some decades of the rosary. This pope who is called "Mary's pope", and who wrote a brilliant, moving book full of devotions to her, that I know about only because my older brother Tony, gave it to me.

Tony, again, is so named because mom made good on her promise to St Anthony. He lives at home, just like I do, and he is one of the most gentle kind men I know. He spends a lot of time at home, when he's not chauffeuring mom around or picking up milk or making the coffee each day or doing other things for me and her. And because he spends a lot of time praying, and not running around in a people pleasing frenzy like I do, I sometimes think he's lonely . . . lonely all right, lonely doing the single most important thing each of us in our own way can do—and that is to pray.

And as I think of that gentle saint for whom he is named, I wonder that my older brother is not a bit like him. I remember him in the front bedroom pantomiming mass as a child. My older sister Mary Ellen and I played altar boy and girl—all this before we got too old to consider participating in such nonsense. And we were right in our eventual de-participation; we were older and were wiser. It is only now, years later, looking from a place where I've been given the grace to bask with wonder at the silly little things children do, to know that they are not silly, but that they are beautiful and perfect, because they are performed from a place of innocence and charm that for too many years I had left—believing wrongly and tragically that my maturity had denied me participation. Only now do I realize how right and pure and perfect was my participation back then. Only now as a re-participant, I know it was not nonsense. Likewise the "rap the wall at the end of each decade" rosary races in the upstairs hallway Mary Ellen and I used to have. Do I not think that Mary or Jesus, (or whatever reality way beyond my ability to conceive these two represent) delighted at the "winner's nose in the air" haughty turn into their room? And even moreso perhaps in little Jimmy's peeved "she cheated!" trudge into bed. OF COURSE they *counted*!

As I sit here and think of the shameful way I sometimes badger my older brother, because of his eating habits or whatever, and of the very Christian way he almost never strikes back, I am still very grateful for, make that infinitely grateful for, the prayers that I know he's never denied me. And there that word *infinitely* firmly fits. In fact is there any other arena from which we finitely limited human beings can be catapulted into the vast wondrous world of the state beyond words we call infinite, than in the world of prayer?

And so in the last two decades, except for the breaks in the concentration of my wordfull agendas, I prayed for my pope. It was only later as I walked back and forth in front of the library waiting to see how my man Smitty was making out with the computer directions I'd left him, did I realize that I should have also prayed for Ratzinger and whoever the cardinals are I think might be leading the pontiff back to the past . . . a past filled with much good but with far too much bad. For Jesus told me it's easy to pray for the good guys, it's praying for the ones you don't like is where the real deal is.

* * *

Holding his fingers about two inches apart, "If it's this fat nobody will buy it." Moving his fingers four inches apart, "if you swell it up a bit with pictures, then everybody will buy it", from the back/side room behind the store called *Favorites* from whence the Gaffney's do their thing, Eddie offered his marketing tip.

The place is set like this; the store, a little room just beyond where from the end seat of a table Ann, or whoever, can watch TV, talk to me, do whatever and still view the store. (Any time you go to *Favorites* and there is any size shape or form of an employee *actually behind the counter,* then something is definitely up.) The dining room is off to the right, the kitchen, out of which Ann prepares the endless run of food or tea or whatever, is beyond the dining room.

Jim McCabe and his lovely wife Josephine were waiting when Eddie (not long after offering his tip) dropped me off. Some really terrible news, that Jim's first cousin down in Dublin is very sick, had just come down. Maybe the telling the history tale to me got his mind off it a bit.

But it didn't take long for Jim to get into it, a mention about the Ulster plantation and he was off. And if you've ever heard a man talk with verve and passion about something he knows and loves, it is a wonderful sight to behold. When at tale's end to my "how long have you been a teacher?" query, it turned out he wasn't, I was more than amazed.

But at the beginning of the tale, the strange "down in Belfast, up in Dublin" Cavanesque thing was in place. I know he told me exactly how that transpired but I lost my first page of notes. But the Old *English* were in Dublin, the Old Irish up here. I do know, however, that this was the lineup, with the north being split mainly among the O'Reilly's in Cavan, the O'Brien's in Tyrone and I think the O'Donnell's in Donegal. The Old English in the south had the better land, and their chieftains were apparently more localized and not as territorial. But the post-split from Rome, Catholic/Protestant situation was not really that bad until Henry the Eighth got a bee in his bonnet and didn't want to be just "Ruler" of Ireland, and king of England, he wanted to be *King* of both. (I think Jim stood up at the point, widened his eyes pointed his glasses, raised up his voice and said, "He wanted to be King!") This was during the time Henry was lopping off wives heads' like carrots in a stew, and the guilt and some syphilis I think, probably had his ire up.

Travel was long and slow in those days and before any armies got marching, Henry was dead and the bee in the bonnet was passed down to Elizabeth I. I don't know how many historians with letters galore at the end of their names, could describe, better than Jim, the tragic irony that the *Flight of the Earls*, O'Donnell and O'Brien, happened *after* Elizabeth had taken the price off their heads. For while the two top cats were away, hiding under the Papal skirt, (because these guys had *stood up* to the king of the blasphemers, they'd been welcomed in Rome like conquering heroes), like mice to an open bag of feed, the Scots and English came down and gobbled up much of the good land. There was a definite Protestant tint to things by now, and the rocky black soil, like that which I saw up in my family's land in Derryvilla in West Cavan was all that got left to the Irish. There's a song *The Black Rocks of Borne* that's all about it.

It gets a bit fuzzy here, the Stuarts get involved, some secession questions and such, but I do remember, that by the time Cromwell arrived, there was an urgency to his madness as the Brits had their hands full over in America, and money was kind of tight. I think it was before Cromwell though that O'Brien's son Owen Roe was doing a good job pushing out the invaders—but he ended up getting poisoned.

But time marches on, and reigns of terror eventually run dry. Cromwell was dead and his son ended up being such a dud, the English decided to go back to monarchy and to bring back Charles I. (Child-rearing can be tough, I guess, when you're busy slaughtering, raping and pillaging a whole island full of people.) But even as the grass was greener for the Scots and Englishmen, down here on the land of NOT their forefathers, it was even greener over in America. So off many of them went, Scottish Presbyterians I believe leading the way, mostly to the southern part of the New World. Alas they apparently brought a lot of their old world fire and brimstone with them, and who knows, maybe because of the warm climate or whatever, it got even hotter . . . fanning the flames of what would become the KKK down the line.

And only a man like Jim who really knows his stuff, could add how unfounded was the, "Why don't you work the fields, instead of cramming up in urban areas?" disgust the New Worlders had for the 17th and 18th century Irish that went over there. The problem was if you were Irish, over here, you couldn't *own* your land. So you see land over there, without the money to buy horses and things, did you no good. And that their Protestant *brothers* were allowed to sell land back to the landlords, and land that was a tad lot better to begin with anyhow, in America too—you can see how the Irish were forced to take a major back seat.

But meanwhile back on the "old sod" Charles and James and Mary's and Scotts and Catholic mothers and such, led us to a point where James II was actually lined on up with the Irish against his brother-in-law William of Orange, who Jim was quick to point out was not all that bad a guy. A Dutchman married to Charles II's daughter, he was probably a much better guy than Jimmy II, who seemed ambivalent about his faith and a lot of other things. But because the French are always against the English, it seems, they were set to march on out against William of Orange. In France, however, some other things were going on. Greed, it seems is universal, and when the French, for whatever reason, decided they wanted the landholdings of the Church, grab them they did. And I guess Pope whoever it was at the time, wasn't on the one about Jesus telling Judas to give their slim purse to the poor when he started making waves tither'n'yon about which way to toss his chips. He didn't like King Louie whatever (it probably was a Louie—they usually were) de-rendering what he claimed had been his . . . .

But back to the facts. I'm pretty sure Jim was up and pacing by now as he laid out the sides; William versus James in the Battle of the Boyne. Seems the stew going on across the channel was such that the French that came over were so tres ambivilante that some went with William and some went with James. In the beginning the battle went well for the Irish, but the void at the top, turned the old tide. And seems Jamie was running before the battle was even over, and Willie of O, won the July 12th day. But like nature hates vacuums, so it seems does history at times like this here. And into the breach a chap name of Sarchfield did gather on up the Irish were left. And at a bridge in a town called Athlone, some very brave men, blew it on up so Orange's pursuit was neatly slowed down. And by the time they got to Limerick, Willie of Orange had a bit of real deep respect for this Sarchfield. Seems right under his nose, some of Sarchfield's men had sneaked into camp and blew up Orange's munitions. Anyway down there in Limerick, William was decent enough and had got to respect Sarchfield enough to let the Irish go back to their land. Problem was because most of the Irish troops (40,000 to 1,000 nearly) went off to fight for hire in France, the Irish were left with no protection. William sailed back across the channel, and into this new vacuum of non-leadership, the haves filled on in. And the Catholic-*owned* part of the land went from like 65% to less than 10%. And that is pretty much as far as we got.

To have been presented a picture of this tale with the accuracy, flair, passion and even love, is something for which I will always be grateful. I'm glad I'll be around long enough to thank Jim McCabe many times.

Being that it's late I'll probably skip St Claire's tomorrow at 7:30. Jim McCabe often goes to the 10:00 at St Pat's; maybe I'll see him there.

When I asked Jim how long he and Eddie Gaffney have known each other, Josephine chimed in "since before they were born." That kind of closeness fills the air here. The delicious meal and wonderful conversation after the lecture were all part of another magnificent day here in Cavan Town. When the topic drifted to the pope and Josephine told me she'd heard he'd been given bad counsel in South America, I realized I should have listened a bit more to my Chilean Marxist friend and fellow-qigong practitioner, Julio, who blasted JP II's anti-Latin American revolutionary rhetoric. But my "don't like communism" conditioning got in the way.

When Josephine said "you can tell you're a McGowan from Cavan," as she heard some of the questions I asked during Jim's brilliant oration, it made me very proud. There is no one in the world more proud to be a McGowan than I, or an American-Irishman, or even a Cavanite of sorts. BUT if that love is not imbedded and rooted in a love for ALL mankind, then it is shortsighted and parochial . . . a drop, well with the McGowans a lot of drops, but certainly not the ocean.

I'm certain I missed a lot, and in my melodramatic way, I wondered if this is when the French Jansonists seeped their poison (one not dissimilar to the fire and brimstone the Scots took across the sea, only a poison named Catholic), into the clergy here. I don't know if it happened then but I know that it happened.

And even though for the most part no longer do crosses go burning deep in the night, the attitude that went with them *is* still around. Maybe too visions of fires of hell if you see a dame's ankle are no longer part of the spirituality here, but scars do get left.

And it's 2:42 AM, and I am going to bed.

Day 16
Saturday

Cold and sunny in Cavan town this morning. But cold and sunny and bright. Is it that the sun is more needed for its warmth in the cold that makes it seem brighter, or is it that the cold air freezes the stuff between us and it?

On a sunny summer day in Philadelphia, many times you can not even see the skyline from a mile away because of the smog. These great ivory towers, brilliant in design and that serve a real purpose, lost from view in the crud.

But in reality what difference does it make if you can see them from a little bit afar? Up the elevators, crammed with the legions marching to the office to do a day's work. Quiet sullen faces, nary a word spoken, cause there's others around. And work like all work (at least such that is not involved with taking from the lowly to give to the high) *is* good work. I think of my sister-in-law, Eileen who used to be really close to me, but now somehow is not. She used to do all my typing until this hunt and peck system became a thing I had to learn. Once I wrote a line that was good but mostly I wrote it for her. The topic was 'what I owe the other' and the teacher who'd assigned it was a kind decent man from the uneev of pa, a place of which the brush of godless intellect, I paint fairly too wide.

The line went like this:

> *I have known countless others . . . some irreligious ones but who in their kindness and innocence speak volumes of the God that's inside.*

And that is Eileen. "Long lean Eileen" as I call her. My ace of a brother Mark became much more of one, once he met her . . . another kind and loving in-law. (One time brother Mark, who can do *everything* mechanic-wise, was litanizing all I can't. "Jesus Christ Jimmy you can't do no plumbing, you can't change a tire, etc . . . : and Eileen punctuated each item with a sure and steady "yeah but he *sure can write*" . . . so you know I LOVE Eileen!) Mark is the one who went down to South Philly on Thanksgiving Day 1997 and brought me to dinner when, in the midst of a run, I'd lent my car to a drug dealer who had not come back. Mark is also the one who co-signed my bank account so I could not make withdrawals to buy the substance that was claiming my life.

So if you can see in an "It's a Wonderful Life" way, where exactly would I be if mom had said yea to the doctor who'd wanted to close that wond-errous womb. And then there is Sally, named after Sarah, at the end of the line. She was so well hid in the womb behind Tommy, her twin, that the new doc of my mother said, "whoa another's in there!"

I don't know if anyone knows, but surely I do, of the warm August night, when during a rollicking party at our home cause the folks weren't there, that it was Sally who'd tucked my falling down drunk self safely in bed. It must have been around 1977 or '78, and when I awoke from that load, the beacon which had shone through a horrid psychotic spin, was then re-lighted with the warm morning sun. And the beacon was this, that which had made it through the awful shock-t's, and the drugs and the drinking and the fear of the she's and the this and the that . . . it was that of my Savior lost and alone, wond'ring what had become of the world he loved so. But the beacon I'd lost in the anti-psyche drug cure they gave me—til the kind loving care of a sister Sal-li.

Then all through the years, through the smog of the booze, through the cold near-death terror of the "hits" in torn seedy rooms, that beacon had tailed me, calling me home. Home as Michael called it, which is here, but not just. And Sally was there at a meeting of good ol AA, a good year 'fore I was ready, as I needed more of the flame. Yes, Sally was there when I shared of a dream of being held by my dad, in the sweet land of sleep. And with unshamed tears in her eyes, did she holdeth me too, in this land of alive. But the greatest of all the things that she did was to open her home, she and her friend Pat, about no less than three and some years ago, when I needed new shelter from the most deadly of storms.

I woke up just now from a single hour of sleep, after I'd trudged through the cold and the yawns to a glad was closed door of dear St Claire's church, and then as Ann told me to, turned 'round and came back. (for'n Saturday morn the mass is at eight.) And aft the dear feeling of sleep that was sound and was pure and was of tiredness from wortwhil'enterprise, did settle my soul, my thought then did drift, to the sleep of a wom who for a day and a night, in my upstairs bedroom, whose sleep was induced by the deadly 'prize of the pipe. The meanest of all the partners, this one . . . but even with she there were moments of kind.

Little Sean, two-and-a-half, and way a guerrier, and Angela's (other and third) grandson, downstairs at breakfast just echoed the majority of the town with his crystal clear "what's he saying?" In his speech and diction and in the way he does the hand slap thing, it appears he's a bit ahead of schedule of the "moose" I call Thomas, mon guerrier nephew in the land 'cross the sea.

Concepta collects me at two to go see, 'Vinne the bushman' over Black Lion way.

I have a dear friend in America who came to Ireland and brought back a book of poetry by Yeats. Today driving out to Black Lion her message inside the book by Yeats that she gave me, "As I can see it Ireland is poetry" came alive to my eyes. And I wrote her a poem (hardly a "Yeats"!) which I'm putting right here.

Nancy

Ameri-cans we all may be,
But how we do go on
'bout polocks, de-gos, harps, et al
tis such a silly yarn

An emerald Isle across the sea
bred many micks like me
Yet I've n'er been there cause of the dearth
of dancing girls—there be

A dear, old friend (a pole, I think) and
wed to an I-tal-lee
Didst make that trip and brought back
a book by a chap named Yeats, Will B

And this book of poems
with hope and charm
She gave to dear old me

Thru time and 'stance and life and chance
Drif-ted apart have we
But this book and note, I touched last
night and peace came unto me

So I read some poems and tried to sleep
but my head buzzed like a bee . . . .
So up I got, and wrote this poem to my
dear, dear friend—Nan-ci

Well it is Saturday night here and it is near nine o'clock and being that I have a bunch of clean clothes now because Angela washed them, dancing girls not exactly, but at least a laugh or two and with nary a jar mind you, I'm off to go find!

* * *

I received an e-mail from my priest friend from the worst part of Philly today, he's the one I mentioned was so sad all the time. Well sad or not, he hates computers almost as much as he hates iniquity, and for him to send me a message, means so much to me you cannot imagine. But he wrote because he cares, because he's a shepherd and I am sheep, and the suggestion he made that I see the Redemptorist fathers, when I make it to Dublin, I surely will take.

Oh speaking of Dublin, the ladies downstairs, (you know these ladies of Cavan Town who read papers and think), said how in Dublin now almost *every* day, someone leaps or stands in front of the trains going into town. But the real kicker is the drivers are getting spooked, on valiums and stuff because there are people *smiling* as the trains are rushing to crush them . . . this also is too frequent to be news.

I drove around near heavenly surrounding up in Glengavin way this ol day, but I'm too lazy to write about it, so I opted instead for this tired cliché'. Sorry

Day 17 Sunday
4:00 AM

I just remembered something. There once was a time, and no coke was involved, when I met a girl just walking round the old park . . . and I invited her in, and she did her 'thing' and I gave $10 and flung her to the night, like a used up cand' wrapper, to the cold and the rain with a half-working umbrella, while my nice'n'warm car sat right down the lane.

And if EVER I USE the bones of a woman for my own selfish gain, I'm different than that not at all in the content but in just the degree.

* * *

8:00 PM

Driving through a lane coming back from the Mullen market (a flea market of sorts) in the North Ireland town Kinawley, across the border from Swanlinbah, with the windmills of Derry Lynn that provide clean natural power for many of the enterprises of the Sean Quinn empire on the right, and the smaller, more hairy sheep up here in the mountain region, on the left, provided a nice mix of Darwinian perfection with responsible 21st century technology. (This Sean Quinn who has a very nice but—for one of the wealthiest men in Ireland ((I've heard both third and sixth))—somewhat modest house, seems quite the working class hero made good. Knowing my penchant to have goofed off quite a bit, and this Quinn's reputation for coming back to check on his employees, even while on holiday, earlier at the Sheridan house I'd said, "I would have lasted about two weeks if I worked for that guy." John Gaffney, always ready to chip in a disparaging word, said "That long?")

And then after seeing Hugh's brand new calf, like *this morning* brand new, hovering under his mom having been licked clean of all the after-birth muck, the beauty and splendor of nature doing her thing hit me again. When I asked Hugh about the birthing process, he explained when six or seven of the cows are near ready, he puts them in a pen, and the bull does his thing. And when I asked who the bull chooses to mate with, he told me only the ones who were ready to give birth. And so out here in the wild there is no 'only for pleasure' aspect in this act of procreation. (Although I am sure it *is,* pleasurable, it would have to be pleasurable, like real pleasurable, for only *it* is the reason the cows, us, and all others keep a travelin' on. In fact it might be even downright tiring if maybe heifer Betsy and Sue are 'ready' around the same time!)

When Hugh told me about this sex only for birth, it reminded me of a book I once read called, *The Autobiography of a Yogi*, and how this extremely holy guy (as in miracle-type stuff holy, including a body that did not decompose), and how his very holy too, parents mated only once every year, and also only when mama Swami was "ready". And I'd remembered thinking that sure is not much fun, "once a year and only to have kids?". Sure can tell I'm an American. But Hugh also said the heffers did not get placed in the pen until they were ready, and completely of age. A natural as can be sort of thing.

Then I remembered how I read in a sociology textbook one time, something like, "the cultural bias of active sexuality only happening well after puberty, is finally being eliminated in the upper and lower socio-economic classes." I'm not making that up—I wish I had the book here because I **did** read it . . . I read it about five times in fact. I know I read it because I remember thinking "what is this guy saying? It's a GOOD thing little 13-yr-old Kalif, is banging little 12-yr-old Tawana in the basement of an abandoned building somewhere, or that little 12-yr-old Drew's screwing little 13-yr-old-Buffy in daddy's pool side cabana up on the Main Line?"

Well I guess if you think little kids aren't much different than bulls or heifers, then that scenario fits. (Although none of those names would be any good for cows.) But ask my little sister, or Father Mac teaching and working in the North Philly ghetto where the screwing has nothing to do with creation, and is more like that of rabbits than it is of cows, or of how the black boys call the children they father, then basically ignore "jewels", how they like this *textbook* summation.

I guess it all comes down to how one views the old Darwinian purge. My view is that when folks reached a point where they were more like folks than apes, and developed brains that could *think*, they might have started to wonder about the source of it all. And as they evolved into us, with brainpower that gave them domain over the heifers and cows and the like, they didn't seem to understand the responsibility of such an evolvement. Their still ape-like behavior started causing problems. Rules had to be made. As they found they got nowhere, perhaps they started to look to the heavens to inspire their progress. I'm no scientist or anthropologist, but this one fits the contours of my own *thought-*out belief. I always believed in God, but circumstances forced me to go a bit further in the search for a stronger faith.

How much further must this world go down before enough of us do the same?

I for one do not believe literally in Adam and Eve, and I know this expels me for the New Christian Churches and their wonderful fellowship, but who in their close-minded insistence that it HAS to be so, scare the living shit out of me. The tape by one of these Church's preachers about his telling his dad for SURE that he's going to hell, was more than enough for me to steer clear of these guys. I have no problem if you believe in Adam and Eve, as long as you don't say that I must.

But I do believe in a lot of the Old Testament as pretty historically accurate, especially from about Moses on. (With all those dudes before then living to be 350 years old and such, I have a real problem.) From David on the tracing the line is pretty darn clear up until Joseph. I can almost see Mary giving that line to Luke—they were real good friends after Jesus died, biblical scholars unlike me have stated. For you see Mary was an in-law; that line down from David went through Joseph. In light of the fact that Dympna Sheridan, the in-law, just a little while ago smoked me in my supposed knowledge about Hugh's family tree, and being how Hugh knows almost nothing, and how my mom and almost all the McGowan women in-laws know the score, I doubt that if ol' St Joe had been around when Luke was doing *the David-to-Joseph* family tree, that he'd have been very much help either.

I go back to the textbook writers and the scholars. If you're looking for the real Pharisees, look no further. Look to your text book writers and the smug professors of the great institutions of learning where you can only be liberal, if you're liberal like them. I've been there too—five Penn professors refused to be the primary readers for my final paper because it didn't fit their scheme. Eventually I was forced to take out what they didn't like, because it suggested a deeply different theory than theirs. I look at the un-returned e-mails and the ignoring of dialogue because what I said was different.

Far and away, a closed mind is *the* most dangerous thing in the world—especially ones closed because they're stuffed with so much intellectual baloney that nothing else can get in, or ones with a bastardized "earning salvation" literal translation of a magnificent story of Love.

For it's the really good schools, like my University of Pennsylvania, who produce the marketing directors, and the screen writers and the heads of industry and the 'at the top' scholars who write the textbooks and then seep down their poison, hidden behind vague concepts the ordinary folk just blindly accept. The infantile masses in their masses and temples just don't know the real score. I sat there last May, on a gray rainy graduation day, and after the perfunctory prayer by the chaplain, one after another said "Fix the world, YOU can do it". And how many left that field and are now in the process of fixing it on their willpower alone—or even more likely fixing the type on the old portfolio.

Of course I'm not talking about all of the teachers I had. Most all were good people and teachers. But when a great author and a true altruist, a professor and Penn graduate, gives a lecture and honestly states that he admires his mother's great Methodist faith, but cannot *intellectually* accept it, and everyone nods, students and teachers alike, can't you see the connection with our wonderful intellectual idealism and the piss in the winds it is netting us?

When did we lose the capacity to open our minds to ALL different schemes? I read every hip, Buddhist-type, New Age thing that came down. And they were good books. Anyone who picks up that *Autobiography of a Yogi* book I mentioned and is not enthralled with that spirituality is crazy. I read everything but the Bible, because it was not hip to read the Bible. Eventually I did though and there I found a beautiful story pointing to the most wonderful peace we ever could know. Plus how can you simply ignore 2,000 years worth of saints and miracles, even more miraculous in the light of the awful hypocrisy the official church was involved with a lot of the time it was going on? And no I do not take the Bible literally! How dare anyone deny good decent people their salvation simply because they don't "to the letter" follow guidelines that were meant to show us how to LOVE!

A good writing tip is to "show and not tell". And as I sit here tonight with tears in my eyes, I know how far I've drifted from this tried'n'true method. But if you want near what I do, to borrow the line from the wonderful sermon of Father Sheridan this morning (whose mom's a McGowan), maybe just say one little prayer to open your heart to let dear God in.

The gospel this morning, by the way, was the one about removing the plank from your eye before removing the stick from the eye of your brother.

Day 18

I woke up this morning and the thought came to me, of the "show and not tell" tip I'd received from a wonderful teacher in that writing class I took last fall. And I thought about the New Testament and how maybe it was not a document trying to tell us we must follow some rules, but that it was about Jesus coming and walking among us to show us how to love.

I know he said he's not here to bring peace and all that, but to rip and to tear up the whole bloody rot, but it seems to me the tearing he did was not at the folk who were struggling a bit with those ten commandments, but more at the folk who were using those ten to distance themselves from the common folk—those who had seemed to forget to know how to love. "If you love me you will keep my commandments." Of course that is true! But for a man and a God to be dying on a cross to have the capacity to love enough to say, "Father forgive them, they know not what they do," do you think he'd deny admission to his so loving arms, of one who *tried* to be good and decent and such, but who maybe, for whatever reason, struggled a bit with those ten? Many times I really struggled with the thing he said not long before those "forgive" words (that to mine eyes opens the world to those so wide and loving arms), the "Father why have you forsaken Me?" part. And to me, a person who's tried and true 12-step trained, and knows how a "bottom" got through can lead, other side, to dizzying heights of happiness, it seems to me those words are when maybe Jesus hit the lowest of his lows, and that only from there, from that low lonely place, was he able to ascend to perhaps the Godliest words he ever did speak.

I guess because it was fresh in my mind, when, last night on the news, that Archbishop of Dublin, now Cardinal Connell reiterated "it's a matter of doctrine that we cannot receive" Irish

Anglican Church communion, I thought of the teachers with words that obscure. I also thought about how as a kid I was scared half to death that I'd drop the blessed host, or how I'd gingerly try to pry it off the roof of my mouth if it got stuck, cause fires of hell waited if I were to tear it before swallowing in one piece. And I thought of my cousin last week and how she spoke of a friend who, as a child like sometime in 1950's, was about to have her Christmas absolutely spoiled because a priest told her she'd have to take a sin AS BAD as going inside a Protestant Church right to the bishop. She thanked God a more decent, loving and logical priest (a missionary as I recall) was there, and that the girl had a mother who could tell her child was hurt, and who got the missionary to talk to the girl, so thoughts of hell fire did not spoil the feast of the day we celebrate the birth of our Lord. Now what if that priest was not there, how do you think that would have made *any* God feel, from any dimension, or place beyond thought who is all about loving and peace in the world, to see a devout child sad and morose, because one of his shepherds told her "she's not invited in" because it's too sinful to sneak in the door of a house of worship on the other side of the tracks?

Then I wondered about Connell's immediate trek over to Mary McAlese's house, and, how now maybe fresh from a trip to Rome, where he'd got a nice dose of Grand Inquisitorial scorn, if he was going to say to this woman who tried to make a gesture trying to unite an island torn apart, "now MAKE SURE you don't do that again!!"

The good cardinal's pronouncement re Mary's doctrinal blunder brought to mind a woman who Angela told me about, who came down here a recent July 12 Orange Day "marching season" weekend. Seems the woman whose life was a wreck, of tranquilizers and fear of who was behind her back, said if this accord does indeed fall apart, she'd see no reason to not end it all.

And I know for us it's THE body and blood and for them a symbol or such, but are you kidding me! And I thought of the content and degree thing that came to me when I awakened on yesterday morning.

* * *

Real live snow was falling as I walked to the office of my AA friend here in town. We'd just had a serious push-shove argument, and my spirituality had punched his spirituality right in the nose. But I immediately went over to make an amend. And while face-to-face was not available as he was out to lunch, my sincere, "make *sure* you tell him the yank said he's sorry" to his secretary, I'm sure will get passed on. And because my good friend is twelve step trained too, the next time we meet I expect we will be okay.

DeMello tells me when we get emotional nothing gets solved, that it even gets worse. Since I began the raising of voice, the mirror beside me reveals the one with the bee in the bonnet, in *this* particular scrum. And seeing how we both stormed off thinking we'd '*won*', I see how no winners *ever* come out of such self righteous, "I see and you don't see" grunts . . . and that it will *always* be that way, until kingdom come.

Seeing little Dallan and his buddies come scurrying out from his daycare-after-school-type thing they have here, reminded me of the little calves romping around in the fields we drove by yesterday. The mothers waiting for their kids, reminded me of the cows not far from the calves, and Hugh's saying if the rough-housing gets to be too much, a loud cow-mommy moo will settle things down. It was even cooler when Hugh told me how if one goes over to his mom for an afternoon snack, the other ones follow suit, right up his back. And I wondered if the daycare people our modern economy necessitates are paid well enough.

On Saturday's trip there was not as many cows, but sheep were all over the place as we made our way to Black Lion. But we made a stop at this place called the "Shannon pot"—a little tiny pool about as big as a baseball pitcher mound—that *is* the beginning of the mighty river Shannon. It really defies logic almost, how this little tiny pool can grow up to be the largest river in the

British Isles. (Already I've had to correct two different Cavanites since I saw it Saturday, who said the longest in *Europe.* That Irish blarney thing you know.) And Hugh yesterday said it used to be much smaller than that that it used to be like about the size of a bucket. But just recently they made it sort of a National Park thing, and pointed about a ten-minute walk path to it. I for one am glad the Irish national whatever, did take the time to do this, so a Yank like me could see this real wonder of nature. But for as long as anyone knows, it's never been totally dried up. The rains of Glangevlin make sure of that.

It seems that underwater springs go into it, and of course the ever-present rain, and the fact it's almost straight downhill in the beginning, gets it off to a head start. And then there's the bogs, that are as wet as can be, and I'm not really sure how much, specifically, they add to the Shannon's ol' flow, but they're essential to the environment over here. I've been told the turf brickets made out of them, which make such wonderful fuel are even being shipped to America.

These bogs are so "people friendly" that you can pick them each year, and they'll grow right on back, so you can pick 'em again. But of course you can guess it, there are certain impatient folks who are strip-mining the bogs. And of course there's the overuse of pesticides. It's already different according to Angela, as there used to be certain types of butterflies she'd see flying about, but the irresponsible strip of the bogs is the main reason they're no longer around.

And into this breach, it seems very cool that a very influential Brit by the name of Bentley is the man who's the major force saving these bogs.

But back to the Shannon. When you see the little trickle you can easily step over, as it comes out of the pod, it amazes, how it goes moving on. It comes real close to the Erin down Belturbet way—on that river's peculiar trek north. But all sorts of little tributes join in the flow as it moseys along through the middle of Erin. And sure enough it ends up where Orange and Sarchfield chose to battle no more, down in lovely old Limerick, and then on out to the world. And I wondered and asked how long it would take, to ride it from where it really gets started all the way to the end. The answer I get, is a very very long time, cause it dibs and it dabs through the Irish *heart*land. It hits no major cities—Dublin's got Liffie, Cork has got Lee—but the Shannon, from the side of a hill up in Cavan, kind of like the way Irishmen will stop and talk to ya, lingers on out to the sea.

I just did my final back-forth walk to Swellen Lake, up the street for a spell. The cold and the rainy sleet, smacking my face . . . the cheery Shannon sonnet above seems from some other time.

Death came from Dublin last Saturday night, a drunk from down that way who'd been expelled from a Cavan club for bothering some girl, twice ran his car over the bouncer who'd expelled him. Everyone says that the one who was killed, a 38-year-old father of four, was really a prince. Michael said that the guy and his wife had got a late start, the fourth of their kids is just 18 months old.

Foot and mouth disease is over in Wales, the virus blows in the wind, no doubt soon to be here. Thousands were killed in San Salvadorian earthquakes.

"Life is a mystery" is how *Awareness* explains it. But my awareness tonight seems as black as that lake I just left. Tomorrow I go to Kilnacrott for a three-day retreat. To either cling to the sad news or the stuff really neat, I know is that which, I must surely avoid. But from where I sit now, that seems impossible.

Day 19
6:00 AM

I'm glad I packed last night, because the sweatpants I've now got on, being huddled all night with all the other clothes, are nice and warm in this "heat-not-on-yet" room on this cold winter day.

I remember getting an e-mail about a man watching the last stages of a caterpillar becoming a butterfly—one of the real splendid treasures of nature—and one that to me doesn't really make any sense. They're like two different beings—one skin is discarded, slimy kinda yucky skin, and from it emerges one of nature's most wonderful treats.

But the man was watching and because the old skin seemed stuck and the butterfly seemed not ready to appear, he decided to help out by providing some extra warmth with a trusty hair dryer, partly to help out and partly because he wanted to watch the miracle of nature take place. And see it he did, but just for a spell. The beautiful butterfly, emerged, flew a few feet—then plunged to its death. For you see you can not only not fool Mother Nature, you can't speed her up.

Last night after prayers and meditation rolled into one (a rosary said while doing the breath and imagining of my Yan Xin Qigong) I still didn't sleep well, I tossed quite a bit. And then came some shakes quite pronounced, and it brought to mind an August middle of the night 3.5 years ago, when the shakes were much worse—almost scary even.

'Twas August again, and I'd been on a run, the third (and the worst) in the last three months after the 4-month 'taste the clean air' of a preliminary release from the pipe. On the way home driving up I-95, I realized how insane I was as I was thinking how I wished I'd had gotten one last good hit. And naturally enough, my mind drifted to the second of those God-given twelve steps, "Came to believe a Power greater than ourselves can restore us to sanity." That step opens the gates to that Power in all different ways—and one that I call "the low road" says you can think of this power as your friends, the AA rooms, anyone who possibly can get you a day sober, just as long as it is somebody/thing else, and you think of this power as greater than you.

And so right then and there, right in my car I said it myself, "time now to go that lowest road route. You've prayed like crazy, you've talked up this God, you've sort of gone back to your bloody old faith, but my 'coming around' had not seemed to do me any good, even with the quakes of that last day of the year, and here I did sit on the edge of the terror, very scared of the dive ALL the way back in." So "low road" I said is the way I will go.

Then later that very night as I lay in my bed, I'll import from my journal what happened.

So I then brushed my teeth, got into my sleeping shorts and got down on my knees with all the passion I could muster (and it wasn't much) and asked God to keep me sober, I buried my head in my hands and asked again and again and again . . . . a lot of stuff hit me . . . I was on my knees for at least 20 minutes doing the best job I could at listening to GOD . . . the 'ask and you shall receive' ditty certainly in the thoughts . . . . when it was I got off my knees and laid down in my bed I am not sure . . . . but as I thought about St Peter and the words 'the gates of hell shall not prevail against it' I felt a very strong, strange tingling sensation over my entire body, my arms, legs, EVERYWHERE and it wasn't just for a flash it was for a good twenty seconds and the first tears of the night came trickling out of the corners of my eyes, as I felt truly insulated against those dreaded gates . . . . truly insulated, protected . . . . and then I thought about all my trying and writing and doing . . . trying writing and doing . . . trying, writing and doing—that maybe I did deserve this and all the prayers on my behalf and OF COURSE I thought of Dad . . . and the word deserve got too complicated and I realized I need not go there . . . . and NOW it is time to sleep . . . man I forgot the most important part . . . 'because you believed that I loved you . . . '

I was in bed for quite a while after all that stuff had happened before I finally got up and wrote it down in my journal. And that last quote about believing God loved me is what poured into my head as those pins and needles tingled . . . and I got up again, after having turned off the computer and having again crawled under the covers to close that night's entry with it.

You'd think after a moment like that, that I'd never go back . . . but back I did go, quite a few more times too, (the next though not for a good 7+ months) because like the caterpillar to a b-fly, I just was not yet ready.

But the most important thing during all those days before and after the big and little relapses, was that I kept coming back to those AA rooms, and I didn't go less, I went MORE with the prayers. And *not one single time* that I did come back, even though, and with good reason, a lot did not like me in those assorted and sundry rooms, not one single time did anyone say, "why even bother, you just have no clue."

So with all of my steps/program talk, if you think I belittle the fellowship and my friends, I hope that you know I do not mean that. My friends and my family and my God, that somehow now in a way I still can't explain, I know, are not now, nor ever have been, anything at all except the same thing, saved my life, time and again. The fellowship, friends and family, in a sense, were the cocoon of protection that kept me alive, 'til the warmth of God's grace could strip enough of the dead skin away to finally *keep me* sober.

Day 19 2:00 PM
Holy Child Abbey
Kilnacrott

The irony that a book called *Sun Dancing*, about Irish Monks and their almost ridiculously stoic existence, specifically a group that sailed to a barren rock off the cold stormy coast of Southwestern Ireland called Skellig Michael, should sit beneath the power pack bringing the power to my laptop computer, not long after a sumptuous meal of meat, potatoes and all else had been served, swirls like the leaflets of snow in the brutal cold winds outside my comfortable room here in this Abbey. But this cold brutal wind here and now at this exact moment of time is exactly what is needed, for it comes from the west and the north pushing back the deadly virus of the foot and mouth from Wales across the channel. If one were to draw up a line from exactly where that Skellig was, off the west coast of Kerry directly across the south part of Ireland, it would almost line up exactly to Wales.

Pretty much all those monks did there, besides doing the arduous chores involved with living in such an ungodly place, was to pray . . . while hankering from the bitterest cold night and day, eating hardly at all, they recited the psalms and such seven times every day.

Now could those very old prayers be a cause for this wind? Do prayers count *that* specifically? Do they travel through decades and centuries too? Could the prayers of those incredibly holy men, be part of the reason this god-awful death to the most innocent of creatures, is not being transferred to the land that they loved?

Again I have nary a clue . . . for prayers are a part of the world I know not about, but if anything could travel through time and through space, it would be that which is aimed at that Power we, in reality, can not really know.

It's amazing how almost no one in Cavan *does not know* for what Kilnacrott is famous. The big college down a piece from this abbey looked empty and abandoned as Jim Hannigan drove me up here today.

Here in the abbey courtyard, set aside by itself is the grave of the priest named Fr. Brendan Smyth, who spent the last five years of his life in a Belfast jail cell convicted of molesting young boys. But the worst of it was, as if anything can be worse that that, was the abbot head guy here knew of the accusations, and said nothing—allowing Smyth to move on, even to go to America, to a town somewhere out Chicago way (I believe).

There's even more. A government came crashing down, that of Prime Minister Reynolds, because a clerk in the Irish equivalent of the Attorney General's Office, stuck a report re Smyth in a drawer somewhere, and too late did the news come to light. Then there was talk that Smyth signed papers himself, to get a job *helping* kids in an area hospital.

So now what was once a nice school is dead as can be, another victim of dirty unearthed Catholic Irish laundry. The trail of the cover-up if a Bernstein and Woodward were here on the scene, might go pretty far up in the Church hierarchy . . . and fallaways fall, as the church seems to march to the past . . . . and it has to be said again and again—they think and they thought what they were doing was right. Centuries of hiding things in the night, is a habit hard to turn around in a short time. And content to degree bothers me here as I think of my job, the having of which had once probably saved my life, and of the non-addressed problems I tossed in the can right before I left. And if I don't think that way how can I love the sinner but not love his sin?

And because I'm a man with a fourth step in my life (the one we review the times we did less than right) it's a lot easier to be not so bloody self-righteous.

Day 20 (Ash Wednesday)

For the monks on Skellig Michael this must have been a not looked forward to day as their self-denial for Lent's 40 days, was almost super-human. Geoffrey Moorehouse's fascinating fiction-based-on-historical-accounts, reveals that the morning's host was almost the only food they ate all day, except with a little reprieve on Sundays—so if ever a prayer could travel through time and through space, maybe it was those of those holy as roley old and young monks.

But in the *Sun Dancing* book there's the story of one guy name of Aedh who did things with even more passion than all of the rest, and this guy did all this in the year of Our Lord 1044. I just noticed now in this book that I read quite a while ago, how the wonderful abbot looking back from a spot after it happened, wished he had done something about Aedh's 'more-intense-than-the-rest' practices when he noticed the marks inflicted by self-flagellation.

For you see this Aedh guy who came by himself to the Skellig in his own little boat, and joined the community, stayed for only a while—he went off on a separate rock to pray by himself, to *really* get close to the Lord. And after fasting way more than anyone else, one day very close to Easter morning, this monk thinking he saw Jesus' face in the sun, took off like a bird to reach for the sublime, but as this wonderful book tells us,

"Exaltation was suddenly transformed into terrible awareness, appalling truth. Slowly enough for the truth to horrify him, the grim rocks and the seething of the sea rose up to meet his fall. His head was split open from tonsure to chin, his brain slattering out like the ordure of a gull. And in that instant he saw before him at last the yawning chasm of his willfulness and pride."

I am constantly reminded by my friends in AA that all that I have is one God-given day. In the Big Book it says "we have a daily reprieve contingent on the maintenance of our spiritual condition." But for someone like me who felt spiritually fit, even more fit than the rest, the example of Aedh, in the ultimate content to "head crashing on rocks" degree, I had better thank God each and every day, that my pride never got me like it did the "holier than thou, pray by himself" monk from long long ago . . . talk about traveling through time and through space. Was it not pride that carried the legendary figures of Adam and Eve out of the Garden and into the cold?

It is six in the morning here on Holy Child Hill, Kilnacrott and in the land cross the sea, in the hills of Kentucky, in a place they call Gethsemani, the first gasp of Ash Wednesday has just happened along. Their first office begins at 3:15 AM, monks praying the psalms back and forth through stretches and yawns. About eight months ago, I stayed for a week in those rolling Kentucky hills in that abbey, where in the smiling faces and warm greetings from the men who stayed there, I found none of the false, or not really the false but more the *over*-piety of an Aedh. I went on a Monday and it was there that I asked my God to take away my pride. (Sometimes you better watch what you ask for, because the next day I wrote a little poem, and the day after that, when I shared it with a priest, I looked and his eyes were flickering asleep.)

The rain kissed the window of my room in that Trappist abbey last August 22. There on the twelfth anniversary of my father's death, the feast day of Mary being made Queen of Heaven, I wrote a poem—the first poem for what I really hope and pray is, the God willing, day-by-day, rest of my life.

The Infiltration

The grace, the qi amassed at the border of
his being
The walls of lust and sloth and ingratitude
Had often times been scaled

Beyond was the abyss-mal moat of his
addiction
Here too, many ford-crossings had been
made

But inside the moat
Close-encountered to the control center of
his will
Lay the imperceptible minefield of his
pride

And seeps and trickles were all that made
their way thru
this unholy place

'twas the abyss that seemed most
damaging tho
But the grace that scaled that namable
wall beyond . . .
Found passage thru the abyss
On the pure yet tortured, enslaved souls
Of the beings immersed therein

But from the willful center
The realization of the pureness and
neediness
of those mired in that muck . . .

. . . added yet more and different (even
less detectable)
land mines of pride into those spaces closest
to his heart—

yet some of the grace still seeped on thru

and as it penetrated the will of the man
and served to alter the ess of his prayers
from—
"Dear God, dear God let the qi, let the
grace
come a poring on in!"

to a far far less lordly

"oh God let me see
how weak I do be". . . .

. . . the seeping became
as wet is to rain

and the man grew to know that grace
ran the show . . .
and seeps and not torrents were all he
could take

and when the takes
turned to makes
of fewer mistakes

. . . the 'kingdom' was safe

* * *

The kind gentle Cavan brogue of Fr. Cusack just roused me from my post-wake, still-in-bed lounge. The nap of an hour or so, he had directly facilitated a while ago, by his climbing a ladder a much older priest had gone to fetch, and then gently but firmly tapping with a hammer, the wood around a glass-enclosed panel above the door that was locked by me—and the keys of which, I'd left inside. Some things really do never change. This really old priest, who's actually right next door, who looked *very* uncomfortable carrying that old wooden ladder—when I thanked him again a little while later, gently informed there really no reason to lock up my door. And I did take that advice.

But because I was locked out my well pre-dawn stroll was extended, some major-league good came with this particular absent-mind bad. For the first time in my life I got up really close to the young and old sheep gathered by the front wall. There were two different groups, one obviously the mother and three little sheep, the other group with black markings, one big and two small. And Hugh's tale of "follow the leader—hungry get fed" I got to see really up close. And being the nosy dude that I am, I got a bit closer. A very pronounced bleat, and the reminder when young are around to not get so close, and that I've heard cows are real gentle, but have not heard one way or the other about these here sheep, convinced me that, no closer up should I get.

And of course I wondered about the foot and mouth thing, and how awful it would be if these lovely creatures of nature would have to get destroyed because of this awful disease. De Mello says if man weren't around nature in all her violence and beauty would simply go on, and though I don't really know where this particular disease came from, I'm betting it's from humans somehow. I also don't know if this major cold front that has much of Ireland's electricity and travel shut down, will help stem the disease's spread. I hope and pray that it does.

But my early morning travels also took me the grave of this Fr. Smyth, all by itself. His date of death, August 21, 1997, was probably the time I was stuck most in the deadly throes of my addiction. At mass later on, mainly because I remembered my sister Mary Ellen's "It's always good to pray for the dead" words, I said some prayers for this poor disturbed man, who took down a nice school and even a government. I remembered how my sponsor always says, as do a lot of other AA's, of the ripple effect of bad things that do not continue, when a drunk works that program and finally puts down that drink. Who can tell if a rigorous fourth step had been part of this man's priestly education and if he'd prayed really hard, perhaps the deep buried source of the poison that had seeped for God knows how long, might have been revealed. Maybe even the terrible string of events this one man effected might never ever have taken place.

I also sauntered over to one of the direct points on that string . . . the closed up college/high school, down the road and across the way. Crows hovered about the vacated building; no rims were on the basketball backboards. The back door to the gym was even open, but I didn't walk in, I felt a bit of fear, I'm not really sure why. I guess light was coming up and I hoped to get back in my room. But the rep of the school was really top-rate, and if they had many teachers like my cousin-in-law Jim Hannigan, it's a pity the place is no more.

* * *

I just came from doing the Psalters with the priests in morning prayer. Father Martin, my next door mate, (the one who lugged up the ladder) has taken me under his wing, and was kind enough to give me a special missal so I could sing along. It's funny here is the first place I've actually sung at mass since I've been in Ireland. In America although in many places the singing is not much, at most masses we really do sing.

It sort of reminds me of my very good friend Jim Houck who said to me one time (he of 95 years old, and who has been, since 1935, an active member of the Oxford Group—name changed to *Moral Rearmament* and then to *Initiatives of Change*) "you Catholics all let your priests do your praying for you.". His assessment rings true especially here where I see the sometimes-yeah-sometimes-no handshakes of peace, and the non-singing in most of the masses.

Indeed it seems in celebration of the liturgy is one place where America has a hand up to over here. I wonder what it's like in Dublin. If Father Mac, who down in North Philly runs a long but really neat mass, with food, being taken up with the bread and the wine each week, and a handshake thing that goes for about 5 minutes, and before the offertory, tells me to check out the Redemptorists down in Dublin, then I'll bet that is at least one pretty progressive port in Erin's old Holy See. And as fate would have it, it's the Redemptorists who put out the *Twelve steps to Deeper Spirituality* pamphlet, I been chortling so much about.

The psalms though, really are neat, especially if you sing them back and forth. If ever there was a place where Jew and Christian and even Muslim, could get together, it would be to sing them in unison. One time when I came back from a relapse again, an AA friend told me to look at one of those psalms, and again was the smack-in-face kind of identification. I'm pretty sure it was this one:

Out of the depths I cry to you O Lord
Lord hear my voice
O let your ears be attentive
To the voice of my pleading.

I remember when a Buddhist guy from California and a real good poet, came to Penn's Writer's House and said he was working on a lyrical modernized translation of some of the psalms. I wish I remembered his name.

Penn really IS a great school and I had almost all very good teachers. The guy who I had trouble with on my capstone, still was kind enough to take me on when no one else would. The guys who really bothered me were the ones who just did not write back, or wrote back half-answers to points I had made—they're the ones that stick in my craw. For a person to be in a position to influence many smart young minds, to be so conditioned to think that anyone who talks about God is a fool, is as dangerous a tool as any can be. Not bad people—blind ones again, as de Mello reminds me.

Effectiveness, *do*ing things, is of course what it's about. But to laugh at a person who prays all the time? Is a Carmelite nun, in a room, in a hovel, eating little and praying a lot, *do*ing? I think Mary even said in one of her visits, that rosaries prevented WWIII. Oh that's right all those documented visits are nonsense. That Lady of Guadeloupe deal with the computer that can't figure the dots in the eyes thing, is a worldwide papist deception. And pretty much anymore you don't even have to skip over those stories on the way to your financial news or the sports because the paltry few guys who control all the press, refuse to print them anymore.

But as I sit here in an abbey, having read more about some of the extremes that monks of old went to, it seems to me when it comes to any form of self-mutilation, you cross the line. But that of course is strictly an opinion of mine. And a legitimate gripe would be that so is the stuff about all the prayers really just an opinion of mine. But these opinions are based on thought out investigation, not blind adherence to the conditioning of a certain dogma, or to a tube or a textbook summation.

It all comes down to—does that to which I assess, make any sense? Well all I can say is that I'm *enjoy*ing my days, I've been to the rack and now I am back, and it took a mysterious Presence which I access in the faith of my choice, that has been instrumental in my trying to follow the golden rule.

When Jesus said I am the Way and the Light, he was telling us if we act like He did, we will be rid of our unhappiness. And if that be so, why not follow real closely His way all the way? But does any logical man, think if some cat in Japan, sits on his hands, and acts like a Christian, he is really gonna be out of luck? . . . and won't be invited to the "kingdom"?.

De Mello tells me when we really drop all our attachments, we will spring into action. And he also says how (or was that Merton said that) we will not be the dancer in this thing called life—no we actually will be danced. And as I look back on this trip and see how I have been *danced,* I revel in all of the fun.

Merton and de Mello . . . when you shake them all out, how much different are they than St. John of the Cross and his dear buddy Theresa of Avila? Or for that matter, the Buddhists. You strip and you strip in an infinite regress and all that's left is the grace. The story goes, that Johnny and T had to be chained down when they really got it going good—or should I say *non*-going. A channel you become of holy, and love and effectiveness . . . and for me, it seems, and of fun. So at holiday's end, when I must pick up and head to some really bad spots, I'll still be having a ball.

I wonder if anyone noticed (except my buddy Coneil) that Jesus first miracle, at the wedding in Cana, was not only to show us how important was marriage, but also that we should have some fun. Imagine a wedding that's run out of booze—and all of a sudden, Super top shelf is a flowin', like jars in the Eagle saloon? And whatever you do, please remember for sure, his mother Mary, told him that was what He should do.

When I went on like this at the Sheridan's the other night, and Anita said "do you really believe that wedding feast of Cana story?" I said yeah, four different gospel writers put it down. Again I was wrong—the wedding feast of Cana is in only John's gospel—which does figure because he and Andrew were the only two of the twelve there. Later that night when I asked Anita, "So you don't believe in the wedding feast of Cana?" a really cool thing happened. Whatever the reality of my great grandmother Sarah is these wondrous days, no doubt smiled at the Sheridan blood immersed in 'Nita's "I didn't say that," reply.

* * *

There was a famous French psychologist named Lacan who is pretty much the cat's meow now among Freudian psychoanalysis. I think he lived until the early 60's. I took a course on him at Penn and his stuff was peculiar but also kind of neat. I heard he was funny as hell when he spoke in person as he went on these long Irish-type asides. Unfortunately none of his speeches, at least as of a few years ago, were translated.

But there was something in his philosophy about a "gaze" and now it's coming back . . . there was also something about how we really never drop our masks but all we can really do is to be aware they are there. And when he spoke of some kind of radical individualism, it reminded me a little bit about de Mello's theory about how the only person you can *really love* is yourself. (You can well imagine Tony D does not go over well with the diehard 'til death do us part' super romantics.) De Mello's view is that I am the only person I can really love because with everyone else I perceive or meet, I have no choice but to put my expectations of what I want that person to be, in the way that I view them. That because I am human, I am incapable of not doing that. So the absolute exquisite beauty and wonder of any other human being, that which is purely and only a kingdom unto itself, while it can dazzle me and make me happy, I can't see completely unfiltered because as soon as I look anywhere but exactly at me, the filter of my expectations blurs the real them.

Just now I am realizing that is probably pretty much the same as what Lacan means when he says the best we can do is to own our own masks.

The point of this was supposed to be, is that when I had this Lacan course, I suggested this gaze thing might be considered God looking over us, and that although my real French-thinking and looking and talking teacher, really did not agree, he did at least say that Lacan in his way of not taking himself too seriously, would not have any problem with *my* saying that. It seems Lacan had a wonderful sense of "your guess is as good as mine" in dealing with anything as complicated as the human mind.

The deal is this though, as you do this, and become aware that everybody else does the same exact filtering thing and that they are just as silly as you in the way they expect so much out of everyone else, that even when their perception is blocked by conditioning and attachments to money, sex, prestige, power and *things*, it is their lack of clarity you abhor and not the people themselves. I do not know if that is the only way one can love people they really don't like, but it is one way—and it's a good way and it sure works for me.

I practice qigong and I read and I pray, so my mind can be sharper. But it can be sharper than the sharpest thing in the world, and still it won't change the fact that I am unable to avoid having my own little filter with which I look at that world—and then I realize, for sure, why de Mello says all over that *Awareness* book, "I'm an ass you're an ass, where's the problem?" Mind you Tony had five Ph D's and spoke nine languages; respectively five and eight more than me.

But the whole Demellan scheme (and Merton, and John of the Cross, and I'm beginning to think maybe this Lacan guy too) is to be aware that filters of outside do not have to be added to your own silly asinine ones. And this little de Mello-type poem I wrote, tries to say that.

Delusion

So I make marks on a piece of paper that are called words
and they try to describe a state that is beyond description
. . . a state called happiness or peace or fulfillment . . . . or God

and I own the impossibility of my task, because to do otherwise
would be to delude. But I also try to convey that delusion engulfs us . . . .
a different delusion . . .
that things that can be described and held and eaten and ridden and screwed and lived in and drunk and
smoked and luxuriously surrounded by . . . . or pondered or figured out about
or measured or aimed or fired—are what happiness is about . . . and that without these we will not be happy . . . .

And why do I do this, why do I write? I can say it is because I am an artist,
and this is what I must do, that my essence screams out for me to do this . . .
but that too seems like nonsense . . . more delusion

I do it because I want you with me . . . in the Light—in the land of non-delusion
. . . like the firestorm that keeps burning as it gobbles up oxygen . . . like the river
growing purer with each non-polluted drop . . . like the forest growing healthy
with each new living tree . . . so it is with me, I long for each of you to be.

. . . . and the reason I want you with me is for my OWN self-interest, because the more people who live lives of freedom, the more happy it will be, and not because there will be more people around who think like me, but because there will be more people around who, when they've dropped their conditioning of having to have, they'll be better able to see how much more full life is for themselves. And automatically more good things will start to be done because people will realize living the 'golden rule' is that which in the long and short run makes themselves happiest.

I just looked this over and I realize what I was going to say, that when I lent my professor *Awareness* he read it in about a week and gave it right back to me, telling me it was 'funny'. That is probably because this professor is conditioned to think anyone with SJ at the end of their name is necessarily in the dark. That is conditioning that is very present in many fine schools. If I'd told this teacher about Tony D's degrees, I doubt it would have changed his mind a bit. And like any and all conditioning, that is wrong and it is dangerous.

I remember my first time reading *Awareness* and as de Mello's was saying to drop all conditioning and attachments, I was thinking he's not going to say our attachment to God, but sure enough he did. (And if you're guessing Ratzinger and Tony did not see eye-to-eye, you are very warm.) Plain as day, the Eastern Indian Jesuit said "our final barrier to God can be our concept of God." And the deal goes something like this if your concept of God, (the Father, Son, Holy Spirit concept included) is too chiseled in stone, the feeling of God can get blocked by your mind. And maybe that is what Jesus meant when he said (in Mark, John and Matthew) "if you blaspheme against the Father, or the Son that can be forgiven, but if you blaspheme against the Spirit, that can not be forgiven." The feeling, the Spirit among men, the doing good things, if you're Christian or not, that *is* the deal. The people who lay down unbending hows as to ways and means to that Feeling, or prideful humanoid thinkers, who either blatantly or surreptitiously tell us God is for dumb unsophisticated old ladies, are in my mind's eye, tied for the lead in our continuing march to our doom. If you go to the Word, and the life that Jesus led, and get a *feeling* for the kind of man that he was, then you can not get too caught up in the exact words, and live as he'd want you to live. Let the ultimate *show*er of how we should live, lead us to the Promised Land.

And maybe there have been many bad times in the crusty Catholic Church, but there also have been many that were good. To me there is a direct line from Peter to John Paul. To deny that is really absurd. But the Church as it stands right here and now, should get more protestant in many of its ways . . . but what the Catholic Church has that no one else does, is Mary. The Protestant observer at Vatican II, when he said (as Jim Hannigan told me) that our devotion to Mary is one thing his church really did envy, Reverend Whoever said him a mouthful. If dad ever knew how much those *say a Hail Mary for me, Jim*'s would end up meaning . . .

—

5:45 PM Kilnacrott

So at the end of a day of my head in the clouds, like Damocles' sword, reality strikes. Per a report on the radio, it seems foot and mouth disease has made it's way into Cavan; not from the wind or not from Wales, but from across the North/South border in Armagh.

The 6:00 PM news here pretty well confirmed that the disease has made its way to Armagh, the Cavan part, please God, was a runaway rumor. With the black-plague-like nature of this disease that can travel with the air, borders and check points too seem like piss in the wind. And it is a **very real** possibility that a very sizable number of the thousands and thousands of sheep and cattle I've seen in my 21 days here, could be dead by disease, or by slaughter by the time I leave.

The sheep that came to Armagh came from Britain herself, about two or three weeks ago. Perhaps the Brits had been at least a tad slow re closing off exports there. Maybe an official with a "close our eyes and don't tell me it's so" attitude stuffed a report he had gotten in the bottom of s drawer somewhere. These ideas are seeping a different "we versus they" virus into the heads of a lot of the people here.

"Do the next right thing" my program tells me. I've already mentioned that I walked around a lot today in the fields where the animals roam. One thing the radio said is folks should not do that. So I mentioned that to Fr. Cusack and he said not to fret.

And of course I think of Hugh, a farmer by trade, and of the cows that know his voice and who moo like crazy as he approaches. I think of their big wet brown/black eyes, and words on a page seem as empty right now as a spit in the breeze. The angel of death, in a very real way, has come through the north and perhaps into the heartland of Erin.

11:00 PM in Kilnacrott now. On the talk show nothing at all about the disease had made it to Cavan. That was, it seems, merely a rumor. Of course there was talk of agents, of "why with all our own sheep, do we get then from England?" And between the lines of "we export a lot too" are hands making loot 'cause that's what hands do. And so now the vicious bitter northwestern winds that brought so much snow and ice yesterday that Dublin's airport was closed for a spell, and that also closed down highways and roads as near here as Mead, is exactly what the doctor ordered.

There seems little hope, if you think about this, that the disease will not make its way into the Republic. The disease is only about 60 miles to our east, and almost literally a stones throw across the border from Cavan right up in Armagh—and the fact that it can fly literally right with the wind—you better believe I am doing some praying.

Day 21 (end of week 3)
Thursday February 28, 2001 4:00 AM

I wonder how the very informed folk in Cavan town have reacted to the disease being here on our Isle. The grim faces of the horde of folk who came for ashes and mass last night, I'm sure weren't there only because it was the first day of this particular year's Lenten season.

I was even thinking of ringing Hugh (*calling* here means stopping by), the person I personally know most in danger from this dreaded disease. But even more so because his locale over Belturbet way is close to the Armagh border. In fact I'm pretty sure the town Kinawley and the flea market we went to on Sunday, were both cross the border in Armagh.

* * *

9:15 AM

"**The Plague is Here**" screamed this morning's headline in the *Irish Independent*—just to give you a idea of how seriously foot and mouth disease is taken over here. This morning's travel had led me to the warmth of the open Adoration chapel, and a book on monastic life. In the book there was a mention that a plague in Ireland's sixth century AD, had been a big cause for the explosion of monastery building and living during that era. Darkness leading to Light. The yin-yang history of mankind.

10:15 AM

This morning's gospel, Luke 9:23, says "If anyone would come after me, he must deny himself and take up his cross and daily follow me."

The founders of AA, who were Oxford Group members before branching off officially into AA (shortly before AA's Big Book was written in 1939—in fact the name was put on the book before on the group), used to practice something called guidance. They did it almost daily . . . taking time to pray and meditate and then to *write down* a daily list of things to do to further God's plan. Day-by-day they did this. Of course there were days that they missed, but I'm sure there were not that many. Practical day-by-day, inspired as possible "carrying of cross". Bob Smith's wife Ann, an Oxford Grouper to the bone, used to call other AA wives to ask if they were also doing their guidance. In the one letter of the Bible's Book of James, which the Oxfords used extensively and which, I repeat, was such a part of early AA, the 'James group' was once a candidate for the fellowship's name, the closest I could come to this was,

"Do not merely listen to the word, and so deceive yourselves. Do what it says. Anyone who listens to the word but does not do what it says is like a man who looks at his face in a mirror, and after looking at himself, goes away and immediately forgets what he looks like."

And as I think about *all* the "I'm *gonna*"s in my life that never seem to get done, I'm hoping and praying maybe some of my 'long ago' namesake's graces will help get me to get moving.

* * *

Back home in America, in Philadelphia exactly, each Monday evening, my home group, one that represents much of the recovery nonsense I've bantered about, allows a group of us folks to have, in their basement, our little *Back to Basics* meeting. Part of the 11th step instruction in the group is precisely about practicing the early member-type guidance. And this group that meets once every week is part of a group that is spreading the word of working the steps of recovery throughout the USA. They're in many cities small and large, they're in AA and CA (Cocaine Anonymous), and in the home where Bill Wilson was born and raised up in Vermont, on the third weekend in April, the B2Bers will have a big pow wow.

And 95-year-old Jim Houck, Oxford/Moral Rearmament veteran, will be there along with quite a large crew. And I will be there too, God willing.

So on this morning, on the day after which Bill Gates was literally almost quaked off a stage in Seattle, and when a train derailed in England killing a bunch of people, and as Ireland's stocks had joined the world-wide plunge, and as officials regarding foot and mouth are claiming he didn't do this, or he should have done that—as Atlas Shrugged-type negligence seemingly is seeping all through the world—I sat there in mass. And as thoughts of the far more progressive churches back home sifted through my head, and the thoughts of how our AA is so much better there too, as the snow swirled by the window outside, like a flash it came upon me, that this America I trash so far and so wide, while really the home of the sickness for sure . . . is also where will start the Only possible cure.

—

I just left the Abbey office where I was trying to help Mary, the girl who works there, with some tips on working Microsoft Excel. So I sent a "help me with Excel" message back home to my dear buddy Jen, who either didn't understand my question or was out too late last night at a Ricky Martin concert or something, because her tips were worth zero. So I actually monkeyed around and, in one Window freeze/framian swoop, found exactly what I was looking for.

It reminded me of my little tirade before I stopped writing this morning. There is a line in the Big Book, a very important one, which reads like this (it is in the part of the book where they talk about helping a new guy.) *"If he thinks he can do the job in some other way, or prefers some other spiritual approach, encourage him to follow his own conscience. We have no monopoly on God; we merely have an approach that worked with us."*

What that line is telling us is that the steps are a means to an end. The end is God. But please note that he says 'some other *spiritual* approach'. And if any AA member leads a spiritual life, whether working steps or not, even if they never set foot in any Church again, then all the better to him. My beef is, why not do what they did to get God in your life? Why not use a practical way that has worked, and get out of the way (as my good friend Father Bill used to say) and let God work his magic? And there is no reason at all that any Tom, Dick or Joe, whether a drunk or not, cannot surely work the same thing. An admission that you can't and belief a power greater than can—and you can pick anything you are powerless over, and that is all that is needed to start.

—

The sides were drawn on the political talk show—on the Irish side, a journalist and a veterinarian, on the Protestant North Ireland side, two different ministers. The moderator fed the flame like a short order cook tossing burgers on a grille. It even got down to denials of facts stated, and to out and out shouting. The foot and mouth virus is creating another disease, a North/South name-calling one—and this one could help to further undermine an already badly stalled peace process. The one very impassioned young lady, the agricultural writer, said there's been no foot and mouth here since her grandparents time. This is a terribly serious matter.

Joe Walsh the Republic's Agricultural minister, besides ripping the sensational headlines said something like "stay away from going to mass, if you're into such things please stay home". They are not the exact words, but that certainly captures the tone. A friend at tonight's AA meeting said that some official, obviously on a different page than Joe, said, "the only thing keeping us free from the disease is the prayers."

And now Saturday night's "both side of the border" vigil prayer session that they usually have here in the abbey, has been cancelled. No cancellation happened though for this evening's fourth edition of a nine-week novena; there must have been 500 people crammed into the church and the chapel besides. The crowd even spilled out into the hallway. And as I mimicked the outstretched palms of the folks as the chasuble (the gold structure holding the exposed host of God) passed by, I was humbled and awed by these people's, out and out, faith. Hard wooden pews were knelt on for the majority of the 45-minute service. *Here* there was plenty of singing, and though most of the people were old, there were quite a few who were not.

Faith—that is what the Irish people seem to have. There were surely no seats open at this event tonight, people literally were crammed inside of the pews. And as the sweet incense rose along with prayer and song to Our Lord and his mother, I felt love for these folks, and had hope that they would carry through.

Day 22 March 2
5:00 AM

I awaken this morning to god-awful cold. The heat that remained in the walls after the heat had gone out two nights ago, has obviously, if you will, left the building. And so about a foot to a mile, I now at least have a glimpse of what it was like for those monks on that rock called Skellig Michael.

Please understand I am hardly the self-flagellant sort, but the way things shook out, you can only imagine the way I beat myself up almost eleven months ago on one **more** morning after—the morning after Sarah'd been part of the prayer that had allowed me to escape the clutch of a different, but personal to me, even more deadly virus than the one that has made its way to this land I've grown truly to love. Maybe the fact that I thought all the people who would say to me "you beat yourself up too much" were wrong, was yet one more vestige of my false and overblown pride.

But there I was in good old Philly-town, on day one *again.* Glum and morose I sat on the El train that took me to work, reading . . . and this morning I was in the *Sun Dancing* book. (Huge traffic tie-ups, in fact, were the only reason I'd chosen not to drive in that morning.) And on this particular morning, the chapter I happened to be reading told of two of those Skellig monks who were being severely punished for some indiscretion. For hours on end they had to stand hands outstretched reciting difficult Celtic scriptural verses. Finally the weaker of the two, Macet, collapsed, banged his head on the floor and thought he'd died. He saw a horrifying vision of hell, but then beyond it he saw the Lord who revealed to him a heavenly place:

". . . bathed in a light much greater than the light of day . . . He wished to join the multitude in this beautiful place, but the Lord led him back the way they had come together. Then paused, held Macet by the shoulders and at last spoke to him. The words were repeated before he understood what was being asked . . .

'Remember the rule of life. What is it we must do, brother?'

Macet sobbed, 'we fall down and we get back up'. Th tears began to dribble down his sunken cheeks. 'we fall down and we get back up, we fall down and we get back up' . . . . babbling incoherently, foaming at the lips, twitching uncontrollably . . . .

The Abbott took him by the hands "yes we fall down and we get back up . . . "

My tears came pouring right then on that old Frankford El—only blocks away and under that ATM card that had never left the drawer—for the umpteenth time this fallen-down man had been aided in his get back up.

So you can only imagine as I sit in an Abbey dating back 900+ years, how much I was moved by the prayers uttered here yesterday night . . . the link to those monks on Skellig Michael more felt than cognized.

* * *

Lounging around downstairs this morning I found a pamphlet and read about St Norbert—the patron saint for this handful of Norbetine brothers and priests who populate this sprawling abbey. Turns out he too got literally knocked off his horse, some time in the early 1100's, and his carefree nobleman party days were over—and he took off to spread the Word, his legacy mainly was about taking it to the streets.

And it dawned on me as I was sitting there, that this is exactly the kind of spirituality those New Christian churches I smoked earlier, are all about. I remember walking down the beach one day and a bunch of black kids were running like sheep in the field, happy as larks, into the beautiful Wildwood sea. I knew the kids looking over them were shepherds from one of these new churches. And they sure enough were—I'm not sure any Church big or small is as active as these in getting down in the trenches with the really poor and the left out. (The same as John Wesley was in the late 18th and early 19th centuries in the British Isles. The Methodist Church, in fact, grew out of his "a little too down and dirty for the starch-shirted Anglicans" legacy.)

But these New Christian Churches preach an excluding message. And when I criticize their "the BOOK as *we* see it" approach, they'd certainly accuse me of the same garbling rhetoric thing I lay at the heels of our intelligentsia. And though I'm sure they could quote me about 50 chapter and verses where Jesus says "you will burn", for my money, "judge not and be not ye be judged" is another of those great loving erasers He left with us.

I personally could care less if these New Christians ever go into a formal church again. In fact I kind of like the outdoor fellowship gigs. But if you pass on a word saying US and no one else, or one that is about staying out of hell and not of experiencing heaven right here, then you're denying yourselves and your followers some peace and a whole lot of good, clean, wholesome fun. But far worse you are NOT spreading the *real* message of the gospel you claim to so bloody well know.

I think of the wonderful fellowship service in Fairmount Park I went to with a friend from work a couple of years ago. I suspect these Churches would not be interested in the "federal money directly to Faith-based agency" program, George Bush introduced in his very first week in office, and maybe they are right. My friend Father Mac down in the middle of North Philly wants no part of this money either; he features a more socialist-based charity structure, modeled on the magnificent work done by Dorothy Day and the Catholic Worker organization out of New York City. And when I hear about "tankers", agents making money on the sheep and cattle smuggling trade, and "blockers" who bid up livestock so only the big money can afford them, and I hear statements like "our competitors are licking their chops", as I did tonight on a truly wonderful Irish program called the Late Late show, and when I hear the words "World Trade Organization" mentioned also, and as I ponder the gravitational pull of money, I wonder, for real, if capitalism can *ever* work. I am certainly no economist, but when someone as smart as Albert Einstein pens a very logical, convincing essay called "Why Socialism" which he did, in, I think, 1953 (and which my good friend Julio, ever the Marxist, passed on to me) I surely have to wonder.

But getting back to cases, and bread and beds and such, for my money (which actually is exactly what federal funds are), a piece of bread in the hand, is a piece of bread in the belly regardless of the source. And the congressman who said, "this (Federal) money can go for bread and a bed, but *not* for Bibles," was 100% correct. This is an issue directly involved with separation of church and state. Among the many extraordinary features of the greatest constitution ever written in the history of mankind, that of the good old US of A, is the wonderful job it did in ensuring that church and state did not mix. One need only look at right here in a place where north = Protestant and south = Catholic, to see the problems inherent of NOT doing just that. But and this is a but of paramount import, bibles or instruction on how to work the twelve step program, could be made available to anyone getting some soup or a meal, if they *choose* to partake. But these bibles and this instruction must be given or performed voluntarily, done by individuals like the AA's of America who give of their time, to take AA into prisons and Drug Rehabs and Detox Units. Of course to monitor this and to make sure there is no coercion or overlap will take monumental effort and some really effective and conscientious folks at the top. And the irony to end all ironies, is that President Bush appointed a teacher from the same University of Pennsylvania institution I so readily slash as being "godless", to head the faith-based program. So you better believe I tried to e-mail this 42-year old whiz kid from Philly's Southwest section, where in my day I downed quite a few, but the address I had did not work.

To be perfectly honest I really don't know where this faith-based program was as I left town, but I do know one of my first stops when I get back home, is to an appointment with the Manhattan director of the Covenant House for abandoned kids. If I'm given the okay, whether Fed money is headed their way or not, I'll try to bring the *Back to Basics* twelve-step program into their wonderful place. And while a majority of these kids have addiction problems, the powerlessness of being a ward to the street, is enough for them to get started. Of course I have an AA friend from out in the Bronx, who has volunteered to take over after the first month. By then a geometric ripple of people who've been through the *Back to Basics* 12-step class, can take it to wherever is deemed fit. And that is exactly how this program has grown from just a few guys to a pretty sizable group in the states.

Day 23 Saturday March 2 1:32 AM
Cavan Town

When I told Eddie Gaffney I'd been at Killnacrott abbey for a few days, among other observations he said, "bless me Father for I have sinned, it's been 10 years since my last confession." I need a good dose of Eddie after having "been to the mountaintop."

So it seems the "foot and mouth" count three days in is still the same—one case only on the island—and that in the North, but just across the border. As I waited to be picked up from Kilnacrott today, the wind was strong but I was relieved it was coming from the west, the proper direction to keep the virus from crossing the Armaugh/ Cavan border. The Irish Times Op-Ed said "It's Providence Keeping the Republic Free of Foot and Mouth", and if you look at the lineup, 3 in Wales, 2 in Scotland, 1in the North, over thirty in Britain, you have to wonder if they haven't a point.

But it's still a major crisis, there's talk that 40-some sheep from the infected area were smuggled over the border, and the scare surely is still fully on. St Patty's Day parades all have been cancelled, as large gatherings can spread it if the virus is on human clothes and or shoes. Talk about irony. This disease brought on by (seems the prevailing thinking) humans feeding cheap undercooked slop to poor defenseless creatures, to fatten them up so we can butcher and eat them, can be spread by us humans but can only harm the creatures we're about to destroy. Perhaps with this and the mad cow disease, nature is telling us we don't need to eat so much damn meat. And I know of the "we need the protein" rap, but what about the millions of vegetarians who seem to get by. (You should see how healthy *and thin*, many of my Chinese no-eat-meat fellow qigong practitioners are!) So just a few days ago, Ash Wednesday as it shakes out, my recently dissolved, "do not eat meat" resolve has been officially re-upped. And if I, per chance, get to see those big black-brown eyes of Hugh's big and small cows again, perhaps I won't feel as guilty.

March 2 8:00 AM

For the very first time this morning I flicked on the tube resting above my bed in the cold, now, but always, loving and cozy room in Angela's B & B, and there is still no foot and mouth in the Republic. 1,000 Irish troops and police guard the borders checking for livestock. There are now reports of the first outbreak on the mainland in Belgium. The British still haven't been able to remove the wreckage of the train crash that claimed 13 lives. Amidst cries on the talk shows of certain farmers not being careful enough, it seems that most of them are.

Angela told me in her son-in-law's place of work, where his accounting firm handles many farmer accounts, the straw to dry off, and the bucket for the disinfectant, is now part of the business' furniture. And even the selling of disinfectant now is infected with the 'make hay now' capitalist greed—a gallon that was L10 as recently as Monday, now in places is selling for 50.

Mass for tomorrow in the North has been called off . . . there's heavy snow in the Donegal spot of the AA conference that, it seems now, I wisely chose to eschew. But per the forecast I saw the wind still blows east, again exactly what now is sorely needed.

Waiting around before I left Kilnacrott yesterday afternoon, for one more time I sauntered over to the lonely grave of the infamous Fr. Brendan Smyth. The man is so hated in Cavan, the transfer and burial of his body from that Belfast jail where he spent the last five years of his life took place in the midst of the night. Nine graves sit side-by-side across from Smyth's that sits all alone—as if his virus could seep through the ground, and infect rags and bones that now are no more.

That his virus was allowed to get across the border, to America even, when people in authority had been told of its existence, is a crime truly hard to believe. I was told a bishop who was suspected of being part of the cover up, had to cancel a speech in New York City because the American Cavan Society protested so loudly.

"It would be better for a man to place a millstone around his neck, and then to be cast in the sea," is what Jesus did say in regard to someone who harms "one of these little ones." And how many were harmed and how far did that geometric disease branch out? . . . and did Smythe become a priest because he was that way? . . . or did he become that way after he became a priest? The answers to all these questions have unfortunately gone with him to the grave.

March 2 18:43 PM

Driving back from McCall's Cross Key's tavern, not far out of town, the melancholy hit me. Eddie'd just dropped off his brother Tom who lives all by himself in the big house they grew up in. We'd been out to Killnacott because, Eddie after working a hard day of house building somewhere, had been kind enough to take me back out there because I'd left the computer power converter, US to Irish, behind.

I guessed the glum had something to do with how he spoke of his mom from one side of the hill had met his dad from the other, and that I, soon enough, would have to move on from the warm loving bosom of old Cavan Town. But it was after a brief nap when I realized Tom did not want to leave the bar mainly because he was lonely . . . and as I curdled all up in a ball from the cold, I realized that I, in spite of all of my friends, was more than a little bit lonely myself.

Day 24 March 3
8:26 AM

The latest I stayed in bed since I've been here by quite bit. The bitter cold is obviously still with us. Last night I was about to make the 20-minute or so walk to the meeting at St. Fellim's but I was too cold . . . and the cold is still with me this morning.

A long chat with Angela last night revealed that some more of my assumptions about mothering in Cavan and Cavan Town were inaccurate. Of the six women giving birth at the time her daughter did about seven months ago, she was the only mother who was wed. She also spoke of how in the clubs up this way, the guys brag of how many girls they bag in one night. Take a girl out, bed her or whatever her on down, and go in and get themselves another. Here too it is contraceptives are pushed . . . the first line of defense, abstinence, is too archaic to be even considered. So like with the foot mouth and the mad cow, we try to head off at the pass, a disease we created . . . and in the fatherless children arena, we are tragically failing.

I think of Hugh's tiny happy, yelping, *fixed* dogs and how as the bolder male barks from inside the tiny dog house as Hugh shakes his fist and says "don't dare you come out." Hugh says the female in there behind him "you can be sure is nipping at his hind legs, edging his yelping on from behind." On these cold nights I wonder how tight those two must bundle and cuddle to stay warm. I'll bet they look almost like one really strange canine-type being. And then there is the story around these parts that Ann Gaffney told me. Seems a swan that swam all summer long right next to a decorative artificial mate and who, when winter came on and the imposter was brought in, almost died of loneliness. So out came Mr. Swan-not-hardly-alive, and beside him (him?) did glide the no longer unhappy mate, and they swam around the lake, happy as can be. How about that one! The Hasbro swan-making company lending a hand to old Mother Nature.

But certainly we humans can't settle for cuddling and company, the *score* is what's on our mind. So what if the majority of folks from one generation back, going back to the dawn of recorded history, for the most part, did cuddle until a real commitment was made. They lived in a bygone backwards era, before sociologists and Howard Stern, and TV told us of a new, advanced and more fun way to live.

Maybe right *there* is our content/degree link to the deplorable actions of the infamous Father Bernard Smyth. His was homosexual excess of course, and the kids were young and didn't know, and the psychological torment much greater. But if you really think about it, is the cumulative effect of our "sex just for kicks" attitude, and our inbreeding this into our young that much less harmful? Is the ripping asunder of family units, and in the ecstasy-filled *rave* clubs where 13-15 year-olds mimic what mommy and daddy are doing in the singles bar down the way, really all that much different? Our borders are flooded with ads and with books, the Internet a cesspool of how and where we can get *it*. A tool that is and can be an instrument of spreading real positive messages is used to gorge mainly, our carnal appetites.

And so on the March Sunday morning in this land 'cross the sea', I did not win nor did I lose at the *game*, we *call* love last night. And in our calling this love is as obscene and glaring a misnomer as there ever has been.

March 4
Midnight

I just trudged up the Bridge street hill for the final time as a resident of Cavan Town. I move out to Jim and cousin Maura house in Cornafean tomorrow. I had to move aside during the same walk down several hours ago, as a crew of young nine/ten year olds whizzed down expertly on their little scooters—just like the things we had as kids. A little tiny white dog looked hilarious bringing up the rear. As I bid Eddie and Ann adieu at the Eagle Tavern, yawning so bad and barely able to keep my eyes open, Eddie said, "your Chinese friends would not be proud of ya." Of course I told Ann and Eddie about the less-required sleep aspect of qigong.

Day 25
March 5, 2001
5:30 AM

They call the Cavan accent flat. I call it earthy—of the earth. Cavan in Irish means "hollow". And in Cavan the county, if you are from Cavan Town, you say you are from Cavan, if from one of the townships, Belturbet, Glengevlin or whatever, you are from there. Kind of like folks from Port Richmond are from there to the locals, but are Philadelphians to the rest of the world. Like the Bronx, or Queens are to New York. And the Cavan (Town) accent is the flattest of the flat. As near as Kells where Avril is from, or Leitrum the next county over, where Phyllis is from—the 'whistles and twirls' or 'other' surround the flat grounded nouns and verbs of the Cavan (Town) ite. As far away as Tipperary, a la Jim Hannigan, the whistles and twirls would remind you of carnival carousal!

To my hearing, Eddie has THE male Cavan accent, and Angela THE female. Very appropriate. And being that Cavan is very close to the East/West mid-geographical point of Ireland, and is, entire island-wise, also in the north/south middle, my supposition many days back, about Cavan being the potential epi-center of a theoretical/spiritual "start here" movement, is somewhat grounded in a physical geography. Perhaps that is also true of the faith of these people . . . **Cavan** the center—and branching out in all directions. That remarkable display of worship I saw last Thursday night at the Killnacrott novena service, was more that of rural Cavanites, (Angela said those farmers really do pray) than of Cavan Town.

But yesterday in the Cavan Town center next to St Patrick's Cathedral, I briefly was exposed to a prayer service, as untraditional as any with which I have ever been involved. Led by an extremely devout visiting priest, this little room of "charismatics", was packed to the rafters. And for the first time in my life I was exposed to the speaking of tongues, the gibberish sounds certain devout gifted people utter, mirroring the Pentecost Sunday birthday feast of the Catholic Church, when 50 days after the Resurrection of Jesus, people from all over the then-known world were gathered in Jerusalem and heard Peter and the early apostles "speaking in words we all can understand, yet we all speak different languages". Hearing this today was weird and mysterious, even kind of spooky. Rapid fire "thank you Jesus, thank you Lord's" became the non-word gibberish, and I heard no faking. Dublinites up for the event, did most of the arm-waving and clapping during the singing, but the Cavanites, most certainly participated. And was a Cavanite named Ann Fitzgerald who had sort of organized the event, and she had jabbered up a storm when holding my hand during a particular hand-hold prayer thing and she also made sure to invite me back.

Something even weirder, though, happened at this event. I'd figured why not practice qigong in the midst of this? My thinking was, "there be's some serious, mysterious presence of this qi that I call grace going on here." So I adopted the "sit on edge of chair open my palms hands up right above my lap, left top of right (for a man, opposite for a woman)" pose, as we, in qigong, are instructed to do. And then only about a half a minute after I did this, the priest, who was situated in a place he certainly could not have seen me, said "why not let's sit up straight in out chair, and put our hands on our laps face up" . . . and then when he asked Lord to help some of us with certain things, and mentioned two different things in the *front* of my mind, I was *way* impressed.

So this Ann Fitzgerald, is someone I surely intend to look up. She, I believe can direct me to this priest, Father Raymond. And you had best believe, I will be there for a big Medjugorje shindig these folks were advertising that will take place in Dublin March 21. (Medjugorje is a little town in Bosnia-used-to-be-Yugoslavia, where apparitions of the Blessed Mother have been taking place for 20 years now. This event in Dublin is in, fact, a 20th year anniversary celebration.)

As I review the going on of these last 24 magical days, (and because St Patrick's day celebrations have been called off), I've decide to move out of Cavan earlier than I'd planned. I'm thinking next Tuesday March 13 of shifting base down to Dublin, and then to make a 3-4 day jaunt down to Galway, Cork and Clare, circling back to Dublin using these on/off bus passes that are available. The Skelligs including Michael, are down near that way, maybe I'll even try taking a jaunt over there.

* * *

Last night on the news, a car bomb exploded near the BBC studios in London. Thank God no one was injured. The head of the Conservative Party MP is on the news every night—blasting away at PM Tony Blair. A Palestinian suicide bomber blew up himself and three Israelis the other day.

The foot-mouth count keeps going up in Britain. In North Ireland it's still at one. The Republic still has been spared.

The weather forecast calls for more cold today, but with a bit of relief. Pouring down rain tomorrow . . . and then a real warm-up trend. The winds will remain from South up to North, perfect to keep the deadly virus away. I've been predicting we're going to get a big "kill-the virus" warm-up on St. Patrick's Day—I hope and pray I'm right.

This will be my final entry into this journal up in my lovely little room in the Bed and Breakfast ran by dear Angela. Later today I move out to Cornafean with my cousin Maura and her husband Jim, and that will really be nice. Jim drives his daughter Assumpta to town each morning and makes 10:00 AM mass. I'll join him each day, do the library and some roaming around, and then cop a ride home around 4:00.

That it will turn out I spent way more of my Ireland journey here, than in any other place, is so right and perfect and appropriate, I cannot even come close to explaining. The final clean and perfectly folded batch of my laundry sat outside my room when I arrived home late yesterday afternoon. An angel of Cavan took me under her wing for the bulk of my Ireland sojourn, and to say I am eternally grateful, in this particular case, does not overstate.

* * *

Sitting in the Internet café, just now, the need to sleep hit—hard. And so I ventured over to one of the lovely little couches they have, and soon nodded off into a deep sleep. For many years now I've been gifted with the ability to re-charge almost-totally-shot mental batteries with as brief as a 10 (even 5)-15 minute nap. That happened just now.

This nap was so deep I was even into a dream . . . and in it, I was being operated on and was in the midst of a life-threatening/saving operation when the power went off. Like that—and in that instant I awoke.

I used to have a recurring dream as a kid and young adult (I have probably not had the dream in over twenty years) but I do remember it. In it, the world was coming to an end, a blue gooky substance that instantly killed if it came into contact with anyone or anything, was spreading all over the earth. You could stay huddled up inside somewhere, but the gook seeped through doorways and windows and whatever, so the temporary reprieve was very temporary. The sweet comfort of staying, netted you death sooner than if you'd moved on.

The best route one could take in this recurrent dream-drama of mine, was to keep moving on—to the spots the gook had not yet reached, for as the stuff was irrepressibly relentless, it also was slow. Homes in places it had not yet reached were temporary havens until the blue gook eventually got there.

Many and most people perished, clutching the familiar comfort of their safe secure spots that in essence were their inevitable/eventual tombs. As for me in this dream, I usually was on the verge of making a break, when the magnificent release of awake shot me out of the peril. It's significance here, I really haven't a clue . . . but the need to move on is certainly a part of the deal.

Back to an exact on-time example, I now shall move on to the Farnham Hotel to meet my good friend and cousin-in-law Jim, and off to the next stop.

Day 26 March 6
Farnasseur House Cornafean

The seven miles from Cavan town out to the lovely little township called Cornafean are some of the most beautiful of God's acres on this entire planet. My cousin's husband Jim knows exactly where to find them. Some of these acres, ones right in the townland, he stopped to record on film. I should have taken a picture of the cows looking at Jim standing on a fence almost literally right in their face, shooting one spot he calls "the veil of Cornafean." Here picturesque little (and not so little) houses dot rolling hills of four or five variant shades of green and they along with scatterings of sheep and of cows, all roll on up into a big mountain range, magnificent and lordly in the distance.

The pictures are part of what now seems a one-man campaign to draw a bit of tourist trade to a Cornafean community whose farming business, due to apathy, government regulations, and threat of BSE (mad cow) and foot and mouth disease and other man-made viruses, is not what it once was.

When I see this work Jim is doing and when he tells of new homes being built and how he'd suggested a more stilt type of building to protect from the very real threat of rain-induced flooding and landslides, and when I see him spend a good two hours attending the family's two beautiful horses, my query "why did you retire from teaching" seems almost laughable.

One of the hats Jim wore about two years ago was to come up with a suitable millennium tribute for Cornafean. (The "to make a long story short" in *this* particular one, came about five minutes in to the near 20-minute yarn.) Seems he'd come up with the idea of a marble oblong structure, highlighting five of the most notable achievements of Cornafean folk. The most famous of the five was Jimmy Joe Riley the man who captained the Cavan Irish football team who won the All-Ireland match held in New York's Polo Grounds in 1947. The original estimate given him of 10-11,000 lbs. just for the stone alone, priced it way out of the townland's fiscal range. But one night coming home from somewhere, a "blown off his course" turn down a wrong lane quite a few miles away, landed Jim in the vast reaches of a quarry, and then the wheels stated to turn. A name of the owner, a "where and what the hell is Cornafean?" response to the first phone call was followed up by another, and soon enough Jim, "the oracle" (a local long-time Cornafean legendary resident), and a third gentleman found themselves in front of the quarry owner. And when one of them started singing "the legend of Jimmy Joe Riley" and the other two gaily joined in, Jim mimed the quarry's owner's literally seemingly being elevated form his chair. When this 'oracle' donated point blank the first L500 of the overall L6 to 7,000 *total* price tag, the township did have the monument—as eventually enough other people followed the oracle's lead. A time capsule stuffed with items from each and every household that chipped in for the cost, is part of the deal.

So here I now sit, very much out in the country. A bit later I'll accompany Jim as he drives his daughter Assumpta into town and to her beautiful all-girls Lady of Loretto school . . . and then we will roam perhaps over to the Shannon River or wherever he deems a good spot.

The school is situated either near or is part of, the massive expanse of what used to be the Lord Farnham estate. Farnham, who was the Protestant landlord who ruled over Cavan town and the surrounding land in the years before the revolt, was it seems, one of the many decent landlords that were part of the story. Jim told me in fact, his family itself, almost went broke feeding the Irish poor during the worst of the famine years. Examples like this, of bad *and* of good, are part of the portrait of each and every landscape from time immemorial. But 'bad' makes "good copy"—it is only when such "bad copy" is not even considered exceptional or wrong anymore, then the notations of goodness and decency, needs, almost by definition, to see more the light of day.

Jim, Maura and Assumpta's adorable little dog Toby, just burst in my room to say hello and to save me, I guess, from one more sermon.

March 6, 6:00 PM

For the first time since I've been in Ireland, fierce cold winds and driving rains from the East are upon us. The latest official guess that foot-mouth virus does NOT transmit through the air, is real good news now. The count on the Irish island is still the same—one in the North, none in the Republic. In England the number is now over 70, and the way they are letting all events go on as scheduled, the British do not seem terribly worried.

Here though, things are quite different . . . events are being cancelled left and right, mats laced with disinfectant grace the doorways of most retail establishments.

In today's news: Mick Jagger admits most nights he sleeps with a hot water bottle, a photographer spent 24 hours in a cold Scottish Church balcony to take pictures of Madonna's baby's christening, Tony Blair calls for an urgent meeting with top-level negotiators, including Taoiseach (the Irish Prime Minister) Bertie Ahern, to address the stalled North/South peace process . . . and then in the last part of the first section, in with world news, is the story of the smiling 13-year old who killed two and injured eleven of his classmates in a San Diego school shooting incident. About 99 weeks later, Columbine II is finally here.

As I think back to then and remember all the scares and the prank calls, there was almost a rush to get to that school year's end with no more tragedies. Thank God we did make it. As can be expected over here, where handguns really are for the most part, illegal, the talk is about America's obsession with guns. At the end of the report there was mention of a UNESCO summit beginning today regarding violence among youth. "Sociologists, psychologists, criminologists, and teachers are to discuss their experiences." The apparently politically correct UNESCO is leaving out clergymen.

But I remember thinking of the one poor Columbine girl who was shot and killed when she refused to denounce Jesus, I wonder if it would have been better for her if she'd never heard of a clergyman. Sacrificing a mortal life to prove to a crazed gun-wielding adolescent the depth of one's faith, seems to me a waste and a shame. Martyrs in the world 2000 years after Christ, pretty much all scare me. The Palestinian whose bomb blast of a suicide, because it took three Israelis with him, I'm certain left him with the belief that he was headed to a final resting place similar to that of the poor girl from Columbine.

Then of course there is the other end of the God/Satan continuum. I recall there was some outcry against Marilyn Manson at the time of the Columbine massacre because at least one of the shooters was a fan. Apparently such outcry was old news by last New Year's Eve, as ol' Marilyn was one of the headliners on MTV's New Year's Eve bash. Never will I forget the only time I stuck around long enough to get a real good dose of Marilyn—one night as I flicked through the channels and stopped as he was a guest with Howard Stern. Seems a kid about 16 or 17 was singing the *sing*er's praise. Marilyn was obviously impressed with this disciple's "I'm really grateful we have someone like you to turn to. All these people trying to shove Jesus Christ down our throat," rap. On hearing the "it's so great to have an alternative", he invited this disciple come to sit up on stage right next to him.

I heard a folk song not long after Columbine, that said blame it on this or blame it on that, but let's "take away the guns". I could not agree more. Anything we can do to control the violence, should be done. The "right to bear arms" plank of the constitution is so non-pertinent today, it is laughable. But the reality is the criminals *have and will get* guns. The need for protection in American cities is a lot more real than I think people over here realize. But attacking the means of the killing and ignoring the cause, is as ridiculous as waiting to decide which way to head for cover until after a hand grenade lands. I wonder if that came up in today's UNESCO session in Paris.

Tonight's news included the floods in Mozambique destroying the habitats of thousands of natives. But as sad as was the scene, seeing hardly-clad obviously very backward native tribesman, being whisked to frightening (to them) helicopters, by white South African soldiers, and to a future and a world they know nothing about, did my heart good.

Contrasting that with the stink of drug-making giants griping about the harm of shipping low-cost HIV drugs to Africa, and the good and the bad of the whole human drama, smacks one in the face—all this there on a continent of an island, that way more half of *is* the Third World. That *any* debt to the banks and the "haves" that these struggling lands have had run up would not be called off in a wash, is a blatant an example of just how *un*enlightened we are, as any I can imagine.

Day 27 March 7

Yesterday's travel of the Jims, Hannigan and McGowan, included a stop to see the former Hannigan housekeeper to bring her water and things. (Another hat Jim apparently wears is to sort of look after this charming woman.) Her name is Mary and she too hails from England. She ended up in Cavan because she and her husband used to holiday here because he loved to fish so much that they came back to live here upon his retiring. Another "long story made short" by Jim informed me of the coincidences ending up with this delightful woman as their hire.

But Mary, now a widow, alas, as well as three other woman in similar circumstances, is being forced from her comfortable little abode—victims too of progress. Seems the owner of the row of nice quaint small houses in the tiny township of Killishandra, wants to make them into something not quite so quaint and to re-sell them to new, richer blood. Fortunately, down the road just a piece, they are putting up low income flats for senior citizens, and Mary will be moving on. In fact the new places will probably be better for her . . . but, exactly as it is with my mom, 'pack rat' Mary will need to bail a considerable amount of 30 years worth of stuff before she moves on. Back in Philly my mom is likewise contemplating such a move as her arthritis and clogged arteries do not suit well the three floors worth of stairs she now traverses each day. But my mom, like Mary, is fortunate enough to have the money selling the house will net, plus some half-decent savings. There, more than here, a person without such a nest-egg, would seem plumb out of luck.

But one thing Mary did save, and I am grateful she did, is an adorable tiny little tale the Hannigan's third child and second of three girls, Aegean, wrote. It seems Mary and her husband almost raised Aegean in the flat next the main residence on the Farnasseur House estate of Jim and Maura. Aegean writes "reams" Maura told me several times, but is not fond of showing them. Well by reading just this one tiny little maybe 200-word piece about her being a little horse, written when she was about 17 years old, I can tell

Aegean has soul and imagination. Without the former, the words could dance across the page . . . but they would then dance right on off with no substance to ground them. And without the latter, though maybe chock full of meaning and content, they'd bog down in detail, and eventually bore. And this Mary the former housekeeper who is a darn good painter (her efforts decorate the walls of the warm little house) has the artistry to sense her former little charge's talent, and is grounded enough in love, to cherish the story. I genuinely hope that some day, if nothing more than in letters, I get to see more of Aegean's prose.

Jim's many charming stories and tales, always have the mark of the Master in guiding his life. Extremely devout, Jim was quick to point out that it was after mass on a Sunday morning when Mary had called about the nanny job. Faith once again, another example of it on this island where it is rock-solid chiseled within.

Day 28, March 8, 2001
End of week 4

On August 21, 1879, on a miserable rainy and windy night, an inexplicable light shone in the small church in the town known as Knock in the middle part of Ireland's County Mayo. 13 townsfolk of varying ages and gender went to the Church and there saw an apparition of Our Lady, Joseph, John the Evangelist and a lamb on an altar surrounded by angels. No words were spoken by any of the figures in the scene, but the angels flew steadily around the lamb throughout the entire approximately two-hour vision.

All 13 of the people there said they saw the exact same thing, and one old lady many years later—on her death bed, was asked at the moment she was coming close to her final breath, if she was telling the truth. Of course she said she was.

Ireland in 1879 was a desperately poor place. Then almost exactly thirty years after the great famine, a smaller one had brought an already staggering land further to her knees. The vision was viewed as a message of hope and of better things to come, as Jesus

Himself, had become the paschal lamb of a sacrifice, insuring the ultimate eternal better days, for those who believed. In the Ireland of this very day, a far more local and immediate way, the lamb could be seen as a symbol for peace and unity. One need only watch the evening news here, and see the North Irish Minister of Agriculture and her Republic counterpart, outlining their joint efforts in preventing the spread of the foot and mouth, to have hope. On Tuesday night Ms. Rodgers, the North Ireland head, was joined by Ian Paisley, the notorious Unionist separatist preacher who also gave Mr. Walsh (from the South) his respect and attention. As a new crucial round of political negotiations gets underway, it would be wise for all participants to pay close heed to their counterparts on the agricultural end.

As we pulled into the sprawling Our Lady of Knock shrine and basilica, where the beautiful little church still stands, and where we attended a lovely little mass at 3:00 PM, Jim was finishing up a delightful tale of an old woman he knew as a child. It seems he and a friend each week, used to visit this widow who lived alone, bringing her things she needed . . . and almost always as they walked up they'd hear her saying the rosary. Many years later, after Jim had moved out, on a weekly visit she'd asked another young friend to clear off the brush leading down to her lane. She also asked her priest and confessor to come and see her on a Saturday so she could be anointed. The priest protested but the woman who was ill, but not seemingly that seriously, insisted. Well Jim's friend's mother was there that next Saturday afternoon, and she saw the old woman whose breath was forced and gasping. But then all of a sudden she sat up in her bed, a beatific smile on her face, and said "Mary I'm coming." She then fell back down dead in her bed. (Her insistence the path be cleared reminded me of how my great grandfather put double doors on his home in Port Richmond so that when the time came, his casket, following his in-house wake would not have to go out the window.) Jim wondered how many of his dear friend's Hail Marys and Our Fathers helped him on his path through the wilderness of life.

Faith . . . beatific deaths . . . Mary . . . rosaries . . . all these things part and parcel of paying homage to that which we do not know. I remember my brother Tommy after being there for the birth of his and his wife Cindy's first child, "it's a miracle." He said it over and over. Of course I know we can trace the blood and the embryonic path, even down to the DNA and all that, but to deny the wonder and the miraculous . . . to lose it in the glut of facts and figures and advances in our capacity to think things out! Of course every single break though we make that serves to further the advancement of civilization and even to make us more comfortable is right and proper and appropriate. But to blindly think this capacity has made us lord and master over all we see is abjectly and demonically wrong . . . and this is kind of arrogance that is leading to our doom. A mind far greater than mine and one dedicated to that advancement, Albert Einstein (did you know his head was *really* that big, because he had a bigger brain that most folk?) admitted powerlessness to the extent to say;

> *"Religion without science is a cripple*
> *Science without religion is blind"*

How many more deaths or destruction must we face before we realize we need Help in our efforts?

But Knock over in County Mayo was not all we saw yesterday. We were in three of Ireland's four provinces in fact. Ulster—the north county and wherein Cavan resides. For a brief spell we were in Fermaugh in the East, Mayo is in the western province Connacht. Next week I head to the south and Lienster. We had evening tea in a beautiful hotel right on the mighty Shannon outside Athlone . . . we saw the castle where Sarchfield's men held off Orange for a spell. We passed the battleground where Cornwallis (yep *that* Cornwallis) demolished a French and Irish Army—squelching an Irish insurrection in 1798. Mighty Britain was apparently determined that the "shot heard round the world," that which had been fired in Lexington in America 23 years prior, would be muffled on the little island right across the channel.

As sightseeing and story hearing and reverent and wonderful and holy days go (the 3:00 PM mass in the same little church of the 1879 apparition, was one of the most charming I've attended since I've been here), yesterday was as good as they get. Literally listening to Jim singing the songs and ballads describing what I was seeing—man!

Who fears to speak of Ninety-Eight?
Who blushes at the name?
While cowards mock the patriot's name
Who hangs his head for shame

He's hardly a knave or half a slave
Who slights his country thus
But true men like you men
Will drink their glass with us

They rode in dark and evil days
To right their native land
They kindled here a living blaze
That nothing can withstand

Alas that might can vanquish right
They fell and passed away
But true men like you men
Are plenty here today.

I remember my mom telling me among the greatest charms of her visit here was listening to the wit and wisdom of the tour guides. To have a one-on-one guide, with every bit as much wit and wisdom (and almost surely more), then toss in a real genuine friendship *and* a Tipperary accent to die for . . . well you can see why I feel so very blessed.

Day 29 March 9

Yesterday's headlines here in Ireland were about the fizzling peace summit, the foot and mouth spreading like wild fire throughout England, along with the complaints that the big Cheltenham racing season was to be postponed, and the also understandable griping that the restrictions on movement of people is crippling the Irish tourism industry over here . . . among others. In the World News page in the *Independent* but not the *Times*, was a brief notation about another school shooting in America, this one netting no deaths though . . . and this in a Catholic school far closer to my home, right up in Williamsport, Pa . . . less than 200 miles from Philadelphia. If anyone thinks America's sickness is limited to the "publics", let him think again. I remember a friend telling me about three different eighth graders from a South Philadelphia Catholic grade school that were pregnant—obviously our advanced rejection of dated cultural norms has made its way into the good old middle class.

And yet other news came via e-mail yesterday—and this real close to home. My sister who teaches right down in the North Philly ghetto, was robbed and car-jacked at knifepoint about five blocks from her school. Thank God she wasn't hurt. But who can blame her for wanting to get out. "Hate the sin not the sinner" musings, this close to the gut are really difficult. Her attacker—probably an addict . . . needing a score. Armed robbery is a big deal, and in the off chance that they do catch him, he'll probably do some real time. Locked away . . . a necessary band-aid, but there is rarely rehabilitation behind all those locked up bars and walls, very little real healing gets done in the still seething sore of the American inner city.

Day 30
March 10

I awaken out here in Cornafean to the sound of squawking crows. (I think). In my fervor to write . . . or even worse to score points with my writing, I realize I've somehow lost or forgotten about the wonder and splendor of living in the country.

The other night I watched Jim put through his paces the larger and more fit of his two horses, the very friendly and very beautiful Tigger. It has been too wet and nasty to actually ride him the last few nights, so Jim held a loose reign on the beautiful bay mare as she ran around in a wide circle—shouting instruction to make sure he kept up a steady pace. Jim explained that because she was in better shape and had more muscles than their smaller horse, the paces he had to put her through were far more strenuous. Ask any great athlete the lengths they go to keep in tip-top physical shape. Later this morning if the rain holds off I hope to get to see one of the girls ride Tigger—doing the jumps and the whole bit.

So here I sit, a nice walk now can reacquaint me with that nature thing a bit, and also can serve perhaps to help get my flabby self a bit more physically toned up.

Day 31 March 11
Sunday

Through the mist a full moon shone down upon us as we emerged from the small but very comfortable and modernized Derryvilla church that my great grandfather Peter had prayed in all those years ago. A youngish priest, perhaps in his forties had said a brisk, song-less yet very reverent mass, including the first "kiss of peace" hand shake I'd seen at a mass since that one foot and mouth case had been discovered in the Irish Isle. (As I look back I realize that day was Ash Wednesday).

My cousin Eugene, the oldest brother of Maura, had *collected* me around 3:00 PM yesterday and had taken me up to Derryvilla. The visit to his first cousin Eugene's home for dinner and then back to his home for chatting and tea with his lovely wife Kathleen (who was a McGowan before and after her marriage) . . . the drive through the countryside, the meeting kids and cousins, the pre-bedding down pool match on the tiny very-sloped little table with

Sean and his fourth child and first son, Porrig—the entire 22 hour or so stay in the exact land my great grandfather roamed, was beyond warm and happy and peaceful and fun. And when we stopped by the little 3-room now-abandoned dwelling that to me looked like a barn, but that was *home* for Eugene and his brother Sean and sisters Margaret and Maura and father Tommy and mother Mary Alice and her mother—and this in the NINETEEN-FORTIES and FIFTIES—it gave me a fuller appreciation for how different and harder was life for my relatives born and bred across the sea.

There were great stories. It seems among my great grand pop Peter's nephews who did not come across the sea, were quite a few characters. I think it was Peter, the son of his brother Owen, who had a real affinity for the 'demon's rum' . . . and as Eugene's home was on the way home from the local pub, oftentimes Uncle Pete stopped to sleep it off a bit before heading home. One particular time he did not stop, but as he was peddling his bike somewhat shakily, he veered into Gene's car as Gene was gingerly trying to pass him. Pete and the bike somehow, went flying through the air and landed upright as can be—right in the top of a hedge. Pete then did come in for a brief respite!

Eugene and I had wonderful conversations in the car the whole time. It is very evident in talking to all my cousins over here that Tommy Owen and Mary Alice's invitation to all their children to think and question—to not blindly accept traditions and values they don't believe in—laid the groundwork for a wonderfully devout, decent and intelligent lineage. My cousins and their children all really do wow me. And again as is the case with seemingly all the McGowan in-law women, my cousins all tell me, Mary Alice is the one I really should have got to know—that she was the one who *really* remembered. And as sad as I am that I did not get to meet Tommy Owen and Mary Alice, I am almost glad my cousin Jimmy instead, did. Jimmy who came here in May of '99 is a lot less obtrusive than me. He and Tommy Owen hit it off famously; I'd suspect a bit more famously than me'n'Tommy would have. But Tommy and Mary Alice now too are amongst that great band of reverent no-longer-mortally-bound McGowans, calling and guiding me Home.

Day 31—March 11 back in Cavan Town 2:15 AM

I just left the Eagle Bar. Ann's heartrending rendition of *Danny Boy* kicked off a major sing-along. The owner/bartender Margaret (who I frequently used to see at 7:30 AM mass at St Claire's) kept the bar open until 1:30 . . . even the 12:00 midnight last call was eased.

A mother, father and three sons named Jergens were among the major contributors to the singing. Ann told me the sing-alongs that used to happen pretty regularly, happen rarely anymore, as the older fellow who used to lead the singing had passed on. But one sho' nuff happened tonight. The second verse of Danny Boy, was the one that got me . . .

And if you come back when all the flowers are dying,
And I am as dead as well dead may be,
You'll come and find the place where I am lying,
And kneel and say an Ave there for me,
And I shall hear though soft you tread above me,
And all my dreams will warmer, sweeter be,
And if you bend and tell me that you love me,
Then I shall sleep in peace until you come to me.

My dear friend for life, Mrs. Ann Gaffney, has the voice of an angel. She hit those real high notes with strength and tone . . . her face reddening in the effort. Later in the proceedings she did *Amazing Grace*. Anyone who's been as lost as I was, and who ends up found in the loving bosom of a family and friends and a town that as recently as 33 days ago I did not even know existed, would have to be amazed, humbled and exhilarated by the grace that led me here.

I regret that my journal of late has deteriorated; laziness the biggest culprit for certain. But perhaps I'd needed a break. Dublin, Cork and the South await. Perhaps I needed to simply soak in the love of family and friends to sustain me in the last two weeks of my trek. The way the Hannigans treated me—even with my cousin Maura the whole week often coming down from a sick bed, still always putting on the happy face—procuring and including fish in the nightly meals for my bogus-vegetarian self . . . the goodbye dinner with Hugh, Dympna and the family tonight—all of this supplied me with plenty.

Day 32
March 12

It is bright and sunny for my final day in Cavan and in Cavan Town. After my final breakfast with her, Angela clasped the GALA (Success in Gaelic) medal she'd given me behind my neck and then returned the 20 lb. note I tried to give her for last night's stay here. I had thought about taking the bus ride up to Omagh, to see the American folk park they have there (and where the 1904 McGowan picture is hanging) but probably will not. I have too many good-byes and such to make in town today.

At 7:30 tomorrow morning I will be on a bus to Dublin. As is the case now while I sit here and write, I suspect the tune of *Danny Boy* will be echoing in my head.

* * *

The Cavan Geneological Center is located in a place called the Cana House, situated far off the street behind the current St Felim's primary school for boys. It is on Farnham Street, almost directly between the bus station and the library. (That proximity to the bus station those 32 days ago, made my "carrying far too heavy of a load" life as it was then, a hell of a lot easier.)

Cana House used to be the jail for the area. And it is not just legend, but fact that there is a tunnel from its "high on a hill" perch, then underground beneath the town, and then opening out on the hill besides St Claire's school on the other side of the village. I know it's not merely legend because Ann told me her boys used to play in the tunnel. "Gallows Hill" was the spot to which the tunnel opened. Thus legend and logic would confirm the accuracy of the tales told me, "in way olden times, a peasant caught stealing cabbage or something from a landlord would be marched into the Cana House jail . . . never to ever again see the light of day except of a few final moments as his cruel unfair fate was quickly carried out when he emerged from the tunnel onto Gallows Hill."

Back on that first day in Cavan, as I sort of staggered around trying to find the Center, a crew of workmen were repairing the front steps and porch. It was a pretty major job. Subsequent stops up there during my stay found not exactly major progress—it was explained to me these workers were civil servants who were paid by the hour. And when I did come on by, of the three men involved with the repairs, a majority of the time, a minority of them, were actually *working*. But on today's final visit and goodbye and picture-taking session with Concepta (Ann O'Riley was on 'holiday'), my personal 'bet' was lost—a perfectly crafted set of new steps, enclosed porch with door and all the trimmings was in place—they had indeed finished before my Cavan town stay was completed.

This time the timing seemed just right for me to stop and say good-bye to Concepta. Because I picked 11:00 AM as my visit time, I got to see the first and probably only hurling match of my stay in Ireland. And though the match was between gym-class 8 to 10 year-old St Fellim's boys, the "whack a ball with a stick to guys on your team (maybe), try to get it past the goalie", theme was still the same. If it's purity and non-professionalism you're looking for in your matches, you can't get much purer than this. But then again the entire hurling/Gaelic football system throughout the Island, county vs. county, level vs. level and where at ALL levels, that there is NO PAY for the players, personally boggles my mind The money from matches and things, goes back into the football and hurling associations . . . . purely and simply to keep the tradition of the games alive.

So as my days in Cavan draw to a close, as I hear the fears regarding the "Celtic Tiger" it would seem to me that if anyone can tame this greedy tiger, it is the Irish. Perhaps the answer President McAlese might have given the "Is there anything about Ireland that will prevent the dollar from becoming *almighty* there?" question I could not figure out how properly to pose when I saw her give a brilliant "Ireland is marching forward," address last May in Philadelphia, could have been that the faith of the Irish people and their dedication to keeping alive traditions so near and dear to all they stand for, may, indeed be the whips needed to contain such an unruly devouring beast.

The goodbye stroll around Cavan town last night led me to a point on the steps leading out of the village and to a vantage point where the sun, making one of somewhat rare appearances of late, peeked trough the clouds and laid its glow on the rooftops and chimneys of this magic and holy little haven. Hopefully the photo from my cheapo disposable camera will capture the beauty and simplicity of the scene. The glare also made its way to the spires of the towns' Catholic and the Protestant cathedrals situated less than a block apart on Farnham Street. These almost matching set of spires reaching up to heaven reminded me of something I heard a charming little English author and humorist named Malcolm Muggeridge say to William F Buckley one time. (I'd happened to catch him on Buckley's *Firing Line* show, one afternoon surfing the channels during a boring football game.) The tiny, grinning octagenarian+'s paraphrased comment was "To me the perfect image of reverence to God would be a church steeple with a single spire reaching up to the sky, and then right next to it, a sculpture of an ugly, contorted gargoyle. The former would represent man's attempt to reach for God and the heavens, the latter would represent his admitted silliness and absurdity in even trying."

* * *

When my cousin Jimmy made his trek here some 22 months ago, the mistaken impression many people in Ireland have about Cavan was expressed by an information guy at the airport when he said in reply to my cous's query, "Cavan? What are you going to find in Cavan?"

Now I know how my good friend and cousin could have responded. "I'm going to find *Ireland* in Cavan," is what he could have said.

Journal 1

Ireland

Part II Dublin

Day 34 March 13, 2001
Swords, Ireland
Suburb of Dublin
Leinster

Going through the colossal clutter that was his house, Eamon Gaffney, the eldest son of Ann and Eddie, came across, for some reason, a hatchet. "And here's a hatchet, in case you want to kill yourself." This absurdity thing, I suppose, runs in the family. Later I'd see the hatchet in the back yard, buried in a half-chopped piece of wood. A la carte or on-time, and not neat little stacks, it seems, would be Eamon's method of accessing his fuel source.

Eamon is the one son who looks a lot like Eddie. His housekeeping instinct I would guess also matches that of his father . . . Eddie's abode, sans Ann, would, I suspect would look very much like this. But Eamon obviously has the decency and good-heartedness of both mom and dad . . . not only did he give me a couch on which to crash for the final two weeks of my stay in Ireland, but he also stopped and picked up my two huge, clumsy overstuffed bags in Cavan four days ago—and brought them here for me. A systems analyst for IBM and a match-winning bridge champion all over the island, North and South, demonstrates that along with the Gaffney wit and kindness, my new host obviously also has a goodly portion of the wisdom.

So here I am in a new spot. My trip into Swords today (after coming down on the 7:30 AM bus from Cavan with Gaffney brother, Noel, a Tuesday—Thursday resident in Eamon's Swords crash pad, and who, along with his lovely wife Theresa, had allowed me to stay my last night in Cavan in their immaculate home,) found a very modern suburban town . . . and one with charm and closeness . . . but one whose pace is a LOT faster than that of Cavan.

But my bus ride into Dublin, and the walk through the center of town to catch the bus out to here, revealed to me a town I know I am going to love. Certainly I will have to be more aware and careful, but I am after all, a city dude . . . and the city of Dublin as many people told me, looks like a fascinating place, and one chock full of things to explore. Indeed the very first monument of which I really took note—a statue towering over a traffic-infested street—was of none other than Charles Parnell—the spurned champion of the near turn-of century Irish cause, and a *cause celebre'* of the portrait of the artist, James Joyce when he was a young man.

Day 35 March 14

So it's Wednesday at 8:30 AM in Swords. Noel came home last night and led a mini-clean-up campaign here and the place looks a lot nicer. A wonderful, insightful and friendly Cavan buddy named Dermot also crashes here. *March Madness* (the name they use for the NCAA college basketball tournament) while pretty much unheard of over here IS 'in the air' between my particular ears. For the first time since 1997 my alma mater, St. Joe's (in Philly of course), is in the *Big Dance* that they call the tourney. Via the wonder of the Internet I will still be in several fill-out-the-bracket pools. St Joe's plays at 7:40 PM Irish time Thursday night. Along with my sight-seeing, I'll try to find a place in Dublin today that might be showing the game. Top-seed Stanford looms if they win game one against Georgia Tech. The coach Phil Martelli is a wonderful man, and something of a friend. He tries to answer every fan letter, even from a nut like me. I stopped to see him last fall before a qigong event on St. Joe's campus. Thank God he was right and I was wrong about the Hawks being good this year!

I will finally get to meet my cousin Margaret. Me, she and a couple of the nieces from Derryvilla, and Aegean from Cornafean will be meeting for dinner. I stupidly picked Thursday night—the night of the St Joe game, but I'll just have to hope they win so I'll get to watch them on Saturday.

* * *

The feeling one gets in their back would be occasional pain or nothing at all . . . you don't hear a person saying their back feels good. At certain times, though, after practicing qigong, I can actually say my back feels *actively good*. Well that sanguine back feeling happened big-time today, and it happened as I was walking through the campus of Trinity College, immediately after I'd practiced qigong in the adoration chapel next to the main church. And that practice had taken place immediately after having just gone to see the Book of Kells.

The Book is an amazing piece of work—my dad was right on with that one. The actual physical book is intact and under glass; some 800 years after its estimated completion, there it sits. By most estimates, it was begun in the 6th century AD, took near 600 years to complete and that at least four different writers and artists collaborated on its creation. "A Light in the Darkness" is how they advertise it, and after viewing this incredibly embroidered, magnificently scripted, Latin version of the four gospels of Jesus, the emotional moment I had in a corner of the showcase room seemed to have an awful lot to do with my father.

After checking out the monumental "Long room" library upstairs from the Kells exhibit, where books ranging from as old as 600 years are stacked floor-to-ceiling in a room about 50-75 yards long, and that, on certain supervised occasions, students can still read, I went to the painfully commercial Kells bookstore and picked up a book on Joyce's father as well as some letters and notes Joyce wrote throughout his life. I did not get very far into the book, but I did get far enough to find out that Joyce's grandfather, also James, married an ex-nun member of Irish freedom hero Daniel O'Connor's family (niece or daughter) who was ten years his senior . . . and also that she was obviously not up to the task of satisfying James Aloyisius' considerable carnal appetite. "You could throw a stick over the wall of the village, and scarce be able to avoid hitting one of his bastard children", was how the extremely dedicated authors of the book, Henderson and Jones, put it. Later on this evening, in the Herald (Ireland's one tabloid paper)'s report on the near epidemic outbreak of social diseases other than HIV coming out of the Dublin bar scene, revealed a different kind of complication that can arise out of wandering eyes and careless appetite stuffing.

* * *

Dublin really is a neat town. The Liffey running right through its middle is unfortunately blocked from view on most vantage points by a 5-foot high stone wall. (Unlike the Chicago River running through the center of Chicago which is always very visible . . . and which as the crow flies, and as I think of it, is, in about 60 hours, to have enough green dye dumped in it for it to be nice and green for St Patty's Day.) Dublin sort of runs in a circle, Abbey Street and O'Connell Blvd are two streets I know best so far. After I left Trinity, I tried unsuccessfully to figure out how to shortcut back to St Kevin's cathedral on Abbey St for 5:45 mass. Finally after asking about 5 different people, I made it. The mass was modern, fairly quick—a brief sermon and the 'kiss of peace' handshake the biggest differences from the mid-week masses I attended in Cavan. The gospel was the one about James and John wanting to be at either side of Jesus up in pearly-gateville. (In this version it's their *mom,* the wife of Zebedee, who is trying to make sure her little darlings get their proper due.) Jesus' "It's not for me to say . . . the first shall be last, the last shall be first . . . the Son of Man has come to serve not to be served . . ." reply, reminded me a lot of the message I've heard from many AA's with long-term sobriety, that "service service, service" was the secret to their success. 'You have to give it away to keep it" is the slogan we cliché-mad AA's have to make the point.

This "service, service" thing also reminds me a bit of what happened with Apostle Paul vs. his old buddy Peter, a few years down the road from James and John's clueless "I wanna be first" pronouncement. Paul had the fire and did service all over the world. (Freud actually thinks Christianity is a fraud perpetrated by Paul—honest! It's in one of his books. *Totem and Taboo* maybe. Robin Williams' line in *Good Will Hunting*, "tomorrow we find out why Freud did enough cocaine to kill a large horse" is *really* one for the ages! Shame ol' Siggy never found NA.) But Peter himself I think rarely left Jerusalem until he got dragged on off to Rome by one of the Caesars. He also only wrote two letters (that made it into the Bible at least.) Maybe even after Jesus' death, Peter was a bit lazy. In one of Paul's letters, calling him Cephas, Paul lays out Pete for sitting with the Jewish Christians and not the commoner new Gentile ones at some early Church function. Seems it didn't take long for the old we-they thing to get started. How about that, Paul, calling out the *man*—the ROCK—Imagine! But Peter took his medicine like a man . . . he didn't go sending off a counter-letter. (Like certain recovery guys I know who bristle and feel the need to explain when their message at a meeting is cross-shared and contradicted—like I did at a meeting today!*)* Peter obviously did have the fire by the end though. The story goes he converted nearly 70 guards while awaiting his crucifixion . . . a medicine, legend has it, that he took *upside down* to demonstrate his humble subservience to his real Lord and Master.

Well here it is 5:00 AM—midnite Philly time. Three hours ago, I called back home to turn in my March Madness picks to the old college chums I knew would be congregated at my buddy Leo's house for the annual pinochle-game, night-before repartee.

Thirty years later, *The Magic Alley Trash Band* still keeping on keeping on. Beast, "the philosopher B" and a dean at Widener University outside Philly, was, as usual, trying to keep the game moving through Quinny's talking. Coniel took my picks—the Gourmet, Ivor and the Whale said hello. Beast was the one who identified our "Cream rises to the top . . . we all met at the bottom," method of finding one another out at St. Joe's. Those philosophers get things right once in a while.

Day 36 March 15

The first gray day since I've been in Dublin. I just realized that these last two days were probably the first of the last 15 or so that it did not rain at all—and that it's been really nice. The weather the tale end of my stay up in Cavan was really typical cold raw Irish winter weather. The weather gods seem to have a way of easing me in to my new Erin digs as I go along.

I have a 10-11 slot over at the library computer in Rathbeale on the other side of the forest and across a neat little stream that runs right through the middle of the Swords area. I have to turn in my electronic picks for my old office's pool. (I have St Joe's going to the Final Four—just in case you're not yet convinced that I'm really crazy!) I also have to look up some addresses and attend to some e-mails. Later tonight is the dinner with my cousin and a bunch of her nieces (three of whom I met up in Derryvilla last weekend). I also have to check out the train schedule, because I'm going to do a one-day trip up to Belfast—probably on Monday or Tuesday and the train up there is a direct two-hour shot. It's funny if you look on a map, Dublin and Belfast are on almost a direct north-south line . . . and not all that far apart either. I'd guess Belfast, distance-wise, is a tad closer to Dublin than is Cavan town.

Day 37 March 16

The same cold gray rainy weather that accompanied my cousin Margaret as she drove me the five-ten miles from her lovely home back here to Swords last night, is here again this morning. I've gotten my fill of real Ireland winter weather the last few weeks.

And in yesterday's paper, news of the first real cold wind of the American economic slowdown slashing the face of the Celtic tiger—*"Intel cuts back $2.2bn Lexlip Expansion"*—was the lead headline in the *Irish Times. "About 1,400 construction workers will lose their jobs on the site of the Fab 24 project, in a development seen as the clearest indication that a slowdown in the US economy could have a serious impact in the Republic."* Of course there are the company spokesman assurances this is just a temporary thing—a delayed project and not a scratched one. Hopefully he was right, but this statement as well as the Times editorial stating this delay was a positive and logical move, to me smacked a bit of "see no evil, hear no evil." But again I am no economist. Nor do I understand the cry for Alan Greenspan to lower interest rates. But everything I read about or hear about Mr. Greenspan, seems to point to a guy who not only really knows the economy, but also to a man whose actions are well thought out and non-panicky. I wonder what will happen when this man with near super-human powers of dedication and concentration, is around no more.

But another item in today's Times really struck my interest. In an editorial by a columnist named Kate Holmquist regaling the dangers of human cloning, for the first time I've heard of a group who call themselves the *Raelians* who fund scientists involved in cloning—and their plans to resurrect a dead 10-month old boy by replacing diseased tissue or whatever, with some borrowed from his DNA-acceptable parents. It takes not too much imagination to ponder the "Brave New World" such 'ordering up' of temperament, or eye color or whatever, might lead. With our seismic advances in the "sex for pleasure only" market, it might not even be too much of an exaggeration to envision a time when old-fashioned random birthing, with its possibility of defects or even of plain old ordinariness, will be something limited to the simple unenlightened folk.

And so on the morning after dining and chatting with as delightful and diverse a group of individuals I could ever imagine,

I bask in *la difference* among my McGowan cousins. I also finally got to meet Margaret, the 4th sibling, of Tommy Owen whose father, Owen, again, was the younger brother—by 17 some years—of my great grandfather Peter. At Margaret's wonderful dinner were her brother Sean's daughter Ashling—auburn haired and fair-skinned; her brother Gene's daughter, dark-haired and really Italian-looking Marie (both these girls are students in Dublin who stay at Margaret's immaculate home). A little later came the Hannigan daughters, my friend Aegean, and her sister Ailbee whom I also met for the first time—and then later still, Ailbee's husband Keerin. All the above are intelligent, inquisitive young persons—and all are between 19 and 24 years of age. The level of discourse, interest and comprehension of this group makes me feel very confident about the future of the McGowan clan here across the sea.

* * *

Lying around a cluttered living room, as my new and gracious host Eamon unsuccessfully surfed the many channels available on Irish TV, trying to get the results of last night's NCAA March Madness, I asked him about the particulars of the events leading up to the Irish independence in 1922. In about two minutes I was watching the very entertaining and marginally-accurate historical movie *Michael Collins*—a very much Hollywood-ized version of the events of exactly that period. I think most people would agree that Collins was the military man behind the guerilla tactics that led to the truce that led to the Free State that was established in 1922—and that became the Republic in 1949. Among the more chilling scenes in the movie—one did happen though—it *is* history. After Collins' guerillas assassinated an entire crew of British intelligence officers who'd been shipped in specifically to fetter out and destroy the revolt, a bloody blind retaliation did take place in Dublin's Commerce Park. British soldiers during a Gaelic football match gunned down one player and 13 civilians. Another fact is also not even a point for argument—Collins was killed in the 4-6 month Irish civil war that took place after the war with Britain was over.

What would be questioned by many people (along with the timing of the events in the movie) is the not-exactly-stated, but certainly insinuated degree of Eamon Dellivera's involvement in Collins' death. Dellivera, who was one of the rebels taken into custody after the failed 1916 taking of the General Post Office revolt that was really the beginning of the war and not the end, would emerge from the ashes as the first real leader of the free Irish people. But Collins' death ostensibly united the warring factions in the civil war—and thus both in life and in death, this giant of a man from West Cork helped make the dream of a free Ireland a possibility.

Watching this movie one day after reading the Irish Declaration of Independence up at the Kells exhibit, penned in 1916, six years before the freedom was attained, touched off a chain-reaction realization of the many remarkable similarities between the Irish and the American revolts from Britain. The wording is very similar as well as the timing and duration of the wars . . . for although the United States the declaration was written in 1776, the fighting did not stop until 1781, the treaty was not signed until 1783. And the guerilla tactics those rebels from across the sea utilized (tactics that mark the American Revolution as the first modern war), mirrored the tactics used here by the Irish some 140 years later. While there were certainly more official pitched battles in our revolt, the guerilla aspect cannot be understated. Refer to General Burgoyne and his crackerjack British army that had been torn and tattered by the tactics of Ethan Allen's "Green Mountain Boys" (of whom Benedict Arnold was one of his most effective generals) and that was defeated by General Gates in the Battle of Saratoga—which was the real turning point in the war as it was this battle that induced France to join the American cause. Then there were the English armies beaten and ambushed by the southern militias and clans after the Brits decided to shift the war theater down there. It was indeed was one of these Southern based armies, a big one under the command of General Cornwallis who ended up at Yorktown down on the Chesapeake peninsula in 1781.

It was the surrender of his army, when DeGrasse's French fleet snuck up from the West Indies preventing his escape to the sea, and George Washington's daring overnight shift of most of his army from up in Philadelphia down to there, to prevent his escape to the north, that marked the end of the American Revolution.

But for us Americans, the break from England was neat and complete. There was no split of sympathies—everyone rallied around Washington—the Dellevera and Michael Collins rolled into one hero of our revolt. It would take 80 years for our internal demons the be released brother-against-brother . . . only our civil was would last 4 long years and it regarded the freedom of certain *people* not states—and all the American blood shed in it, is almost an ocean to a drop compared to the one over here. Yet the Irish blood shed at the hands of their former brothers-in-arms, was real and intense. 47 of the Republican leaders were caught and executed by the Free Staters during the brief Civil War. How many of those executions took place after Collins' ambush and the peace treaty signed almost six months later, I do not know. But I do know the Irish, including Dellevera rallied around the fallen hero—even the English sang his praises. Who is to make the call? Maybe Collins in death, saved more Irish lives than anyone can really imagine.

A long time ago—early on in this journal—I spoke of the glorious gray of being human. And when one looks at the many variant colors and hues and marching off to wars and glories and defeats and demoralizing throughout all history, but particularly that of those on this magnificent but so complicated little island—lines in the sand or defined stands of right or wrong seems even more impossible. The Real IRA still seems to be holding out for a totally united and *free* Ireland—that as long as there is still a North Ireland, the struggle is not finished. And some people up Cavan way suggested to me rather strongly that there are a pretty substantial number of people up in the north, those in Armaugh, in Fermanaugh, up in Derry, in Belfast even, who would probably choose to join the Republic if they had their druthers. When I asked Eamon about this (Eamon who by the way, about 10 minutes into my watching the Collins movie, handed me a floppy disc with all the info from last night's games INCLUDING St. Joe's win—realizing how much it meant to me—he'd emailed his office to get me the info) his "who cares, let the English worry about up there, the roads are nicer, Brtish/North Irish taxes pay for the huge welfare population," response, I realized, was a colossal mouthful. In this day and age who really does care? To view the mutual effective cooperation of North and South fighting this foot and mouth disease—maybe the English should sit up and take note—maybe so too should the negotiators of the ongoing peace process. In this post-colonial era, does any logical person really think the British will sweep in and take back the Republic if we lay down our arms?—with all they have going on? Of course the presence of the many iniquities Catholics still face up there, has to be addressed. But men like Sein Fein's Gerry Adams are doing a remarkable job peacefully addressing those issues. But is it not time we noticed and embraced what we have in common and chose not to cling to tired, dated, chiseled-in-Old World-conditioning differences? It's cool and neat and okay the roads are better in the North—who cares if we keep the Gaelic on our road signs down here? Some day maybe instead of an Orange Day when the Catholics flee, maybe we could have an Orange/Green day . . . when we could celebrate William's victory *and* the Independence of the Republic. Now that is a real brave new world! Maybe even pick a new day for it. July 4th has a nice ring to it. Do you think U2 would go for a big "unity concert" in Slieve castle at the same time say Elton John, and maybe Paul McCartney and maybe Mark Knopfler were playing at Wembley? Better yet flip-flop the venues—the Brits here, the Irish there. Do you think those blokes would go for it? Just for fun maybe in Yankee Stadium or something, Bruce Springsteen and maybe John Fogerty or (gah) In Sync could be yuking it up . . . . some zydeco gig in New Orleans perhaps, some blues in Chicago—charity of choice for sure. Maybe the whole world would notice.

Maybe it really is time we starting thinking "out of the box".

Day 38 March 17
St Patrick's Day 2001

On this bitter bleak St. Patty's Day I recall one probably about 40 years ago—then I walked in the parade with my father and the *Ancient Order of Hibernian* group in Philly's St Patrick's Day parade. It was a Sunday (as Philly always has their parade the Sunday before the 17th) and the main things I remember about the day was walking in front of Mayor Tate's review stand and then later playing the slot machine back at the AOH club in Northeast Philly's Oxford Circle section. I guess I even had the gambling "bug" then, as I remember having to be dragged from the club's slot-machine, one-armed bandit. The addiction thing already in evidence.

It's funny how things work out—how if you are clear and are graced enough, you can review the there of your life and kind of see how it got you here . . . how a/b/c/d etc got to exactly right now. And as absolutely essential it is for us to live and be in this exact moment, it is hardly idle musing or a waste of time to review one's steps to see the circumstances that led a person to the place he is now. This actually is what we in recovery do with that fourth step and fifth step. For such a perusal led me to see how the lessening of my chronic acting out in my alcohol addiction after my college years—years when it was a good weekend if I did not black out drinking both nights—progressed not with the bottle, but with the gambling, and then with the gambling and the prostitutes.

It is little wonder a good AA member and writer and educator in Philly, the guy who helped get the *Rehab after Work* program started there, told me my 2+ years of "clean/sober time" that I had back when I met him, was really a mirage in that it had included a drift back towards the bet and the paid-for babes. I have since grown to believe that as far as my lust addiction went, the paid-for babes would have been no different for me than if I'd been more successful and resolute in my search for a 'port in the storm' carnal relationship in or out of the AA rooms.

In those 12-step rooms, 'hooking up' is so prevalent, they call it 13th stepping. I am reminded of a girl with considerable consecutive sober-time at an AA convention saying "Ours is a completely physical relationship. He gets his I get mine. If he finds better, fine. If I do I'm out of there too." She sponsors many young women. Then there was the fairly young, quite attractive, 'slipper and slider' from my neighborhood back in Philly. She, who'd been in several *committed* relationships over her many years in AA, hung herself New Year's Day last. Several years ago it was a different perennial party girl who'd done herself in. She, whose New Year's Eve dancin' shakin' booty I coveted so did not make it until St. Valentine's Day. Her January suicide, if I remember, did not even involve the formality of going back to the dreaded "drink or drug." I wonder how many "sober" guys who'd pounded them, paraded past her no longer enticing bones.

Then there was a guy at the other end of the spectrum, down there with me and the other outside-looking-in non-closers. A year of morose, "All right I guess, at least I ain't drinkin'"s before he did pick up one and then put himself down. That a fellowship born on the bedrock of Christian principles is devolving into a storehouse of fodder to satisfy the instinctual drives of its members, becoming a mirror of the mayhem on the outside, is unconscionable. And in my brief time here, I can already see the AA of Ireland is much the same.

Just now I remember a good friend from my home group—one who had, at one time (about five years ago I think) accumulated more than ten years of drink/drug clean time. He was funny and witty and charming and always ready to befriend the new guy (just like he did me), and had married a wonderful recovering woman. But he never really did "put down" the bet and after he and the woman parented three strong handsome kids, he eventually left her and, then eventually, went back out to the booze and the drugs. And he did come back and back, and back, but each time back, he was never without a comely recovering girl on his arm, or without talk of who he was betting that weekend. Finally he came back no more. I bid my condolences to that bereaved former wife only a week or so before I came to Ireland. Liver disease was the official cause.

So here I sit. I was spared. This particular moment is very cool (in fact it's kind of freezing!—I still haven't figured out how to start a damn fire!) All the variant stuff got me exactly here. Somewhere over in New York's Hudson Valley a dear former friend is probably in the midst of a sound sleep. I met this guy my first sober anniversary . . . two weeks short of exactly eight years ago today—at the retreat house called Graymoor in New York's Bear mountain—the place where my father changed plans and decided to come home for the Christmas of 1940. My essential pursuit of *his* spirituality, about a year after that first visit would net me a magnificent and ostentatious 'find". But the summer after that January 1995 "I'm sorry dad", moment of peace and presence and clarity, my friend would utter something very prophetic. For as I left his Hudson Valley, Wappinger Falls home to head up to Saratoga racetrack for the best American thoroughbred racing had (and has) to offer, he said to me, "You know those ponies are only another crack pipe for you, don't you?" I didn't know that then. I sure do now.

So wouldn't you know it, as I trod all over Dublin yesterday, trying unsuccessfully to find a venue that might have today's St Joe/Stanford game on TV, didn't I venture into a betting shop? . . . and didn't I go up to place a bet—only to sheepishly walk away when I found out it was a *dog* race I'd *expertly* handicapped from the racing form hanging on the bet shop wall. I'm quite certain no real immediate harm would have come from placing the bet. (Other that the L10 I'd have been out—did you ever try to handicap a *dog* race? My old favorite betting partner, taking note of the lightning speed with which the race goes off and is then over, did accurately characterize the experience, "RIIING . . . YOU LOSE!") But in light of the subsequent VERY *dog-day* afternoons my past performances of betting may very well have lead to, (an a/b/c cause/effect schema that many of my friends in recovery have strongly suggested is in place for me), is it not really crazy that I went into there? Thank God I came out with the L10 note and a fresh dose of "what are you, an asshole?" recant.

I simply had to add this. Being that everyone here is still asleep, I decided to do a clothes washing to get me through the remainder of my trip. (When I climbed out of them last night my dungarees were approaching "standing-up-straight" status.) But naturally I had to first take the load of wash already in the washer that is stashed out back in the garage. And naturally I had to transfer it to the dryer next to it—the one with the extension cord leading from it into the house and into this room here, in this the most bachelor of all bachelor pads. And then after putting my wash in the washer, I decided to fold the load that naturally had been in the dryer. The amount of lint on the clothes precipitated a trek back out to the garage where I uncovered the dryer's lint tray with a good three-four inch perfectly rounded *pie* of lint. I can't wait to show the guys.

Day 39 March 18

The thing I miss least about drinking is being hungover. And March 18th used to be a hangover day extraordinaire. So this morning as I sit here at 8:00 AM working on my second piece of toast and second cup of tea—on this the morning after an imbibe-less pub crawl through the various Swords drinking establishments, I revel in the lack of the aching head etc. (NB if anyone wants to see the best, most eloquent description of a hangover—I strongly suggest you pick up Tom Wolfe's *Bonfire of the Vanities.*)

And so it goes. Dermott, his fiancée (a *lovely* West Cork gal in for the weekend) and me had a delightful night—and here's one for you—we interrupted our local pub crawl with a delicious East Indian meal in Sword's first class Indian restaurant. Thus on St Patrick's Day on my first trip to Ireland—ham and cabbage be damned—nan bread, bhaji and pakora were the order of the day. The cancellation of the parades and such because of the foot and mouth this year really took a lot of the luster off the celebration . . . one reason I stayed in Swords yesterday. That I had the delightful company of Dermott and his fiancée' (as a car that said "no" kept them from making the planned ride up to Cavan) was also part of the reason. The local pubs were crawling with folk . . . I'll bet more that a few nasty hangovers are being suffered through this gray Irish day.

For the first time since last Wednesday, earlier today I visited one of those meetings that allowed me to bid adieu to the hangovers and introduced me to the joyous way of living I enjoy right now. And my supposition that the AA in Dublin might be more progressive and step conscious than up in Cavan, proved correct—and this especially, dramatically and delightfully, was the case with the speaker at this meeting I attended. William D was the speaker's name and he has been sober for 31 years—and among his many pearls of wisdom was the statement, "If you're not interested in doing the steps, then what are you doing here?!"

I'd made my way out to this meeting through a sort of dodgy part of town down in North Central Dublin, by a very circuitous route. Before I'd left the house on the 9:40 bus into town, my meeting list revealed this 4:00 PM (1600 over here) meeting as the only Sunday midday meeting in Dublin. Arriving in town about 10:20—I found very near deserted streets. If you want a "quiet nobody around" Dublin, try before 11:00 AM on a Sunday if St. Patty's Day happened to be on a Saturday—parade or no parade! I was in town, because I'd had enough of Swords the day before, and because on Friday when I popped into Trinity's adoration chapel, I'd met two young ladies who invited me to attend today's 12:00 noon meeting of *The Dublin International Church of Christ.* Because they were cute, because they usually feed you at these gigs, and also because of my newfound commitment to ecumenism, I decided to go. With about an hour-and-a-half to kill before the service, I scooped around looking for a Catholic mass to go to first. Some older gentleman gathered up his cane, and led me out to the street to point toward the same church I've been to several times already down in Dublin. (One thing I've definitely noticed in Dublin—and that is that although the pace is much faster than up in Cavan, the people are just as friendly and helpful. Directions for lost Yanks, *all over* Ireland are almost never strictly verbal. I don't know how many times, I've been led around a corner or whatever to be *showed* how to get there—and I'd be willing to wager that will be the case also when I venture up to Belfast next week.)

But after following my new friends' directions, my subsequent trek over to St Kevin's revealed the next mass as a solemn in Latin job beginning at 11:00 am. So I ambled around in search of a different Church—and when the next bloke pointed me towards the Abbey Cathedral across from Parnell Square, I did not let the fact that this was to be a Presbyterian service deter me. Call this my "ecumenical day" I guess. And so I sat through the service. Quite literally—I cannot imagine going to a less enthusiastic service—the brilliant organ playing sure did not inspire much singing. Even the choir standing in the front was barely audible. The readings and the preaching were quite good, there was a baptism of an adorable little black baby, but all in all I was hardly impressed. As the preacher said that one of the components of Paul's message was that it worked, I could not help but think about how here and in churches all over the world, can you really say that is the case anymore. I think of my good friend Jim Houck, the 95-year old Oxford Group/Moral Rearmament member's saying in that western Maryland drawl, "Jim you gotta stop smoking that crack. You gotta be like St Paul up there in Philadelphia."

Because of the length of the service I was late getting to the next one—and that next service, *The International Church of Christ* one, was at the other end of the old enthusiasm continuum. In the second floor room of the secular ATGWU Building, there was a very "give me that old time religion" feel to the rhythmic, singing and clapping of hands. And in actuality these new Christian churches at the beginning of this 21st century, exactly like Buchman and the Oxford Group members in the beginning of the last one, have turned to the Bible to get back to that first Century Christianity. These new Christian churches basically use the whole Bible, but seemingly, especially the New Testament, to find their answers. But that is it—the Bible in toto; that is their only source of direction—for the 2,000 years of accumulated knowledge since, spiritual or otherwise, they seem to have little time. To me that speaks of closed minds.

And the Bibleheads say
it is there in the Book
you need only there look
and obey or be cooked.

But these people could not have been more friendly or open or kind . . . and when I mentioned to the main speaker, a brilliant inspirational guy named Tony I'd guess to be about 25 years old, my "judge ye not, be not ye judged" qualms about his Church's message, he said he would never feel the right to condemn anybody—even though in his preaching, it seemed to me he did. But even more impressive was the guy who left with me and with whom I had a spot of tea and who took the time to get out his Dublin map to give me exact directions to the AA meeting I'd never have found otherwise—for he gave me a very reassuring "we're learning as we go along" answer to some of my questions about his Church. His, "Hopefully another member took him aside and corrected him," reassurance when I mentioned to him about the two different tapes by big shot speakers in the fellowship that had bothered me—one in which the guy told his father he was going to hell . . . the other "unless you baptized in a Church like this, you're out of luck", made me feel a bit better about this entire group. And I will keep my appointment with this guy—to meet in front of the Trinity College main gate at 6:00 PM Tuesday.

Another appointment I hope to keep is with the new AA friend Willie I mentioned earlier. I will go to the 8:30 PM meeting this Saturday night at the same locale of this afternoon's meeting. My brief but enlightening tme spent with this gent, (he gave me a ride back into town after the meering) makes me think their may be some validity to his *humble* "this is the best meeting in the world" assessment. My thinking right now is to time my return home from Galway et al for Saturday in the early evening and to take him up on his offer for a ride from the bus stop to the meeting.

Day 40
March 19 St. Joseph's feast day.

I got that one memorized because it meant a day off when I was in grade school—thanks to the St Joe nuns who taught us. Until about 6th grade I think we had St Patrick's day off also—two days off out of three when you're in grade school is heaven. (In one of the most delicious slices of Catholicana of which I ever partook, one time in a restaurant, my buddy Gregory heartily disagreed with my, "man doesn't that roast beef smell good," assessment. "Roast beef is the worst smelling food in the world. It equals Sunday night and school the next day. Fried fish coming out of fans in an alley way—Friday night no school for two days—now that's a great smell.")

I guess today would be the correct day to regretfully add that my alma mater, St. Joe, went down to Stanford Saturday night. My cousin Jimmy e-mailed me and told me of the heroic effort—battling back from a 14 point deficit to actually tie with a minute left. Marvin O'Connor, a black kid from North Philly had 37, and was given a standing ovation when he fouled out in the last minute. (Jimmy called him an "Irishman from Simon Gratz High.") My mom on the phone yesterday said she was crying—she said everybody was. Temple—another Philly school—is still alive though. I've now officially switched bandwagons.

But here in Ireland, St Patrick's Day on a Saturday equals a bank, official holiday on Monday—today was that off day. And a strange day it was for me. I ventured up to Swords village, half ready to take the 45 minute bus ride into Dublin, but then changed my mind. Eamon had decided to defrost his little refrigerator, a task apparently that had not been done since around the Ice Age, and so I instead picked up a few things and doubled back to help with that chore . . . well the chore still is not all done. It almost is, I'm hoping time and perhaps some early morning sun will loosen the small amount of remaining ice so I can bring the 'fridge in here before I go into town tomorrow.

As my little trip heads into its last week, and having viewed *Ryan's Daughter* for the first time last night (another one out of Eamon's pretty substantial video collection) the passion thing, the longing thing—that has been seeping in my thoughts pretty strongly lately, is really upon me right now. That the lovely dark Irish stewardess from the Aer Lingus flight on the way over here, apparently had a change of heart from when she gave me her number during the stopover in Shannon to when I called last week, surely part of the melancholy!

This poem I wrote on the column of a book riding home on the El last fall is very appropriately titled.

Honesty

Lofty words not wholly meant
sanguine sounds guise l'autr'agends

false resolve made to dissolve
closet wants I daren't expose

this nose that goes in front de face
the here'n'now beneath the blouz

the grasp the take the satisfy
the tortured mumbled "why-o-why"

forever is a lovely state
are goose-bump chills so holy great?

The hunger of a lonely man

a warm caress
some eyes that melt
twisted limbs and passion pelts

if here today'n'gone tomor
I do not really care

but this sublime shall go undone
squelched shall it be—mon chase de fun

the endless waiting . . . .
. . . for the 'one'

So alas my girl of my dreams has still not appeared. And as much as I long for the physical connection, it is the emotional one I want even more—it's been far too long since someone wrapped arms around me only because they wanted to . . . the idea of a she whose romantic interest is only in me is so alluring. Call me an incurable romantic but I do not think the fade of the newness necessarily erodes the feeling itself . . . and no it is not only about sex, ask any couple who've been together for a long healthy and relatively happy time—and they will tell you it is not even primarily about the sex. True the rush of the new is as great a one as almost any other. A Faculty Staff Assistance counselor at Penn told me this new romance rush is often one that many people, men usually more than women, dedicate their lives pursuing. Anybody go to any single bars lately? And the guys who feign the *real thing* in their pursuit of a fresh and comely new conquests—these, to me, are the lowest of the many snakes in the grass in our present world's garden of Hedon. Good God is that what we're really here for?

It's funny how things shake out. I remember one I did care about, and was cared about back. It was brief but intense—and not really all that physical. And she was there for the last couple of months at the end of the devastating run that spanned most of the year 1997. In fact it might have been much worse had she not been there. But I do know she could not keep me sober, and it was the realization she was gone December 31 three years back that precipitated my "screw it" prowl to get high. But that prowl somehow netted no finds. And the subsequent blown-off-my-horse feeling that More than luck was involved in those non-finds in a very real way was the beginning of the journey that led me to here. The near five months I stayed sober after that moment, when I'd been unable to get 20 days before, was another 'beginning of the rest of my life'. The ensuing relapses, as painful and confounding as they were, were visits to the madness, not emersion therein.

Tomorrow is another day—the first day of my last week in Ireland. And as usual I've left more than half of the "what I was *gonna* do," column, to that last week. Another Penn FSAP counselor (all of them were very good) once told me, "Jim, you'll never be an 'A' personality with organized 'to do' lists and things. But you will get things done. Usually with your back up against the wall . . . but you will get them done. Don't try to change who you are, make the best and the most out of who you are." Amen dear Nancy—wherever you are.

Day 41 March 20

The howling winds outside felt even worse when I was just in them. "March winds" really do seem more severe over here in Ireland. And the lamb like weather early in this month, has sho 'nuff given way to some lionish cold as the month winds down.

Thus the story in today's *Irish Times* of how the misgivings of local environmental groups to the establishment of energy producing windmills are being ignored by the real powers that be, is, for my money, a positive development. This kind of force should be utilized! Natural, pollutant-free, literally God-given, energy is not to be squelched by activists trying to salvage the supposed purity of the countryside. These windmills actually are kind of sleek, modern and even a little bit neat looking. To try to block the creation of them is absurd. Kerry (the county in which the protests are being howled) will still be very beautiful with their presence. And that the Irish government and people seem to have a wonderful connection with their land and environment leads me to believe that there will not be an excessive over-implementation of these devices. One need only look at Sean Quinn's sprinkling of windmills dotting the Cavan countryside, taking little or nothing from the beauty, to realize there is not all that much about which to worry.

Land and country . . . responsibility to Nature . . . even-headed leadership regarding the issues touching these—to me, these are among the greatest qualities of the Irish people. When Jim Hannigan took me on the wonderful tour over to Knock, we passed a thriving power plant. When I asked what fuel generated the power, I was flabbergasted when I was told "peat." And of course on a tiny island where it is far easier to keep a handle on the energy and environmental needs than it is in America, I am still very impressed that there is no nuclear energy used here.

People don't squander and waste—that is the biggest difference between here and America. (Eamon going across the street chopping up blown down trees for firewood might be taking this a bit far, but who's counting. Ya man is one thrifty Cavanite!) *People* especially don't get squandered and used up here—and even though that seems to be changing from what I have seen and read, Dublin's decadence, in comparison to America's, is like Lourdes to Sodom and Gomorrah . . . or maybe to Vegas and LA. But then again I've not been around at the end of the night in the bars and clubs . . . maybe I try too hard to paint here good and there bad. Reading my e-mails, thinking about going here or there—finally 40 days later, I realize how homesick I am.

Day 42 March 21

The wind outside sounds a little like cannons booming in the distance.

Yesterday I had my first real introduction to Grafton Street—the now garish commercialized car-traffic-less cobblestoned street that extends from the back of Trinity College and empties out into the mouth of St Stephan's Green. The youngster with an electric guitar I passed on the way played, "Stairway to Heaven." (at 3:00 PM *to*, he was playing it. At 5:00 PM *fro*—he *still* was—I know it's a long song, but . . .) "Crossing Stephan's, that is my green" reads the inscription on the bust of James Joyce near the park's South Center side—almost directly in front of the University chapel. You could almost draw a straight line—Trinity, Grafton, Joyce's bust, the chapel . . . but when Joyce turned his back on that chapel, there is little or no evidence he ever turned back.

TS Eliot once called Joyce the most moral man he ever met. Does the fact that Joyce denied its existence bar him that stairway to heaven? Most certainly not my call. (A point I reiterated to my new Church of Christ chums yesterday.)

When I look at Joyce's 1882-1941 life-span, it almost exactly matches that of my grandfather Owen . . . Owen was born in March of 1984 and died on October 30th of that same 1941 year in which Joyce died in January. As I've read about Joyce's final Christmas—it seems it was probably his last happy moment. Exiled from Paris to Zurich at the approaching drums of the Nazi madness, he nestled in the loving bosom of his immediate family for a few glorious weeks. His ever-present stomach problems resurfaced with a vengeance there, and they claimed his life.

That very same Christmas was when my father returned home to Philadelphia and Port Richmond to likewise, rest in the bosom of his immediate family.

Seems my Aunt Nat had done wonders filling in for her namesake mom, who'd passed away some eight years earlier. My Aunt Nat was only thirteen when she took over the unofficial woman of the house duties. But Owen, my dad's dad, as was often the way with the McGowan men, probably started to come apart a bit after his woman died. There was talk of deep financial woes because of an unexpected huge payment to the water department because he'd failed to keep receipts for cash payments he'd made in person. I wonder how many roams of the Graymoor hills and prayers and kind gentler thoughts served to penetrate my dad's hurt at his pained relationship with his dad. I wonder about the day he put aside the "not just this minute" procrastination, and chose to go post the "I'm sorry dad" letter, that was surely the reason for the "I'm sorry too" return letter by Owen that I also read. I suspect that note had so much to do with the unexpected return of the prodigiously moral and thoughtful son. My dad and his dad were allotted eleven months to cement the amend—a thought bringing tears to my eyes as I sit here and write.

As I stated, Dad would meet his *Natalie*, my mom, not long after coming home. But as I ponder the lack of clergy in the descendants of Peter and Sarah, it dawns on me that perhaps we sons and daughters of Cavan, in a sense, need that earthy natural connection of a mate. Up through my dad's generation, the wholesome righteous meld of *one* man and *one* woman was not even something to question. On that wonderful day a few years back when the crew of us had descended on the old 'hood, as the conversation turned to the recently passed on Wilt Chamberlain and his boast of 10,000 women, my uncle Jim Flynn proudly stated, "that leaves me 9,999 behind." Imagine someone from my generation saying that? I don't know how many times my mom has said to me, that amidst the singing and laughing and general chicanery at McGowan parties, lewd talk, especially in front of the women, was the only taboo.

But for my father and Owen, and also too for the vast majority of those McGowans through their respective generations, as deeply and passionately as was the love for their immediate and extended families, it was in the infinite extension to *all* people that their faith and belief in God not only facilitates, but demands, lay the real strength of their love and conviction. It would seem to me that any solely human want or hunger to such a connection, regardless of how altruistic or sincere, is simply not enough. One need only look at the abyss surrounding us to appreciate the folly of our purely intellectual solutions. Intellectually I can trace a family tree or DNA. What I have in common with *all* mankind requires belief in something larger than that which I can *conceive.* And Joyce for all his unquestioned genius seemingly denied his participation in such a connection. Perhaps in his lifelong regret that his daughter was never able to live up to her potential, or to ever beat her psychosis, was the greatest, most tragic effect to the cause of his intellectual arrogance.

Lacan could hint at, and certainly Jung could openly speak of that 'oceanic' feeling, coming from a Source Higher than our own thinking capabilities, but Joyce would not. And when I read of the depth and passion in the love Joyce's father's had for him, even at the expense of his other children, the shallowness of his particular pool of love becomes apparent to me. As I make these comparisons between Joyce and my father and me, it seems the biggest difference is that Joyce was denied a real rich spiritual lineage. A philandering grandfather and an overly pious grandmother who became almost a recluse when she became a widow; a robust, intelligent, charming father who definitely drank too much and whose love for him seemingly bordered on the parasitic; a schooling and training that left very much to be desired. *Portrait of the Artist as a Young Man* revealed no Father St John the Baptist types. I look at my father, and besides Fr. St J, he no doubt had many other inspiring progressive clerics down Nativity way. But mostly he had Sarah and Peter and Owen and Natalie and lots of actively believing immediate relatives in his wake. But Joyce too, like the McGowans, seemingly needed that union with a mate, and to his dear Nora, he was seemingly every bit as true as was anyone in my family to their mates. For any Church to demand that its clergy be denied such a union, a demand denied by the majority of the world and one with absolutely no justification from a Bible on which it claims to base its morality—who is to say Joyce's turning away was unjustified?

How many sons of preacher men were never born? How many Brendan Smyths can be laid at the feet of this demand?

The tragedy of Joyce, seems to me that he could not divorce the excesses of the purveyors of God's Word, from that Word—or from God himself. As I said I do not know what went on in the mind and soul of this complicated genius, but of the things he wrote that I have read, Joyce seemed to perceive a world that was not the province of some 'can't be *figured*' Power somewhere. But then again Joyce was a writer, an artist. He never claimed to be, nor wanted to be, the point man or brunt of a philosophical school. The intelligentsia has laid that wreath at his feet. At a time he was already world-renowned he eschewed the riches contributing to contemporary publications could have brought him, to spend almost 20 years writing what would become *Finegan's Wake*. I've been told that in it, he tried to speak a "universal" language. Perhaps, before I sling any more arrows his way, I should try harder to read it. And maybe too, Joyce's turning away from a tradition and faith that had grown old and stale was the proper thing to do . . . again it is not for me to make that call.

Day 44
March 23

Friday of my last weekend in Ireland. I head home next Tuesday. And as it looks right now, I may spend Friday and Saturday night in a little seaside resort kind of town called Dunleery just a few miles south of Dublin. There are too many things I still want to do in Dublin to head elsewhere (like Cork or Galway). I still want to head out to the Marianella Center in Rathgar, where the Redemptorist Fathers are, and to which my friend Fr. Mac suggested I go when he bid me his blessing before I came over here. Rathgar is also south of Dublin—but still in the Dublin City limits—a walk or a bus will get me there. The DART elevated train system will get me out to Dunleery in about 20 minutes—and there is a DART stop very near the AA meeting I want to make sure to attend Saturday Night.

All this Rathgar/Dart/Dunleery traveling information was given to me by a charming lady I met on the 41 bus ride home from town out here to Swords last night. It started with her telling me there is a Joyce center in Dunleery. But it was this lady who also told me of the first confirmed case of foot and mouth disease in the Republic. And it was found right here on the east coast—in the county of Louth—in a spot actually not too far north of right here where I sit. Louth is Ireland's smallest county, I had never even heard of it until now—but it lies exactly on the almost direct North/South line between Belfast and Dublin. The story is the case appeared on a farm on a peninsula and the slaughter of neighboring sheep and cattle has already begun. I hope and pray that the considerable North-South cooperation will continue and will keep the virus localized. The current count in England of 453 confirmed, and near 500,000 slaughtered, is testimony to the "too-little-to-late" policy that went down over there. On TV last night, an English farmer lamented, "let Tony Blair come out here and get that smell of burning flesh in his nose and in his chest—then let him tell me this is under control".

Yesterday I picked up a London Times and not an Irish one—and though a lot sleazier, it is a very good paper. Among the topics covered was that of an angry Anglican bishop complaining about the stink the Roman Catholics are putting up over this communion thing. It seems Blair himself is married to a Catholic, and how he now must be careful about receiving communion in the *others'* Sunday Church service—the media glare you know. I'm reminded of the tale by the Irish Anglican priest in his *Late Late Show* debate with a Catholic priest a few weeks back. A Catholic Italian was marrying a woman from his Protestant church. To avoid possible embarrassment, the Anglican priest had no communion at all during the service. And when the Catholic priest punctuated the Anglican's tale of the Italian father saying, "I was disappointed, I was looking forward to receiving communion, I'd asked my local bishop and he'd said 'no problem'" with a "well, he was wrong," I was more than a little bit troubled. This very conservative, very intelligent and well-spoken Catholic priest did not come off as loving or as open-minded as did his Irish-Anglican counterpart. But in his closing "*unfortunately* a Catholic can not receive communion in the Church of Ireland *yet,*" remark, I heard an open door, mind and heart that did my heart good. The italics are mine—and to me they represent a prayer as important as any the handsome young firebrand of a priest has ever uttered.

So prayer it was, I uttered last night as once more as I took a 15-minute solitary-in-the-rain stroll up from Swords town center to the River Valley neighborhood where Eamon's house is. Out came the rosaries—the ones blessed by the pope and that I'd picked up at the October 7, "Our Lady of the Rosary" feast day celebration at St. Peter's Church/cathedral at 5th and Girard, right on the edge of North Philadelphia's barrio/ghetto . . . on that day when I first heard of Our Lady of Knock. And I prayed the rosary just like Our Lady has asked us to do so many times. I thought about how intently I'd prayed for release from the foot and mouth while I was up in Cavan, but that since I've been down here, have not really thought or prayed about it much.

Prayer, fasting, self-denial—when one of the first speakers at the magnificent "Thanks Dear Gospa" Medjugorje 1981-2001 concert/lecture I attended two night ago (NOT three nights ago—as I mistakenly thought/wished it was. My trek there Tuesday and the discovery that I was 25 hours early, set off this whole "never left Dublin" mode I am now in) spoke of self-denial, my incendiary comments about forced Church celibacy, tightened round my neck like a too tight tie. But then I thought some more—how much self-denial is involved with following rules you're coerced to follow? Rules that have driven a wedge between our Church and almost all the others. I would sincerely hope and pray that if the day ever came when Roman Catholic priests were allowed to marry, a goodly number of them would *choose* to make even that sacrifice and denial of self in the name of their Savior who gave his all for us.

Someone told me that in one of the Orthodox Catholic Churches, only the priests who choose celibacy move up the ranks to bishop and the like. To me that seems like a wonderful idea. Of course there would be problems with married clergy, among the biggest, the lure of certain women who would no doubt get a kick out of getting Fr so-and-so to bed her down. But other churches seem to get over the problems. Then of course how many Brendan Smyth-type problems would be eliminated if priests could marry? But probably most important of all, how many kind warm, loving, instinctive words of advice, or gentle caresses or hugs, bred in genuine selfless love, would there be available to a tired married priest arriving home after a difficult day attending the flock? (Not to mention the colossal good woman priests themselves could do tending to those flocks.) I'm reminded of the wife of Connor Flynn, the Philadelphian who brought AA to Ireland. Willie D told me it was she who suggested "why not go start an AA meeting" when bad weather put a damper on his golf vacation here. His trip to a hospital found him a gentleman named Percival. Percival was a friend of Willie's and he died recently with a ton of sober years behind him. Then there was Bill Wilson, who before he met

Bob Smith was frustrated and perturbed after going oh-for-six months trying to get anybody sober. It was his wife who suggested "but Bill, *you* haven't wanted to drink. Don't you see that it *is* working?"

Bill Wilson, Bob Smith, Connor Flynn—1900 years later . . . acting like first century Christians, taking a message partly born out of a Bible book called James and using it to pull poor suffering souls from the abyss of a bottle.

8:00 AM. the first bird chirp of the day just graced my ears. Time to head off to somewhere . . . .

* * *

The gospel read today at St. Theresa's, right off Grafton Street, was about the golden rule. When asked which was the greatest commandment, Jesus answered "love God with your whole heart and soul and mind and body and love your neighbor as yourself." Before today, however, I never noticed that the person who answers Jesus' formula back to him, and who says "yes I can see how those two are the great commandments," and to whom Jesus replied "you are very close to the Kingdom," was a Scribe. It was one of the only times in all the gospels that I remember Jesus saying something good about one of the Jewish church elders or leaders. The way I always remember thinking about the gospels is that only the simple Jewish folk embraced Jesus, that none of their Church's hierarchy did—and that pretty much *all* the Jews, high and low, turned on him that first Good Friday.

Now I am realizing that was not so—Joseph of Armithea, he, who supplied the tomb where Jesus was laid, as I recall was a Jewish church leader. It was on Good Friday almost exactly eight years ago, that I heard more than about Joseph than just his name. It was April 4, 1993 when some North Jersey radio station was telling his tale as I sped from Graymoor down to my home group to celebrate my first one-year sober anniversary. I wonder, throughout the ages, how widespread and intense has "the Jews were the baddies, the Christians the goodies," conditioning gummed up the flow of that "love neighbor as yourself" second half of that formula? In a course at Penn we studied a wonderful book called *Number Our Days* about very old Jewish people living out their remaining days at an adult center in Venice California. They recalled how as children living in the ghettos of Poland, it was during Holy Week when the violence heaped on them by the *Christian* children and adults was most intense.

And the real irony was and is; the God of the first part of that formula, He, to be loved "with whole heart and soul", is and always was the same for these two great religions. The status of the emissary Jesus, is where all the difference lies. Here again, for us to concentrate on what we have in common, and not in what is different, could be so helpful. Perhaps in our Catholic grade schools we should have stressed that the early first Christians were necessarily *all* Jews—the same as one clump of those *publics* in the school down the road. Indeed Mary was, and to my knowledge, never stopped being, one very holy devout Jew. If anyone knew the Torah, it was she. If I recall, she was never there when folks pointed out how Jesus and his grisly mates were ignoring certain of the Jewish rituals regarding eating and things. I always thought of Mary as being the epitome of politeness and reverence—I can't see her ignoring the washing and purification rituals of her Jewish faith. Certainly James, this guy who wrote the book of James, who, I reiterate, many Biblical scholars claim was her son, was very Jewish. The Book of James, for goodness sake, is addressed to the twelve tribes of Israel . . . and Jesus is mentioned only one time after the introduction. I invite my good devout Jewish friend to perhaps take a look at this book, and at its simple practical spirituality—even if it is in the dreaded *New* Testament.

Yet how often so we all do this—blindly cling to the tenants of our religion instead of finding out what is good and of common ground in theirs? As I recall my staunch "my spirituality is better than yours," argument a few weeks back with my friend up in Cavan, I own my own still clinging self-righteousness. But as I bask in the grace bestowed me from those twelve steps of Alcoholics Anonymous, (one of, which guided he and I to immediately mend our fences), I revel in the wide open doors that the adding of that *as I understand Him* after that God, has effected. I think it was a "James" from Philadelphia—a chap with a decidedly agnostic bent—who insisted on that "as I understand Him," caveat. Added to which, I take heart in the fact that our founders too, learned as they went along. It was Dr. Silkworth, the heroic doctor who'd treated Bill Wilson, who suggested Bill's early failures at getting anybody sober, could very well have been because he pounded the God talk too heavily on these suffering newcomers; that he should maybe talk more about his drinking.

But alas as I look around a world and at all the killing in the name of God, the Jews and the Christians seem to not be fighting each other each as much any more . . . now they both, respectively, seem to be battling the Muslims. In Israel and Palestine, in the Balkans, in all the places where militant purified hard liners battle farmers or peasants—from Saddam Hussein to Ayatollah whoever, to the terrorist forces of Osama bin Laden—it is the Nation of Islam that seems to be in the thick of the fighting. And on a wall in Dublin Castle, in the Chester Beatty Library where I viewed what might be the most magnificent display of tributes to God *of all kinds* of people's understandings, in Qur'an II:235, I read the following words of Mohammed:

"There is no God but He—the Living—the Everlasting. Slumber never ceases Him, nor does sleep. To Him belongs all the heaven and the Earth.

Who is there can intercede with Him, save by His leave. He knows what lies before them and what is after them. And they will comprehend nothing of His knowledge except as He wills. His throne comprises heaven and earth. For He is All-high, All-glorious."

Again same God at the top. The Koran, I've been told, contains elements of both the Old and New Testament. How much thought or "where's the common ground and not the difference," went into the thinking of the West and Rome as they launched unsuccessful crusade after crusade to wrestle the Holy Land back from these *heathens.* How many years and centuries of 'my God is different than yours' conditioning is behind the suicide bombings and burned flags and seething hatred? And when Malcolm X went to Mecca and saw the light and came back to America preaching the real Islam message of love and not hate—his very own lieutenants, blinded by the myopia of their own particular 'we', from the light of *All* that had come to him, did X in.

The library is one of the fixtures in Dublin Castle. Chester Beatty, for whom it was named, was an American of Irish descent who made a great fortune developing a unique system for mining. Colorado, Alaska, and Africa were some of the places he went plying his trade. But miner's disease (a serious throat ailment) and his love for England brought him across the Atlantic in 1911. A very rich man, he developed a deep love and appreciation for the Orient—near and far. And when England's post WWII monetary policies began to burrow too heavily into his fortune—he came to Ireland. In 1957 he would become the only man ever named an "honorary citizen of Ireland", and upon his death in 1968 (at the age of 93) he would leave his entire collection of art and books to Ireland.

The collection of these original books and manuscripts on display for free every day in the castle is amazing. There is a Koran written in 800 AD—*very* legible. There are Chinese doctrines and manuscripts dated 400 AD. There is a PAGE from John's gospel in the first century. I hate to say it, but the book of Kells exhibit pales in comparison to this one; talk about calligraphy and embroidery! But the fascinating thing to me was the early Christian books and artifacts. Magnificent gospel accounts written by Syrians in 200 BC and the like. (Many gospel accounts were from that period. Somewhere in, I think, the fourth century those written by Matthew, Mark, Luke and John were chosen to go in the Bible. And theirs emphatically spoke of the death *and physical* Resurrection of Jesus. That Peter and Thomas' gospels do not specifically mention it, and that Peter's mentions something about men carrying a body away in the middle of the night from near where the tomb of Jesus was, do, as some Biblical scholars have suggested, make a pretty strong case that the Resurrection was not a literal/physical one. I don't believe that . . . far more literature before and after suggests it was physical. But in reality who cares? It is the *message* of Jesus that is what's important. As an AA friend once suggested I listen for the message and not the mess at AA meetings, I think of the *mess* and ripping asunder of that message through the years by folk demanding that Jesus' resurrection was a physical one.)

The Beatty display though, was mind boggling. And the notation on the wall about how Christian missionaries in this modern day allow the inclusion of ethnic traditions into their teachings of Christ, it reminded me of a book called "*I Rigobertu*" that I read in the same *Oral History* course at Penn where I'd read *Number Our Days*. This wonderful book, about a heroic Guatemalan Indian woman contained an account of how the Catholic missionaries in her country had done just that. But then when I read about how the Jesuits when taking the word to China in the 16th century, were denied permission by Rome to incorporate the very moral and practical aspects of Confucianism into their teaching, it reminded me how Rome was unfortunately, not always so open minded. And even now, today, as I recall a Trinity priest earlier today telling me how Rome has recently placed de Mello's *Awareness*, on the "not recommended to read" list—I cringe at the thought of yet one more Jesuit censured by Rome. As my good buddy from America, Feudi, just e-mailed me, de Mello can join Copernicus, Galileo and de Chardin on a pretty heady list. Imagine censoring writings by men of God! Still fighting off the heresies. I agree that de Chardin (as I understand him) had it wrong—his philosophy that we sort of *evolve* into God was off. But everything, we DO and all the knowledge and skill and wisdom we accumulate is proper and worthwhile—and is in accord with God's will—that part of de Chardin was dead-on accurate. But our function is not becoming God, it is doing as He wills.

On a website that comes out of Little Rock Arkansas, each day I receive a beautiful little de Mello snippet on various aspects of spirituality. It just so happens that yesterday's had morsels by both these men my Church has chosen to censure. The subject, appropriately was:

HUMANITY

Much advance publicity was made for the address the
Master would deliver on "The Destruction of the
World" and a large crowd gathered at the monastery grounds
to hear him.

The address was over in less than a minute. All he said was:

"These things will destroy the human race:
politics without principle, progress without compassion,
wealth without work,
learning without silence,
religion without fearlessness
and worship without awareness."

Anthony de Mello, S.J.

MORSEL: The day will come when after harnessing space, the winds, the tides and gravitation, we shall harness the energies of love. And on that day, for the second time in the history of the world, we shall have discovered fire.—Pierre Teilhard de Chardin

The heresies: how much do we really know about them? Is that too strong a word to use for what Rome contends de Mello and de Chardin spoke? How dare anyone ban people from writing what they believe is the truth regarding our Creator!

Look at our church's past. The early Church in her zeal to get away from Roman pagan idol worship pretty much banned pictures and statues. The New Church of God crowd naturally is hot into this kind of thing . . . and I'm sure they'd say the secession from Peter was already out the window by the time the Church tune changed and Clement of Alexandria called God "the Great Artist" in 250 AD. Gregory the Great in 500 or thereabouts called images the "Book of the Laity". Then when this staunch resistance to images resurfaced in the latter part of the first century, it was then regarded as a heresy! It was a big part of a heresy even—the Bogomil heresy . . . and this heresy flourished in a place pretty big in the news lately—a place called Bosnia. These Bosnians, already discontented with how Rome intruded on their Christianity, readily became Muslims after the Ottoman conquest of the region. A few centuries down the road, Luther was big on the "lose the pictures" movement. "A Hundred Years" was the name they gave to the European war that followed; in Bosnia and the Balkans they are still fighting one just like it.

Yet I wonder, why and how does a painting or a piece of music or a word written or one uttered in deference to the glory of God, replace the God as the object of the praise? Is not art one of the only places we can get to that is stripped of the idol-worship of our intellect? When I read the particulars of Da Vinci's *Last Supper* out in Kilnacrott—of the details of the bread and spilled wine on the table, of how the turned up palms of one of the twelve underline the pointing fingers of the apostle beside him—the art, the search, the beauty, the love of God expressed in those details, simply overwhelmed me. Freud did a psychoanalysis of Da Vinci—from across the centuries, and it was actually pretty well presented. But to me, his conclusion that it was in the sublimation of his sexual instinct that Leonardo was able to create such magnificent art, was wrong. Freud limited his horizons to the terminate box of psycho and sexual. Talk about drops in the ocean. DaVinci, it seems to me, went to a place Freud denied because he could not conjure it.

For years I jotted down notes and poems, the morose artist . . . ambling about in the aimless ether of my own intellect. Fiery scathing words some: cool, sweet and flowing, others. But the fire was without warmth, the waters cold and bracing until the asbestos-like cloak of my pride was ripped away. There beneath it, in the Art beneath the art, was/is, again, not the glowing spark of *arriving*, rather the sweet caress of having never left: Home. Always was and always will be. Eternity now . . . the kingdom IN my heart—not *will* be.

It is very late and I am very tired. I'm also still in Swords. The folly of leaving here hit me as I showered this morning. This drift into losing things mode (today it was my *12 Steps to Deeper Spirituality* pamphlet), and the thought of lugging my laptop through a bad part of town, convinced me to stay put. The Marianella trip today was a bust; the Dunleery trip I'll take tomorrow.

The foot and mouth thing is huge. "12,500 Animals to be Slaughtered Today . . ." read the headline in *The Irish Times*. When a farmer said his one cow seemed like he knew something was wrong—that they are so instinctive, all I could think about was the big black eyes of the cows in Hugh's barn.

Now they're back saying maybe the virus IS spread in the air . . . there's still much not knowing re the foot and mouth. That the farm on which this case was discovered is on a little peninsula makes isolating the area a bit easier and that is a good thing.

3:27 AM . . . . 10:30 Friday night in Philly. 6 weeks ago this journey and the journal began. The journal nears its conclusion, the journey is ongoing. Everything that happened led me to here. And here is good.

Day 45
March 24

My twin brother and sister's birthday: Tommy and Sally. Sally would be glad that I am going to write about Cougar—she grew to love him dearly in the year and a half, me and he lived with her and her friend Pat. It was she who drove us out to the Somers Point, New Jersey vet a year and a half ago when the arthritis finally got so bad it seemed inhumane to keep him alive.

To the blind person sitting next to me on the bus out to Rathgar yesterday, whose retriever guide dog named Billie was of the same breed, I said "my retriever Cougar was a watchdog to my heart and soul."

It was October 2 1997, the year of my "using" despair and discontent. Cougar and I were sitting on the beach in Ocean City, New Jersey on a mid-week afternoon because my boss at work had given me a two-month paid sick leave five weeks earlier to get myself straightened out. This instead of the pink slip I'd earned. The eight-day post-Labor Day stay in the Rehab had been wrapped by trips to the copman (and the accompanying women.) Three days before and after I was getting high. I had taken the incredibly kind "Let's us be Jim's Rehab" offer of Renee, the wife of my friend from college, and first AA sponsor, Jack. Renee and Jack had given me and Cougar the downstairs apartment of their home in the safe quiet, *dry* haven that is OC.

Cougs sat by my side that glorious Indian Summer afternoon, (I remember the exact date because the temperature hit 80 that day, and the swim-inducing surf temperature hit 70) when a girl who'd recently lost a dog, punctuated the big fuss she'd made over Cougar with the remark, "He's really an angel in disguise you know." My God how that comment got the wheels turning. Like little Billie on the bus (who, because he was off-duty, his owner said it was okay to pet him) Cougar *loved* being made a fuss over.

The angel reference that October day, brought back thoughts of that just-past summer when I was farther into my addiction than ever . . . and Cougar was with me the whole time—dying as I was dying, getting better as I got better. He'd lie clumped up in a ball in a corner, under-noticed and underfed as I paraded one woman after another to the upstairs room of my little row house . . . up to my little bedroom to smoke crack and only very rarely to act out sexually.

But even with the mistreatment, on those horrible 'next mornings' or afternoons or evenings or whenevers—as in whenever the money would run out, as I'd lie on the downstairs couch wallowing in self-pity and despair, he'd still walk over and put his head on my chest . . . looking, panting, almost suggesting "how about a little walk to clear your head"—and up I would sometimes get, and walk and pray and ponder and think "maybe *this* is the time I'll stop." Obviously it wasn't. And there were all those other walks on those nights I was struggling not to, but then as I'd head not towards the park, but up towards Broad Street to find the hers and the hits . . . and he'd linger behind . . . tilting his head looking as if to say "not that way . . . the park is over here", it was like he knew. And usually I'd have to go back across the street and physically get him started in the other direction—in the wrong direction.

But even though the trip to Ocean City was not the end—within two weeks I found what I was looking for 15 miles north up in Atlantic City—it was sort of the beginning of the end. The chronic using stopped down there—the loads were briefer and more spread out . . . both me and Cougar sort of came back to life. The arthritis medicine I'd started him on, plus the nightly massages of his hind legs, put a little life back into his steps . . . steps that had become strained and hobbled. We walked the beach and we hung out and bonded probably more than we ever had before—he was as happy as he'd been in many years.

And of course he was beside me on that unforgettable walk on that warm windy last day of that year. I was 18 days clean at the time and I'd moved up to my sister and her friend Pat's Far Northeast home to get out of South Philly. It was right and proper that my little angel was beside me when I was overwhelmed with the sense that the "luck" I'd just had in not finding a using partner had come from that Higher Power for whom I'd so desperately searched. That New Year was the real beginning of the end—but alas it was not *the* end. The demon pride still had to be slain. The first relapse came four months later . . . it was about the sixth, 16 months after that, when Cougar's days were drawing to an end.

It's funny how dogs know, how animals seem to know when the time is near. And quite a few crying whimpering false alarms had occurred in the months preceding that July 25, 1999 Saturday morning when Sally and I finally took him to his no-more-pain

Big Sleep. But as fate would have it, about three weeks earlier, the last time I'd walked Cougar around the long Far Northeast block where our residence was, Cougar chose the long way home. The entire twist and turn block probably takes in ¾ of a mile—and on the way three different groups of kids—one at each end and one in the middle, always regularly made a big ol' fuss over Cougs. But as the arthritis had begun to get real bad again, I'd go just to the base of the block and turn around—the whole block-long walk was too much. However as I made the about face that time—a time which would turn out to be the last time we made that walk, he didn't follow—he walked on to kid groups two and three—it was if he knew it was time to bid final adieus.

There is never a "right" time to go back to smoking crack. Just like there is never a "right" time for an alcoholic to stop drinking. I remember all those years thinking, "well, after Labor Day, or after the Super Bowl, or after St Patty's Day"—such thinking is nonsense—you stop when you stop. But for me, choosing that July '99 period to pick up again was particularly disadvantageous. The last week of that July, the whole family was congregating down the shore for my other sister, Mary Ellen's, birthday. My half-a-day vacation Thursday and all day Friday and Monday were supposed to be about vacationing with my family. The pipe, the hit, the crack however trumps all . . . filial or any other considerations mean nothing, and the half a day that Thursday turned into a load. I'd switched vehicles with Sally the night before so I'd have her van to transport Cougar, as the arthritis had made it impossible for him to get comfortable in the back seat of my car anymore. But after packing up and loading him in the van, I took $150 I'd cash-advanced on my credit card earlier and prowled through a bad neighborhood looking for a "player". (This sometimes-interrupted run had begun about two weeks prior.) Eventually I found one and as we camped out in this little dingy back bedroom of a glorified hithouse, Cougs sat in the back of the stifling van on a near 100° day. I cracked the front window so he'd get some air . . . but he was out there a good three hours before the $ ran out. And when I got out there, he was not in the back, he was scrunched up by the front door trying to get more air. I stopped at a gas station nearby to get him some water as I made my belated trip down the shore. By that night when we got down there, he seemed okay. We took a couple of very slow walks and he drank a lot of water.

The next day, that Friday, he seemed normal . . . perhaps a bit slower, not that interested in eating, but seemingly okay. But he did bark quite a few times—not an in pain bark but a "pay attention to me" bark . . . which was way out of character for him . . . almost like he knew. And one of those barks elicited a good 10-15 minute very tender moment on the lawn out in front of Sally's shore house. He put his head right in my lap and I gently petted him. It was almost like he was purring "no grudges boss, I still love you". In the middle of the night, though, the barking started up again and this barking had a real pained tint to it, so I got up and petted him and hung out with him . . . even slept on the couch in the living room where he was. In the morning we took a very, very slow walk, and of course I snapped at him when he refused to eat again . . . but when he refused to even eat a piece of straight ground beef—I knew something was up. The whining, in-pain whimpering and barking started soon after. These plus the refusal to eat, hard-time breathing symptoms all were part of what the vet had told me were signals that it "was time". So I made a few calls, found a very humane Vet's office out on Route 9 just outside of town—Sally drove the van and I stayed in the back with him and then through the entire ordeal . . . and Cougar was finally at rest.

So the memory of him curled up against that side van door in a panting, struggling-for-air hump, is one I have to live with. Many people have suggested it had been time for a while before then—that he was in pain more that not. Who knows, and speaking of *knowing*, dogs are not supposed to be all that great in that department . . . but they sure enough know how to love and to love selflessly. And if given the choice of a month or two of extra living in his pained state vs. sacrificing himself to a painful dehydrated demise so that his beloved master might finally get better, I'm quite sure it would have been a no-brainer for Cougar. The demon who'd been right on my shoulder vacated for a spell after that Saturday morning. And although I could not tell anyone in my family about what had happened, sharing the pain with a sponsor and some friends in recovery when I got home did help a lot. The next two days though, I was in the exact right place—in the warm bosom of my incredibly wonderful immediate family (including my nieces and nephew)—to ease the pain of losing my very literal *best* friend.

It was last fall when I found out that October 2 is the day the Church chooses to call the feast day of all guardian angels. Mike the Monk says we should know our guardian angels—that we should talk to them and have names for them. Sorry Mike, for me, I only really *knew* one of them . . . .

* * *

On my last Saturday in Ireland, the weather was nice for the first time in a while. No rain, not cold. Minimal wind. As I walked through the New York-ish throng on the street, outside the Killarney Grille, my near every day spot for tea and a scone, a bag-piper who calls himself "the Highlander" was blowing out *Amazing Grace.* I shared a table and had a chat with a nice girl from Wales who'd just spent a year in Australia. Figuring out her accent was impossible!

As I crossed over the O'Connell Street Bridge to Dublin's South Side, I came across a gentleman selling his own books of poetry and essays. In our very nice chat, he told me that morning, his "poor me nobody's buying my stuff" musings were tempered by his looking at a dandelion being perfectly content being just what it was—and how he made a similar connection—his literature meant much to himself—he needed no outside support. His comment reminded me of Thomas Merton's "Song of the Birds" . . . in which to his admiration of the way the birds simply sing and fly and live, the birds replied "and even that is too much."

It was a truly wonderful day in Dublin. I made my way over to Trinity—ready to practice my Qigong in earnest for the first time in a couple of days, but the adoration room I'd made my Qigong spot, was shut tight. So I walked on past the football fields, and as I did, the sense that it was here, Joyce in the *Portrait,* had watched his country-type buddy (the guy might even have been from Cavan!) excel at athletics, really enthralled me. But Joyce who was amazed by and admired this guy's devout worship and by his Fenian spirit and by the way he clung to his Gaelic language, simply could not intellectually accept it.

Merton, likewise had been a card-carrying member of the intellectual elite in his school, Ivy League *Columbia* in the 1930's. After his tune-turning conversion, in *The Seven Story Mountain,* he said some things about "poor Columbia" . . . specifically because of the way she clung to her intellectual anvils. On different sides of the Big Pond, brain power preeminent.

But brainpower, that for me involves the access and usage of my God-given gifts, is exactly what this Qigong practice I was scouting around looking for a place to do, is all about. And so right there on a park bench besides the field not being used—a bit removed from the crowds who'd gathered to watch the *Trinity vs. Satltanains* Grade 3 rugby match, I practiced Qigong—Yan Xin Qigong that is. And the thought hit me that it's nice practicing outdoors as it is easier to imagine the sun or moon light entering the tiempo point in the top of my head (as we are instructed to do) if it actually is! A lot of thoughts hit me while I was sitting there. My mind wanders frequently during Qigong practice, like it has done for all of the meditation methods I tried in the past. But I did as instructed, and went back to the breathing. Minds in meditation are not supposed to wander—that is the whole deal. They are supposed to be trained. And that to me is one of the beauties of Qigong. We have specific things we are instructed to do with our minds as we sit there breathing in and out. That is why the more advanced practitioners are so adamant about calling Qigong a practice and not a meditation—I look forward to getting back home and practicing again with a tape that verbalizes those instructions.

Again I go back to de Mello. As a Jesuit and a native of India, who wrote a whole book on meditation practice, (back before the Church started finding his spirituality a bit *too* Eastern and dodgy)—how much time do you think he spent effectively meditating? The Buddhists and Hindus who, like John of the Cross and Avila—actually at times get lifted off the ground, do you not think they are getting anywhere? And de Mello *never ever* denied Jesus! When I said to that priest who told me of the official Church censuring of it, that Jesus is all over that *Awareness* book—he was surprised—and if he did not burn his copy—maybe he could find the references. Then there is the other end of the spectrum: the brilliant writer I was in class with last fall who told me to send her no more *Awareness* snippets because she "don't want to hear about Jesus." Does anyone in the Church's hierarchy have any clue as to how many people there are out there exactly like her? And still—two thousand years later, we censure and monitor the things our shepherds say to the flock—why? "We teach Resurrection through the risen Christ," I was told by the priest who notified me about the *Awareness* banning. As I sit here in passionate agreement that Jesus IS the way out of the abyss, I hope and pray that the Church to whose return for me has elicited so many magnificent moments of peace and clarity, will grow to realize those arms extended on the cross are meant to invite ALL people . . . that open-minded thinking and pondering and theorizing about the quite literal "Greatest Story Ever Told" is not an exercise restricted to only a certain enlightened elite.

It is actually Sunday morning **Day 45, March 25**—I cheated a bit—I wanted to finish up yesterday's thoughts that I was too tired and lazy to do last night. And as has often been the case here—the writing took me to a whole different place than I expected to go. Today is my second to last full day in Ireland. I never made it to Dunleery. I'm still thinking about Belfast tomorrow—I have tickets for the play in town with my cousins for 8:00 PM tomorrow night.

But while I wait for the water to heat up so I can take a shower, as I find myself still in this Eastern mode—and again put off my Qigong practice, I look back to the time when my Qigong practice was most consistent and intense. And ironically it was last August at Gethsemani, the place Merton made famous—in what I hopefully and humbly believe was the first week of the rest of my life. The retreat was from August 21-25. The irony and appropriateness that I was doing it in the monastery made famous by Merton, the man probably more responsible for bridging the gap between Eastern and Western spirituality than any other, has come me upon more and more as my journey has continued. The first day there I sat on a bench under a tree practicing by memory—then returning to my room and did the closing procedure with the tape. I diligently practiced Qigong—the middle three days listening to the entire one-hour tape. But on my final day there, alone in the near-darkness between the stark, Spartan, unadorned stone cinder block walls of the Church/chapel—high up in the balcony—I practiced again. For the only time that week I'd awakened in time to say the 3:15 AM morning office with the monks who live there and it was after the office, that I practiced. The smell and the silence and the reverence were among the things I imagined seeping into my waiting, open pores. It was a magical time.

Then there was more irony the day after I left that holy mountain. At mass in a very old, very traditional Cincinnati church called St. Mary's, the first church that I'd been in since I was a kid where you kneel down to receive communion (first until I got to Ireland that is), in the first reading from the Old Testament book of Ezekiel, a very holy and blessed prophet named Elijah, spoke of a dream he had of the New Jerusalem in the clouds . . . and of a fresh wind coming in from the *Eastern* gate. The East, where the word God is seemingly eschewed in the spirituality. For how many years and centuries have men killed one another claiming to they *know* God and that their brand of spirituality is the only means to His graces?

Sitting beside me in that church was my sister Mary Ellen—the one who almost exactly one year prior had driven me the 2.5 hours from her Cincinnati home to this Gethsemani place that until then, I'd known only by reputation. Mary Ellen whose prayer and good thoughts on my behalf I'm sure have been a large part of my recovery. Mary Ellen the one who every time I tell her I admire her "dad-like" faith, humbly and honestly says "I don't think my faith is that strong" . . . Mary Ellen the one who thanked me for telling her I go to mass often down in Drexel University's little Mother Katherine chapel had induced her to go to lunchtime masses also. Mary Ellen the one I fight with a lot less now, a happenstance that is so cool. My older traditional Catholic sister, however, had little time for the excerpted *Qigong and Christianity* piece I'd left behind when she'd driven me to Gethsemani that preceding Monday.

———

April 23, 2000

Qigong and Christianity

Church was crowded today because it was Easter Sunday, maybe the holiest day of the year in the Christian/Catholic religion. And when we prayed for the parish's other priest who was in the hospital with heart problems, and for the woman who so magnificently leads us in song each week and who is suffering from breast cancer, it struck me how much the mind/body benefits of Qigong could help these two kind devout people.

In this old church in Philly's Fishtown section that I regularly attend, the maybe 150 people there today was about three times the normal crowd. But because the crowd was so large, and because the Church was so nicely ornamented with Easter flowers etc and because they used the old fashioned organ this week (and not a guitar), and because the scent of incense filled the place, I thought about mass and life and belief in the world in the middle ages of the West. Then life was certainly simpler, there was only ONE Christian Church—the Catholic one, and people lived and believed and did not question. And for the most part their lives were simple and happy enough.

But I also thought about how this era was also known as the "Dark Ages" and when you think of the oppression of the masses during this era, of people being born as serfs serving often brutal feudal lords and of living and dying a life from which there was no escape, the description seems pretty accurate. In many cases the priests were among the wealthiest of the folks around. So the accusation that the Church, in their call to the people to essentially put up with hardship and pain in THIS life in order to know peace and happiness in the next, was instrumental in maintaining the inequity of the status quo, is probably an accurate one. When you are OF the "haves" you frequently like the status to remain quo.

Therefore when the Enlightenment of the 16th, 17th and 18th centuries arrived, the Church was an appropriate target. And many of the rules the new Christian churches wanted changed, needed changing. But the end-result of all this revolt was not a more equitable viable accurate method of following and worshiping the teaching of Jesus Christ (the real aim of Christianity), what resulted was diversion, hate, destruction and death . . . and this diversion hath carried on even into the present day.

But this little essay is not supposed to be a summation of the breakdown of Western Christianity, it is supposed to be a treatise of some of my experiences in the 13 months I have been practicing Yan Xin Qigong. But for me separating Yan Xin Qigong from my spiritual journey, from my Catholic/Christian faith, is impossible. And when Qigong tells me "virtue is the essence", to me they describe the essence of Christianity. And when they tell me living a life of open honest kindness and decency is 70 to 30% more important than the actual practice, I am reminded of how many time Jesus expressed the idea that being good to your neighbor was far more important that ostentatious displays of reverence.

I thought back to last December, when after researching Qigong and reading the literature, how my practice "took off" when I began to think of the qi I was receiving as being the grace of God. The literature I speak of is Collectana Volume Nine and a section where people from three different Eastern and Western religious traditions (including a Christian) spoke of how Qigong, instead of detracting from, actually enhanced their religious practice.

I think of how perhaps the most moving practicing moment I'd even known, happened when I practiced in the chapel where, one hour each week I sit in front of the exposed Blessed Sacrament. (The host representing Jesus in his saying to his disciples the night before he was crucified, "This is my body which will be given up for you.") That day as I did the closing part of the practice and slowly moved my hands back and forth, the only part of me that I could realize was that movement, it was like "I" had disappeared. I was lost in a blanket of white that permeated the surroundings. And that week (like every other week I practice there without the tape and for perhaps 30 to 40 minutes), I imagined the qi coming directly from that host . . . the very real representative of my God. There is a Zen Buddhist teaching that goes "don't seek the truth, just drop your opinions." And that day, that moment, I felt like the opinions and all the other parts of me had been dropped. And the qi had helped me to do this dropping. In that absence I was far more aware of my sharing of the Great Reality of us all. For that moment I felt "the union between humankind the universe" that Dr. Yan Xin mentions.

Then of course was that electrifying Chinese New Year night up at the Philadelphia XYQ center when Dr Yan Xin had said "we are ALL brothers and now is the time for East and West to come together". And I thought of a different day when during group practice and the pain in my back was real and intense and I tried to think of my mother's painful neuropathy-afflicted feet so my pain might lighten hers (as a more experienced practitioner had suggested I do), but instead the image of a Chinese woman in a rice paddy ladened with a heavy yoke, came into my head.

But as I sat in church this Easter morning taking part in the celebration as thoughts of the positive aspects of Qigong accompanied my negative thoughts of the Western Dark ages, I thought too of the maybe even darker ages of the East. That there, despite the presence of great Qigong masters throughout the land, for the most part, did not violent war lords control and enslave a backward, unenlightened people? Indeed had not a violent horde from Mongolia under Genghis Khan swept through Europe and helped plunge her into that 'dark age"? And indeed did not this unjust archaic state of affairs carry on well into the China of this century?

As I sit here this morning, I take heart in the fact that I have shed my western/capitalist skin enough to realize that the communist system that the forces of economics and history has brought to power in the

People's Republic of China today is probably a more equitable one than ever existed there before. But as I swim in the largesse of America and being an American, I think of Dr Yan Xin's words about enhancing the common will of the whole world. And that thought to me conveys the exact same message as Jesus did when He said, "what you did for the least of my brothers, you did also for me."

When Dr Yan Xin makes the point that being 7,000 years old, Qigong predates any and all organized religions by a considerable amount, he is accurate. It predates the earthly visit of Jesus by 5,000 years. It even predates, I believe, the estimated time Adam and Eve were supposed to have been in the Garden of Eden. But as far as I know, according to official church doctrine today, that Adam/Eve tale no longer HAS to be considered literally true. Instead it is a parable allegorically representing a time that as man evolved, he became so involved with sinful non-loving-of-his-neighbor behavior, that he was banished from those beatific surroundings. In the Judeo/Christian tradition a messiah would arrive on earth to redeem us of those sins and allow us to reclaim our heavenly realm. For us Christians, Jesus was that messiah. The redemption took place on that cross, and in the Resurrection that we celebrate on Easter, we are welcomed back Home.

Qigong tells me that "everyone is our teacher". And when I read of a practitioner from Delaware describing how Volume 17 Common Qigong Questions and Answers helped her in her religion/Qigong understanding, I quickly borrowed it from my chapter. And having reviewed it, I think of last year and a very brief but enlightening conversation I had with a very old Chinese doctor whom I met at the Christmas party of a friend. Almost out of nowhere, he expressed his difficulties with the Western/Christian concept of original sin. And then on page three of that volume 17, when I read, "In the beginning Qigong was based on the premise that human nature was naturally kind", I see a similar attitude. To be perfectly honest I am not even sure if the concept of original sin, per se, is in the Bible. But I certainly can see how distracting this particularly religious abstraction can be.

Over eight years ago, re the paper with which I closed my first writing course at Penn, an inspirational altruistic teacher made the following comment "By the light of my religion, the only unpardonable sin would be for you to not shine your light upon the world." Yan Xin Qigong has not only allotted me the energy to do this, it has also helped reveal to me how inseparable, from all my brothers and sisters, the real essence of my light is.

———

An older Chinese man at a Christmas party in Delaware planted the seed that original sin seems unreasonable. Original sin—where did it come from? Why and how do we have it? Did Jesus ever mention it? Is it only from the fact that our supposed original parents were tossed from the Garden and thus we were then all henceforth born with the indelible mark on our souls that ONLY baptism by the Holy Mother Church could eradicate? Is that where the competition started? Adam and Eve were supposedly expelled from the Garden for wanting to know as much as God. Has it ever occurred to anyone how deadly and damaging the "through the centuries" bites of that apple are represented by all those who claim *only* they know the way back to Him?

* * *

Well my man Eamon just got up; it's like almost noon—I still got to get that shower—and I'd like to get to mass somewhere today—and Eamon said they do have a noon mass at the ultra-modern church right around the corner. The shower and shave will have to wait.

* * *

The gospel today was about the Prodigal Son. Being that Mother's Day in Ireland was today, the tall thin priest who said a very brisk reverend mass, took a different angle on the story. He spoke on about the son who'd been good all along—making the point that we should never forget to appreciate the good people in our lives—like our mothers. It was a good mass and the enthusiasm of the kids at its end madly rushing up to get the Mother's Day daisies left over from the children's mass at 10:00 AM, provided a nice contrast to the latecomers standing bored and impatient in the back of the church.

Town (Dublin) was crowded but nothing like Saturday. At the 4:00 PM AA meeting, a statue of Mary, the grandest mother of them all, sat behind the speakers. The final picture in my second disposable camera of the trip was of me and Willie in front of the famous picture of Bill Wilson and Bob Smith talking to AA member # 3, as he sits despondent on the side of a hospital bed. This picture I was told, was a painting done by the charming little guy who'd chaired the previous night's meeting. Willie's contention that this is the best meeting in the world holds a lot of water with this particular Yank. God willing, my overture to my new friend for life that maybe he be the speaker next at Philly's big annual Round-up, will come to pass.

I walked the 15 or so minutes back into town after the meeting with a guy named Mike who has 5 months sober and who was through the ringer the night before. But he stayed sober—and he did not punch out his cousin who knocked on his door at 4:00 AM, woman in tow, E'd out of his mind, wanting to use his place. He took my address and I'm sure he'll write. More importantly at the meeting he'd spoken with a certain white-haired gentleman with 31 years sober named Willie D about his becoming his sponsor. Mike, who was telling me about some "dive off a cliff with a rope around you" type-thing he did a few weeks ago, sure seems to be enjoying not drinking. I feel pretty confident he will have seven more sober days under his belt when he follows the direction he was given by Willie and does come back to that meeting next week.

At the meeting today, at other end of the "happy, joyous and free" continuim, was a girl who was the mother of two, and whose bruised nose and near all meeting nod, may have meant her two days sober claim was not exactly true. She was so sad—speaking of Mother's Day and what an empty day it was for *her* mom with a drunk for a husband and with two sons who are drug addicts. This poor suffering girl, a mother herself, washed the cups and saucers after the meeting. Some people you really root for—just hoping they get it—she sure is one of those to me.

Earlier that day, heading across to the South Side of the Liffey (and Dublin), I walked down a relatively empty Grafton Street—past the spot where, the day before, a well-dressed mother, father and two children all laughed unashamedly at a curbside preacher who was hoarse and red-faced talking about Jesus and Calvary . . . past the spot where Steve the piper had moved shop and was again doing *Amazing Grace* . . . past the spot where Mr. *Stairway to Heaven* had not been at his usual post . . . eventually making it down to the University church, and to the beautiful little Mary chapel off to the side. I was only on decade one of the rosary when the "last call" lights flickered. Mary the Queen of Heaven.

In the Knock apparition tears trickled down the side of her cheeks. John the Evangelist pointed at "the Book", Joseph, her husband, stood by—angels flew around the paschal lamb. John was the only male disciple who made it to the foot of the cross, he who wrote the "gospel of Love," he of whom Jesus said "Mother behold thy son." Maybe 1879 years later, on an island that had long been a rock of faith, and one which had loved Mary so, maybe we were being told to look at the book a little closer—and not to just keep looking it at the way we had been. (I know of one 16-year old girl who'd left the island forever just three years prior to that apparition . . . and this little girl named Sarah's devotion to that mother would never waver.)

* * *

At the big Medjugoree event last week, I asked an Anglican priest who was hanging around in the lobby, (but not for the concert) what his Church thought about the Immacualte Conception: the Catholic dictum that Mary was the only person ever born without original sin. Obviously he did not think much of it. I suspect there is not much Biblical back-up for this one either . . . exactly like the "she was a virgin her whole life" one. And the Catholic reasoning goes, in Greek the word cousin is pretty much interchangable with brother and sister—ergo biblical references to Jesus' brothers and sisters actually meant cousin. But if you really think about it, does not the impact and signifigance of the very hard lesson Jesus was trying to impart there when he does say "brother and sister (and mother)", get a lot watered down if you put cousin in that spot? I happen to have the Book right besde me here . . . I'll even give you the verse-line thing. It's in Mark 4:15 31-36

"Then Jesus' mother and brothers and sisters arrived. Standing outside, they sent someone in to call him. A crowd was sititng around him and they told him, "Your brothers and sisters are outside looking for you."

"Who are my mother and my brothers?" he asked.

Then he looked at those seated in a circle around Him. "Here are my mother and my brothers. Whoever does God's will is my brother and sister and mother."

I ask you—how much weight, how hard a message is that if you substitute *cousin* for brother and sister there? I further bid you see he says "Whoever does God's will," *not* whoever follows me. Jesus was teaching us a very hard lesson that day—that Universal brotherhood takes precedence even over the immediate family . . . and that only the grace of His Father can guide us to that kind of Love. And in the loving little row home on Ann Street that splendid Christmas season 61 years ago, my father knew this lesson. Across a great ocean, the patriarch of a different warm loving family, exiled in a strange land, unfortunately did not. The author of "the most significant book of the 20th century", did not realize the Ireland he left, represented a Family it was his choice to be part of no more.

But why is it so important to the Catholic Church that Mary be a virgin her whole life? How much of the Catholic "sex is dirty" implicatation that bothered Joyce and me and God knows how many other thousands of people throughout the last however many years it's been since they came up with that idea, come out of that interpretation? How much of the backlash rampart abyss of decadence we see about us, came out of it also?

"Brother*s* and sisters waiting"—as a devout Jew, do you not think Mary would have mothered quite a few children to a man who was her loyal and faithful husband? Did that angel Gabriel ever say anything about *after* she mothered that first child "without man"? Of course she was a virgin again by the time of Jesus' public life—devout Jewish widows 2,000 years ago did not get into sex-included outside-of-marriage *relationships*. And of course she was a virgin when Jesus was born—the whole Christian mystique revolves on that—I think the Old Testament even prophesied it. And even if you cannot "intellectually accept" that, can you at least accept that Jesus was the Messiah? . . . or at the very least that his teaching and example and direction that we seek the will of the loving Father is good for us? I am reminded of a heroin addict friend I met in the rooms . . . a very intelligent man who goes all the way back to the beatnick days. His rap to me was that being a real existentialist is a lot harder than believing in God. Right on my man! I, for one am not strong or smart enough to EXIST without a Higher Power. But in today's world the existentialist has, in a large degree, been replaced by the *stuff*essentailist.

But why the insistnce that Mary *always* remained a virgin? Jim McCabe after his stirring history lesson to, spoke a mouthful when he said, "She was one of us." Mary—the one who always comes down in the visions . . . she told us in one visit that the Assumption *had happened*—why did she never say the same about her virginity? Mary—a human being who earned the title queen of heaven simply because no one ever lived who was more humbly diligent in following God's will. Mary—probably the best human being that ever walked this planet. And when last Christmas I thanked Mike the Monk for bringing her into my spirituality, I uttered my own epitaph. If ever there was a person who should have brought as many people as Nature would allow into the world, it was she. Mary the Blessed Virgin, *and* the Blessed *Mother.* Do you think her beatific glow was shining down on that bruised and beaten girl washing those cups and saucers at that meeting yesterday? Do you think she hopes and prays that the fellowship partially based on a book written by a Jew who was very possibly her son, will help pull this one also out of the abyss?

So I offer a different scenario than the *cousins* one my Church does. What if one of Jesus brothers, this devout and holy younger guy named James, did come to see Jesus and was turned away? What if he were a sensitive type—one who might have had a hard time accepting the fact that his older brother turned out to be *the* Messiah. Imagine an older brother, one who was probably unusually good, but one with whom you still got into arguments, and whom you still saw get into scraps and things . . . imagine all that and to then find out he's going around preaching that he *is the deliverer* about which your religion had been prophesizing for a few thousand years? And maybe you hear all this and you're not quite buying. Many weren't buying in those days. I've been told there were a lot of folk around claiming to be the Messiah in Jesus' time. And then you go to see what all the fuss is about and big brother shoos you away. And maybe you go away and pout . . . maybe you ignore his big return to Jerusalem as you have your own family and kids now. And then you feel a cringe of pain when you find out what they did to him—but then you find out about another sling—"Mother behold thy son" said to one of this motley crew of the Law-breakers big brother hung out with. And maybe you cling to your faith, your strong devout Jewish faith. Maybe you stay away from the growing fire spreading out from these followers of your brother who you heard rose again but who, now, really *is* off the earth. And almost surely Mary your mother did keep in touch, and surely she always gently did say "It is true James, he WAS the Son of God. I know because I was a virgin when he was born." And maybe finally, maybe even late in his life, (they estimate the *Book of James* was written in the latter part of the first century) you, who maybe took over your father's carpenter business, went to your mom and said "Mom I finally do believe; you helped finally convince me. But of what I've heard and read so far, I see no workmanlike way to keep the faith. I wrote this little thing . . . I'm sure you'll know what to do with it."

Fiction?—probably . . . but not necessarily. And maybe Mary never told us about it because we had to figure it out for ourselves. We were supposed to utilize our God-given capacity to think—not to blindly follow dicta handed down by men—no matter high and mighty they set themslves up to be.

Mary—the Queen of Heaven. Do you know how much *more* masses mean to me now after hearing Eileen Reid from the Medjugorje tribute say, "Mass and the Eucharist—that is the way you stay close to my son!"? The quake in Ms. Reid's voice made me a believer that she really was quoting Mary directly.

Holy Mary, Mother of God, pray for us sinners . . . .

Day 46
March 26

My second to last day in Erin.

There are a LOT of gorgeous women in Dublin—there are a lot of gorgeous women most eveywhere. Sleek, maybe cosmetically enhanced, maybe not. In Dublin, there are a lot more women arm-in-arm than there are up in Cavan. But down here, the nuance definitely denotes a different kind of *friendship*. In a world where 'getting off' has become an end in itself, the flip flop of genderfication is also rampart and somewhat understandable. "If a she or a he gets me *there* better, by all means go for it" is the logic. I am hardly a homophobe—the slimy heterosexual champion men I see prowling the singles scene I find more offensive than loyal gay couples—with the likes of the 'studs', no wonder women often look to each other. A big spread about a girls-only hotel or spa was in the other day's paper—a foxy brunette in a tight business suit was seductively blowing cigar smoke at the camera. I wonder how many women-women relationships are as much about cuddling and comraderie as they are about sex—I'd suspect quite a few.

When did it become SO weird and stupid to love cuddling. When did a non-*score* date start being only for squares? I remember a time when I fumbled through a night with a comely blonde, part drunkeness, part worry about my at-the-time social disease status, but mostly clumsiness, preventing anything from *happening*—and the next time I saw her, "oh yeah, you were that guy—that nice night we just cuddled." What is wrong with cuddling for a while . . . until you're pretty darn sure, you're with the really right one.

"It's getting near dawn . . ." The darkness outside leads me to believe there will be not much of a sunrise out there this morning. I think I'll go for a little stroll anyway.

But while on the topic of beautiful women, I have to mention the "North Foxes". I met them in a big bar-restaurant on O'Connell Street Saturday night—they were from Belfast and were down here to see a redhot "boy's band" called *West Life*. Anyway they talked back when I intruded on their conversation. I even got my picture taken with two of them—and I wrote and gave them the following *awful* poem.

The North Foxes gathered
to view a band of boys
they cal-ed ol' West Life

The older chap from the West
Was lifened by their charm

Tomorrow will be Sunday
Then Mon
Then dreaded Tues

. . . and off the older chap will fly
. . . a little lighter . . .

because you were so kind

And even though I promised you ladies, I think I'll not make it up to Befast today—not enough time. And speaking of the north, seems my man Paisley changed back his tune. As soon as the Louth foot and mouth news broke, he was screaming to close the border tight. Thank God the more sane voice of Bryn Rodgers is up there!

One bird is chirping out back. There's black and white birds called magpies all over the place over here. I think they serve the same purpose as pigeons—but are way cuter. Ireland has a load of really sharp looking birds—I saw them at the Natural History museum Saturday. I think I'll cross the street and have a closer look at some of these magpies . . . if they are like pigeons, then, necessarily, I suppose, they are "theiving".

The fierce March wind was back on my last full day in Ireland. By the time I left Benediction in the Trinity University Chapel off St Stephens Green, it had diminished, but the drizzle/rain had returned. It really rains a lot over here, but rarely are there downpours—only once on the day we went to Knock did a dowpour hit—and that for only a few minutes.

Waiting for my cousins to show up to see Paul Mercier's tremendous play *All Down the Line* at the Peacock Theater on Abbey Lane, I walked down to look at the Liffey River one more time. I was on the North Side, it was flowing left to right so that meant it flowed west. And it was flowing fast. The Lee through Cork comes in off the Atlantic Ocean, I'll bet it travels east.

The Shannon—south, the Erin—north, the Liffey—west, the Lee—east. The natural ecological symmetry of Ireland again.

My not going to Cork last week was a big faux pas of this trip. So too was the non-trip up to Belfast. On the news today, seeing the throngs gathered to celebrate the 100th anniversary of the NON-ecumeniclal fundamentalist Presbyterrian Church Ian Paisley made famous, made me realize how shallow and specious are my suppositions about the healing going on between North and South. I had no business not going there myself to see what it was like.

But I suspect I'd have found mostly just people up Belfast—people just trying to get by. I'm sure mostly I would have found friendly talkative folks. In Cork I would surely have found the same. (There too I'd have found one more Gaffney—*and "takkin"* in general, hard as hell to understand.)

Earlier a crew of folks, a busload full, in fact, of students from Denmark had jammed the 41 bus for what would be my final ride on it into Dublin. And the lovely youngster named Mette who sat next to me reminded me of a Denmark girl who was a fellow student in my capstone class at Penn in the fall of '99. Even though she had a baby during the semester, she finished in December—unlike me who just got under the May deadline to graduate.

She, her husband and their adorable and *huge*, and hugley happy baby were among the guests at the lovely going away party my very capable, very kind and very patient Penn instructor threw for us February a year ago. And for this "guerrier" par exellance though only three months old—I bought a Philadelphia sweatshirt. Two days later, I was e-mailed a picture of this incredibly healthy happy baby, in the Philly sweatshirt—sleeves rolled up a bunch to make the shirt sort of fit. This couple, in their, unobliterated by seemingly any societal norms or conditioning, seem as fit mates and parents as I could ever imagine. I'll bet it's been a long time since either has been inside a church—to the utopian ideal of John Lennon's *Imagine;* Christain and Christina, seemingly live their lives.

On the way in today, because I was actually looking out the window at the time, on the outskirts of the city proper, was Dublin's Crowe Field . . . here where a massacre took place 80 some years ago. The hurling and Irish football matches will start happening again soon in the wake of the foot and mouth restriction being lifted. A little before that, we'd passed the spot where they are filming scenes for the *Bloody Sunday* movie now being made. Bloody Sunday refers to a far more recent massacre, one occuring in 1972 where shots were fired into a crowd of Catholic protestors killing seven. The "they shot first . . . no they did" accusations are still being made. A far more recent tragedy—but one still in the past. Do both sides think they'd be *chicken* to really let it go?

When an older gentleman who sat behind me remarked as the crowd of young Danes got off the bus in the lower scale North Central neighborhood—home to hostels and cheaper spots to stay—"With the bags, you really got to be careful. Dublin is changing", it reminded me of a story of the daughter of a friend of my mother who was robbed of all her luggage and money soon after arriving for a weeklong vacation in San Francisco. She was bruised, beaten and crying whan a gay man approached her. Then he and his partner took her in, lent her money for clothes and were her personal tour guides for a vacation she'll never forget. The story goes they are still friends. Is there anything in the world more important than being kind?

The memories that come back as you try to drink in a life, unencumberd by the baggage no longer needed. At benediction yesterday, I remembered the freezing eighth grade Sunday when the high school I'd call home the very next year was playing for the Catholic League football title across town from my Northeast Philly home in the South Phlly frozen mausoleum we called Municipal Stadium. Eleven o'clock mass was the one where we choirboys gathered to sing the Gloria and Creed and the this and that in the one High Mass we had each week at good old Resurrection. After mass, at Benediction, we'd sing the Tantum Ergo and the Sancta-whatevee before we'd close with the lovely *Holy God we Praise thy Name*—a hymn I still love—partly because it brings to mind Sunday mornings and a time when life was simpler and easier. But that week, because of the game, me and my buddy Eddie Grogan and I had made plans to go to early 8:45 Children's mass so we could blow out after communion and before Benediction. Being a dope fiend of sorts even then, and certainly a pretty lazy lad, I figured sister would let me go even if I skipped Children's mass—*two* masses in one day, come on now. But sister took not the bait. Eddie got sprung after communion, I ran like a cat out the cage, when she did let me go, not after communion, but after mass and before Benediction. But I was too late—by the time I made the less than 10 minute walk to the Grogans' house, the gang had already left. The cold and the shattered look on my sniveling face, no doubt moved Eddie's mom and older brother Artie to pity. Artie drove me all the way across town—a good 45 minutes—and I caught Eddie and his dad and the rest of the crew in the parking lot.

I remember how glad I was that Mr. Grogan's pull as a chief in the fire department, netted us a heated room at halftime, to give us some needed shelter from the cold. Today, Eddie is a fire chief, has several kids, and has a still very attractive wife. His one daughter who is in a league I umpire (and who like Eddie did as a kid, has a penchant for drawing walks) I was told, took like every other award when she graduated from a private Catholic girl's high school a few years back. Artie is a husband and father and has been teaching philosophy for over twenty years at a little Catholic Commuter college in Philly's Northeast section—a spot where I attend many AA meetings. His brother Jimmy, who lives real near my mom's house where I now reside, told me not long before I left for Ireland (when I ran into him at the cleaner) "He's reallllI deep" when I asked him about Artie. He also told me he's now living at the old family house that I walk by frequently on my nightime strolls. I'll now make it a point to stop in.

Another brother Johnny, went up 'til right near the end, before an 11th hour decision to not become a priest. I remember him and a shorter stumpier guy coming to see our eight or seventh grade class talking up being a priest. He was so cool and so funny—kidding the shorter guy about not being able to play basketball—I remember thinking "he'll be a really good priest." Just now I remember a seventh grade trucking all the way across town on buses, els, and trolley cars—to go swimming in the pool in the massive St Charles seminary—Johnny must have sponsored that trip. Johnny now too is in the fire department—married with kids. His mom who graduated in the same Hallahan class as my mom, has bone atrophy, lives with the oldest sister and stopped going to seniors after her husband died.

The waters of time trickling under the bridge.

I think it was between 7th and 8th grade when Eddie went away to some camp; the same camp, the previous summer, I'd made an 11th hour decision to eschew. The charming and beautiful school nusre (Miss Testa, if memory serves me), had arranged for me to get in as the bad financial times had hit for us by then. Eddie met *girls* at the camp . . . got a new circle of friends and kind of drifted away from our crowd. I often wondered how my life would have turned out if I'd gone to that camp, if I hadn't backed out because I was so afraid of "new". I remember in the dull times that summer, thinking, "maybe I should have gone to that camp—even if black kids would be there." I wonder no more though—or I should say I *worry about* it no more—I'm here right now, and now is good.

Perhaps that is the most blatant thing we ALL have in common, that none of us can live in any other moment than the one exactly at hand. I guess it's all about how much real happiness you're doing nets you.

It's 5:00 AM now, **Day 47 March 27, 2001.**

The last one, has dawned. The howling wind outside promises a beaut for a weather day. My plane leaves aroud 16:00. (Today's the last bloody day I'll need to read time like that for a while.)

Mercier 's wonderful play last night centered around a Dublin family trying to get by in the new climate of the early-mid eighties. (My cousin told me Mercier is from Cavan.) Mom and dad hold onto their old values—and with charm and wit and a certain degree of progressiveness, try to provide guidance to the entirely new breed they still call their own. Like Ann and Eddie have for 30 years now, mom and dad still sneak off to Galway for "holidays". An older brother who's made it pretty big in London brings home a charming girl, but one of a different, higher caste. Immediately before and soon after mothering a daughter, this wonderful woman breaks out in alone and unexpected tears. Something is definitely amiss. But like Shaw's *Pygmalion* and not the *My Fair Lady* play and movie version, she and her husband, these two very decent people, but from other sides of the tracks, do not go the route. At play's end, they are divorced and he is dating his long ago love.

Next in line is a daughter who's scared to death to move on. After a string of many beaus, she marries finally, but refuses to let go the home ties.Two kids later, in a rousing passionate argument scene, her husband in the outside garage, cradles a picture he never knew she painted—never knew she could—and in the cooperative awareness that they never really *saw* each other, she finally leaves the nest to go *with* her man.

The youngest son, a hilarious 80's punk rock'n'roller shocks them all by really making it last with the New Age fruit and fern disciple—whose child he fathered, *before* they got married.

The lead character is the second daughter, a woman revolutionary and visionary of sorts who is taken in and over by many of the men and women whose causes she championed. The verbal battle with her mom re her dubious stances for eveyone *but* the family is one of the play's best scenes. She is seen at the end having come out of a mental breakdown and is teaching the underpriviledged in London. But the play's kicker is that all the action is wrapped between visits of her boyhood love, Johnny—hardly a genius—but his long ago vow to her to never be dishonest and never to intentionally hurt, he assures her he'd always kept, even as his fiancee waits in the car to whisk him back to his Galway computer job. The honest, sincere "you're always welcome here," Mr Walsh offers to Johnny, before mom packs things for the heroine to take back to London, closed our a show for the ages . . . the acting and writing really spectacular.

The Walsh's are a family that love one another—depite all the bemishes, just like the McGowans. But like the McGowans, like a lot of Irish families, there seemed to be not too much hugging. I remember way back then, the way I *protestethed too much* at the counselor whose care I was under after the trip to the shock treatments and subsequent mania, "oh yeah, now you're gonna say because we didn't go kissy-facing and hugging all over the place is why I'm like this!" In my first crack at fiction my heroine, Maggie Fahy, an attractive, twice divorced mother of the bride, but dateless at the wedding because she'd finally dumped her latest charming cad, thinks "why did our affection have to be so expressionlessly *understood*?" My family hugs more now—my sister Sallly leads the way.

I spoke with Ann last night late when I got home and I told her my older sister Mary Ellen is coming to Ireland in May—I hope to talk her into stopping in to visit Cavan—and to maybe even stay with Angela.

Last night, it was certainly a charge sitting between three cousins representing the lineage of Tommy Owen and Mary Alice—the keepers of the Derryvilla flame that flickered, but always remained lit for my great grandfather Peter. Margaret, their daughter sat on my left, on my right were their son Sean's daughter Angling, and, their son Gene's daughter, Marie. (Aegean of the other, Maura, was sick with the flu and could not make it.) Viewing the hilarious scene where the youngest daughter speaks of looking in the abandoned farmhouse where Mom grew up, while sitting in a theater in *Dublin* with three "country girls", was very cool.

Across the sea I have nieces and cousins who match them both in looks and somewhat in temperament.

———

Last night in the Café Kyelemore (before the play) I sat with two Christians whose mission is helping chidren of drug addicts and alcoholics. They offer the 'good news' of the Bible to salve their wounds. In so many words I suggested they to try to heal the wounds any way they can. Christians are always good to run into on the road. They always want to talk, they are always extremely polite and thoughtful, the women, are often cute, and they sho' nuff KNOW that Bible. These lovely ladies clued me in that James indeed *was* in the Bible—in the Acts of the Apostles . . . that he headed the Jewish/Christian Church in the first days after Christ. As I think about it, James, and a lot of other folk might have changed their tune that first Pentecost. Seeing thousands of folks hearing the same foreign words being understood in their native tongues, seems to me, would change a lot of people's minds. The 'head start' supplied by that first-day-extraordinaire, was no doubt, a necessary "big push jumping off point" for the fledgling Church. Same with the not-spoken, but somewhat implied "the end is next Tuesday" preaching of the early disciples. Whatever it takes, ya know.

The AA member who spoke Saturday night, he who painted the Bill, Bob Smith and AA #3 picture, repeated the tale of how Dr. Silkworth told Bill Wilson, "Lay off the Bible—talk about how sick you were." On Sunday Willie D., Mr. "WORK the steps", himself, said when he first got in the "rooms" he was too sick to work anything. A cup of coffee, a, "I know what you're going through" an act of kindness, helped him to stay alive. What we addicts and alkys have is "we been there."

The world is a radically different place than it was 2,000 years ago; it is, in fact, a radically different place than it was just 40 years ago. To be kind, to not judge, to not demand anyone believe or not believe, but to do rightly. I guess it all comes down to how far I can get with any or all of these ideals of my own accord. The experience of my own life is I got nowhere until the grace from Other got to me. I'm twelve step trained; without God I am nothing.

But most of all the kindness. Never was Jesus unkind to anyone who was down. I look at all the kindness that's been heaped on me—what about Cavan? What about the Gaffneys—Noel called last night to say goodbye. Last week I felt bad having wolfed down the only can of tuna fish in the fridge—instead of complaining, this morning Eamon had four such cans in the fridge.

Across the sea in a dingy little apartment not far from my sister's house, two addicts are right now probably trying to figure out how to get a hit of crack. Both of these, at different times, told me "no thanks" when an "I've been clean for a while," accompanied my "let's get loaded" attempt to pick them up. Crackheads—people for whom the next hit is all that matters, turnng down dollars and a load because they didn't want to see some stranger get stuck like they are. Are they Christians? Was it four or five different times that happened to me?

I remember one summer night, last year or the year before, as I drove past scores of black kids skipping rope, or squealing after an ice cream truck, or of older folks sitting and talking on the steps—of folks being folks—the thought of what the likes of me was dong to their already poor, less-than worlds . . . where was that *love* without which St. Paul said my faith is "nothing"? And on that particular night, I did make it home. I did not the next however. Still I did not realize 'home' was not the safe, big house in nice white Northeast Philly . . . but that it was a far broader, non-physical place. And I would have to go back to the darkness again and again, before I realized that unless I actively participated in the freeing of all my brothers from their addictions and hate and conditioning, and invited them to share in the bright and benevolent 'Home' of the 'kingdom in our hearts,' I was doomed to return to the decayed hovels where the only landlord was the rapacious pipe.

Also across the sea, my suicidal buddy from way back in the beginning of this tale is back out drinking. I finally called and got through yesterday—and in the sadness in his near-deaf father's voice, you could almost hear Hank Williams "I'm so lonesome I could cry." Each other is all they got. Dad a widower; son, a divorcee—I suspect his visitation rights to his adorable 10-year old daughter, have been stripped with all the recent drinking. But he's still alive—and I'll bet and hope and pray he'll keep coming back. And then there's Sally's neighbors—an older invalid couple—not a call, not a card, not a note not a nothing did I send them. Yesterday was supposed to be the day I'd write letters to my friends up in Cavan. Think any of them ever got written? The self-centerdness still abounds. My last day—for how many family members do you think I have not bought any gifts?

It sounds like both the brutal wind and the slashing rain out there. Why do I feel so empty? My triumphant exit and return home, right now feels more like a dull thud . . . .

———

Me and my big mouth. The slight drizzle of my fifteen minute walk to the Rathbeale library—across the park and woods—had, by the time I left, turned into a steady, drenching, rain. I missed the bus by about a second and by the time I got into Swords to pick up my pictures and get a bite to eat I was soaked.

The one-hour reserved free Internet time with which I began most of my days here in Swords, this morning found an e-mail from my friend Patty, who is the wife of my college buddy Joe, and who along with their two daughters, treat me like a king each time I visit them in their Columbia, Md. home. One night as we were discussing God and heaven et al, their older daughter Megan, who is a freshman in high school now, and who is a delight and a wonderful writer and painter, said "I'm glad they have purgatory. I'm not good enough to go to right to heaven." I don't know if I ever heard anything so cool. She loves the guys, and if she finds a "Johnny"—type, I hope she keeps him. But like the heroine last night, she has a wonderful rock of a family to help her back if she ends up getting hurt. Speedy (Joe's *real* name to we Trash Bandees), who probably last did his Easter duty when he was a freshman in high school, and who nonetheless unashamedly went up and received communion when we went to mass later that day, in his inimitable fashion, said "religion is a crutch. Purgatory is a crutch within a crutch." I'm laughing right now just thinking about it.

Anyway I wrote Patty back that I'll be down some time in April—on my way to the Outer Banks to see my friends Nancy and Rob, and after I pop in and see Jim Houck who is also on the way in his Timonium, Maryland home.

On the way into town, I got out of the rain for a second to grab a paper. I could not help but notice the tabloid picture of Pamela Sue Anderson and some other actress arm in arm, spilling out of their respective tops. Seems last night was Oscar night and these two, both currently single, were just girls out to have fun. Pamela, whose home movie video having oral sex with her ex-husband and *Motley Crue* rock star has near legend status in America—it and the physical endowment of her ex used to be a source of many ha-ha's on Pam Sue's frequent guest spots on the Howard Stern show—because of the plentitude of sycophants within, and the dearth of covering without, spilled out a bit more than did her chum. Her friend's joking and buttoning her up were a big part of the story. "We'll have a few laughs and be home early—like 7:00 AM," her buddy said.

The pictures I got from the camera shop were considerably different. The shot of the rooftops of Cavan town as the sun was just going down, did come out great. But the two best pictures were of Eddie and of little Dallan. I ruined most of the ones I was in, because, for some reason, I can't smile in front of a camera. I even screwed up the "North foxes" picture.

While in town and hoping to get out of the rain, and because this story turned out to be such a Mary tribute, I headed over to the little, old but beautiful St Columbine Church to say a rosary. I was mighty glad the doors were open. The heat was on and I had enough sense to drape my soaked jacket over the radiator as I knelt down to say the rosary. My very local prayer to stop the rain was not answered—but after leaving the Church, a cab did pull down the street as I trudged up. As for the rest of the prayers, time will tell.

Well what of my little Marian scenario? What nets it for us if we strip the virginity belt off Mary and accept and be glad that James and Jude and whoever else were her children? Well we could start here in Ireland or maybe England—maybe some open-minded Anglican minister with sentiments like the "envied our devotion to Mary" observer from Vatican II long ago, and could start leaning a bit towards praying to Mary. And maybe a real open-minded and bold padre could even consider putting a statue of her in his church. And at a big ecumenical CON-celebrated mass perhaps, an Irish Catholic priest and an Irish Anglican priest could do a service together. The Catholic giving communion to the Catholics, the Anglican to the Anglicans. Do you think anybody would go? I know literally hosts of folks up in Cavan who'd travel quite a distance for such a celebration. I'm sure there are many Catholic priests who would go for the job—one I remember, from Cork I think, who wrote a letter that priests should, from the pulpit, speak out against Cardinal Connell's actions regarding President McAlese, for sure, would. It would take a very holy, very courageous and open-minded Anglican prelate to open that door. As we say in AA, that door once cracked open can eventually become a floodgate for grace.

But then what would this do say for, the Jewish people—perhaps they could look at those first Christians and realize all of them were Jews—some more, some less committed to the old Law, but all of them deeply committed to the granddaddy of those laws—the ten commandments. And maybe in their growing realization that Mary was probably the most devout Jew who ever lived, before and after she bore a son many people thought and believed was the Messiah, an honor she earned by her incredible devout holiness in prayer and deed to the Old Jewish way, they will also realize she might be worth praying to (or more exactly *through).* And maybe the Moslems will review their fascinating Koran and will grow to realize that their God, the God of Abraham and David and Jesus *and* Mohammed would never condone a jihad, or holy war—that any killing of any human being is wrong—and maybe they too will see how really special this Mary was. I was told their Koran has an entire book written about her . . . and that the idea for the rosary came from the prayer beads the Crusades had found the Moslems used to pray.

Who knows perhaps, in a bog somewhere, a young Irish Protestant boy or girl might some day be saying a prayer to this mysterious lady her pastor just started talking about—and maybe he or she also, would be granted a visit by the single most wonderful human being who ever walked this planet—the *woman* who earned the title "queen of Heaven".

And maybe somewhere in a isolated spot in the desert somewhere a little Jewish boy will befriend a little Arab boy . . .

maybe far away from the guns and killing, these two will discover they are just kids, just people—that they are really the same. And maybe they'll say that little short prayer a new radical rabbi or mullah has started teaching them:

> *"Hail Mary full of grace, The Lord is with thee.*
> *Blessed art thou amongst women*
> *And blessed is the fruit of thy womb Jesus*
> *Holy Mary Mother of God pray for us sinners*
> *now and at the hour of our death. Amen"*

And maybe they too will see a beautiful lady in the sky.

* * *

Tears came as we pulled off the runway at Shannon. The stopover from Dublin was long enough to get more duty-free stuff. I doubled back because I'd forgot to pick up something for Pat in whose house I was given the room three years and four months ago, back when I desperately needed shelter from that South Philly storm. But lifting off the ground, I knew the gig was finally up. It will be a while till the next time I plant my feet on Irish soil.

I was on the right side of the plane so I was able to see where the Shannon lingered on out to the sea. My brother Mark and my cousin Jimmy are supposed to be waiting for me at Newark Airport. I suspect Jimmy might be a no-show, the day-long beer-drinking, watching the Temple NCAA game party at Mark's, might have had something to do with the "I'll be there and with the kids" promise.

But there or not, Jimmy knows something is going on here—something about family and rightness and being a McGowan. Last fall, his son Owen, whom he named after my grandfather, sat next to me at a funeral for a wonderful man and writer and friend of the family—a man named John O'Riordan. Aunt Betty, who has that motherly instinct in spades, had made it a point to introduce me to him at her husband, my Uncle Jim's funeral some 25 months ago. She knew he was a man I should talk to "A Catholic, an Irishman, and a Philadelphian" is how the priest in the packed church in Northeast Philly called St Martin's, referred to Mr. O'Riordan, who was also a writer and a politician.

Four nights after that funeral, Jimmy arranged for himself, me, my mom, his mom and sister Trudy (the one my age, who, as a kid, used to hide in the back of her dad's station wagon with me, also scared by the July 4th fireworks), to go see a dynamite Irish rock band called *Solis*. When at the little dinner beforehand, Aunt Betty said "John would have loved that funeral." I said "didn't you think it was a little long, with the five or six eulogies?" In the classic understated Aunt Betty humor, she replied "You obviously didn't talk to John that often."

Aunt Betty loves England, the royal family and all that—and she is absolutely correct in admiring ALL that little island has done throughout the ages. Who knows, maybe now that England's colonial days are over, maybe in the spirit of Gladstone and the other prime ministers and movers and shakers who throughout the 19th century did promote home rule and better conditions for the Irish, maybe Tony Blair, who for my money is one hell of a prime minister, should offer a worldwide ninth step type apology to the Irish. I'm sure the equally competent Birdie Ahern would accept. Prince Charles and Mary McAleese would, I'm sure, be interested in getting involved. How much wind would go blowing out of the sails of the Paisleys and real IRA's with such a gesture? It boggled my mind how every single Irishman I met who lived in London—and I met a bunch of them—while admitting its difficulties, simply loved the place and it's people. Why not trumpet from the rooftops our brotherhood and all we have in common?

And while we're in such ninth-step forgiveness mode, perhaps John Paul II—another wonderful leader and shepherd—Mary's pope they call him—in the spirit of ALL-mankind brotherhood, could follow up his historic and heroic apology to the Jews with one to the Moslems for the crusades. Maybe Rome could even offer to mediate talks—and to offer round-the-clock prayer vigils inviting all and any to pray as the talks were going on. I'll bet they'd have no problem filling up the middle of the night slots for that.

Catholics, Protestants, Jews and Moslems—in the same city at the same time—talking and praying for peace. If that's too much Church and State for anyone, does anyone really think the message of Abraham and Jesus and Mohammed was not about peace and brotherhood? Doing God's will, those who do THAT are who Jesus called his brothers and sister, and it seems to me all three of those major religions have a lot to say about doing God's will—and the irony to end all ironies—none of the three *ever* claimed the God at the top was any different.

"We don't want to give the enemy anything to use . . . we don't air our own dirty laundry" were two of the other snippets offered me from the Trinity priest who'd told me "we preach salvation through the risen Christ," and who seemed a bit wary of my agenda in this book. Is the aim of the Catholic Church really to promote salvation only one way? Is that also the aim of Paisley's separatist Presbyterians? Is that the aim of the New Church of Christ crowd? No wonder in the East, they want no part of us! Someone told me Gandhi once said, "If Christians acted like Christians, I'd be a Christian." I do not know that he said that, but if he did, that might be the best single line uttered in the 20th century—that or maybe, "Can I get you a cup of coffee? Don't worry about the shaking, you should have seen me my first day . . . ."

* * *

I'm home now. Shoulda slept for like a day but I'm awake somehow. It's 3:30 AM Philly time.

As the plane neared Newark International, I sat looking out the windows at clouds puffed and glowing beatific red from the setting sun, tears welled up again as I envisioned a "Unity Day" exchanging of plaques between Mary Mac and bonnie Prince Charles, Mary's saying something like "In memory of all the English who tried a better way, we thank you . . . and we apologize for the shedding of innocent blood we caused . . ." Charles' saying something like "For all the pain and anguish we've inflicted on our Irish brethren through the ages . . . we apologize . . ." And then Paul, Ringo, and George leading a group of younger singers in a rocking version of Lennon's *Instant Kharma* . . . and having the concert timed so that simultaneously, U2 in Slieve and Bob Dylan Zimmerman, the other premier author of my generation, could also be quoting his British brother, in a venue somewhere in Palestine—a little town called Bethlehem maybe.

About twenty million things swirled through my head in the last few days as to how to end this journal . . . and while the editing, making sense work that awaits me will be colossal—I know the content part of this story must end soon.

I was right about Sally and the room—it is spotless.

An ulcer is back on mom's other foot now—on the other big toe. She told Mark the other day, she never really feels that good anymore. The sobs and shakes when she hugged me, I suspect were not only of joy. One of the things that always bothered me about Joyce's *Portrait's* Dedalus, is when he refused to do his Easter duty just for his mom's sake (as one of his buddies suggested he do)—his philosophical stance was that strong. He should have been more like Speedy. And as I envision the American portion of this pilgrimage, the heated "what about the family" conversation between Mrs. Walsh and her rebel of a daughter echos in my head.

But I don't think mom will begrudge my leaving. In my good-bye note to her before I left I said something about, that last joyful mystery and how this trip I'd envisioned was about being about both my father's business. But her blessing is not something I'll ever take lightly.

It is all about love—I think we all know that. "But I don't believe in God," a beautiful little cousin said to me one time. She is a devoted, caring single mom, but one who's fought the booze and drugs and psychosis for most of her life. I told her to think about her and her child—to follow the love.

Only last week did I notice that the gospel's' prodigal son did not return home until a great famine had crossed the land. The crashing stock market, foot and mouth on the continent, the fanatical hate and violence all over the globe, the runaway addiction and decadence. I for sure don't know where we're headed, but if you're into Armageddon scenarios read the letter in *Revelations* to the angel from the church in Philadelphia . . . .

The girl who sat beside me flying home is the sister of an old "down the shore" drinking buddy from days gone by. She read some of my stuff and can't wait for the book—she too hates the way the Church treats women. Her and her two buddies drove 900 miles in eleven days. Two bent fenders and a damaged ancient wall later, they confirmed the sagacity of my "I'd sooner jump off the cliffs of Mohr," response, when people asked me if I was going to hire a car on an island full of hills and only stick-shifts, and folks who drive quite crazily on the wrong side of the road. She did go to Belfast, her family came from there and she told me the women of Belfast are keeping the peace and the church alive up there. I'm sure she is accurate.

Her brother is a writer and took the route in life I often thought I should have—Temple U, journalism major, writing for a small periodical, Master's degree, writing for a big outfit—he's married now with three kids. But I really don't worry about that stuff anymore—it seems a long time ago I said something about the folly of regrets . . . It's time to move on.

Journal 2

Back In America

Next day
March 29, 2001

Having no job to go to, made today really feel like "the first day of the rest of my life." As long as the money holds out, I'll enjoy it.

To get to the Wednesday Big Book study at my sponsor's house in Port Richmond, I had to drive right past the house my great grandfather built, as it is only four doors away. We were on the *Into Action* chapter and a lot of our discussion centered on the difference between a spiritual experience and a spiritual awakening. And while the distinction is something of a semantic one, in general, "experience" refers to those of the powerful "knock you off your horse" feelings, while "awakening" refers to a gradual lasting awareness of Godly influence in your life. From repeated personal experience I am one who can vouch for the fact that A does not necessarily equal B.

I got real emotional (as in *pissed*!) at the meeting when my sponsor's cousin Jerry suggested it didn't matter what I thought. But we are both 12-step trained, he apologized and we shook hands immediately, and two more times before I left. Jerry is also a semi-regular at Mike the Monk's prayer group.

The big news in Philly is about how an Irish homicide captain had gotten another cop to cover his tracks after he'd torn up a city vehicle driving stone drunk one night. Monday our Dublin-born police captain John Timmony, had tersely answered reporter questions suggesting that his discipline had been insufficient in the matter. "A good night's sleep can do wonders" was what our black mayor, John Street, had said about why he thought the commissioner had changed his tune on Tuesday. The drunk captain was busted to lieutenant and night-time duty somewhere. Street also assigned an appropriately diverse task force, headed by a black female professor from Temple, to review discipline within our town's police force. The almost perfunctory "bring in a federal task force to study the situation" cry of the black clergy crew, and the Fraternal Order of Police's "he did *not* stand by his man," denouncement is seemingly recognized by both sides, for the saber rattling that it is. Thus quick dirty laundry airing and appropriate about face doing, seems to have defused what could have been a very difficult situation. My impression that in these two vitally important posts, mayor and police commissioner, we in Philly, are blessed at the moment with very good men, was further fortified today.

Timmony, by the way, spoke at a communion breakfast I attended last year—and then left immediately to go speak at a Protestant luncheon. Mayor Street is likewise an active member of one of Philly's bigger black churches.

On the international scene though, things are not so rosy. Pie in the sky musings about a chummy feel good concert in Palestine seemed downright silly in light of Israeli air strikes precipitated by recent Arab suicide bombing. Yasir Arafat, the PLO chief, said something like "chances for peace are now gone".

In the worst days of my addiction, some people suggested that I had not gotten low enough, that I had not bottomed to the extent that I needed if I were to ever get and stay sober. Such advice is about as bad as bad can be—can you picture Jesus saying "go out and sin some more and then come back to me." What about our world though, how low must we go?

* * *

Mom just got up now, her Sixers got dumped again last night, so she'll be a bit upset. The first words out of her mouth to me will be "did you sleep?" . . . and I did, a little. It seems I don't need too much sleep anymore. In a couple of hours I'll drive her down for her 3-4 hour volunteer stint at the hospital—and she'll tell me this and she'll tell me that.

Mom tells of lots of things, and as much as she's not enthralled at the world of today, there is no looking back in horror—she muddles along, ambling a lot more now with the toe. Like the mighty Shannon, mom lingers a ton these days . . . and "stop and talk to you"!—I can only imagine the blabber with her "bus buddies" for all those years when she'd schlep out on dark cold winter mornings (or on bright sunny ones) all the way out to West Philly to man that hospital information desk.

March 30, 2001
Friday

On the trusty old IBM my friend Lisa from work gave me, now in the corner of the room after my sister Sally's rearranging here, I found the last pre-Ireland entries from the journal I've been keeping like forever.

I am leaving it *sic* or whatever they call that when the misspelling and punctuation does not get fixed. (Which reminds me of something my buddy Jack, my first sponsor, told me a while back. He ran into another buddy from college, Pat McCool, who asked him if he'd gotten any e-mails lately from F. Scott *Misspeller.*)

February 6, 2001 Tuesday

Ask larry c re b2b book.
Go to sister silva's
Write helen betz
Go to hup for cd, call irish edition & go there
Go to fr mcn's after calling . . .
Go to nativity leave stuff for mrs white
Find out info re joe klein and his son

February 03, 2001 *Saturday*

and so a nice little piece to take over to my good buddy Jane, Editor of the Irish Edition. From there I'll traverse down to see fr mc n for 5:00 PM mass.

The Revisit *February 3, 2001*

125 Years ago, Peter McGowan and Sarah Sheridan left their homeland, a green and poor little land called Ireland. I do not know the particulars of what awaited them here, I can only make guesses. But I know that Peter at least, HAD little in the way of material riches. Nor do I know if they knew each other before they left. That they were wed six years later, and considering that the Irish of that era (or anybody else for that matter) hardly rushed into marriage, and that the crossings for folks from their County Cavan were not all that regular, would make it seem very possible that they met on the boat that carried them here.

The McGowan scenario for earning the money to pay for the long, terribly arduous voyage was to sell the family horse and big picture window from their farmhouse. The family would make do with a donkey (or whatever) and a less sturdy, less attractive window until the conglomerate McGowan emeigres sent enough money back home to purchase another horse and another window—which could then be sold for another ticket, etc. I am not really certain how many others of the clan of my great grandfather used this little scheme to come here. But I am pretty certain Peter and his older brother Frank, before him, did use it.

Sarah would never see the place of her birth again. But Peter, in 1928, one year after her death, along with Sade, the youngest of his nine children did get to go home. Three years before his death, it must have been a particularly chilling and thrilling time for him—to walk the land he'd left more than 50 years earlier—land that was now McGowan land, and not indentured rental property of some English (or Protestant Irish) landlord.

In five days I leave for the land they left behind. I will walk the land they both walked. I've been in contact with descendants of both families that still reside on the exact same plots of ground they did. A little over a week ago, I walked away from a safe, secure but hardly lucrative job to dedicate this portion of my life to writing a book that will largely be about honoring their memory. My material circumstances, while hardly extravagant, are surely worlds more bountiful than were theirs those 125 years ago. And yet the fear and second-guessing, like fog over a sumptuous morning sunrise, has served to blur the beauty of my quest.

Apples of Gold, the meditation book that sits beside my bedroom computer offered this little morsel this morning:

> *For the test of the heart is trouble,*
> *and it always comes with the years.*
> *And the smile that is worth the praises*
> *of earth, is the smile that shines*
> *through the tears.*

The tears and the smiles of late, have been almost neck-to-neck as far as frequency goes. But in reality, the tears seem closer to those of joy than of pain. But what I have been granted, is, at least a smidgen of the faith these two must have brought with them; faith in my God and subsequently in myself, that I will be okay . . . and without that, this is a journey I would not even consider undertaking.

Life goes on. Today I woke up after 4 hours sleep—WIDE awake. (beware the snooze at the forthcoming meeting, mon ami!) If I keep on trying, the road will open up for me. If I keep my eye fixed on the REAL prize.

Way way way more stuff gots to get did around here. At least sis ain't coming home which is actually a shame. But makes this room situation a bit less shaky.

The first item above is a sort of daily 'to do' list. It is a chore we are instructed to do as part of our 11th prayer and meditation work. AA's founders were adamant about doing this Oxford Group kind of thing on a near daily basis. They'd pray, then write—then weed and edit for worldly vs. Godly thoughts. At the *Back to Basics* classes we give out a wonderful *How to Listen to God* pamphlet describing exactly how we go about doing this. Of that list above, most of those items got done—truly a rarity!

It's funny how things work out . . . in my little wild little Marian schema presented a while back, I forgot to mention that even if none of that praying to Mary stuff happens, if little groups of recovering folk or whatever, can take our simple *Back to Basics* 'work the steps' message, and try to bring it to anyone interested in bettering themselves, then, person-by-person, institution by institution, nation by nation, the world really can start to become a better place.

The Revisit piece was something I took over to my friend Jane the editor of *The Irish Edition*, a wonderful local paper that has published a few things I've written, including several things about my family.

So the beat really does go on. I made the rounds today down at Penn. I stopped in my office and got a big hug from Marge and Jen and Carmella (who somehow was wearing her red shoes I always made a fuss over.) I got a huge hug from Sandy, appropriately named Greene, who has been feeding me the most delicious collard greens anyone ever *et* (as they say in Ireland) for the past 18 years now, and whose Irish cross medallion given to me before I left, was on the side of my jeff cap for the entire Ireland vacation. Sandy wondered if I was wearing the sneaks I had on when I was over there because she didn't want me bringing that "hoof and foof" over here. Her old roomie and good friend G-L-O-R-I-AEEE,

Glooo-ri-a also gave me a hug. Katie and BJ who I've known like forever were still working away. I kidded 'parrot-head' Marianne about Jimmy Buffet coming to town. Nancy my old boss, true to form, was not big on a show of outward affection, Tom "the Big Kahuna" as he calls himself, and whose management style might be called "Papa Bear caring", gave me a hearty handshake. I saw Julia, who through the years bequeathed to me, hundreds of lunches and probably thousands of prayers. (Like mom, she is a St. Anthony fan—the life-size statue of him in her living room is an almost-shocking reminder of such!) I stopped up in A/P to see Lisa (of the computer) and Steve and Tonya and Darlene. I had a long involved chat with my Christian friend Drew, had lunch with Bob and Brian and his wife Kathy and GOJUS Kimmy-baby. . . .

I stopped at the Presbyterian Medical Center after-care treatment place that was there for me when I needed it, to see about bringing *Back to Basics* down there.

I stopped in and saw Kris, my Penn MLA teacher, and told her what I was up to—her damn-near bubbling excitement was hardly a feign. I stopped at the *Writers House* to get on the computer to do my e-mail and have their mailing list sent to my active e-mail address as the work one is no more.

I did not stop in and see Fr. Brinkman at the Drexel University Neuman Center, but will soon enough. My brother Tony (who, when I told him my "Mary was born the same as everybody else" rap last night, had made the very appropriate comment that Mary in her having been chosen by God to fulfill the role of mother of Jesus, and that in the special super-devoutness of her parents St. Anne and St. Joachim, probably was almost immaculate in her conception) had saved me a piece from the *Catholic Standard and Times* about Fr. Brinkman. Fr. B says a little mass each day at 1:00 PM at in the Katherine Drexel chapel—only two blocks from where my office is (WAS!). I went on an average, about four out of every ten days, I'd guess. He was just given the national award as the best priest in the country at doing what he does—bringing the Catholic ministry to students on non-Catholic campuses. He is well loved at Drexel, and the little Thursday night dinners he sponsors right in the Neuman Center, are attended by as many as 100 students—Catholic, non-Catholic, mass goer or not, even believer or not. And when I read the comment by an engineering senior student, first re the dinners, *"It's become a hot spot, You see the most prominent student leaders on campus mingling and talking. I think it has been Fr. Brinkman's dream to get to this point,"* I thought that was so cool. But when I read further on her comment, *"He's done tons of stuff for me during some of the toughest times of my life,"* all I could think about was all of my "one-day back" confessions, when I'd call or e-mail and he would get back, and I'd go see him, head down and repentant again, and his absolution would be accompanied by sound, kind, non-judgmental advice—and how much better I'd feel when I walked out. *"Change the center point of the pendulum maybe"* he suggested one time. Raising his hand, *"you go way up here in your spirituality,"* then swinging the arm down and back the other way, *"but you go flying to crazy places when you go the other."* I'm not sure which time he offered that particular guidance, but I thought about it a lot, and when I made the mental commitment to make that center point just staying sober for one day, and not writing or doing this or that, things did get better.

Fr. B—another wonderful shepherd who was put in my path. Tony also told me Pope John Paul II, the grand-daddy of all the shepherds, served a similar campus ministry-type post when a young priest in Krakow.

Re JP II, I told Tony the story I read one week in Mattingly's column about a tale a real big shot Jewish Rabbi told about the pope. Seems this rabbi was also Polish and he told of how back in Poland during the war, a Jewish couple on the way to their Auschwitz extermination, had left their infant child with a Catholic couple. After the war, the Catholic couple brought this orphan boy, who'd been raised Catholic, to the pope (then a parish priest) to have him baptized. But when JP asked if there had been any religious requests made by the parents, when he was told the parents did ask to have the son raised Jewish, he refused to do the baptism. The young boy would become, the story went, a devout practicing Jew. And if anywhere in this journal, I gave the impression that I do not love and admire this wonderful brilliant Polish pope we now have well then that impression I gave out was wrong.

And so here it is the penultimate day of March . . . year of our Lord 2001. (I always wanted to use that word penultimate in my writing somewhere, and here it is. A ridiculous stretch, but who's counting.) The pelting rain outside my window just started again. I think this morning, I'll do a formal guidance list. The NCAA championship game is next Monday night and that is the one-year anniversary of the night I did not go across town and get my ATM card so the crack run would continue—the night an image of Sarah crept into my prayer. Routing through all this crap up here yesterday, I found one of those little tiny 3" by 3" Day's Inn pads from that night—scrawled in pencil were words that, in a sense, were the beginning of this book.

Across the sea I genuinely hope and pray, the foot and mouth count is still just one in the North, one in the South. I can't call over there right now—it's the middle of the night. I don't have all that many phone numbers either—I lost my address book towards the end of my Dublin adventures. I do get e-mail messages almost every day from Michael Smith though, he shows most of my e-mails to the staff at the library . . . yesterday I asked him to stop up to see Angela and explain the lost address book was why I didn't call on Mother's Day.

My e-mail is not working on my laptop for some reason—but that is okay. In fact I'm going to cancel my AOL account and continue to do my e-mailing in libraries or the Writer's House or wherever . . . gets me out of the house. The librarian at our local library was talking about they are going to make a movie of "Bartleby the Scrivener." Now I would prefer to see that one!

My sister Mary Ellen is going to Ireland in a couple of weeks . . . ironically staying in the little ocean town of Dunleery, south of Dublin, I never got around to getting to. She *is* hiring a car (God help Ireland!), and she is going to make it up to Cavan. I'm going to try to make sure she stays at least one night there—maybe even in the very same room in Angela's B and B. Ann Gaffney knows she's coming. When I said "my sister's so hyper, she makes me seem calm, Ann said something like "That's impossible. She'd fly off the planet if she was."

It's about 8:00 AM now—my mom just got up wondering, "Who's cooking bacon on a Friday during Lent?"

April 2, 2001
Monday

The NCAA championship game is tonight. Last year it was on the night I escaped the pipe and that Day's Inn room. Actually that crackerjack of a game (if you"ll pardon the expression) between Florida and Michigan State, did help me get my mind off the awful matter at hand.

So it goes. On the wall sitting next to me is my story from the November 29, 1999 *Philadelphia Inquirer.* This newspaper I criticize frequently for being so non-God oriented, printed these closing paragraphs. (A good friend gave me a framed copy of the article as a Christmas gift that year.)

The incidence of recovery is, however, way down in contemporary 12-step programs. In today's secular age the notion of a Higher Power seems passe. We look for drugs, counseling, behavior modification, anything to keep away from the dreaded G-word. And yet from where I sit, with this crack thing, this life-defying demon never has there been more of a need on a power greater than oneself to survive.

Kids growing up in essentially godless households turn to the fun and freedom of "ecstasy" because they've learned that this world is all that matters. They turn on the tube and are inundated with looking and feeling good. I hope they somehow learn otherwise before it is too late.

The sentiments expressed there did not become false or lose their value merely because I got high again after I wrote them. That I got high after them was because I was too enamoured of the words to humbly thank the Source from whence they had flowed. Nor were the words written below—many years ago—probably even before the relapse year of 1997.

The River of Life

Permanence . . .
Certitude . . .
Exactitude . . . .
Pulchritude . . .

These are all maya—illusion.

We are all flux and fluidity
We are rivers and brooks
—ever flowing.

The permanent among us
those exact, those defined
Seal their permeant membranes
with the mortar of things.

And yet this flow is not
without meaning—
not some meaningless run-off
through the valley of time

The waters conjoin
The essences merge
And head both to
And yet fro . . . the Ultimate Source

So turn in your dams
your erection that seal
For the River of Life
must flow where it will.

The flow, the river, the way. My personal flow was through the deadly rapids of addiction and alcoholism . . . due to God's grace and mercy I emerged in the safe calm waters on the other side.

One translation of the Tao is The Way. If one thinks in terms of this Way being the will of God, then there really is a point of sameness, of comaraderie, of unity, of love, of a point where the joining or the hugging or the dialogue can begin . . . but mostly it is a point where the praying emphatically and consistently for the same thing can occur. In Lao Tzu's *Way of Life*, the sort-of bible of Taoism, # 40 reads:

The movement of the Way is a return
In weakness lies it's major usefulness
From What-is all the world of things were born
But What-is sprang from what is not.

Jesus came down and walked among us to show us how far astray from this *Way* or Path or Will of God we had drifted. HIS message, if taken and "cut scraped, rubbed, melted" and all those other things the Buddha told us to do with all messages will reveal REAL peace and happiness—not much of the assorted rubbish humans have turned it into. But His message also, is just a pointer. If we think it is IT, then we are wrong, we never get IT . . . we get glimpses, we get peace, we get happiness—REAL happiness—not the crap we have been conditioned to think is the real thing. But we don't ever, get the whole picture—and if we think we do we are wrong! Buddha put this in rather extreme terms "If you see the Buddha, kill him." If you got IT, you got an illusion, because we and our brilliant, conceptual, getting-more'n'more-computer-like minds cannot, no matter how much we try to convince ourselves we can, ever conceptualize the wonder and magnificence of God.

My dear sweet cousin Aegean, (my God how I miss her embarrassed little smile) thought this one would make a great rap song . . .

ETERNITY?

E-ter-ni-ty
it seems to me
lasts way way way too long . . . .

And though I can't conceive
can I
still believe
in such an endless song?

Is it va-ni-ty
or the will to be
that makes me want
to never punt
as long as time do be?

And now speakin of bein
will my bein good
in this world's
neigh-bor-hood
insure this time immemor
be splendid galore -

will I dance with the saints
will I be a ti-fic shine
from head to behind
will the n'er-ending gliver
keep me free from all shivers?

And of course there's the other
If I'd been a bad brudder
will this means that I shudder
midst the fiery crudder

and one day to anudder
in the hell way down under?

I don't know, I don't know
nor do you nor's Joe Blow
(ev'n if Joe read the "Book"
cover to cover
and ov back and then under)

I can tell you this
I 'scaped a mean
man made-ian abyss
cause I believed
in the diss
re a timeliss De-iss

And so I do feel my song
will go on, on and on
but the tune of the tun-in
ain't for me or for you'n
to ev'n try to be clu-in

and if my dance now seems grand
*as if a part of de **Plan***
and the opp-sit of bland
and means reach out my hand
and puts some chutz in my pan . . . .

Then who gives a goddman
how long be's its span

but if this belief serves
to enhance
mon e'er great 'I am' stance
- then it serves up a sham

. . . but on thee other hand
if it has the effect
that I'm one small connect
on the great cosmic set . . .
The same as the rest

in the chance for success
in my n'er-ending quest
to bring right to my nest...

then it earns the name zest

and so believe what you will
and if some night there's a chill
as you ponder the still
as you lower your will
...and Else makes yer eyes fill

then get up and rejoice
soon sure return will the noise

but that Moment you had
might be had, had and had
for like... E-ver-more
and...that...
ain't half bad...

Lo and behold whilst looking for my little Eternity ditty, I came across this one. I wrote it last fall and the title is a central tenet of Qigong:

Divinity is the will of all the people . . . .

Everything is of the Way
even the discipline to stay on the Way
even the pained tortured times when it seems we are not on the Way
—is
of the Way

But this doe not mean one does not try,
that one does not exert effort,
that in the times one finds himself in conditions where hate, inequality and idolatry exist
that he does not try to either eradicate the injustice
or to extricate himself from the overindulgence.

What it does mean is that even as one tries,
if his efforts lose their effortness
if he then knows he can
(in fact even then does!) . . . .
bask in the cool cleansing flow and the glow of the Way . . . .

that in the realization of its n'er evaporating presence
and of our inevitable eventual immersion (or reimmersion) therein,
we go that way automatically and steadfastly . . . .
and we draw others with us because the natural way of the Way is all-participating

And could any gravitational pull be stronger than that of All?

God's plan for us, the Tao, the Way, the Buddha-nature—
all painfully inadequate words we use to try to describe that which is beyond description . . . .
and in its vast vast kingdom of all that is, ever was, and that ever will be—indefinable
it contains, engulfs, digests and gurgitates the comparative microscopic
drop-in-an-ocean-like sliver of reality we call the definable

But of course we will fight the pull,
we will avoid the flow . . . .
our laughable preoccupation with the snares and cares
of our magnificently defined and refined physical bodies,
leaves us little time and even less concern for distracting musings
about things as silly as Ways or flows or paths or indefinable

By definition practically (and practically-speaking)
of what import specifically could anything be that is indefinable?

All this too (I guess you knew)
is also of the Way . . .

And so off to the spa, the gym and the skim . . . .
read your great books of how to hook and to crook . . . .
get ahead, get some head—by your nose be on led . . . .
for the more that you stuff—the quicker you're stuffed . . . .
for only when stuffed will most of us choose—a much simpler way . . . .

when we've had way too much we no longer will clutch
. . . and fall we all will into the simple sanguine
of the with-the-flow-go we call Way . . . .

The Bible tells us eventually the Good will win out. I'm sure the texts of the great religions of the East say the same thing. That is why real mystics are never bothered by the rinky dink nonsense going on around us.

The very first paragraph of *Awareness* reads:

> *Spirituality means waking up. Most people even though they don't know it, are asleep. They're born asleep, they live asleep, they die in their sleep, they marry in their sleep, they breed children in their sleep; they die in their sleep without ever waking up. They never understand the loveliness and beauty we call human. You know all mystics—Catholic, Christian, non-Christian, no matter what their theology, no matter what their*

> *religion, are unanimous on one thing: that all is well, all is well. Though everything is a mess, all is well. Strange paradox, to be sure. But tragically most people never get to see that all is well because they are asleep. They are having a nightmare.*

Way back last August Fr, Kelty the venerable little writer and monk in Gethsemani, as I went on and on about how bad things were, simply said, *"things are good now, people have money. When things are good, it's a bad time for religion. There are many good young priests around, things will get better."* I can't wait to go see Fr. Kelty next month.

* * *

Well it is now Tuesday. Duke won the NCAA final game last night so I didn't with the Trash Band pool. But I split 2nd and 3rd, which means I won $20. (My picking Arizona to go real far helped me pick up points lost on the good ol' Hawks of St Joe's.) Considering that one year ago I went through about $600 on the Sunday and Monday of the tournament, and that this year I also made $100 umpiring Sunday—that makes me $720 to the good compared to this time a year ago. (Kind of the inverse of how my mutual funds are going.) The good times for me are every day now. The badder times for this grimy yet lovely old world, seem to be just beginning. Foot and mouth is now cropping up in little cells all over the continent, they're now going to start testing sheep in the Carolina's. The stock market keeps going down . . . and I am going to be heading downtown.

April 4
Wednesday
6:00 AM

It's still pitch black dark outside—Daylight Saving Time now.

April 4 a huge date in my life. My "sober date" three different times. Nine years ago the first time—the day I woke up in a hotel room in Atlantic City—the day after my buddy and first AA sponsor, Jack,'s wedding. The crack had entered my life in a big way by then. That day, however, I needed it not. I was just plain old drunk, although ten days earlier, I'd been smoking up a storm.

That's the crazy thing about crack—there is very little heroin-like physical-type need to do it not long after you put it down. The "my drug's worser than your drug" 'tude of a lot of heroin users, is, I guess, because of this. Watching this dynamic in a Rehab is actually quite hilarious. You think the Irish Catholics and Protestants are crazy!

Two years ago, April 4 happened to fall on Easter Sunday—that was the day I ventured down to Nativity where my friend Nick and his family gave me to eat. I saw Nick last Saturday night at a meeting. His hellacious heroin kicks still, unfortunately, very much part of his picture.

April 4 one year ago I woke up right here the morning after Sarah's image helped me escape the hotel room about 3 miles away. I did make it to work that next day . . . even got started on the capstone rewrite after work. (And it WAS AFTER!)

But that night in that room, as the money I'd had was gone, the drama centered on that ATM card. There really was little doubt I would go and get it. As I said before, when you're on a crack run, and there is any means to continue, it is a very rare occurrence that you stop. The pipe is like that; the hit trumps all. In a story I wrote about my crack cocaine addiction that had been published six months earlier, I described it like this:

> *And yet describing the actual "hit" seems near impossible. There is an instantaneous euphoric "rush"—there can be no questioning that. And that is what you keep chasing—that very first one, you never get there again, but you get close—so you keep trying. But instantaneous is not a strong enough word to describe just how temporary the rush is . . . for even as you are exhaling, the concern for that next one is taking hold. This*

manic fixation with "more, and mine" pretty much describes that "crack mentality". With the clarity of lines formed on a mirror, that mentality is etched on the faces of users everywhere . . . leaning over a bureau or table, or a slab of anything in the bowels of an abandoned building . . . the intensity, the concentration the "don't waste any," the "don't take mine!"—it is sick—it defies sanity.

There is something truly demonic about crack cocaine, about smoking coke. My best friend in recovery, Larry, and the man who has helped me more than any other in my ongoing battle with my addiction, (the one who first took me through the *Back to Basics* step class in December of '97) had had his own little fling with the pipe. So did his brother. This brother was a legend on the streets of the down and out Kensington section of Philadelphia. He'd been called "the dinosaur" as he'd survived, even, at times, flourished, as an alcoholic, a heroin addict, a whatever, for over thirty years. But one night while smoking crack with Larry, he had said "This is the big one, buddy. This is one that's gonna take everything down. This is the devil."

And as I sat in that hotel room that night, I felt very much like it was the devil tugging at one end of my psyche. Back and forth I went. Like a rope being stretched between two powerful adversaries, my decision of whether or not to go get the card and continue the load went yea then nay.

'You ALREADY are IN the load why not get your money's worth. You can get sober again tomorrow, you've done it before."

"You've not really done that much damage so far; IF you stop now and go home, your mom won't find out. You won't again put her through the living hell of her son being back there. You'll get a decent night's sleep. You won't end up calling in sick tomorrow; work won't find out . . . "

And then back to the thought of the smoke curling up that pipe and into my mouth . . . the hit, the glorious hit.

And then the other side—echoing in my head—words spoken to me almost exactly three years previous, as I was just about to embark on the worst seven-month crack run of my life:

"Every time you get high, you're more likely to keep getting high."

My God the degree to which, in my case, those words of warning had proven true! And now I could add words from my own experience:

> *"This empty despair you feel right now and that horrible moment when that pipe went dry about an hour ago, that will only happen again when the next three hundred dollars or so is gone . . . and then it will be worse . . . "*

The mental battle went like that. But that is the grim reality of smoking coke. There is never satiation. The more you smoke, the more you want to smoke—no matter how long you smoke, nor how much you have spent. Not one single time in all the hours I'd spent getting high, not once for all the thousands of dollars I'd spent on crack, had a run ended with a, "Gee that was nice . . . now to kick back and relax . . ." feeling.

But even with all the monumental evidence heaped on the side of not continuing the lure of the hit seemed to be winning the day. And along with the smoking, there were the visions of kinky illicit sex. Despite the fact that this almost never actually happened, the anticipation of it continued to be part of the lure.

So there I sat . . . . a confused, scared, lost soul, watching the moments flicker away. And so I prayed. I did what the people in AA told me to do. I asked God to help me. (That I did not do everything they told me, like to call somebody to get me out of there, was a testimony to how much I really didn't want to stop.)

Again, there was certainly no "great awakening" that night. That I kind of felt Sarah's presence was not really any great shake. The miraculous thing that did happen was that I did get out. I did make it home. In fact when I did get home, the second half of that NCAA title game was just getting started. I didn't watch the end though, I just trudged upstairs and crashed—if I said a thank you prayer before I crawled in bed hurt, crushed, beaten, battered, I don't remember.

A night to remember always—the dark and then the dawn.

This April 4, I have more consecutive 'clean time' at this particular spot on the calendar—in this artificial but very efficient way we use to measure and cardon up this immeasurable, uncardonable thing we call time—than I have had in quite a while. Being in the light and no longer being whiplashed from the dark, I enjoy the peace of a relatively even keel.

Last night I got home from Mike the Monk's and found an e-mail from John Timpane down at the *Inquirer*, asking me to write about Daryl Strawberry—here is what I wrote:

Daryl—Keep coming back

Last Sunday morning, umpiring in a sobriety softball league over in Jersey, I watched a left-handed hitter by the name of Johnny, after struggling for his first five or six doubleheader at-bats, smack a home run over the right field fence. But this was not the home run I think of when I think of Johnny—no that was one he hit last year, when he turned his hips perfectly on a low inside pitch and walloped it into the trees behind that same fence. Watching that swing, up close and personal I finally knew why the real good lefty power hitters love those low inside pitches.

If anyone ever saw the beauty of Daryl Strawberry turning on such a pitch, bringing the fat of the bat down on the ball, flicking his wrists, the bat twirling with the speed and precision of a baton—and then viewing the ball disappear into the stands or the night—then they know the tragedy and the waste of a magnificent God-given talent—but even worse they know the tragedy of a life being chucked aside.

I do not know how many chances Daryl has had. BUT contrary to what I hear many people saying, he is not hopeless. I know the pipe, I've been there—I know what it's like to push anything and everything aside in chase of that next hit. But I also know that as long as a human being still breathes, as long as he still keeps trying and keeps, as they say in the rooms of recovery, "coming back", then he always has a chance. If Daryl Strawberry even lowers his will to the extent that the grace of God can gain entry, then he too, like any other addict, can recover.

Days and night in rehabs or in jail cells are all good days for an addict. They are good days because they are clean ones. BUT they serve little real lasting use, unless the addict uses those clean days and nights, working the 12-step program that is designed specifically to effect the entry of that grace. The fellowship is fine . . . the camaraderie great, the meetings are wonderful, but all of these are mere eyewash, the recovery comes from working the steps.

There is no guarantee however that recovery will happen for anyone. For Daryl Strawberry the fame and fortune he knew may be too great an obstacle to overcome—nothing blocks the entry of God's graces more than pride. He may run out of chances before the miracle happens. Refer to David Ruffin, whose John Doe carcass was dumped in front of the Hospital of the Univ. of Pa emergency room a few years back, about fame and fortune and the pipe. Think of Len Bias.

I don't know the particulars of Darryl Strawberry's religious beliefs or that of his family's. Religion does not necessarily equate to a connection with a Higher Power, but it certainly helps. Most people who make it to the rooms of recovery are pretty well convinced they were prayed in there by someone. I sure do believe it about myself.

18 months ago the Inquirer was kind enough to publish a story I wrote about my crack cocaine addiction. Perhaps the 'getting published' thing, served to add yet one more layer to the thick wall of wordily pride

I've built over the years. As far as I can tell the pride was the cause to the effect of my relapse that was to take place about four months later. Irony of ironies, last April 3, I sat in a hotel room as Michigan State and Florida battled it out for the NCAA championship—trying to not go get the ATM card across town and continue that "goodbye clean time" crack run I'd been on for that day and the one before. Somehow, some way I did not go get the card, my prayer was answered—I did make it home.

Whatever you do Darryl keep coming back—Home is at yours (and all of ours, by the way) beckoned call.

Seems the *Inquirer* thinks of me as their "crack" reporter. I got no problem with that—I just wish they would give more heed to some of the other things I write. My *Emperor's New Clothes* ditty after Slick Willie's final 'state-of-the-Union" speech, I thought was a killer! Plus I can use the $200 . . . my car needs 4 new tires and an axle—to the tune of about $700. (This "fear on financial insecurity leaving" thing might start getting a little tight. I'm glad I'm umpiring today, tomorrow and whatever other days.)

Mike the Monk is leaving for Italy today. Of course Rome is on the itinerary. If JP II knew how holy ol' Mike is, he would grant him an audience. But because Mike is leaving, at last night's session, a lovely girl named Mary came to give Mike a bunch of gifts. Mary is as kind and as sweet as can be, but me'n'she do bump heads on the importance of working the steps. Last night in the little post-reading sharing portion of the meeting, Mary spoke of having been given the gift of really feeling that Jesus "had her back." I know why she looked so peaceful.

Things do work out if you believe and you keep trying. "I can't, He can, I'll let Him" . . . is one way we slogan-mad AA's use to describe the steps. How much lower the world must go until they realize they can't, I suppose, remains to be seen.

April 5, 2001

Driving up to see my friend Mitch speak at a meeting up in Philly's Northwestern suburbs where he now lives, I stopped the car to call and apologize to Wally of the *Back to Basics* event in Vermont for the tone of my e-mail letter to him. It seems they are calling the event *Back to Basics for Christian Alcoholics*. That letter had triggered a nasty response, and a nasty one back from me, etc, etc. Seems I'd gotten the wrong idea simply from the name of the conference. In this Vermont conference, they are going to use the New Testament, (James, I'm sure a part of it a least,) to teach the steps. Also in the works is a conference for Muslims using the Koran and one for Jews using the Old Testament.

AA's Big Book quotes Herbert Spencer "one way we will remain in constant ignorance is through contempt before investigation". I was guilty again of this regarding the Vermont conference. And Wally's approach made me realize that, in my little round-the-clock prayers for peace scenario mentioned a ways back, how much broader and wiser would be rosaries *and* readings from the Old Testament *and* from the Koran. And with that, my beloved pontiff, he who sponsored a Lou Reed and Amy Lennox concert, I'd suspect would have no problem.

I live and learn and change and grow because to not do so would mean that I am stagnating and dying. For the first time since I've been back in America, I really practiced Qigong this morning—with the tape for a good 40 minutes. I do this because it also is an attempt to make myself wiser and healthier.

Under my arm is a painful abscess. Later today I'll check with a doctor. These abscesses seem to come and go with me—my very efficient Penn physician, seems to not think them that big a deal—he suggests I cut down on the caffeine and acidic foods . . . I haven't yet. On last January 10 my birthday, the abscess was in a much more delicate and painful spot . . . but until it was ready to burst, my at-home doctoring did me no good—the same was true last October when I had one on my ear. But pop they did when the time was right—and the relief was amazing. (January 10, nine years ago, for the final time, God willing, I was an overnight guest of "Philly's Finest"—a different kind of abscess/obsess had me then.)

Way back near the beginning of my Ireland adventure, Hugh explained to me the particulars of the stopped up water piping system in the farmland near his home. The electronic sensor that reopens the valve that keeps the water flowing needs a steady enough flow over it to keep the valve open. A slight trickle just would not do. And because of seepage somewhere along the line, the flow had become too weak to trigger the sensor. So Hugh, to the consternation of many of his neighbors, those especially without back-up water sources, had to close the water off completely to allow enough pressure to build for the water flow to re-trigger the sensor. By midnight of the evening of my visit, Hugh's return to the station found a build-up strong enough to let the flow go. And there, only a few miles from when the mighty Shannon flows out of an almost miraculously ne'er dry tiny little "pot," Hugh released the waters and his friends and neighbors' baths and spigots had running water again.

The seepage from the flow of good and decency in the world about us these days needs be chronicled no more. But nothing will ever stop the Flow . . . no man-made dams of greed and lust and hate and ignorance and prejudice can ever stop it.

Yesterday as I walked past the shopping centers over on Cottman Avenue a few miles from here (that were being built when I was a kid) still there amidst the pigeons, were the inexplicable "sea gulls of Gimbel's parking lot." Even though they've now moved across the street and the Gimbel's is now a Sears and was several things in between, that is what I still call them. 60+ miles from the ocean, I've never ever been able to figure out why they hang out there . . . . but hang out there they have for as long as I can remember. And as the image of my dad in that blue bathing suit he wore for about a hundred years, half in and half out of a wave he was riding perfectly seeps into my consciousness, I think perhaps the gulls were always trying to tell me to come back to the sea, the flow—that the water really is fine.

I remember the time, not long after my dad had died, walking around thinking that he and John Lennon, whose October 9 birthday is three days before dad's October 12 one, were somehow united now. "Death sure makes strange bedfellows" is what I had thought—as my dad would have probably liked Lennon about as much as he liked being called "Shorty". Instant Kharma indeed.

April 8, 2001
Palm Sunday

Going through the Stations of the Cross this year (the first time I've done that in a long time), I noticed that the "women" stations surround the Simon of Cyrene station, the 5th. Mary is the fourth, Veronica wiping Jesus face is the 6th, and the women of Jerusalem weeping for him is the 8th. If anyone wants a little more evidence of the preeminence of women in the Jesus story, they can look to the gender of the folk who were with him there for that trudge up to Calvary—and then can fast forward a few days to Mary Magdalene being the first person to see the risen Lord.

But today at mass for the first time, I really took note of what Jesus said to these loyal Jewish women who believed and followed Him. (A CBS network special called *Jesus* from last year, that I guess did not get good enough ratings to bring it back this year, I thought, presented a wonderful portrait of the life of Jesus. I read where the pope shared this view. And in this special, instead of the entire city of Jerusalem shouting "crucify Him", this show presented the scene as a handful of carefully placed "plants" whipping a small gathering into the appearance of a frenzied mob.) But from where exactly my head is at these days, the words he spoke to these women take on added significance.

"Daughters of Jerusalem, do not weep for me, weep for yourselves and your children. For the time will come when you will say, Blessed are the barren women, the wombs that never bore and the breasts that never nursed. Then they will say to the mountains, 'Fall on us', and to the hills, 'Cover us'

For if men do these things when the tree is green, what will happen when it is dry?"

Was Jesus speaking of the day when we will call his own mother barren? When we will insist that the greatest woman, for my money, who ever lived . . . bore only one child—and he through a miraculous intercession? . . . When to claim, for some reason, and to make it a central facet of religious doctrine, a supposition with no Biblical corroboration, with even, in fact, contrary Biblical corroboration—that their Mary was a virgin her whole life?

But even more so, perhaps Jesus was speaking of a time when, via abortion and massive contraception, we reached a point in our civilization where the real end of sexual intercourse, procreation, would be considered an unwanted annoyance . . . that the act itself would be considered our end-all. I wonder if any marketing genius considered calling those new abortion pills "golden calves".

Back and forth I go, seeking the sweet solace of a middle ground.

Again I go back to Joyce's *Portrait* and how when in a tortured recall of his would-be love's flirtation with a young handsome priest, his hero Dedalus calls himself *"a priest of the eternal imagination, transmuting the daily bread of experience into the radiant body of ever*living *life,"* I wonder how many broken homes, and abandoned children, and blasted lovers, and aborted babies, and teenage suicides and shot-up bodies in high school cafeterias—have been sacrificed to this god of ever*living* life. But as I ponder the blight of Joyce's 'church', I think of the thorny path leading up to it . . . one of concubines and "bad popes", and Inquisitions, and gay liaisons and the millions of dollars of out-of-court settlements and countless broken lives spreading like a Malthusian virus from out the tattered psyches of violated little boys. And when I read of the young flirting handsome priest, I think of two priests I had in high school strolling down a seaside boardwalk in their civvies, carefully admonishing us NOT to call them "Father." Then another priest from my high school comes to mind. Our senior guidance counselor would eventually be busted for his sexual involvement with certain students.

But while the prostitutes for young Joyce would mark the beginning of his emancipation—for me they would mark the beginning of my descent into the hellish black hole of crack cocaine addiction. Then I think of a priest friend of mine who fell prey to that same addiction, as I envision a cold lonely night in a rectory somewhere, with that urge coming on accompanied by a torrent of lust . . . and his struggle with recovery does not surprise me.

Recovery has come for me though—from that satanic lair of abandoned buildings and decayed hithouses, from a despair so deep and dark I knew not if I'd ever escape, the beatific light of God's Love would finally draw me back to the surface. And this Light that filtered through, came pouring in those stained glass windows I'd turned my back on all those years ago. For it would be there, in safe bosom of my beloved Catholic Church, with *all* her past *and present* deficiencies, where the grace finally gained ascendance.

April 12, 2001
Wednesday

Spy Wednesday—they call it in the Church—the day Judas took the 40 pieces of silver to the Pharisees and set up the betrayal of Jesus. Not long ago someone mentioned to me that Jesus goaded Judas into setting him up to fulfill the scriptures. I'm not sure who said it, or what the basis of their supposition was, but it seemed typical of the half-truth kind of things about the Jesus story that cumulatively lend an aura (or an excuse) to not accept the whole thing.

Another such half-truth I heard last summer was that there was a second agenda behind Paul's mission of taking the Word to the world—that there was profit or something involved. Yeah, Paul, who by the time he was martyred had a face ugly and misshapen from all the beatings and stonings, really made out like a bandit in his ministering. I do believe that in the language of those early Christians, there was a bit of a spin that the world was going to end like the following Tuesday. Peter and Paul and Timothy and the boys did, I suppose, need something big to get them going. But in reality, in comparison to Eternity, each of our silly little 70-80 years on this planet *is* next Tuesday—a *hiccup,* I frequently call it.

The weather outside today is cold and rainy—Ireland weather. The sunny 80 degree weather of Monday seems a different season. Then, an afternoon umpiring stint right on Philadelphia's beautiful Benjamin Franklin Parkway, was followed up by a stroll into town for 5:15 mass at old St. John's, (the center city church with the St. Ant statue my mom 'wore out' with prayers for dad) that was my mom's as a child. And the brogue of the woman who led one of the decades of the post-mass rosary, induced me to go up and speak with her. Ann, a Mayo native, was more than willing to talk. She'd earned her passage here feeding pigs and doing other duties—and all of this some 40 years ago. This brogues sure do hang on for some people.

But as Ann went on about the other things she did to earn money in her younger days in Ireland, I shifted into American "in a hurry" mode . . . . and so I missed some very interesting details because I was in a hurry to go nowhere in particular. The unnecessary extravagance of the $10 cup of coffee and bowl of soup at the outdoor café on the way back up the Parkway to my car, could have waited. I'll be back for the 5:15 at St. John's soon enough, I'm sure Ann's a regular there—I'll hopefully get a second chance at listening better.

April 13, 2001
Holy Thursday

At the Big Book study at Jamie's house last night, we did not get very far with the book, but our discussion of the 10th and 11th steps was deep and worthwhile. *"What we have is a daily reprieve contingent on our spiritual fitness,"* the book reads. Only one paragraph prior to that we are told, in regards to drinking that, as we work these steps and approach that spiritual awakening, with regards to that first drink *"it is a s if we are we are placed in a position of neutrality. We have not even sworn off. The problem has been removed for us."* This message seems a far cry from the "stay away from people, places and things at all costs" message I hear frequently in the AA rooms these days. Later in the book, in the "Helping others" chapter, we are told, *"we will go to the worst place on earth, if we can be helpful".*

Last week as I drove my car to a shop right up the street from the park where I knew I could find the last girl with whom I got high, I quite literally asked God to continue to protect her—that some day soon, hopefully that I will be able to go in there and maybe help her—but that now I am not yet ready. For that poor addicted and trapped soul has a "prayer bench" right there in her living room. A Bible sits on it there almost directly between where she and I did our thing, pipewise and body wise just last August. There she prays each morning—before she goes out to do her business—doing whatever is necessary to feed the devil of an addiction inside her.

As days of doing active positive things go, yesterday was a good one for me, I did the stations and a rosary down at Father Mac's church before the little 5:00 PM mass in the sacristy. I also went to a regular AA meeting before the Big Book study and to Qigong practice after the study. In the Big Book it was again stressed how vital it is to take the 12-step message to another alcoholic who suffers—and perhaps the best thing I did yesterday was to get the phone number of the guy just back with four days sober. Now I can call him. The number of times I've given out *my* number to no avail, is probably well over 100.

But something else important happened yesterday; the brief glance at a couple of probable "players" on my way down to mass, turned into a something of a lingering look. "Farther from or closer to" that first drink is where our program tells us we have to go, there is no treading water or remaining the same. And if I do not review my thoughts and actions, if I do not analyze how and why in one week I was asking God's forgiveness for not yet being ready to put my hand near the flame, and one week later was entertaining thoughts (however embryonic) of how warm and comfy that flame might be, then I am not doing what is right and proper, I am headed in the wrong direction.

"Where have you been my blue-eyed son, where will you go now my darling young one?" Dylan's query rings fresh in my head as I review all that has happened—but mostly, at present, of this treatise that I am writing.

Today they're contemplating calling in the National Guard in Cincinnati to quell racial tension. Eleven people were shot dead outside of San Diego—this time old people. 45 were killed in a soccer game riot in South Africa. An article by Clarence Page of the Chicago Tribune, last week laments the environmental carnage involved with Bush's policies. If Bush really is going to "hands off" trickle-down Republicanism, what will that do to our world? Is it the nature of capitalism itself to justify any-and-all activity in the name of profit? Does he really think morality will guide the actions of the coal, oil or whatever barons?

At Mike the Monk's last night, Bobby N, the good friend who gave me the *Sex Love Anonymous* Big Book that helped me so much last fall, addressed my probing pronouncements, *"I've been there questioning all that stuff . . . but I came back to my faith because I found peace there. I accept their doctrines."* At mass at Father Mac's yesterday a well educated and wise gentleman told me that not even a majority of Biblical scholars, Catholic or otherwise, think James was Jesus' brother. And the words of the priest back in Ireland echo again in my head "We don't want to give the enemy anything to use against the Church."

So here it is Holy Thursday morning. 40 or so years ago how I loved this morning—because I didn't have to get up and go to school. But the passion play of the ensuing two days was on my mind. After the Gloria at Thursday's mass, the organ would be turned off. There would be no accompanying music for all the choir singing we had to do until Easter midnight mass—the endless litany on Good Friday was the biggest pain. And even in my "no school" euphoria, the day was tinged in sadness in the anticipated two-three day recreation of all that had happened to my savior Jesus. And as I ponder these incendiary words I write about His church, I wonder, are these new different swipes of the whip I administer to His torn and tattered flesh? Or am I really trying to help him with that cross . . . am I trying to expose all the world to his tender love—quite, almost literally, through the incredible love, kindness and strength of his magnificent mother?

So tonight and on Sunday, I will go to that Church of my youth for services—to Resurrection. Tomorrow I will mirror my steps from one year ago and attend the wonderful so ecumenical-in-nature Good Friday services down at Penn. Perhaps I'll even fast the entire day again.

But mostly I will take heart (and soul) in my unshaken belief that nothing I believe or have written takes away from the beauty, wonder and truth of all these rituals of my faith—that wonderful faith of my father. And that as the priest walks down that aisle on Easter Sunday morning, the holy anthem "Alleluia, Alleluia" will again ring out the sorrow—and ring in the joy.

April 13, 2001
Friday morning 4:00 AM

Good Friday morning.

Seemingly a whole choir-full of birds chirp in perfect harmony outside my window.

Nowhere Man was playing on my radio as I drove up Almond Street on my way home last night. A back-up on I-95 had convinced me to take the alternate route up from Center City through Port Richmond—and because of this I'd decided to stop by and see my cousin Susan.

Susan's grandfather Frank was my dad's first cousin—he was the oldest brother of the Jim who was my dad's best friend. His nine children and their offspring made for a huge contingent of McGowans at last year's picnic. Many of these whom I never knew, now mainly because of Susan's involvement, are a wonderful part of my life.

Frank struggled with alcohol his entire adult life; but he left behind a family deeply committed to each other, with a keen awareness of the paramount importance of filial closeness. Susan and I discussed how important that bond of love is, and also of how important is the faith of parents for us varying prodigals in our individual treks into the wilderness of life. And when this lovely talented and immensely energetic cousin spoke of how, especially the mothers keep that fire of faith going—I told her about how Angela, my angel back in Cavan, spoke of how when the kids come along, the mothers usually find their way back to the church.

Doesn't have a point of view
Knows not where he's going to
Isn't he a bit like me and you

I don't know how many times I've heard in the AA rooms, "I was going to do this and was going to do that, but I just could not get off the bar stool." My particular variation on the theme was "after I stop drinking . . . I'll do this or that, but I could never stop drinking."

But eight years ago I had stopped drinking. The "no major changes for the first year" period was over for me. I celebrated my very first sober anniversary with the first of many visits to the Graymoor Retreat House at which my father had had such a change of heart 53 years prior. Eight years ago Good Friday was April 4—my first sober anniversary—it marked the first time in my adult life I was able to say I've not drank or drugged for an entire year. One year into sobriety I was ready to take on the world. And on the last day of that first sober year—Holy Thursday—part of the mass ritual at Graymoor, just like last night at Sts. Agatha and James, was a priest actually getting down and washing folks' feet—mirroring what Jesus had done 2000 years ago.

"Love and service" the two words to which, our co-founder, Bob Smith said the AA program can be reduced—that seemingly was the message Jesus' feet washing imparted.

These two items however were obviously not at the top of my list that night eight years ago—getting ahead and getting a mate were. I was in the running for a new, different exciting job in the University; I finally had got around to dating a girl I'd liked (a lawyer whose father had access to a private box at Saratoga!) By July both the girl and job were history—the melancholia probably began to sift in by then, and though the only drink or drug that would pass my lips for the next two and three-quarter years would be one hit on a crack pipe, the pouting and discontent would eventually skid my path back "out there".

But on that Holy Thursday night way back then, all seemed very well. And that night in the Graymoor visitor's lounge I made friends with those two guys—both from Queens—who I thought for sure would be friends for life. One of them, as I left the retreat in mid-stream after Friday dinner, carried my bag down to my car. But time, circumstances and my unkind words in a letter to him have come between us . . . I truly believe that eventually time will heal this wound also. I can only hope and pray that it will do so while both of us still are breathing.

Love and Service. As usual Peter, (in the gospel reading according to John last night) spoke up. When he resisted Jesus washing his feet, Jesus more or less told him, "if you can't let me do this and aren't ready to do this for others, then you miss the point." So Peter caved in again—and apparently had nice clean feet for a pretty eventful next twelve hours or so—for his little nap with buddies James and John as Jesus sweat tears of blood just a ways off in Gethsemani's garden—for his lopping off the ear of a servant of a high priest soon after—and then through the three abject denials—all before the first crow caw of the morning. Of the four Passion accounts, only Luke's mentions Jesus and Peter's eyes meeting after that third most passionate, "No I don't know him!" And that is because Luke was the only one who covered Jesus life as a reporter—his whole gospel was written from accounts of others—John and

Matthew were of the twelve, Mark was an adolescent follower. (Only Mark mentions the one follower running away so scared he lost his cloak. I'll give you exactly one guess which "naked in the night" follower, young Mark, Peter's sidekick of sorts, was writing about.) Peter must have told Luke about Jesus looking at him.

Peter ran away and cried after looking into those eyes—and it was in a tape given to me by a follower of a powerful preacher from the bright spanking new-ageish Calvary chapel not far from here, where I learned of that particular account of that first Good Friday pre-dawn. And it was to this chapel I went on a Monday night three summers ago, after circumstances only, had prevented what might have been a disaster of a load from taking place three days earlier. On that preceding Friday afternoon my boss would not allow me to leave early, a request made not because I was ill (as I said), but because I wanted to return to a load that had begun a night earlier. And so instead of working on that particular Friday afternoon (one that turned out to be a darn *good* Friday), I wrote an impassioned piece about how my boss's action coupled with my envisioning of the face of Jesus had delivered me from that particular obsession. And that direct from that treatise, I immediately drove down to South Philly to score, seemed emblematic that my pen, like Peter's sword, was of the wrong stuff. As it came to pass, for my last $5, I was given a piece of plaster and not coke (the no ATM card 'shielding' was already in place and I'd got out of work too late to get to a bank)—and so without the consummation of my will and all else that first hit would have triggered, I never made good on my "I'll be down later" call I'd made to a using partner in Atlantic City—where there in the casinos, my regular credit card could access all the cash I wanted. I called a recovering friend instead—and he took me out to dinner, and the following Monday over to that Calvary chapel.

The same tape spoke of how Peter was a much quieter, more subdued person in his encounters with Jesus after the Resurrection. In that last meal together, Peter stayed in the background and cooked the fish. Three times Jesus asked Peter if he loved him . . . . "feed my lambs . . . . take care of my sheep . . . . feed my sheep . . ." were the retorts Jesus gave to the three "of course I love you" replies of Peter. Three *yeas* to match the three Good Friday morn *nays*. Seems Jesus wanted to wipe clean his rock of a buddy's slate. Love and service indeed.

The Holy Thursdays of my recent life. Two years ago that was the night of my visit to Mitch's dying mom Bert—the night after Mitch had performed the Seder for her. Last year I was less than two weeks clean and the wolf of my addiction again was howling. A post qigong and tai-chi practice, one hour "prowl" had netted no finds . . . and a powerful case of the shakes as I drove through one 'hood into the next, apparently shook enough sense into me to make it home. The following night on Good Friday, the shakes returned—good shakes. Were they the "spontaneous movements" sometimes brought on by Qigong practice? I have nary a clue.

This year—more than eight months sober time preceded Holy Week. It is different, it is better, the glory of a day sober is more special if it comes on the back of many that preceded it. But a day is a day, "we have a daily reprieve based on our spiritual condition."

Sitting in church last night but even more so last Sunday, I wondered about what my changed beliefs about original sin and such do to my take on the rituals. And of course the idea of baptism is a magnificent one—a true and beautiful sacrament—not one of cleansing a little child of some unearned inherited blemish, but one of initiation, of unity of blending, into the glorious Mystical Body of Christ. As a kid I was way more impressed with that Baltimore catechism representation of those all-different-colored little faces drawn into Jesus' torso, than the "milk bottle" thing. The Biblical evidence is there for this—the holy holy man Simeon as Jesus the Jewish child was *presented* in the temple and, his telling Mary her heart will be pierced because of him. All this in Luke—the reporter—he was supposed to have been very close to Mary; my brother tells me the "black Madonna" (that is the image the church uses for Our Lady of Perpetual Hope), is closest to his drawing or representation of what she really looked like.

Mary again . . . I always seem to come back to Mary.

* * *

Last night there just happened to be another Qigong introductory event down at Penn. This was one of the best I've seen. Dr Frank Zhu, the man whose spiel most sold me at a similar event almost exactly two years ago, did the presenting. And in his stressing of the Qigong "regard everyone as you teacher, be kind and compassionate and humble towards all", principle, one can draw an easy parallel to the 'Love and service" feet washing by Jesus.

But Qigong is not about religion . . . or really about anything emotional like that. It is a practice by which we enhance our capability to think and feel and be connected. Perhaps I'm wrong about the emotional part, but a friend Patrick, in whose home I will practice later today, told me "if I'm emotional, I'm not practicing properly." He's been practicing longer and way more effectively than me, so I'll take his word for it.

Now when the emotional moments hit during practice, I do not feed into them, I just let them go. I get back to the breathing and the counting. I follow to tape's instructions and imagine my thinking coming from that tiempo point in the middle of my forehead. "If you practice Qigong and you believe in a religion, new Light will come to your belief"—I keep going back to that quote of Dr Yan Xin. My emotional moments are fast and furious these days. The extensive purging and cleaning house I have done, leads me to believe these moments are more real than false anymore; there is more room for grace to enter—just as promised in AA's *12 Steps and 12 Traditions* book discussion of the second step.

One of my questions to Dr. Zhu at the event today, was in regards to a mistaken impression I'd mentioned in my Qigong/ Christianity piece from a year ago. For Qigong masters did not "roam the countryside" during the dark ages. Qigong for many centuries was an individual person-to-person practice—it has been "brought out of the caves" so to speak and presented in big qi-emitting lectures only since around 1980. And my question to Dr Zhu was about why the recent unwrapping of the practice. Dr Zhu's response was that while I was correct in my impression, one reason *was* that now we now can scientifically measure the effects of qi transmission (which has been done via electro-magnetic experiments and such) but that there was a second reason: that now the world needs Qigong. And when he said this, the closing lines of a paper I wrote two years ago comes to mind:

> *The Mystical Body of Christ, the Chinese Tao, the Qigong qi, the Buddhist "Self-realization", Merton's Palace of Nowhere, the Muslim or the Quaker's "Inner Light", Buber's I-Thou dynamic, all point to the same place—to the unity and brotherhood of mankind found deep within our souls—that which can be our destiny. And yet two thousand years later, despite all the words and prayers and sentiments, and all the nations formed and deformed, and all the blood let, and all the everything else . . . we seem farther apart than ever. The never-absent gap between the 'haves and have-nots" seemingly gets larger. Our greatest 'progress' has been in the creation of things . . . these we cling to with a fervor that would make the most righteous evangelist proud. And perhaps if this meteoric growth in our physical capability to make things, (prominently including weapons) is not accompanied by at least a minimal complementary growth in our spiritual dimension, then we will march to our man-made Armageddon. And whether or not we do, is perhaps dependent on how much each and every one of us seeks, finds and marches to the cosmic tune of his own righteous destiny.*

———

As I think now of the Penn professor's insistence that all religions are *not* the same . . . I wish I'd been a little better prepared to have argued the point a bit.

April 14, 2001
Holy Saturday

I look at the "sell" reference re the Qigong presentation above, and I wonder is that what I am doing here—am I trying to sell something? And the answer is—of course I am. I am trying to sell peace and happiness and brotherhood—just like a lot of people. But I am pitching that we need belief in and reverence and prayer to a Power greater than ourselves, if we are to achieve it. There is certainly nothing new there. That I embrace the right-leaning Marian spirituality of my Catholic Church and the leftist Demellan eastern mode might be a new slant—good—that simply is the way it shook out for me. When my cousin Susan pointed out how Mary's hands were faced differently at Knock than in all her other apparitions—not palms upward to heaven—but one pointing towards the lamb and the other to Joseph beside her, it maybe provided more fuel for my argument about Mary having other children. Someone else could certainly argue otherwise. That is not my concern. I ask no one to buy my theories; I only invite you to think. A good and devout friend who does not agree with my stance on Mary's lifelong virginity, made the very valid point that Jesus on the cross, would not have 'given Mary away' to apostle John if he'd had brothers and sisters.

So here it is Holy Saturday. Yesterday's Good Friday services were nowhere near as emotional for me as they were a year ago. But then again they did not have to be. A year ago I was less than 3 weeks sober. As the priest rested that cross beside me on his way up the aisle, I was only about 16 hours removed from coming very close to reentering the abyss—that day I needed the emotional "thank God" upheaval. One of the many wonderful tools of the AA program, however, is exactly about "staying on an even keel—not getting too high or too low." Thus yesterday's services, and Qigong practice after, and an AA meeting after, and the dinner after—were all wonderful and positive actions—and their 'even keelness' took nothing away from their splendor. Even the pre-bed rosary walk was pretty calm. De Mello's words about emotionalism stifling our effectiveness, is another example of his spirituality mirroring the program. No wonder his "because they do the same thing in there that I do" response years back—which is what someone in recovery who had known him, e-mailed me was de

Mello's response when he'd asked why he'd wanted to go with him to an Open AA meeting.

It looks as if today is going to be a beautiful sunny day. I could not access two letters back to Ireland that I wrote yesterday because there is something wrong with the disc I'd copied them to. (I have no printer here in my room—I floppy on over to the local library to print.) I'll try a different disc today. I'll be getting over $600 back from my income tax and that is cool. The money will take care of itself. I'm thinking I will not put off the Pittsburgh, Cincinnati, Kentucky, Chicago—Akron on the way back—post Mother's Day junket. June 9-11 is AA Founder's weekend in Akron. My money situation is better than I thought.

* * *

The Supreme's *Love Child* was playing on the radio as I drove up Northeast Philly's Frankford Avenue from the apartment complex where two Holy Saturdays ago, I'd spent smoking crack. "Love child, so different from the rest . . ." is how in the song Diana Ross described what it was like growing up as a child born out of wedlock. How far, baby, have we come from that? I think of the ex-Spice Girl (Nasty?) I saw on the *Late Late Show* back in Ireland . . . . and how she spoke of her daughter and her charities being the most important things in her life—and this only moments after speaking of how the tabloid stories didn't bother her all that much because, in them, all her ex-lovers agreed on her acumen between the sheets. A long way indeed.

The two girls I'd smoked with and who had lived in the apartment complex had moved out though . . . people move on. They were the ones who at different times had either said no or had not tried to talk me into it, when they'd been the ones I'd found as I was ready to bid adieu to a period of sober time. I was going to give them a copy of the Strawberry *Inquirer* article and tell them about a church not too far away that had a lot of Cocaine Anonymous meetings. If it is meant to be, our paths will cross again some day.

Easter Sunday
April 15, 2001

Walking back from finally catching a sunrise, I walked by a young couple and their two small children. All of them were really dolled up in Easter outfit finery—both mom and the daughter were wearing pretty, wide-brim flowered hats. They were walking into the Protestant Church down the street. ("Mrs. Crawford's Church" my mom had always called it. Mrs. Crawford who worshiped there, resided three houses down, lived to be near 100, never weighed more than 100, and never, that I remembered, was anything but sweet and smiling and gentle. Her stoop was the meeting place of the chattering ladies when I was a kid. She once told mom, "when you try to wake up Mark, you wake up everybody on the block but Mark." Mrs. C was so nice that even a statement like that did not come across as offensive.)

On this gorgeous morning the little about-two-year-old boy must have been impressed by the bird chirping. "Birdies, mommy" was how he put it. When I remarked how in tune they were, his older sister proudly raised four fingers my way and said "I'm four", " . . . she's real shy" is how the father put it. I was reminded of the little black kid walking downtown one time, pulling his finger back from a smoking grate as his mother about ten feet behind raised her eyes to me after she'd said, "I KNOW you didn't put your finger on that thing!"

He learned soon enough I suppose.

Dropping my friend Bob off the past two nights down in the Frankford neighborhood where I used to live, I noticed the slew of "for sale" signs absent from his street. His black next door neighbors, he said were among the nicest people he ever met. And so it appears in at least one little Philly neighborhood, the "they're coming" fear-induced exodus is over. On an integrated block of nice row houses, my good friend Bob now lives. And I recall a black and white kid, each in green Cohoxin football uniforms crawling through a hole in the fence down in the still-very-white Port Richmond neighborhood in which my dad grew up. As Carl Sanburg put it "The people will survive."

Last night's drop-off was after watching a fascinating movie called *Memento*. (SO if you get nothing else from this account, you got tips on one great play, *All Down the Line*, and two movies *Memento* and *The Butcher Boy*. My man Eamon G, by the way, when I told him my "I'm gonna get the whole world to pray to Mary" agenda of the book, in true Eamonian fashion, said, "Oh so you're gonna turn the whole world into butcher boys, are ya?" You'll have to see the movie if you want to get the line.)

But one of the things the main character, Leonard, says in *Memento* is "If you can't remember something, that doesn't mean it didn't happen." And immediately I thought of Alzheimer's and the incredibly lame excuse I and other people use for not visiting, "they won't remember my being there anyway." Of course I thought of my Alzheimer-stricken Aunt El, my dad's last remaining sibling—and my godmother. The last time I saw her was last October—I really think I'll make good on my Easter Monday plan to go see her again. (This not working thing is really wonderful.)

As fate would have it, yesterday's "too late" visit to my old using partners had been precipitated by the fact that the adoration chapel where I spend most Saturday afternoons doing my 3-4 PM stint in the 24-hour Blessed Sacrament vigil St Katherine of Sienna's parish keeps, was closed. The Holy Saturday "Jesus is absent" thing you know. But being that I had to go back towards that exact part of town for the 7:00 PM Holy Family AA meeting, and being that I'd felt a bit guilty about the brevity of my visit to Sally's invalid neighbors, Ann and Ed, I stopped back later. On the second stop to see them I brought with me a piece I'd written exactly one year ago . . . 12 days after I'd escaped the *Days Inn.*

April 15, 2000
And the executioner's face is always well hidden . . . .

Two weeks ago yesterday I went to a viewing for a kid who died in a hotel room from a shotgun blast. The official word was that it was a suicide. His cousin and friend (the person I went to the funeral to see) thought that was bullshit—that even though the kid was a drug addict and alcoholic, he was not the one to pull the trigger, that he'd been executed because of unpaid gambling debts. The official book is pretty much closed now—we probably will never know.

The route I took to that AM viewing was through a pretty serious ghetto—down a street where 'players' frequently roamed. And when I say player I mean prostitutes—and in my case, specifically prostitutes who smoke crack cocaine . . . . for I am an addict, and two weeks ago the call of the hit was very strong. And even though it was a workday and I was on a 'lunch hour' of sorts that morning, I stopped a girl I thought was a player—I was ready. Fortunately she turned out to be just a regular woman—and I made it back to the office. My plus five months of 'clean' time that I had accumulated during this run of sobriety was safe. It would be gone before the end of the weekend. The two day later prowl eventually netted me a 'find'—and I was back with/in the pipe. Somehow I got out the very next day. I've not been high since. My clean 'time' is now twelve days, and for seven of them now the obsession has been lifted, the lure seems far away . . . for that I am very grateful.

I did not know this young man who died—I went to the viewing to comfort a 20-year old girl who was and is a very good friend of mine from AA. And although this young lady is only 20 years old, she has accumulated three consecutive years of 'clean' time and I've always looked up her as a model of sobriety and optimism. I never did see her that day; she arrived at the viewing later than I did. We did communicate later, via e-mail and a little bit via the telephone. The next time I would actually see her was last night at an AA anniversary. At this event however, her optimism was noticeably absent . . . . it seems a guy with whom she'd had a relationship and who'd broken it off only one day earlier, was at this anniversary with a different sober girl. I believe this guy also had about three or four years of consecutive sober time.

Also on hand last night, in fact one of the speakers, was a man who though only in his 40's has accumulated 27 years of consecutive sober time . . . he is something of an AA legend. His pitch accentuated all that he had acquired during this long sober run. One of those acquisitions he did not mention was a sharp-looking little wife . . . perhaps he left her out because he'd lost her since. I used to see her at all the functions. No more though, they are now either divorced or separated. He was not the first guy to lose this girl however, before she met him she'd been in a relationship with a man 'Mr. 27 years' had sponsored in AA. This sponsee had introduced them . . . and it has been many years since I last saw this other guy, but that night I did see him, the hate and bitterness he expressed towards this AA guru was real and intense.

Also in attendance at the anniversary was a chic-ly dressed urbane and quite foxy woman I've never seen before. She and "'Mr. 27 years" seemed sort of hooked up. A few tables over was another women whom I see at many AA functions. I believe she has had relationships with several AA guys. A few weeks ago at a bigger AA event down at the Jersey shore, I saw this young lady a few times with this guru. I have no idea if anything happened between them that weekend, but the hurt in her face was quite apparent as he cavorted about with the comelier, more polished women.

The final two actors in this passion play of life of which I was a part last night was a very attractive woman I kind of like . . . the feeling is decidedly Un*mutual. The shoulder she gave me, was as cold as cold could be. She has four years of sobriety, works a very good program, so I'd wanted to introduce her to player number last, this young girl I brought to the anniversary who's just coming around AA for the first time. Ms. 'four years' was not interested though, she was seemingly not in a very good mood. Perhaps the sour mood was because of the absence of any men at this function who fit her 'shopping list'. Maybe she thought of the previous year's anniversary and the tall handsome date she'd then had. I do not know, I didn't really get to talk to her. Perhaps the cold shoulder was because I'd gotten high again, maybe my "crying wolf" as I speak so often about God and morality and such, and then keep going out and getting high, was why she wanted no part of me. Maybe she thought it should not be an 18-year-old* girl *I was helping . . . . maybe she is right.*

And so now it is that next day . . . I can click another sober day on the old calendar. It was not fun being the last person to stand up (when they hit 11 days) at this anniversary's oldest-to-newest "countdown" of sobriety-time . . . . nor was it fun last fall when I stood up at a different anniversary at six. It was and is humbling. But for me, humbling is a good thing. For as I view, from my self-righteous mountaintop of celibacy, the debilitating goings-on down in the decayed valley of sexual immorality below, the "better than" screen I place between me and my fellow AA's, helps keeps me in the dark. And though gratitude alone should be my attitude towards my-not-exactly voluntary non-participation in the sexual jungle I see around me, it is not. For it is from atop this lofty holier-than-thou mount, right past the play-and-play-alike romps in the 'rooms', to the decadent denizens of prostitutes and crack to whence I descend when the "going gets rough". And my claim that these human beings I drag down farther into the muck with me are already down and out and not recovering people trying to stay sober, is as grotesque and contrived a rationalization as could be. 2000 years ago, when Jesus uttered the words "what you did for the least of my brothers, you did also for me," there was no segregated hierarchy involved with that word least.

I will leave soon to go across town and visit my father's last remaining sibling, my godmother Aunt Eleanor. She is in a beautiful upscale facility specifically designed to treat people with Alzheimer's disease. My Aunt EL was a beautiful and popular young lady in the financially tough yet happy 1930's in the McGowan-infested squares of Port Richmond. She was wed at 20 and a mother at 21 . . . probably specifically because in those days, at least in my traditional Irish Catholic family a "walk down the aisle" proceeded the end to which dating and romancing etc led. And the product of that early union, my first cousin Eleanor, would grow up to be, pure and simply the most physically beautiful woman I have ever personally known. She also had a grace and a charm and a decency and kindness that matched her looks. She would marry a man almost as handsome as she, a charming dashing dark Irishman cut in the Tyrone Power mode, named Frank. He too was a wonderful guy, a St Joe grad, like me . . . I got to know them pretty well as I babysat their four children when I was a young teenager.

But the husband would get caught up big-time in the mid-late 60's "God is dead" movement. Both he and El were heavy drinkers too—at family functions they often were among the most inebriated there. Frank would meet his end on a cold rainy night on a slick Connecticut highway. There was no booze involved, it was a weeknight and he was on his way home from work. Little El (as everyone in the family knew her—even though she was a statuesque, perfectly shaped 5' 9" or 10') kept it together for quite a few years after that, but gradually started to come apart. And when the coming apart began to take place and the stories and the rumors began to make their way through the grapevine of the family, I wondered if misgivings about Frank and his beliefs and the potential guilty verdict they might have elicited from the eternal court were part of her problem. If the letter I wanted to write to her to speak of this ever got sent, I really don't remember, I kind of think it didn't. "Gonna, wanna, shoulda"—the procrastination which has plagued me near all of my days was much in evidence then.

The booze eventually did become a problem for El though . . . there would be several days on end "no one knew where she was" benders . . . culminated by one where as a pedestrian, she was hit by a car. The damage from that accident plus the alcohol had caused severe brain damage and she would spend the last 15 years of her life in a rest home. She died about a year and a week ago.

. . . . and so now the visit to see my Aunt El has taken place. The deterioration from my last visit only 6 weeks ago was readily apparent. She soon will go on 'hospice care'; a term used to denote Medicare kicking in money for care as a patient nears the end. This visit was not as easy as the last. Easy mentions of the old days and her popularity had little effect. She did not seem to recognize me and was almost hostile. She wanted no parts of my pretentious self-indulgent little poem. I mentioned

the old neighborhood and that seemed to trigger a desperate determined "I want to go home" response. So when she got up to go I just walked along side. One good thing about people with Alzheimer's is that when they come up with an idea that ain't a real good one, they forget it pretty quick. We got up and sat down twice. So then I merely sat there with her. She nodded off, I nodded off. I looked at her and saw my dad's face when he neared the end of his Alzheimer's. I silently prayed that she would know some peace. And when she came out of her longest nap, I asked her if she remembered the Hail Mary and I said how my dad always used to say to me, "Jim say a Hail Mary for me, will ya." And so I did—right there—I said one for him and for her. And for some reason, maybe because she saw the wet in my eyes, but for whatever reason, she softened a bit. For the first time in a couple of days in fact, she even ate her lunch—a whole grilled cheese sandwich (minus the crust of course!) AND an entire piece of cake. And when I got up to leave and I told her I loved her, I think she knew I meant it. And when I clutched her hand and kissed her forehead, I was rewarded with that wonderful smile . . . the trademark little crinkles around those beautiful eyes (eyes I never realized looked so much like my dad's) were there, a kingdom of their own amidst the wrinkles. And I realized as I drove home that a spin in the hay with the most beautiful woman in the world could not have warmed the cockles of my heart as much as that smile did.

So my dear Aunt El will rest in peace soon enough. She knew all too little of this peace in this life. She was still young when she became a widow for the first time. She lost that first husband, the father of her only two children, while she was still in her thirties. Her second husband was a successful lawyer but also was vain and cruel. Her divorce from him was the first in the family and caused quite a stir. I believe he was dead before she married a third husband—that husband died over fifteen years ago. Her only other child Joe, like his sister, exceedingly handsome and charming, died of a heart attack shoveling snow in his 50th year.

One year ago on April 5th, the day after Easter I sat in a pew next to her daughter, little El,'s coffin. I had one day sober again at the time. And as I sat there she was somehow connected to this "I CAN stay sober for ONE day at a time" thought I had—and that "this was the time I was going to get it." I was wrong again. Now one year later I have that same sober date . . . the same one I had when I came into the rooms of AA eight years ago.

Of course all four of Little El's children were at the funeral. All are successful, married and are parents—they and their spouses and kids are among the nicest people you'd ever want to meet. When I see El's kids (and her kids' kids), I am reminded of an e-mail I received not too long ago—of a discovery made by a forest ranger cleaning up after a Northern California forest fire. What he found was a dead charred burnt-to-a-crisp bird, its wings frozen in ash but fully extended. And when the ranger pushed it over, out from under those wings, four little chicks flew to safety. In like manner, I think of my beautiful and beauteous cousin Eleanor—she also kept it together long enough to know that her young were safe.

The title of this little essay comes from a song that has another line that goes ". . . . but I'll know my song well before I start singing . . . " I sometimes wonder if my song is the right one, or even more so if I worry too much about the 'song' and not enough about the people to whom I sing. But mostly I suspect my problem is about the absence of real humble gratitude to the Source of my song and my everything else.

The kid they found in that hotel room was not graced with the traditional, "mother/father dutifully guide them" family that all my cousins and I were. Nor was the young girl I brought with me to this anniversary last night, nor was my jilted in-pain 20-yr old friend . . . nor was the woman who had no time for me. But the latter three have been exposed to Alcoholics Anonymous and the 12-steps of recovery . . . and a way of life that is supposed to be all about Christian caring and fellowship and not about using each other to stuff appetites. From the deepest crevices of my being, almost like the earth quaking, my heart reverberates in the feeling that, more than anything else, my generation's stark rejection of the idea that the art of making love is an act reserved ONLY for a man and a woman who have made a sacred vow to each other is at the root of all our problems. Maybe if I STAY sober, some day I will 'shout it from the top of the highest of mountains . . . .'

Aunt El came out of her little bad spell soon after. She started eating again, the hospice care was postponed and by the time I'd see her the next October she was doing a lot better.

* * *

A little after midnight—Easter Sunday just ended.

The $40 price tag for Easter dinner at the country club of which my brother Tommy is a member was like nothing in light of the warmth and delight of having dinner with him, his wife Cindy, his four children, my mom, my brother Mark and his wife Eileen, and my brother Tony and my sister Sally. (That my sister Mary Ellen is in Cincinnati and that her two daughters were also not there was a real shame.) A major 'food hangover' is now my companion—a result of overstuffing myself at the sumptuous buffet.

Perhaps it is my imagination, (probably it is my imagination,) but Tommy's youngest, Caroline, she who was not yet born that brutal summer of '97 when my trips up to his house provided those so necessary moments of shelter from the storm, to me has eyes as blue and skin as soft and milky white as only one other person I ever remember—and that was my first cousin Eleanor. And maybe too it was just my imagination but the first time I really looked into those eyes, perhaps a month or two after the March 19, 1999 day they were part of the magnificent little bundle that came into this world, from behind them I noticed an inexplicable glimmer of recognition. And I imagined that glimmer has something to do with "little El" who had died about one week after Caroline was born. I suppose there is nothing wrong with positive imagining. Last night Caroline was thoroughly enjoying the little hand slap thing—and her older sister Caitlin, was *still* saying I did it wrong.

The rain is falling pretty steady out my window now. As promised by the weatherman, the absolutely magnificent day gave way to a rainy miserable night. Ireland-type weather will be with us for a few days now. An umbrella and the "Nature Conservatory" hooded rain jacket that I carried to and from Ireland without ever having once used it, will make the little rosary walk I am about to take a bit more palatable.

The bad weather reminds me of a eulogy story spoken at Little El's funeral two Easter Mondays ago—about how as a child her daughter was really sad that it rained on Easter because the beautiful Easter dress El had made for her would have to be covered by a jacket. *"Think of the kids with dresses not as pretty as yours. Because of the rain now, they won't feel embarrassed by having dresses not so nice."* That's the kind of woman El was. I heard one more story about her—this from, Toby, a friend of my sister's who was in the same Catholic High School class as El. What she told me was that several of the nuns had been really tough on El . . . that they must have figured someone that smart and that beautiful and that kind, had to be something of a fraud. But what amazed Toby was the absolute grace and poise and charm with which El handled the mistreatment.

Special is nowhere near special enough of a word to describe my dear departed first cousin.

But I'm reminded of how *un*special my still-struggling friend Steve feels. He is the one whose dad I spoke to over while I was over in Ireland. This Easter afternoon, he drank "about 4 or 5 shots" to take the sting out of the loneliness. He has a job now—from 10 PM until 7 in the morning at Home Depot. I believed him when, this afternoon, he told me he'd drink no more today.

I told him to go home and write down all the reasons he was sad and lonely and depressed—maybe this will begin the process where he can some day get to the point that he realizes the tattered coats of depression and loneliness are temporary coverings that will fade away in time. I told him to do this and to then maybe offer to take his father out for Easter dinner at a diner somewhere.

Hank Williams sure had that one right—lonesomeness sure *can* make ya cry.

April 18, 2001
Tuesday

Yesterday afternoon I attended at a lecture down at Penn's bookstore given by a Penn MD named Andrew Newberg who'd written a book called *Why God Won't Go Away.*

When I mentioned how his work takes some sting out of my "Penn is a typical Ivy League hotbed for godless intellectualism," supposition, he wondered where I got that impression, that Penn is really hot on the topic of scientifically measuring spirituality. Good for Penn. Bad for me and the over-blowing of my Joshua horn at walls that are already seemingly coming down.

What Newberg is doing down at Penn is de Chardinish evolutionary magnificence to the hilt. That he and his partner persuaded Tibetan monks and Franciscan nuns to allow themselves to literally have their brains tapped while doing their meditation, is in my eyes, beyond cool. And what Dr. Newburg and his unfortunately recently deceased associate, Eugene D'Aquili, found when they did this was . . . that in the areas of the brain used to specifically "keep tabs on the you/not you dichotomy", the activity was way down, when, first the monks and then the nuns, reached their peak meditative state. The authors thus found it perfectly logical that the eight Tibetan meditators description of what happened during meditation was all about feelings of oneness with the Universe, or that the nuns description of the moment as a "tangible sense of the closeness of God".

"What would happen if the OAA (Outer association area that they called it) *had no information upon which to work? we wondered. Would it continue to search for the limits of the self? With no information flowing in from the senses, the OAA wouldn't be able to find any boundaries. What would the brain make of that? Would the orientation area interpret its failure to find the borderline between self and the*

outside world to mean that such a distinction doesn't exist? In this case the brain would have no choice but to perceive that the self is endless and intimately interwoven with everyone and everything the mind senses, And the perception would feel absolutely real . . .

In the words of the Hindu Upanishads

"Forgetting that they were ever separate rivers,
So do all creatures lose their seperateness
When they at last merge into"

(This direct quote from the book is on pgs 6 and 7, At this late date I'm not going to get involved with footnotes.)

Science and religion. Again I quote Einstein:

"Science without religion is blind
Religion without science is a cripple"

Among the attendees at Newberg's lecture was a gentleman who thought it "silly" that people think of euphoric states the nuns spoke of as coming from God. I was one of several other attendees who phrased my 'question' as a forum to contradict this guy. But this guy did stick around after the lecture—he was going to talk to Dr Newburg. I gave him a Yan Xin Qigong flyer, telling him "these guys meditate like crazy, and they think I'm crazy with all my Qigong/God talk." There is absolutely nothing wrong with thinking your way to spirituality or God—even if you refuse to call it God. But again it's got to be something capitalized you get to—it's got to be bigger and better and of a different ballpark that the plain ol' gray matter . . . that matters . . . like infinitely even . . . . The "deeper spirituality" pamphlet gave me the idea that a person could even work the steps *into* a belief in God. The unbelief could be the first step admission over which a person is powerless, then the paradoxical second step jump in belief in any power greater . . . then to make that decision and then go through the 4-9 action steps, and see what happens. Even if belief does not result, living the program would almost surely make anyone's life a lot better . . . one need only refer to the handful of atheistically bent, sober recovered alcoholics I know for proof.

* * *

The car radio told me it was 3:50 by the time I got off the El in Frankford after the lecture. Parking at Penn is a royal pain. Plus I get to nap and read a bit on the El. A book that was given to me by Father Mac called *Taking Sides-the Education of a Militant Mind* is what I am currently reading. But I'm going to take it back to Mac as it is painfully boring. (Like a nap per every three pages boring.) I'll have to go to another of author Michael Harrington's many works to try to capture the gist of the his socialist/atheistic philosophy. But in his introduction when he states he taught the first political science class he ever attended because the president at Queens College was on the lookout for stimulating teachers regardless of degrees, I got a strong sense of how godless intellectualism made its way in our University system. I could give less of a crap about "formal qualifications", but I wonder how open was the mind that found Harrington so "stimulating".

But because the El ride was so slow and because I'd puttered around down at Penn so long, I was too late getting home to cover the 4:15 game I was supposed to umpire all the way up in Bucks County—well north of the city. A father or assistant coach (or maybe nobody) having to umpire their game, made for an even colder afternoon for a bunch of little girls from St. John Bosco and some other school who'd gathered to play. My apology phone call was a major case of "closing the barn door after the horse got out." That "Get a watch" thing just jumped up a notch or two on my "to do" list.

As that list gets longer and things don't get knocked off it, I wonder am I getting closer to or farther from that first drink. And then I wonder am I being too hard on myself. As I drift into the next day, it is now **April 19 Thursday morning at 6:00 AM** and I realize this journal will go on for at least a little while. The "keep writing, what's the rush for publication" words of that New York agent resonate beautifully. As the birds chirp sweetly out my window, the "look at the birds in the field, does not to Lord take care of them. Do you not think he'd take care of you, his most prized creation?" paraphrased scripture reading, echoes just as sweetly in my head.

And so I will head off to California on the super cheap rates they have through June. There, in the Napa Valley, I will find Helen Betz, the niece of my father's mother, Natalie Devlin McGowan. Helen is 91 still sharp as a tack and keeps in touch with my mom (who else?) via nice involved once-a-year-at-Christmas letters. I'll also make the Pittsburgh, Chicago, Cincinnati, Kentucky, Chicago, Akron trip after a week back home following Mother's Day. The Outer Banks trip will end the Saturday before.

But in the meantime, after this weekend's trip up to Vermont etc, I will stay close to Penn. Penn really is a special place. One day *Why We Can't Get Rid of God*, the next, Tom Wolfe. Yes *that* Tom Wolfe spoke yesterday and his delightful, fast, witty, never boring spiel, was exactly what I'd expect of him. "Some form of reporting is needed in all writing" was the part of TW's pitch with which Mailer, Updike, Irving—the *real* novelists—seem to have a problem. The vehemence of their critiques of Wolfe's latest work were really something. One of them, I think Mailer, likened reading Wolfe to making love to a 300-lb woman . . . to which the thin-as-a-rail, white-suit-with-spats-southern-gentleman-stylish-to-a-fault TW replied, "I happen to know that Mailer *does* sleep with 300-lb women." Methinks Wolfe would be more approving of this account that Mailer or the boys.

As I left the place, having chowed down on the major good and Penn-proper buffet, Wolfe was still stuck in the line of people who, not-so-surreptitiously, wanted his ear personally—the way it always happens at these gigs. I sort of rudely butted in, complimenting that *Bonfire of the Vanities* hangover description.

He smiled back "Oh that was one I had to get from other peoples' input."

Wolfe is writing a book on college living so he's hanging out on college campuses for a bit. I sure hope I run into him down at Penn some time in the next couple of weeks. I'd love to take him to Callahan's Grille—right across the Schuylkyll River from Penn in the section known as Schuylkyll—and owned by my good buddy Mike Callahan. A stone's throw away from Penn—a neighborhood bar to the max—and as far removed from the proper toufou-ish buffet at the Writer's House as Wolfe is from Updike. Callahan can hang big time. In some of my more notorious "cross the line" loads back in the day, he got stuck with me as the other members of our drinking/traveling crew had vacated or gone off to other pursuits. My back was watched by he a plenty—it might have been broken once or twice otherwise. He also is a piss. One night coming out of his local church, his wife wondered about a bunch of guys standing around smoking cigarettes. Turns out it was the break of the Friday night AA meeting that is held there. "Oh, they're those AA guys," I can picture the side-of-the-mouth delivery he uses for the real good ones, "you go there if you want a cigarette, a cup of coffee, or a cliché". TW would get a major kick out of MC.

And so now it is time to pack and head on up to the town in the northeastern Pennsylvania mountain region called *Jim Thorpe* to see Judge Latrelle—then off to Manhattan tomorrow and Vermont for the weekend—then friend Jackie B in Long Island and the band moe. in Jersey on Monday. My mom and my brother Mark and his wife Eileen are on their way to the Virgin Islands to attend the wedding of their (and my) friend Joan, affectionately know as Soeve'. Mom's foot is seemingly getting worse. And I'm beginning to get a bit concerned about the care she is receiving by her podiatrist—particularly his foot-dragging re getting a nurse in here to dress it each day. I wonder if his Medicare reimbursement would be cut if such an action would be taken. When the actions in question are as close to home as the health of my mother, the intensity of my growing realization that I need question the motives of anyone whose primary concern in life is profit, is heightened greatly.

The bad toe is on the other foot from the one I wrote about last August.

Assumptions about my mom's foot

I wonder when was the last time the full moon fell exactly on August 15th. As the full moon glares clearly above right now, and my mom lies peacefully and comfortably in her bed down the hall, it seems very cool that it happened this year.

My mom is 81 years old. She has arthritis, diabetes, clogged arteries and God knows what else. Aug 15 is the day the feast of the Assumption of the Blessed Mother is celebrated by the Catholic Church. Of all the feast days it is probably the one that most invokes "you're putting me on" s . . . it is surely the one the Protestant Christian Churches most readily disposed of. The deal is that Mary, the Blessed Mother of Jesus was assumed into heaven, spirit AND body—sans decay. There is no Biblical corroboration of this, so the real Bible-quoters of the New REAL CHRISTIAN churches see this baby a prime example of the banal idol worshipping they deem Catholicism to be.

But for the CATHOLIC Catholics, it is a big deal. Being that it is the only holy day of the summer, we who have access to the Jersey shore can get involved with an after-mass "procession to the sea"—with the priests going out in boats and all the folks getting sprinkled with blessed ocean water and the like. And today, less that 24 hours after my mom had spent the afternoon in an off-shore emergency room due to a "false alarm" tightness in her chest, my sister wheeled her down to the beach for this procession. She walked the rest of the way to the water, and even though they were covered, for the first time in two summers, she placed her feet in the Atlantic Ocean . . . and she loved it . . . she was really moved by the whole thing.

How much, if any, actual physical healing got done in this is doubtful . . . if the feet are any less wounded, if the arteries are any less clogged—but I will tell you this, my mom's spirit certainly seems lifted . . . and I sure as hell know mine is. And I do know about one year ago her doctor told her that he really did not think that the diabetic ulcer on her big toe would ever heal—and that today what was an approximately quarter-sized red infected hole is now a barely discernible almost completely healed, skin-colored sliver. I do not know if rubbing the flower that had sat on the case wherein the remains of St. Theresa of the Little Flower rested on her visit to Philadelphia last fall, on to that foot had anything to do with this healing. Her proud careful and exceedingly efficient podiatrist most surely would not think so. Who knows? I know it was on the day that would have been my dad's 86th birthday that the flower was given to me. And I do know it was at least several weeks after that when the wound finally began to close. In God's time anyone?

Knowing certainly is cool. If we did not know one plus one equaled two, we never would have emerged from the caves. But I'll take believing along with my knowing. I know my life has much more meaning because of it—it is much more exciting and intriguing. When you get right down to it, a computer can know—it takes a person to believe.

* * *

While the prayers for her have been rather strong and intense lately, other thoughts that have crossed my mind, like fasting, are being ignored. Driving up 95 after dropping off the crew at the airport this morning, I thought about words I spoke at a meeting last night—about how the steps take me to an admission of weakness and not to garnering of personal strength. That thought frames the "faith can move a mountain, but you better bring your shovel" dilemma I struggle with so often. It is not from the pricks of the rose bushes on the flowers of Theresa where the healing power comes, it comes from the sharing of the microscopic sliver of my faith to the boundless faith and reverence she had—a faith that was demonstrated in the actions and sacrifices she, in her lifetime, made. That my actual doing and sacrifices, on a daily basis, are coming up a bit short, can be a good thing though—*if* they demonstrate that there is still too much *me* in my spirituality.

It is late, I gotta go . . . I'll take TW's word for it "If I'm done my three triple-spaced pages a day limit . . . . I'll quit in mid-sentence."

Friday
April 20, 2001
Somerset, New Jersey
4:00 AM

Going out to get the laptop out of my car, I realized my niece's computer and the floppy disc in my bag would do the trick. Unlike way back on February 8th, it certainly was not cold in the apartment. And even though I'd only been asleep for about four hours the "should I get up and write" back and forth battle had been relatively brief. (The "well you can manually write it down and then transpose later" option had never really been one—I simply hate transposing. In fact, I had the nerve to ask my sister-in-law to type the written entry from my trip up to Derryvilla last month. La Pidgeone—still typing for me after all these years. Her buddies nickname for my lanky, oft-spacey sis-in-law is 'the space pigeon'. Thus my "I should carry a tape recorder as I drive" thought I'd had as I'd driven up to this part of the world yesterday, I know now, is a scratch. This is of course, as is most nearly everything else, subject to change.)

Jim Thorpe, Pa and an afternoon with Judge Latrelle had been stop one of this particular junket. Again, just like when I'd come up here in the summer of 99, I'd been treated like royalty. I even stretched out on the floor of the Judge's chambers for one of my little naps while he scanned certain of the pictures of my Ireland trip. That he is to go to Ireland in September and meet Concepta and Dympna and the others delights me to no end. It was on a visit to the judge in July of 99 when in discussing how hurt I was at the negative reaction of some of my relatives to the first version of this story, when his sage counsel, "This is *your* story, Jim . . . if you don't write it that way, it won't work," helped me immensely.

Dynamite directions and I-287 had made the trip across New Jersey to here and Elizabeth's apartment in this big beautiful old house, on Elizabeth Street in Bound Brook New Jersey, a piece of cake. I just remembered how when I'm on that second joyful mystery, Mary's visit to her cousin Elizabeth, I usually think about going to Cincinnati to see my sister Mary Ellen, Elizabeth's mom.

Mary Ellen should be in Ireland now. Again I sure hope she decides to include Cavan in her travel plans. A visit with the McGowan and Sheridan relatives, and Angela and the Gaffneys and Michael Smith and the rest of the characters and sights and smells of Cavan can really do wonders for a person's soul. The judge is in for a real treat next fall.

Where I will be next fall, is really sort of up in the air right now. I doubt I'll be working in *Smiley Burgers* as did Leonard end up doing in the movie *American Beauty* that Eliz and I watched last night. I can now add one more example of my closed minded assness to the old list. My, "I don't need to see another movie glorifying illicit sex" edict was way off base. *AB* was wonderful.

To me, the theme of the move to me was not too dissimilar from the "It all comes out in the wash" one I've pretty well adopted lately. Fr. Kelty sure has a good sense for it—so too, it seems, does my niece Elizabeth. About a year ago as I sort of pondered the "should I or shouldn't I" leave the job thing to just about everybody or anybody who'd listen, Elizabeth wrote back something like, "I hate to quote Nike, but maybe you should 'just do it.'" Last night her advice was "end the book". That advice I'll take—this little trip will be it.

During the movie last night, my niece's father Paul telephoned. It was in that summer of '99 that Paul, who was divorced from my sister more than 25 years ago, finally got around to making amends—only a few weeks after I'd visited the judge in Jim Thorpe that first time actually. Mary Ellen's choosing to share that amends letter with the entire family provided some amazing healing for us all. I, for one on the day we put Cougar down, was in need of much healing that day. And that Elizabeth and Laura, her older sister and my godchild, were included in that entire family unit that was there for me, helped immensely. Laura who works for environmental issues in Washington DC, and who really loves nature and animals and the like, was really torn up when we took Cougar away. Somehow the intensity of her tears made mine sting a little less.

So as I lay there in bed just a little spell ago, pondering Lenny's beatific post-shot-in-his-brain musings, I purposely popped into my head, visions of Cougs speeding across the football field down in Philly's Wissanoming Park where I used to walk him. Heaven really does not have to wait, you might say. Then, there's also always dad in that blue bathing suit . . . .

April 21, 2001
East Dorsett, Vermont

On page 112 in the "first *new Catechism of the Catholic Church* in more that 400 years" (a direct quote from the back cover—400 years! Is THAT how old that Baltimore thing we read was? I'd think not actually because Baltimore as of 400 years ago, I'd think, was only the name of some Lord chasing after foxes over in England somewhere . . . but I digress.), under the heading **Man's First Sin,** is the following:

> *Man, first tempted by the devil, let his trust in his Creator die in his heart and, abusing his freedom, disobeyed God's command. This is what man's first sin consisted of. All subsequent sin would be disobedience toward God and lack of trust in his goodness.*

In that statement I find a somewhat open-minded and reasonable way of dealing with the issue of original sin. Unfortunately I also found many references to the sins of our 'first parents' Adam and Eve that insinuate but do not exactly say, that a literal interpretation on the garden of Eden story is required. The worse thing I found on the topic was on page 110:

> *The Church, which has the mind of Christ, knows very well that we cannot tamper with the revelation of original sin without undermining the mystery of Christ.*

In chronological order; in claiming the Church, HAS the mind of Christ—I find dangerous presumption; in the words *we cannot tamper* I find censorship; and in the unwritten but implied horror of "undermining the mystery of Christ", I find the deadly "we preach salvation through the risen Christ" competition I heard from the priest back in Ireland.

I'd driven directly from my niece's apartment to Graymoor, because the two stops I'd intended to make in Manhattan had not panned out and it was a nice in-between place to break up the ride to my eventual destination—here in Vermont and the *Back to Basics* weekend seminar at the Bill Wilson House in East Dorsett.

But really I went to Graymoor because I wanted to talk to a priest about my dogmatic concerns. A priest friend directed me to the new catechism. Mike the monk's words about how de Chardin had got into trouble because he never consulted a spiritual director have not fallen of deaf ears. For someone like me, whose difficulty at listening was a paramount cause to the effect of all those relapses, it would seem obvious that getting opinions of others is important. (One sponsor told me I *nod* well.)

As for what I found in the section on the *always* virginity of Mary, I found nothing substantial, hardly anything even quotable—I found that we have the document, but nothing really about why we do. The "*Jesus is Mary's only son, but her spiritual motherhood extends to all men whom he indeed came to save*" quote, on page 142 did not do much for me.

To be perfectly honest, I'd hoped and expected to find a more open-minded treatment of these Church dogmas that trouble me so.

There was a time way back in the day, the summer of '71, I think, and a few of us were riding down the Ocean City shore for the day. My buddy Leo, for whatever reason, decided to spend the day acting out *The Mr. Big Shit Show.* Leo, of course was the lead character, *Mr. Big Shit*, and he was patterned on a little kid show clowns or whatever . . . the "big shit" name referred to how the logical man would react to the pearls of wisdom handed down by these characters. So Leo, in an extremely high-pitched voice, dropped such pearls for the entire day. And to even point further to the banality and blowhardedness of his remarks, he'd introduce each comment with "Well, well . . . WELL . . ." I was the trusty sidekick—a Boo-Boo-from-The-Yogi-Bear-Show-sounding character named *Little Fuck-up*. Other players popped in and out of the "show" . . . I was there pretty steady. And Leo, whose ability to sustain idiocy was legendary (ask Beast who had to listen to him'n'Gregory do the "Pete . . . repeat" thing for an entire different 1.5 hour ride down the shore one time) really kept it up.

Among Mr. Big Shit's gems was . . . . "*Did you ever wonder why dogs sniff each others assholes?"*

"no, Mr. Big Shit, WHY do dogs sniff each other's assholes?'

"well, well . . . WELLLL little fuck-up, you see wayyyy back in the beginning of time allll the dogs had a convention. But it reaaaallly stunk in the convention. So the chairman told all the dogs to go hang their assholes out in the coat room. But then there was a biiiiig fire at the convention and the dogs ran out and grabbed whatever asshole they could. To this day, they're still checking if they have the right one."

Later towards the end of the day, being a fine interlocutor, not to mention a *great* "little fuck-up", I posed this query to Mr. BS, *"Mr. Big Shit why do dogs have such long tongues . . . . ?"*

"Well, well . . . . WELLL little fuck up, wayyyy back in the beginning of time, a dog went and licked what it thought was a piece of candy. But it turned out to be a piece of gum . . . and his tongue got allll stretched trying to lick it up."

Being the have to know kind of guy I am, even as "little fuck-up", I wondered, *"But Mr. Big-shit, that was one dog way back in the beginning of time, Why do ALL dogs have long tongues?"*

And as I sit here right now and think about it, in a Lacanian, Ann Gaffneyish "in the absurdity is the answer" sort of way, Leo, Mr., Big Shit himself's response of, *"well, well, WELL little fuck-up . . . allll the other dogs did it too,"* frames my problem with the whole, "they did it, we're guilty too" original sin thing.

April 22, 2001
Sunday morning 2:45 AM
East Dorsett, Vermont

Listening to the perfect harmony of the crickets outside, I think about nature tapes people listen to so they can relax—and it calls to mind the time me and Soeve' were sitting in the outside bar of the Springfield Inn down the Jersey shore town of Sea Isle City. There, Joan (Soeve), in reference to the nice breeze blowing in off the ocean, said, "man that breeze feels so good. It's almost like artificial air conditioning."

Howard, the little Jewish guy who named her, (her real last name is not all that close to Soeve—but he based her nickname on that and it stuck) is among the crew that went down to the Virgin Islands for her wedding. That he, Sandy (another co-habitant of the old shore houses I used to be in), Joan's dynamite parents and family will all be there, will make the time a lot nicer for my mom. Sandy, Soeve and Howard were among those invited to my mom's big 80th birthday bash two years ago—they are that much a part of the family. Soeve' husband, *is* her hubby by now, also was there and he too is a real nice guy.

Howard was an absolute riot on the video at mom's party—back in the day, he and me shared many a hilarious load together. I was not all that great on the video. The wolves of my addiction howled even that night. I came real close to getting high right after the party was over even. But I put it off—did what I was told—five minutes from success. And after a brief deep nap, I woke up free and refreshed—went down to the midnight meeting and shared about how grateful I was.

Two weeks later, on the Sunday of the Super Bowl, I came a lot closer to the flame. I'd found out that a new ATM card had arrived the previous day and was ready to roll. Somehow though, I didn't. I was five some months sober at the time and figured I was ready to have access to cash. I was wrong. The shielding in place that AA's Big Book states is "doomed to failure", because I'd not changed enough. For two more months I did the "yea-nay" cha-cha with that first hit. The Holy Saturday load that year was the second shoe of the first that had fallen eight days prior.

ALL this part of the process of my life—and in fact of my recovery. IF I am here—then that is the only way to view there—as a necessary part of the process. I had to go through the pain until I DID enough (as in working the steps—*again and again*) to allow the grace of God to enter. And for me, and for a lot if us I'd suspect, the final straw was that buried, hidden imperceptible pride that had to be gotten through.

What is it, if not pride, that prevents most of us from getting down on out knees and saying an actual *praye*r? We'll chant, we'll ponder, we'll meditate, we'll read all kinds of things, we'll 'think kind thoughts' but we will not pray. And what we really will not do is that simple little Oxford Group-type daily guidance thing, where we find out what God had in store for us on that particular day.

But all this too is part of the process of the world's recovery. We had to go through the Inquisitions and the Reformations and the Hitlers and Stalins and all the other assorted pains and inequities to get to here. But all during those times, in the decency and goodness, saintliness even, of a lot of the people, the hand of God was apparent. John of the Cross and Theresa of Avila, I've been told, were around during a time when Rome was at one of its lowest moments. Like the experiments at Penn almost, perhaps the absence of outer peace, induced them to go inward—and there they found something similar to what they've been finding in the East for years. But even the Buddhist message—how bad has that message also been butchered? A devout Buddhist monk I met at Gethsemani told me the incredibly holy man of *Autobiography of a Yogi* would be appalled at the cesspool of moral infidelity in the California fellowship he left behind. The monk is also a psychotherapist who ministers to the monks at Gethsemani several weeks each year. He's no longer a Catholic though, and I felt bad for him when he'd remain behind at communion last August. He'd make it to almost all of the offices too, but was denied, or chose to deny himself, the body and blood of Christ.

All part of the process—this cesspool of today of which I speak is too part of the process, Joyce had to question; the intellectuals had to do their thing. Even Howard Stern. "Until you are stuffed." The lovely girl I met via the Internet last summer said to me, "Stern serves a purpose." I didn't dwell on what she meant. But this girl didn't fit my shopping list, and when I saw her with another seemingly nice guy one night, I chose not to even say hello. Perhaps she does not *know* she does not *need* a man to be happy . . . certainly it is not always pleasant to be alone, but in the end we are really alone. DeMello quotes George Bernard Shaw, who, when at a boring cocktail party, was asked "are you enjoying yourself?" responded "that is the *only* thing I am enjoying here."

And of course I can say that—I can quote a thousand daily meditations that make the point but do I mean it? Have I really bought out of the *need*—of our society's preoccupation with sex? I think of Richard Gere, the famed Buddhist, for whom Cindy Crawford was not even good enough. Certainly I know not what went down with them but I know I've seen Ms Crawford on the Jay Leno Show and she seems like a pretty decent down-to-earth woman. (If any super-model can be down to earth!) Thoughts of Ted Turner maybe trolling the singles bars in Atlanta tickles me no end. Jane Fonda I heard left to become a "Christian" . . . which is fine and dandy but I hope she's not joined a "have to get baptized as an adult and if you don't you're not saved" cult. Although noting the ideological extremism to which Jane tends to lean, I expect that's right where she is. (You should have heard the deafening silence at the *Christian Back to Basics* meeting yesterday when I suggested the "burying the talons" gospel might have been Jesus' way of telling us to not ONLY USE the Bible!) Jane, whose *legend* of a dad went through four or five or six wives—and who did not even tell his kids about the suicide of wife number one—their mother . . . the trickle-down effect of our enslavement to instinct. Compare him and his life to Jimmy Cagney or Jimmy Stewart, or other *squares* who, like the swans, kept the same mate for life.

I'm sure Ted, the self-proclaimed high priest of the New Age (he paid for a World Symposium on global spirituality a while back, making himself the main speaker) who, again, controls about half of our media, would never stoop so low as to simply call up Heidi Fleisch. Charlie Sheen, bless his soul, who even tried marriage, even if it only lasted about twenty minutes, was at least honest enough to go there. Charlie, whose typecast "wooo, you mean you got like a lesbian thing going on here," line in *Being John Malkovich* brought tears of laughter to my eyes, one night forced the f—word in on an appearance on the Dennis Miller Show with more frequency than does Dennis drop inappropriate metaphors on Monday Night Football. And Dennis, whose opening night salvo about how a Higher Power had changed the whole world of quarterback Curt Warner absolutely knocked my socks off, regardless of what he says about God or religion is at least a thinking social critic. Same with Dennis Leary . . . . same with Chris Rock, whose *"MartinlutherKing . . . martinlutherking . . . . all he ever talked about was non-violence, non-violence . . . . well I'll tell you this . . . you go the ANY MartinLutherKing boulevard or street or avenue anywhere in this country and you gon' find the most violent muthafuckin street in the city"* rap near forced me to pull over my car one Martin Luther King day, I was laughing so hard.

But then there is the real high priest of egomania, of stuffing and gorging of self . . . good old Howard, who from his lofty throne at NBC sends his poison out each morning as his hordes of followers gobble it up in the same way the poor defenseless sheep and cattle become foot and mouth or mad cow victims because of the cheap slop fed to them by we 'profit is king' heathens.

Even Dylan in his long storied career has gone through women like sweat socks. You were right Bob that society babe should *not* have let other people get her kicks for her . . . but how many kicks did you and/or your entourage get out of her svelte lithesome body? But then there was Lennon. I was one of the majority of the world who said, "what does he see in Yoko?" Yoko who, during his drinking, drugging, "hang out with Neilsen" carousing days, even set John up with a beautiful young Eurasian friend so he could stuff himself full, provided him finally with the proper shelter from the storm. Take *Julia* about his mom, and *Woman* about Yoko, and you can see how and why John became the giant of a man he was. But he chose to live among the *people*, and he paid the ultimate price. If you think about it though, his tenure here surely was the penultimate—for if ever anyone deserved to "shine on like the moon and the sun and the stars," it was he.

But have I finally really bought out of the *have to have* in regards to women and sex? I think of that last using partner—she was the best, the most talented at the sexual acting-out part. But on my part, nothing happened. Perhaps it was the presence of her prayer bench right next to us. I didn't smoke *that much* coke that day. And no, Woody, it was not a bad thing but a good one that my *drive* got diverted that day . . . that my conscience got in the way. I might not be sober today otherwise . . . I might not even be alive. I'd suspect your *Everything You Wanted To Know About Sex* pathetic little conscience/priest, never impedes as you make love to your step-daughter/wife. My money, for what its worth, will never be shelled out to see any of your new stuff—not unless I hear about a sincere amends made to Mia Farrow . . . and to that daughter/wife for the jaundiced view of family and decency you pound into her. For someone to write a love story as warm and moving as *Broadway Danny Rose*, and to then do what you did, frankly turns my stomach.

I think of that day—that last load. After the pipe had run dry, she wanted me to take her across town to see a concert. She would even have paid. But I could never go on that kind of *date* with a prostitute. Talk about owing an apology.

Then and now.

I suspect, foot problems or not, mom will come home Tuesday in a lot better spirits than she was when I dropped her and Mark and Eileen off at the airport some 93 hours ago. I lit candles for her in front of both the statues of St. Anthony and of St. Teresa of the Little Flower in the tiny beautiful little St. Jerome's Church up the street from here. I think of Tony as mom's "everything" saint, and Theresa as taking care of her foot. No crime in that, I suppose.

I went to the little church last night for 7:00 mass. And because it is so small, the statue of Anthony sits right next to the kneeler on the left hand side—the Mary side. (And I'm reminded of how my buddy Jimmy Kelly in reference to which side you sit on when you go to a baseball game says "when you're born you get stamped 'first base or third base.'"—I'm a third base guy). But in this church, on the "Mary side" the Mary statue is smaller and is embedded into a carved-out-in-the-stucco alcove high up above. And directly below her is a statue of Joseph holding the baby Jesus. On the right side of the church, normally the St Joseph (3d base) side, in the same alcove spot is a statue of the Sacred Heart of Jesus . . . . no other statue is below it, but next to the kneeler in front, are the candles and the smaller statue of Theresa—and her customary holding of the flowers. I guess this artistry is kind of appropriate because Mary pretty much always says in her apparitions to pray to Jesus, in one I think, even specifically, to His Sacred Heart. And I'm reminded of the girl from the New Christian Church back in Ireland who when I mentioned Mary, went busily scurrying through her Bible for *proof* that Mary was not that big of a deal . . . that she prays to *Jesus only*.

I never really thought about the relationship of Jesus to Joseph. I think of that wonderful *Jesus* movie that was on CBS for last but not this Easter time. Right before he starts his public life, Jesus is shown as a carpenter beyond compare—a customer is heartily admiring the work he'd done. I'd think he got that way with*out* heavenly intercession, that it was more the result of dutifully copying the work of his stepfather Joseph. I wonder if perhaps, this book of James author, who maybe was another son of Joseph, likewise learned the carpenter trade real well. And maybe viewing the goings on as head of the Christian/Jewish community in Jerusalem, he saw and heard the various letters and books that were going around about Jesus. And maybe what he noticed was missing was a carpenter-practical-type approach to perceiving and doing God's will.

So he wrote a book about it.

8:45 PM

It seems funny that I've struggled so with the when and how to end this book, considering that a major spiel in it is about taking the twelve steps to the world, and that I just sat though a closing meeting of this *Back to Basics* group who are doing such a magnificent job of doing just that. Last night at the Saturday night speaker meeting, my 95-year-old chum James Houck mentioned how his two-way "Listening to God" approach that we B2Bers do, was always the cornerstone of the *Oxford Group*/turned *Moral Rearmament*/now called *Initiatives of Change*. This practical no-nonsense, nuts'n'bolts way to have God guide our actions each and every day, is such a cornerstone of Jim's spirituality, that the sort-of biography Wally P wrote about him is called *How to Listen to God—A Guide for Successful Living through the Practice of Two-way Prayer*.

Jim's guidance has led him many places . . . and last night as he asked for questions after his magnificent 45-minute "never-for-a-moment dull" share, when I reminded him of a story he'd told me previously, I found out it had taken him to a place I'd never heard about before. What I'd reminded him about was a story he'd told me about a woman named Madame Irene Laurie who had been one of the fiercest French resistance fighters in WWII, but who when invited to a post-war peace summit, got ready to walk out when she heard German being spoken there. Well the story goes, after speaking to Frank Buchmam, the Northeastern Pennsylvania preacher who'd founded the Oxford Group movement, Madame Laurie did not leave the conference but returned to her room for three days. And when she emerged her "I apologize to the German people for my hatred of them" speech, Konrad Adenauer, the first chancellor of West Germany, claimed, more than anything else, paved the way for the post-WW II peace in Western Europe. But last night Jim went one further. It seems he (himself), this Madame Laurie, a black stevedore from New York named Smalls and an American Indian, both of whose lives had also been changed by the Oxford Group, all went to North

Ireland some time in the 70's to talk to the head of the IRA. (Buchman was dead by this time so he was not included in this Oxford Groupian *Village People* of sorts.) They never made it into Belfast though—it was too hot—but the IRA head did come out to see them. As a result of this meeting, a bombing scheduled for the next day was called off. And the IRA head who made many trips to America, to speak among other places, to dock workers in both New York and Baltimore, often spoke of how much that meeting had changed his life.

"New people, new nations, a new world," was Buchman's mantra. As Jim says it, he was not all that interested in saving souls. Delicious and important irony that the "return to first century Christianity" movement that came at the beginning of the 20th century was about a practical way to make the world a better place and NOT about saving souls . . . and that the "return" movement coming at its end is all about this getting saved. It seems to me I read or heard somewhere that we *all* already *were* saved when Jesus took that hit on the cross for us.

Besides Jim and me at this closing meeting were Bonnie and Ozzie who run the Wilson House Bed and Breakfast. They both gave up successful comfortable careers to spend their lives volunteering to run the place. Wally's wife was also there and she and her husband both shared on Friday night how their life's work has left them in such bad financial straits, it recently took some *It's a Wonderful Life*-type contributions to lift them from financial ruin. The other people at the meeting were a big guy named Rick, who along with his wife Kathy, spend a large part of their vacations volunteering at the Wilson House. Also there was a wonderful minister from Texas named Mike, who recently lost his post at the sprawling River Bend Baptist Church in Austin Texas. His recent guidance has led him to a place where he is not going to pursue another formal minister position for a while.

This Mike whose honest, poignant, open sharing the whole weekend had really added to the conference, shared last night, that to many of the people who'd come to him throughout the weekend, he'd replied that he too was kind of stuck. And just now when he shared that his guidance on Friday morning was to be "open to anything the whole weekend" . . . I asked him to maybe pray to Mary—that her messages are always about the love and healing power of her Son. And I told all these wonderful decent Christian people of God, that certainly I would say a rosary for them. And that is exactly what I am going to do right now.

April 23, 20001
Monday

With undue pleasure I now click Vermont off of that list of those states of the 50 that I have never seen. I did not know if it was fog or actual clouds that clung like moss to a rolling stone, to the ravines and gullies in the mountain, as we drove to'n'fro a 5:00 AM prayer session at the Benedictine Westin monastery on the other side of the mountain from here in East Dorsett yesterday morning. Someone shared Friday night that Vermont is the birthplace of both Bill Wilson and Dr Bob, and Ebbie Thatcher and Roland Hazzard . . . all those pioneers who got AA started. Seems Ebbie though, after being sprung from jail by Hazzard and then taking the message to Wilson, got drunk again and would be in and out of the program for the rest of his life. The beginning of his slipping away was where I picked up the *My Name is Bill W* movie that was, with stupefying irony, on TV here when I got back to this room last night.

I'd intended to leave here yesterday to spend time with good friends in Poughkeepsie but did not because I forgot their phone number. (I figured I'd keep the old phone book where I'd found that number, safely in my toiletry bag—the same toiletry bag sitting on my bed back in Philly.) And so I think I'll hang around a bit today—maybe go to the Ethan Allen museum over in Bennington, perhaps to the Robert Frost museum just up the road in Manchester.

I did make arrangements to meet my two sober buddies down in Red Bank NJ tonight—we're going to see some band called moe. that hardly anyone has ever heard of (except for a fanatical bunch of Moe-rons—their name not mine And that is not a punctuation error there with that period in the middle of a sentence above. This band ID's itself as moe.— with a small m and with a period on the end.)

The two guys I'm meeting are Grateful Dave, a word play on both his gratitude for being sober, and his allegiance to the Grateful Dead, and Jackie B. who hails from Long Island. I met Jack at the Garden State Young People's AA conference, I think, eight years ago. Dave whom I met at the Downingtown Young People's Conference not long after, is heavily involved in Native American Indian spirituality. Jackie who has Buddhist leanings, is an even bigger deadhead leftover than Dave. If you think moe. might be a deadhead spin-off band, down to the endless jams and loooong concerts, you are way warm. I really can't wait 'til tonight!!

Back to the movie last night though, among the last words that the far more humble Bob Smith says to the firebrand Wilson, are "For God's sake Bill whatever you do keep it simple." But the other thing he says, "one foot in front to the other" are exactly the words my old friend I'd met at Graymoor that first one-year sober anniversary said to me. (The same guy who later told me the bet was "just another crack pipe"). And my buddy, whose about ten years of sobriety at the time outdistanced mine by nine, took exaggerated, "one foot in front of another" strides—kind of similar to the old hippie "keep on trucking" posters—as he offered that advice to me. As things turn out, that old buddy's been on my mind a lot up here—first of all because of my stop down at Graymoor, but even more so because Rick, the volunteer at the Wilson House, bears a remarkable physical resemblance to him. A further irony is that Rick, who has a digital camera to die for, and who *already* gave me a disc with the pictures he just took, lives only about 45 minutes from Graymoor. So I told him about the first week in August Franciscan Nature retreat I make each year, that my old chum usually makes also. So, God willing, if they both make it, when they meet each other, it'll be like they're looking in a mirror.

That will be a big weekend for me, come to think of it, two days later I'll be celebrating a year sober again. It's funny how things work out, at our little sit-around guidance sharing session this morning, Wally's, "I'm walking this path, not sure where it will take me, but I must keep going," was real close to the thoughts I had nine years and two weeks ago I guess. Then I was one week sober for the first time—and I was walking down by the sea on the Friday night of Philly's big AA Intergroup weekend round-up in Cape May, New Jersey. An hour or so earlier, I was, for the first of what would turn out to be several times, the last guy to stand-up in the longest-to-newest sobriety countdown. There was no shame involved then, but there were goose-pimps and wonder and splendor, at the rousing, rollicking "keep coming back" 500-strong standing ovation. Moments later the thought that went along with the chills and thrills of that walk by the sea (of which thoughts of my dad were definitely a part) was, "You're not really sure where you are going, but finally you are heading in the right direction."

April 24, 2001
Tuesday (back in Philly)

moe. was great. They opened with a dynamite Bo Didley-type rocker called *St. Augustine*—the town not the saint. Ya man Chuck and Al can *play* guitar. Didn't I say something earlier about the folly of "contempt prior to investigation." . . .

Having just hung three loads of "out-of-the-dryer-but-still-not-quite-dry-but-still-too-late-to-prevent-the-wrinkles" clothes on the basement line and then seeing the bright sunshine outside, reminds me of Soeve's "artificial air conditioning" line. It also reminds me of how nice it must be that across the ocean, the makeshift hanging-from-the-ceiling-in-the-kitchen contraption Ann Gaffney uses to hang clothes, has now surely given way to the outside line. Michael Smith's "the weather's fine" message was the first of 39 e-mails I looked at this morning. He told me he met my sister too—and that she was going to be heading out to visit the Sheridans. Then Ann's son e-mailed me and told me his mom accompanied Mary Ellen on the visit. She really *is* in good hands over there.

* * *

It was three years ago, sometime in late March I think, when I first met Jim Houck. The event, a one-day seminar promoting Back to Basics was titled *Barriers to Bridges*. The day ended on an almost miraculous note. It seems right before they closed shop, Jim spoke up and said that the young man he'd taken through the 4th and 5th inventory steps had something to say. And what this about 30-year old guy, who was about six or seven years sober at the time, said was something that prior to his talk with Jim, he'd never shared with anyone before. Seems years back when one of the first black families moved in to his starting-to-change-neighborhood, he'd done something really rotten to their property. He was on the other side of the room and spoke in a very low tone, so I did not get exactly what he said. The black girl who was on that side of the room, surely did hear it though—and when they subsequently hugged, the theme of the days' event was enacted right before our eyes.

Yesterday sitting out on the front porch, the little girl whose single mom moved back into the home next door some time ago, rode bikes and played with her new buddy. So inseparable are these two they remind me of the "butcher boy" and the buddy he lost that set off the whole dastardly chain of events.

There is not a lot of love lost between ours and this family with whom we've shared a driveway for like thirty years now. The mom rarely speaks to us. Surely it's not still about the bottle of whiskey my sister stole out of their house sometime in the early 70's. For the three daughters though, all of whom are back home now, we usually at least exchange greetings. Such was not the case yesterday though. When the younger daughter—eyes forward—chose not to notice me when she came home, I said nothing either. In this case a barrier remained one—it had not become a bridge.

Life indeed does go on. Mom's foot really did look a bit better this morning. Her attitude was also way improved because the Sixers bounced back from a horrible first game/round-one loss and whipped the Pacers. Their star, Allen Iverson, had 45. The "Answer"s near-100% changed behavior from one year ago is almost all of the reason the Sixers ended up with the second best record in the league this year. Iverson who comes from a bad downtrodden ghetto in Hampton Virginia has never been a saint—he even did some time for his part in a race riot that took place in a bowling alley down there when he was a high school senior.

I guess it was a little over a year ago, I think near the end of the regular season when there was a little blip in the paper about one of Allen's buddies getting killed down in the 'hood—the pipe I believed was involved. A few days later he got tossed from a game screaming at the referee as he was carried out. I remember not long after I wrote him a letter. (I write a LOT of letters—ask Coach Martelli out at St. Joe's.) And in the letter, after my perfunctory "I been there with the pipe"—I probably enclosed the Nov '99 Inquirer article—I said "maybe you were screaming not just at the ref but at a world and a system that keeps the brothers that can't hoop it up like you can, down there". Letters—words on a page—I do try.

The word is that Allen's engaged to the mother of his two children, the younger an adorable little son, he sometimes brings, doo-ragged up a storm, to post-game press conferences. Iverson's December *"All the stuff that went down last year did not come out of the air. And I was in the wrong like 99% of the time"* speech set the tone for this magical season. His *"where's my coach, where's my coach"* rap while accepting the all-star MVP trophy was Chip Hilton stuff.

The Phillies are 4.5 games in first. Larry Bowa, the hero from the late 70-early 80's Phils golden years who they brought home to coach the team this year, is yanking pitchers quicker than little Dallan went bursting out the *Favorite's* door when we hopped the bus to go watch his uncles play soccer back in Cavan. They swept Turner's Braves over the weekend. I keep telling everybody, "remember 93" (when the Phils made it to the World Series)!

April 26, 2001
6:00 AM

Popping out from the covers was easy this morning. Putting the period on the end of a sentence is much easier than beginning one. The world has convinced us that living a life trying as best as we can to discern and then do God's will net us a life that is like serving a sentence. The world is wrong.

The little 5th and 6th grade St. Matt's girls I umpired yesterday afternoon (an intramural St Matt vs St Matt's tilt of sorts) were beyond cute. So too were the little Jewish boys I umpped immediately after up in the plush suburb of Upper Moreland.

The young girl I took to that anniversary a little over a year ago, I think left St. Matt's probably only five or six years ago. I overheard someone say she is back sober just a few weeks now. Zanax is her thing. And her talks of suicide attempts seem to have lessened quite a bit as she *does* keep coming back.

At the regular Beginner's meeting at my home group, her latest little boyfriend was there. Before I left for Ireland she told me he'd dumped her, "they always dump me," she added. Her ex is a nice kid—hangs around with a crew of the younger guys at the group—they go on various sober adventures—shooting paint at each other trips—they even go on "road trip" meeting spins up to New York or out into the 'burbs every now and then. They seem stay sober for a while, get drunk and then come back. They're always *sort of looking* for babes, which is pretty much exactly what I did all the time—before I went to Ireland, that is. Over there the Demellan scheme finally took hold—I'd looked at it long enough to realize that what I was doing was not making me happy . . . that I did not *have to have a* she to be happy.

My little friend's ex-beau once told me a parable about his uncle. Seems the guy was sober for a while, met a cute little women in recovery, moved in with her, but after she left him, he started drinking and doing heroin again and then died of an overdose. There but for the grace of God go I.

I used to pick this kid up on Friday nights at the end of his 3-11 shift in a downtown hotel at which he used to work . . . sheltering him from the "dope fiend express" which is what he called the El ride home at that time on Friday nights. He once told me he doesn't read much, but I asked him if he'd read *my* book. His "Yeah man I'd read *that* one!" confirmed him as a friend of mine for life.

April 27, 2001

I can hear the birds outside and am reminded of a portion of the meditation I wrote last Saturday morning up in Vermont

.

Birds chirp
The water flows
I wonder if I worry too much about being poetic

To live each and every moment
To allow the fade of the last chirp
give birth to a different one – from a different bird
a different kind of bird

Birds of a feather may flock together
yet they seem to have no problem
with birds of a different feather
joining in . . .

the flock the glory of oneness and unity and brotherhood

Yesterday was not the best for me. I lost my wallet. Got on the pity pot real bad at all the non-returned e-mails and calls and perceived cold shoulders. And on the way home, driving up from the Big Book meeting at my home group, I kind of lost it. "Where is some help, an attaboy from THIS world . . .". Then when I woke up this morning, in the way that happiness (or spirituality or awareness or however you want to phrase it) is not a linear commodity, I realized the "attaboy," I'd been looking for had already been had.

Seems this guy Billy, who goes to my home group almost every night, and who's sober maybe about ten years, but who though not a big fan of *Back to Basics,* does share about how he had to change to stay sober, and that it was, the steps that allowed him to change, told me after the meeting "you sound good Jimmy, you sound like you're on the right track." It seems he liked what I'd had to say. I was the first to share, and reading the *How it Works* fifth chapter, which goes from a beginning-type statement that the only people who cannot get and stay sober are people who "*are constitutionally incapable of being honest with themselves*" all the way through the inventory process, including the sexual inventory, had set up my sharing about all the years I'd been coming to meetings sort of trying to get/find a woman and that somehow this hidden agenda had stopped in Ireland, that somehow while over there I realized that this was keeping me from being happy.

DeMello tells me that the only way to be happy is to just keep looking, keep trying to become aware . . . that only when I realize what I am doing is making me miserable will I stop doing it. That if I try to pull up the old Ayn-Randian boot straps and do it myself, I'll only get frustrated. And I've finally realized that is what I kind of have been doing for a mighty long time now—I've been looking. From the little guy walking around in the May procession thinking, "man that sound system sure sucks, but that is some deal that all those folks from all those places with the weird names heard what Peter and the rest were saying in their *own* language" . . . to the not-that-much-less-little guy, hurt and perturbed that he was not invited to any of those 8th-grade make-out parties . . . to the guy who went off to high school and snuck off at lunch-time to go to communion, and wondered why he didn't have the gumption to join the school paper . . . to the guy who went off to college and who read Joyce's *Portrait* and listened to all the "it makes no sense" cafeteria clatter, and who then said 'bye-bye' to the old Catholic-pie . . . to the guy who graduated and ended up in the shock-treatment chair . . . to the guy who went back to work and who fell in love a few times, and who then fell headfirst into the rocks of addiction and despair . . . . to the guy who ended up in AA . . . and then to the home of his fore-family and to now back in the bosom of his immediate family – all the time I've been 'looking'.

And as a chirp and a caw and a distant bark or two resound out my back window, it is an immensely nice feeling to realize that I *am* happy . . . . .

April 29, 2001
Sunday morning 6:00 AM

One thing they suggest in AA is to not get all kinds of sponsors, to stick with one, because with multiple guides, you might go bouncing all over the place looking for advice until you find what you *want to* hear.

I suppose that is why Jim Houck's Oxford Group *How to Listen to God* pamphlet kind of guidance is so essential to their life/world changing agenda. And if I cannot trust my *own* thoughts preceded by a devout prayer, and then tested by qualities as Godly as Honesty, Unselfishness, Purity and Love, then I might as well head back to the caves. I can sit in one, read my Bible all day and stay out of trouble . . . then eventually venture out, only Bible in hand, and try to teach the masses the *right* way. And probably what will happen is the same thing that happened to Bill Wilson for the first five months of his recovery, when his preaching netted zero successes—before he met Bob Smith—the helpees will listen politely, say that "stuff happened 2,000 years ago", and eventually head back into the bar or to whatever hurtful way they feature.

But anyway, one might accuse me of this "look under every rock for the answer you want to hear," approach in my seeking out a more palatable explanation for the Church's original sin doctrine. As legitimate as that argument may be, yesterday's odyssey did uncover an explanation I could more readily accept. For at Philadelphia's version of St. Jerome's parish, at a little games for kids party-thing, a priest named Father Crehan used the words "a genetic predisposition to sin" in his explanation of original sin. Baptism is an access to grace way of taking away that predisposition. This disposition to sin . . . I sho' nuff know we grow into. But to regard it in that light, it takes the "he's soiled" out of the make-up of a precious and preciously pure, newborn child. This interpretation certainly removes that "limbo" doctrine the Church used to spout but does no more—the one about babies who die before being baptized going there because without the dip in the baptismal font, heaven is not for them. Talk about a travesty of a teaching! No wonder Joyce and so may others turned away. How much love is in that doctrine?

Father Mac(from down in North Philly,) who is quite a biblical scholar himself, told me a wonderful story about St Jerome. Seems Jerome was an early Church father who sometime in the fourth century AD, along with a translation of the four gospels, also did a biography of the authors. In the bio of St. John, the only apostle to not be martyred (a prophecy Jesus spoke of at the end of his, John's gospel, by the way), he speaks of how each year the early Church fathers would fetch up the very old John from the island where he was living out the rest of his days. And each year John would say the same one brief thing. "Little children, love one another." The story further goes that finally one of the early members asked John, "why do you say that same one thing, year after year?" Perhaps Albert Camus' secular humanist crew, might whet their whistle on John's "because if you do that, it will be enough," response. Maybe all the existentialists could take note of how many more times Jesus referred to himself and the Son of *Man* than the Son of *God*.

The sacraments, including baptism, are all about grace. Father Crehan told me the embryonic reuniting with the Catholics and Lutherans has a lot to do with the sacraments. I think of the magnificent way Carolyn Myss in *Anatomy of the Spirit* allies the seven Eastern energy chakras to the seven sacraments. I gotta look into these Lutherans . . . Buchman was a Lutheran clergyman. A

Lutheran columnist named Wible wrote a wonderful, reporter-like account of the events at Medjugorge. Grateful Dave's father, who is open-minded enough to have sat in with his son for American Indian sweat lodges, is also a Lutheran minister. For sure he and his wife's *Bed and Breakfast* up in Erie, Pa will be a stop on one of my tours soon enough. Mr. Grateful Dave, somehow, thinks Jesus was one of six—four boys and two girls, if I'm not mistaken.

Indeed the beat does go on . . . yesterday's travels in a walk home from the library, took me down the exact street on which I took those May procession strolls all those years ago. My friend Fr. Bill, who eight-and-a-half years ago, during my very first fifth step told me, "maybe some day you will write something" again told me to be patient and relax . . . "in God's time" he said. That is exactly what he is doing with the 12-step center my diocese is sponsoring. The al-anon meeting he's gotten started right in Reso's old convent, is exemplary of the "cell-planting" method he's adopted. God's input in this decision, whether Bill practices formal guidance or not, is very apparent.

Later on, my journey, after the stop at St, Jerome's, took me over to my 3:00 PM adoration stint. There, speaking with a wonderful young priest named Fr. Coffey, when I said how it seems to me that there have been enough baptisms gone around in the last 2000 years to cover everybody, he said *"Yes maybe that was the what the water that flowed with the blood out from Jesus' side on the cross was about."* Right ON Father . . . . again seems I heard somewhere we were all saved when Jesus died for us . . . . seems again to me it is all about realizing we are.

Full circle is a nice way to close things out, I suppose. The penultimate stop on last night's tour was to a beef'n'beer in the same school hall where I once was the General Services Rep for the Saturday AA meeting they have there that's called *The Hand of God.* The benefit was for a stroke-stricken friend of my work buddy Bob, and was a rousing success. Lisa and Kevin at whose home I was fed and given an envelope with a chipped-in $175 in it on the same night as my "Sunday-before Ireland" brunch with my family, were there as were Bob and his wife Marty. Right afterward I went to my home group for the midnight meeting, but after doing a non-job of fighting off sleep I left at the break. But I did give my friend John Q a ride home. John *is* something of a miracle. He's been sober now since January 1, 1998—except for a few hits on one joint about a year and a half ago. For 25-30 years before that John was a semi-street person, coming to meetings mainly for the coffee, the warmth and an occasional hand-out. Never, ever, did he panhandle aggressively. John did go through *Back to Basics* in February of that turnaround year of my life, 1998, and even though the chances of him doing daily guidance are about even with those of my buddy Gregory doing a novena, he *stays* sober.

John's brother Tom and one of the Trash Band originals, was one of the four 'skip-mass' pinochle players with Chuck and Gregory all those years ago. TQ was one of the funniest MATBers, and was sort of the guru of our Northeast Philly contingent. But he could also be very tough with the old quips. I remember him singing/saying to me in St Joe's cafeteria "and you know that something's happening but you don't know what it is, do you Master Bates."

And guess what, I still don't. But now I really believe that there is a Power that *does* know . . . and in the effort to try to decipher and then to **do** the little or not-so-little things He knows are best for me, I will, in the end (and for that matter in the beginning and during the during), experience all the real happiness a man could ever want. And my contribution to this world shall be exactly what it was supposed to have been.

Full Circle. When you think about it, there is no closure in any circle. You come to a point and you're in a circle that actually goes around again.

In a little while I'll head over and umpire in the Sobriety softball league. If finished in time I'll head over to my home group and humbly see about getting *Back to Basics* reinstated. The "fire and brimstone—how dare you bounce us out of here!" speech I was going to give, I've decided was a bad idea.

I have my wallet back. Friday's adventures started with an e-mail message that my wallet had been turned in down at Penn. Such "extra mile" kindness reminded me of what a lady over in Ireland had said when I was going on and on about how cute the Irish children are. *"American children, I'm sure are very cute too."*

I'm also reminded of the dude with a very pronounced New Yawk accent and schnoz who sacrificed a green light to make sure I got his "take a right, a right, and a right" directions to get on the Jersey turnpike last Monday as I headed down to Red Bank and moe. On Friday night last, flicking through the dials I found another New Yawker with a very pronounced nose conducting a thoughtful, sleazseless interview with a very pretty actress. In the interview he led her to discuss how important the love of her immediate family has been in her rise to success.

De Mello says the most dangerous thing in the world is a closed mind. It seems to me if one keeps an open mind and tries to be kind and decent and loving, that eventually they will get *happy.* Maybe the Buddhists are right, maybe it takes a lot of lifetimes. For my money, such thinking tends to make one not diligent enough about taking care of this lifetime—the only one we have any real control of after all. In my *Pie in the Sky* poem I put it like this:

And the Buddhist he chants
For him many a chance
He can reach for the sky
Or come back as a fly . . .
depending on his last try

April 30, 2001
3:00 AM
Final entry (finally!)

The events of the movie *Memento* run in almost exact inverse chronological order—that which happens last is presented first . . .

the earlier events—at least those in the hero's post accident trauma period, are presented last. The irony is delicious and pronounced, that, likewise, as the flow of my little tale takes on the question of Baptism, yesterday's events should bring me back to St Leo's Church and the church in which I was baptized—the very church Mr. B, Tom Q, and Gregory avoided all those years ago. The irony is that the last time I was in that church, was almost surely on that baptismal day, 49 years and about three months ago (and now that I think about it, and was held in the arms of my beautiful Aunt El.) We moved up here to Resurrection when I was a month old. About a hundred times, I've heard my mom say, *"it was so warm that winter the men doing the moving wore short sleeves."* And for whatever reason, in these four or five years of my rejoining the flock, as I've made mass in a lot of the various churches around town, especially up here in the Northeast area, I've never gone to St. Leo's.

The reason I was at St Leo's was for the confirmation of the son of Bob N, the Mike the Monk's regular, and sponsor of my sponsor, who gave me the *Sex Love Anonymous* Big Book. I even drove Mike to'n'fro the lunch/party after, and we had a deep discussion about spiritual directors and the pope and other things. I told him how absolutely delighted I was to have found Father Crehan from St. Jerome's, whose previous post ironically, was in the Port Richmond parish of St Anne's where my great grandparents Peter and Sarah, were wed 120 years ago. And now that I think of it, it was an Ireland (and Mayo) native with the same last name as Tom and John Q, who moved from St Anne's up the road a piece to Nativity. In fact it was his incredible faith and charm and wit and connections that helped Nativity become a reality. The story goes, in 1883 after a huge storm had knocked down the original wall that had gone up, it was Father Q who went to the people to help get the rebuilding accomplished. And Peter was one of many late 19th century Irish émigrés who answered the call.

It is 4:00 AM now. The first bird of the morning is chirping quietly. I know more sleep is in order before today's activities kick in. High up on my 'to do' guidance list is to mail the family picnic letter out to the portion of my cousins I've been assigned.

My sister is back home from Ireland. She had a ball. Ironically my mid-day stop home on Saturday, found e-mails only from her, Gregory, and two of my other best friends in the world—Nancy (of the poem *Nancy*) and Lisa who now lives in Chicago. Nanc, Lis and I were constant companions in the days we all worked at Penn. Nancy, whose February 26 birth date, I just found out is also Sarah's, and her husband Rob will be seeing my face in their Nagshead home next Monday. Lisa, her husband John and dog Gracie (and Chicago) will have to wait until August to be graced by my presence. (I AM kidding!) My plans to go there soon, have been changed—as May, June and July are prime umpiring season. That gig is pretty much up by August.

Back to Basics is back in at my home group. We'll re-kick off in June. The kinder gentler approach worked, my fellows could not have been nicer. My rather volatile sharing about my sexual addiction at a different meeting last night, and some perhaps-unwarranted finger pointing, did net some negative cross sharing. When I asked about bringing B2B to a long-term Rehab, I was given an extremely cold shoulder. All stuff I'll have to live with.

Tonight at 7:00 I'll go down to the Intergroup Special Event committee to try and plant the seed of bringing Willie D over from Dublin to speak at next year's round-up—which happens to fall on St Patrick's Day weekend. God willing, at that sobriety countdown, I'll be able to stand up at 18 months.

At 4:15 today, I'll be up in the 'burbs at a different Nativity parish, the one where my Jewish buddy Mitch's daughter goes (his wife is a darling Italian Catholic) to umpire. Mike the Monk is going to get me some info on *Jews for Jesus*.

Last night's rosary walk was very nice—if a bit yawn heavy. Mike's telling me that Mary was 16 when the angel Gabriel came to her, made me think she was probably about 40 when her son, Jesus, was hung on the cross. Mary didn't stop doing God's will after that, her duties just changed. In fact she may have been a little more involved between the crucifixion and Pentecost than she was after that wedding feast of Cana . . . when as Jim Hannigan so expertly noted, Mary, in an almost giving-away gesture, went to Capernham with Jesus and his disciples. It's in John 2;13 and in my translation it reads *"After this he went down to Capernham with his mother and brothers and disciples"*—more evidence that Jesus was not an only child. But after that Mary fades from the picture. Her son and his disciples did the active preaching. Just like she always reminds us in her apparitions, it's her Son we need to go to. I'm quite sure she was there in the room on Pentecost Sunday, when the Holy Spirit, with howling wind fervor, came sweeping into their beings . . . but then again she fades away. She goes back to being a good Jewish women, and a mom of sorts, I suspect, to all the boys. Imagine Luke coming by all the time peppering her for information. Luke, the physician, they think caught the fire when he administered to Paul after one of his stonings.

And Mary as I think of it, kind of faded from this story after I left Vermont. It just happened that way—honest—pretty much all this book/story just happened.

But last night as I thought of Mary's age, and of how the strictures of age and circumstance have now evaporated for her and dad and Sarah, the eyes got very moist again . . . a bit of daydreaming though, preceded that very last bead. But I came back to earth just in time to answer again that little *"say a Hail Mary for me, will ya?"* request dad made so frequently to me.

Book III

Their Legacy

Of the people in the picture . . .

Anne lived the longest. She was **90 years old** when she **died in 1982**. She is in the left center of the 1904 picture, sitting next to her father; sitting on the left in the 1928 picture that leads this chapter. She was, I suppose, the first "modern" McGowan woman; a success in her own right before marrying a wealthy and wise *gentleman* named Whinney who would both love and be fascinated by "the McGowans." She was a bridge champion, would play with the masters; she had a lot and gave copiously.

For the first couple of family picnics, that triumph of an event began in 1977 and that carries on until today, though almost totally blind and dependent, she was alert to the doting, near icon/legend status she was given. She was our last living breathing bridge to our heritage.

The "roaring twenty" gathering at the big house on Monmouth St., where that1928 picture was taken might have been the zenith moment for the McGowan's in America. 13 months before the crash of '29, the times were fun, fast and lucrative for the burgeoning clan. In that picture included here, of those included in the 1904 photo: Sarah, Peter Sr., Jim and Sade are absent. Sarah had died 11 months earlier. Jim had died in 1918; Sade and Peter were in Ireland that day—the trip partially financed with money Anne had earned in a Florida real estate deal. Joe Sheridan, a nephew of Sarah's and a scholar and gentleman extraordinaire, who lived with the family on Monmouth St and who we know all too little about, is included in the '28 photo.

Anne was probably the smartest of her siblings. She was a bridge champion who played with the masters. (Including a match down at Philly's prestigious Wanamaker Room with Omar Shariff and Chares Goren). She ended up taking her 'master' points and began a bridge club in the family. I remember as a kid on days when I'd stay home from school, either sick or sorta sick, listening to the clatter of the "Bridge club", thinking how much actual bridge can they be learning with all that racket going on . . . my dad's observation "watch when any three or more women get together in a group, you'll see at least two of them talking" reverberating in my ears.

Anne married late, she was still dating Milt Whinney who owned a trucking company when the '28 picture was taken. They had two children, Joe, who currently lives with his wife in a suburb not far north of Philly, and Mary who with her husband Cy, lives down by the Jersey shore.

When Mary started dating Cy whose real name is Mario Ciboldi, Anne was not exactly clicking her heels . . . the vowel on the end of the name thing you know. Eventually she came around to love Cy, it would be almost impossible not to. In the 1983 Dublin St Patrick's Day parade in which my parents were part of a large family contingent that walked, the fun-loving, gregarious Cy was "King Kelly" for the day, and he headed their group's parade contingent with sparkle galore.

The story goes when Mary and Cy were "courting", a lot of Saturday night dates consisted of Cy and Mary carting Anne over to sister Mame's apartment to sit and chat and drink beer. And when Mame would suggest, "well Anne, it's getting late, I think Cy is tired." Anne would answer for all saying, "Oh they're not tired. Let's have another beer." Mame rarely would argue with her younger, far more assertive sister, so she, Cy and Mary would indeed have another.

Anne did have her problems, both with the booze and depression—particularly in her later years. And as a brilliant, thinking woman, she surely puzzled about the Nature of things. I don't know how many times I heard my mom quote her, "without my faith, what use is anything." Such musings are not those of one with blind non-thinking adherence to any doctrine.

She and Joe went through some stormy seas themselves, but by the time of his deathbed conversion to Catholicism, they were a couple that was *together* in the strongest sense of the word.

Sade (Sarah) would go next (English has no word the denote *next* going backwards . . . . so hopefully you'll forgive the ongoing syntactic error.) She was 73 when she **died in February of 1970.** Sade was one who would argue and stand up to her older more domineering sis. She knew a lot about almost everything and if she found a philosophical stance she felt important, would bow down to no one, woman or man.

Sade was not shy with the booze either, and loved her cigarettes. There's a story about when she moved out of Port Richmond up to Philadelphia's Juniata section where she had to put up with the loooong sermons of the pastor there, her comment was, "it wouldn't be so bad, if they put ashtrays at the end of the pews." And the cigs and the beer probably had a lot to do with the hospital admission that was supposed to be not that big a deal, but that ended up being the end.

Sade was a huge part of the lives of so many of her nieces and nephews—and the children of those nieces and nephews. I think it kind of ironic the way she spread the wealth of her knowledge, wit and charm equally throughout the family. Grand daughters of her brothers' Frank, and Owen—and of both her sisters seemed closest to her. My first cousin El was from Owen's brood (I've heard my mom say about a million times, Little El's husband Frank could not believe how much Sade knew about baseball) . . . my cousin Nancy and Patty were from Frank's and maybe the closest of all, my dear cousin Patsy, was from Mame's. Many or at least most of these were part of the round-the-clock vigil during that final hospital stay. Patsy's dad Jimmy, who also was always real close to Sade, and Anne's daughter Mary, were likewise there for the constant company she had at Philly's Northeastern Hospital.

I think Sade would have liked to marry . . . but she seemed to have gotten lost in the times and the shuffle. She, in a sense, almost as much as Bennie (even more so after he died), was her brother

Eddie's "right-hand man" in the numbers business. She too was a whiz with numbers. Maybe the men she met in those circumstances were not of the right stuff. After WWII, it seemed she wanted to keep the fairly large "numbers" business that Eddie had ran out of the Monmouth St. house going. But the times had changed, and Sade had to change with them. It was 1950 when she was the last to leave the big long house on Monmoth Street. With the house that had been the anchor to them all no longer part of their holdings, the McGowan in Port Richmond era, was really over. I supopse it was appropriate that her song in the mandatory sing-alongs at the McGowan parties would be the Irish lullaby "Turaluralura."

Sade, for sure, was named for Sarah. I suspect she was the child most like her mother. Faith, wit, wisdom, compassion, a passion for fun and for folk—the best of my family's qualities—Sarah and her precious independent little namesake, seemed to have them aplenty.

Mame (Mary), the oldest girl, was 73 when she **died in 1961.** It seems fitting Sarah's first girl would be named for Mary. (Ironically enough, I suppose, Mame's birth date is December 8—the feast of the Immaculate Conception.) She occupies the same right of center spot in the 1928 picture that she did in the 1904 photo. Her love of fun and laughter would be topped only by her capacity for kindness. She married a fixer, a carpenter by the name of Flynn, whose complementary tendency to give without receiving, would make for an oft difficult and struggling life, but one never devoid of optimism and mirth and happiness. That her song at the McGowan sing-alongs was "Don't put the cork in the bottle," was very appropriate.

It's funny that I remember the visits as a child to Mame's apartment, but hardly remember at all going to Sade's. But I do remember going to Mame's . . . I do remember that smile and the near-ecstatic way she would gobble me up with hugs and kisses. I remember how stupendously happy dad seemed during those visits . . . so happy to be showing off his little clan to his beloved aunt.

Mame was all about fun and love and laughter. But she too, though fiercely dedicated to her family, quite obviously knew that ALL were her brothers and sisters . . . and in one endearing tale that demonstrated this, a temporal reward was involved.

Seems that after having many Port Richmond addresses in the 20's and 30's the often-struggling Flynn clan finally found a place to call home. Largely through the connections of my grandfather Owen, Mame, Jimmy and their four boys were among the first families to move into the spanking new Hill Creek development in Philadelphia's Northeast section. The proprietor of the development was a gentleman named Joe Devine. When sober he was a capable, conscientious administrator. But very frequently he was not sober—he was an alcoholic and because of his antics when drunk, the community disliked him immensely and shunned and avoided him. All the community that is, except Mame. When she'd see him staggering down the street she'd invite him in, feed him some coffee, let him sleep it off on her couch. For this, she often was ostracized and talked about by her neighbors. But that did not really matter, what mattered was that she saw a fellow soul in pain or in trouble and she helped him. It was the way she was raised . . . it was the way she lived her life.

By the early 50s the boys had moved out, Jimmy had died and Mame had been out of Hill Creek for a number of years, living with one son or the other. She told the boys she'd like to have her own place. One of them suggested they try the one-bedroom units at Hill Creek, but upon checking though, they found a 50-name waiting list. They decided to look up old Joe Devine who it turned out had gone to AA and gotten sober . . . he'd gotten his life very together and now was the man heading all these developments throughout the city. When he found out Mame was looking to move back to Hill Creek, ("*Mame* wants an apartment!"), she jumped up to # two on the list and was moved in within a month.

She'd have "her own digs", and much company and fun and activity until her death in 1961.

I've asked some of the AA old-timers around my area if they remember Joe, and I've gotten quite a few "yes"s. "A good guy, a kidder with a great sense of humor . . . would do anything for you . . ." were among the things I've heard. That ripple effect of a drunk that stays sober. Who knows maybe one of those individual acts of kindness by Mame prevented one of his loads from being *the real* bad one.

Mame loved her four boys, but she always wanted a girl. The story goes she near clicked her heels when her first-born son Jim's first child was a girl. I know not what the celestial equivalent of a heel-click is, but I know Mame now does it and more in the sharing of the woman that eldest daughter of Jimmy became. (I'd suspect that twinge of melancholy marking that ever-present smile, is also gone.) I guess as much as anybody in or out of the family, that oldest daughter, my cousin Patsy, is my soul mate.

Pats who teaches computers in a local Catholic grade school is so tuned in to her faith that the 13 computers in her lab are all named after saints. I chuckle right now thinking how she told me she finds herself saying, "that goddamn John Bosco is down again!" She also once shared that she too always felt Sarah was the spiritual head of our family. But the most honest thing my dear cousin ever told me is that she lives her steadfast, consistently kind and devout life, basically by rote—that any fire her faith might have given her, she lost a long time ago.

The story goes that Dr. Bob, AA's co-founder, a kind, gentle man—even when a drunk, people basically liked him—always wanted to have one of those "burning bush" kind of spiritual awakenings like the one that began Wilson, the other co-founder's, recovery. Wilson was the ego to Smith's humility . . . even after sober, Bill W admitted the "traditions" grew out of the need to protect AA from big idead, big mouths like himself. There was no need to spell out the irony of this tale to my smart-as-all-get-out Flynn cousin . . . nor is there any reason to question the hand-of-God influence that Sunday afternoon in October '00 when Patsy was the next person I met, following the last time I came *really close* to again tasting the flame. For it was her that I saw, and with whom I took that walk around the two miles of Lincoln High School when I came off I-95 after *not* making the u-turn to go back to the player I'd just seen in a badder part of town.

"It all comes out in the wash", might be an apropos sub-title for this tale. And for Mame and Jimmy, and all the parents of my grand-dad's generation who instilled into their children a strong sense of decency, reverence, honor and devotion, the thought of how they now share in those ripples of righteousness marking the ongoing flow of the descendants of Peter and Sarah through the oft-rabid rapids of the world as we now know it . . . their praises need loudly to be sung.

Almost exactly 17 years passed between Mame's death and the death of the last of the men of Peter and Sarah's brood. Longevity was not part of the deal for the first generation of McGowen men in America. Owen, my granddad, was the only one to see his 50th birthday. When **Peter died** in **December of 1944**, he was only 47. He and Eddie, the little mischievous bookends moved from the bottom of the 1904 picture, to the top in 1928. Peter wearing glasses, has the upper right-hand spot.

Pete and his wife Anne had four children . . . and the struggles for the family were immense. I was told they lived in 10 different residences in 18 years . . . early morning or middle of the night "beat the landlord" moves part of their landscape. The kids at times went from school to the entire-family Monmouth St home site to find out where they were living. Little Bernard, the eldest, sometime had to go track dad down at the club or a bar to get a dollar or two so he, his mom, his little brother and two little sisters could eat that night.

Yet it was Bern who, more than anyone else, awakened the genealogical spirit among our family. Way back in the 70's, before the advent of specialized programs and the like, he put the first family tree together. Manually via lines on a page extending down from the top, at that first glorious family picnic in 1977, we got to trace from whence we came. He dug out the pictures . . . asked question, had others dig out pictures. Who knows, maybe in the same way the nuns and the monks in Dr. Newburg's experiments were wired to go cosmic in their search for community, the lack of a strong sense of an individual nuclear family, drove Bern to broaden his horizon a bit . . . and in doing so opened up the eyes of all we McGowans to the glory of our heritage.

But Bern had help with getting that first picnic going . . . and in the all-corners participating way things used to happen in our family, descendants from all the crew were involved. Mame's son Jimmy had almost as much to do with getting things going as did Bern. Jimmy was the letter writer for the picnics, and he, almost single handedly kept things going after Bern's death in 1988. I guess Jimmy's from the get-go involvement, was how the Flynns got to have green as their picnic shirt color. Pete's crew is the "yellows" . . . we of Owen's wear red . . . Frank's wear dark blue . . . and Anne's, light blue. Anne's daughter Mary was also there in the early formulating days, as were Betty and Jim from Frank's; my first cousin Pete represented Owen.

Last June was the 25th (or 26th) installment of the picnic. We missed only once—in 1999. Seems we of the "committee" to whom Jimmy handed over the reins a few years back, dropped the ball a bit. But in the year 2,000 we were up and running . . . bigger and better than ever. And a huge, amazingly accurate and detailed family tree is now a prized exhibit at the picnic. And as fate would have it, the cousin we have to thank for this (an actual DOer amongst all us TALKers) is likewise, a descendant of ol' Peter. For my cousin Terry, a yellow extraordinaire, is the daughter of Pete's daughter Dot.

The greens, the reds, the yellows and the blues still gather once a year . . . and it is a treat mainly for the kids . . . races, games galore. And when I made my way up to see the McGowans in Derryvilla, the faces of the kids there reminded me so much of the smiling faces on top raised out chests adorned with 1st, 2nd and 3rd place ribbons I see each year.

Blessed is nowhere near strong enough of a word to describe how I feel to be included in the family that I am.

Eddie was only **44** when he died in **July of the same 1944** year as Pete. The little bookend bros connection was carried even unto the timing of their respective deaths. And for both of them, excessive lifestyles certainly were contributing factors.

There are more stories about him that any of them. Called "Big Eddie" by near everyone, he was an imposing gregarious character—was a bootlegger, a bookie, a bar owner. He would never marry, live kind of fast, and die kind of young. The most famous story is the one about him scaling the Polo Grounds in New York wall at the 1927 Notre Dame/Army game as one extra showed up at the train heading up there and his refusal that anyone would go home. He would have a lot, nowhere near as much as he pretended (if you were a big shot and a bookie, the pretending was part of the deal), but there was no pretending in his occasional slip of a $5 or a $10 to his struggling married siblings. In his later years, the very extra weight he carried no doubt had much to do with the heart attack he suffered while playing with nieces and nephews down the Jersey shore. From this he never recovered, so, in a sense, the closest thing we had in the family to a "godfather" matched the Marlon Brando character from Mario Puzo's spellbinding book and movie in cause of death.

Eddie never married, but did have a lifelong "partner". An example of how my family was not always so open-minded was how this partner was not exactly welcomed with open arms. Seems my family back then took that "sanctity of marriage" thing pretty seriously. But Eddie still was an integral part of the McGowan lives down in Port Richmond. 'Twas Eddie who turned the big garage in back the house on Monmouth St. into the rollicking "Howard Taft Club" speakeasy of the late 20's. Was also Eddie who broke the jaw of the gent who'd helped himself to a keg sitting outside the club. (Was also in this club where my uncle Jim, knowing full well the only difference between the variant "brands" of whiskey was the amount of caramel and coloring he'd earlier doctored the home made base with, remembered chuckling as he washed glasses while certain patrons chose of one of the more "expensive" ones.) It was also Eddie who along with Bennie opened the B and E bar down below Richmond Street near the river after the club closed. And it was Eddie and Bennie who'd finally come across with a quarter or dime so the little nieces or nephews who frequently dropped in "just to say hello," could go scurrying off to the movies or wherever.

In another picture taken that September 1928 day, Eddie and Owen are seen holding a keg . . . other laughing, smiling family members are pouring from bottles of homemade whiskey. "A celebration of the end of prohibition three years early,"was how one uncle described the party that day. Eddie for all his wit and charm, was not a real popular guy with the local police. If not for his brother Owen's connections and influence, "Big Eddie" would have spent many more days and nights behind bars (the vertical kind!) Indeed maybe the only man to whom Eddie showed any deference, badge-wearing or not, was to his brother "the Chief."

The big car behind the family in the 1928 picture of course belonged to Eddie. It was this car that his brother Frank's son, Frank, used to collect the "numbers". Frank was an Eddie "wannabe" but never quite made it. The poster on the pole in the background read, "Al Smith for President." It was not until I went to Cavan that I found out Smith was not only Catholic, but that he was also Irish and also of Cavan descent. So you can only imagine the backing the Democrat Smith had in my family . . . even if Owen was an influential Republican committeeman.

I often wonder about Eddie . . . and what his relationship with Sarah and Peter was like. I wonder if they worried about his taking the wrong path in life. Perhaps in their knowledge that Eddie never seemed to deviate from being decent and kind, they had faith that it all would work out in the end. Who is to know . . . that whatever their respective realities, far beyond the microscopically finite limits of our cognition, now are, I can only hope they are together. Perhaps life, and in the way we choose to conduct *our lives*, can and does affect the lives of those who came before us. God knows I pray for Eddie enough. As visions come to me of him rolling across the Monmouth Street living room, going south or north depending on the way the radio announced the direction the Fighting Irish of Notre Dame were marching, his little nephews, one week Michigan, one week Navy, the next Purdue getting literally rolled over as the Irish moved toward pay dirt . . . sometimes getting banged up pretty good but never complaining about it . . . Sade calling in from the other room to take it easy . . . it occurs to me that perhaps the size and breadth of the Ultimate Comic Party may depend on how well each of us mortals "carries the ball" on each of our allotted sets of downs. But it also occurs to me that the separation 'tween the living and the dead, is only a perceptual one . . . that the Party IS and always was . . . that we only, and just, have to realize it.

Owen, my grandfather, was **56** when he **died** on **October 30, 1941**. He moves from the upper right-hand corner in the 1904 picture, to the center in the 1928 photo. And with the parents gone, in the center he belonged—for Owen truly *was* "the Chief". Not only did he frequently cover for his brother Eddie (and Pete) with the local constabulary, or did he arrange better lodging for his younger sister's family . . . in every sense of the word he was "the man", not only for his family, but also in a broader sense, for the whole neighborhood. Mirroring the actions of his mother from days gone by, I was told that during the depression he arranged to have food and other needed supplies distributed to the poorer families in the area. Fittingly his death that marked the essential end of the McGowan in Port Richmond era, would take place only five weeks before the Pearl Harbor attack that would mark the end of the world as we then knew it.

Owen's world however, really started to come apart on October 2, 1934 . . . for on that day, his wife Natalie Devlin McGowan, died. That petulant little letter he wrote to my dad six years later displayed a hurt that even for that long, had never gone away. I know all too little about my fraternal grandmother. I am told she was very neat, even fastidious . . . that her home and her garden were near perfectly kept. Some of my dad's more exacting habits I expect came from her influence. i.e. his dressing ritual—tee shirt on, then careful combing of hair, *then* shirt on . . . making pullover shirts a *non-put-on-a* as far as pop's ol' gift list went.

But I suspect Owen's trips down to Byrne's Tavern at Richmond and Westmoreland where he and many of the movers and shakers of the Philly political scene talked and drank and made arrangements, became stays longer than necessary after he no longer had a devoted wife waiting at home. The negligence in the bill-paying details that helped get Owen into bad financial straits, almost surely would have been avoided if Natalie had been around. And even as remarkable a job as did the namesake daughter, my Aunt Natalie, perform becoming "lady of the house" at the ripe old age of 13, she surely could not have completely filled her mom's shoes. The hero worshipping way Nat loved her dad, my mom experienced that first and only time she would ever see Owen . . . for she told me she does not know if she ever saw anyone look as sad as did Nat the day of his funeral. If you knew my Aunt Nat, though, and how fully and richly she always represented the *opposite* of sad; the tale is even more remarkable. Indeed if you saw the way my dad's face would beam at Natalie's simple "Hi ya Jim!" each year as he carried in a chair or a cooler to the picnic at which Nat and her husband Paul and their two children Nat and Paul were almost always among the first arrivees, you knew a little bit about how "Irish eyes could steal your heart away . . . ."

But on that October day in 1941, the heaviness in Nat's heart probably had at least something to do with the regrets Owen carried with him to his grave. As fate would have it, my dad also would know the same pain of having never owned his house. They "can take it away just because they feel like it" attitude that many first generation Irish-Americans had regarding the mortgage man, probably made Owen's indentured status even more traumatic.

But for both Owen and my father, their lives were ultimate triumphs. I have heard it said that my father's choice to have so many kids was a wrong one—that this *Irish Catholic* thing was in part responsible for his worldly woes. Likewise, because in the story I wrote about him several years ago I spoke of these woes, so many of my relatives found the story "too negative," the point surely has been missed. For my father's quest, his destiny, truly were not concerned with things of this world. The regrets for material riches not achieved were not for himself but for us, his children. His really was a different, more noble agenda. And even if Owen's faith was not of the same pondering, penetrating strain as my dad's, such an Ultimate agenda surely also was his. Again for Owen and his second-born son, in the sharing of the way their earthly-bound lineage *try* to live righteous loving, lives (amidst varying degrees of "in the flock" status), their eternity must be that much more beatific. Conversely but importantly, some of my lowest moments would come on the mornings after particularly gruesome nights of "acting out". Then, with all the mental resolve I could muster, I would jettison any flickering thoughts of how my life was affecting dad's Eternity. For it seems to me the whole "whew I made it to the Heavenly side" or "curses I didn't" manner in which the Christian/ Catholics view the separation of the living and the dead, is a bit too orderly, exclusive and exacting. How could my dad not suffer some purgatorial misgiving as his son lived a life so contrary to all he stood for?

But all this too is history—in the past. In my fervent belief that my dad and my grand-dad were two of the more brilliant points of light in the Loving Beacon which eventually did draw me up from the abyss, in our mutual and eternal participation in the carrying out of God's plan, we need not wait until I turn in my worldly cloak for us to be *together.*

For some reason, though, it was not until I went to Ireland, did my grandfather become more to me than just a handsome rugged face in a picture. Maybe it was all the lakes and the way he loved to fish . . . maybe it is because, as was so often the case with 19th century Irishmen, Owen the first-born son was named after his grandfather . . . and that that grandfather was the "Red Oiney" for whom our strain of Derryvilla McGowans are named. Oiney was the way they pronounced Owen . . . and he had red hair—that simple.

As it turned out my grandfather was the only one of his first generation American siblings to carry on that naming tradition. My dad's older brother, the first-born, is named Peter. Dad's younger brother is Eugene, which I also found out in Ireland, is Irish for Owen. Waiting 'til the end of the line to name one after the father is another Irish naming tool I've noticed. For whatever reason, it was of Owen's lineage where the closest to entering the religious life took place. Uncle Pete spent time in the seminary in the 30's, but came out. And when my mom tells me that Pete *always* had a girlfriend, and that even after he married, he rarely socialized without his wife (my one Aunt Dot), the reason for his coming out seems pretty apparent. Then it was Uncle Gene's only child, my cousin Dottie, who went the whole religious route and became a nun. The irony here is that Gene's wife, my other Aunt Dot (the *comical Aunt Dot* we called her because she was/is a riot!) wasn't even Catholic. Dottie ended up leaving the order however, and now lives and teaches school down in Maryland, very near where my buddy Jim Houck lives. Hopefully some day we will make good on our plans to meet up.

My uncles Pete and Gene lived in the same hundred block, two streets from each other and only a few blocks west of the house I grew up in. And being that Pete was my sister Mary Ellen's godfather, part of our Christmas ritual each year was his gift-bearing visit. I always remember him coming in and saying to my dad in his wonderful deep baritone voice, "Merry Christmas, Seamus", and I remember thinking that sounded so cool.

Pete and Dot had six boys, and the second youngest, my cousin Johnny, was a great athlete . . . and his son Sean is probably even a greater one. As the starting quarterback on a pass-happy local Catholic High School team, there is a lot of interest in him by various colleges. For some reason when I visited the home of the Sean McGowan in Derryvilla, in Cavan, in Ireland, the connection with Sean's long-legged, soccer-playing son, Porrig, and the son of my cousin Johnny, struck me. God willing some day these cousins from across the sea can get to see each other play.

The house on 2618 Ann Street where Owen raised his family is still very much there. But when I go by it, as I frequently do, it saddens me that I almost never see anyone there. For "back in the day" it was apparently the hubbub of activity. In the park across the street, my dad's gang hung out. It was also in this park where the younger guys who worked for the variant bookies would hang and play "three-card Annie" waiting for the three-digit daily "number" to work itself out as it was based on the winner of a certain three of the races at the local track that day. My Uncle Ed (Peter's younger son) told me that he did not get involved in the card game . . . he'd kill the time buying a couple of penny cigarettes and going and smoking them with my Aunt Natalie.

Several years ago, in the winter of '98 fresh from the New Year release from the most deadly clutches of my addiction, as an assignment for a fascinating Penn course *America in the 30's*, I sat on a bench in that little park reading James Agee's spellbinding *And Let Us Now Praise Famous Men.* And the words, *"Their father and mother before them were, in their time, the children each of different parents who in their time were each children of parents . . . it will continue for a long while: no one knows where it will end."*, filled me with a great sense of nostalgia. Agee was exactly correct . . . we do not know where it will end. But what and they who came before, can and should be our teachers. And for me, many of those teachers were also blood . . . and for all and any of the variant deficiencies that carried down my family tree, that kindness and decency to *all* folk and that reverence to the loving God who gave us all our All, also came down, fills me with a gratitude greater than I could ever express. Agee's closing poem fits them better than I could ever say it.

> *"Let us now praise famous men . . . .*
> *And some there be which have no memorial, who perished as though they had never been . . .*
> *But these were merciful men . . . and their glory shall not be blotted out . . . .*
> *Their bodies are buried in peace: but their name liveth for evermore."*

Frank, who moves from the top center in the 1904 photo, to being seated at the far right in 1928, **was one week short of his 50th birthday when he died on October 10, 1937.** He was a real whiz with numbers, and this skill was a great asset in both his fields of endeavor, insurance and real estate. Unfortunately both those fields were dependent on the booming times of a strong economy. So when the Great Depression hit, Frank was the McGowan hit hardest. Apparently not as strong or resilient as the rest, this brilliant, handsome and charming man was thrust into a depression of his own . . . and it seems it was one from which he never escaped.

But his children and their children certainly knew or learned "how to hang". The third oldest, my dad's great friend, Uncle Jim, (nickname "Abner" because a blonde named Daisy from the neighborhood seemed to have her eye on him) was only 16 when he gave up a high school basketball scholarship to go to work and help out at home. Frank the eldest, (nicknamed "Cohen" because of his large nose) was pretty much on his own by then, heavily involved in Eddie's numbers business. But the drink and the lifestyle were already becoming problems for him . . . throughout the rest of his life his family would try to no avail, to get him off the booze. John (nicknamed "Moose" and I don't know why) made his way down to the Philadelphia Navy Yard, where he ended up a supervisor. His younger brother Joe would eventually follow him there . . . and likewise follow him to an early grave from lung disease at the expense of the exposed asbestos that, in those days, no one knew was so deadly. The irony here is that Frank's irresponsibility when John repeatedly procured him employment there, eventually cost him those jobs, but saved him his life.

Sally was the only girl and with her black hair, high cheekbones, exquisite bearing and sparkling eyes, was a true "dark Irish" beauty. Her Aunt Anne sort of took her under her wing. It seems Sally and her first cousin, my godmother Aunt El (more of a light Irish beauty), were more or less the unspoken "belles of the ball" as far as the ladies of my dad's generation of McGowans went.

And boy did the boys of Frank's brood procreate . . . Frank had nine, Jim had nine, John and Joe had six . . . Sally would marry a Philly basketball legend named Obie O'Brien and had a boy and a girl. Obie coached the basketball team at LaSalle High, a private Catholic school up in Philly's suburbs for-like-ever. My dad told me that his Catholic champ team of 1955 even gave Wilt Chamberlain's super-powered Overbrook team a real battle in the City title game . . . for a half at least. Sally's nephew Jimmy, by the way, who was a star b-ball player himself and a compatriot of mine out at St Joe's in the early 70's, now coaches the Boston Celtics.

People tell me that in the first picnic back in 1977 pretty much this whole gang was there . . . I really don't remember. But as the years went on, only the offspring of Moose and Abner attended with any regularity. In the slow days of the early-mid 90's in fact, it was Moose's son, John, who, with his own money often, was more responsible than anyone in keeping the picnic going.

Life can be strange at times, but for whatever reason Jim and John (Abner and Moose) went many years without speaking to one another. But at the funeral of perhaps my dad's best friend growing up, the lanky left-handed power-hitting first baseman of the Cardinals baseball team that was the pride of the neighborhood, Bud Fenningham, Jim saw John there and thought "this is crazy". And they soon reconnected and mended fences well before Moose's life was sadly cut short. (As it turns out one of Bud Fenningham's sons, Jimmy, is married to the sister of my brother Tommy's wife, Cindy. If you're a Catholic from Philadelphia, especially one with ties to Port Richmond, the world *really is* a small place!)

I guess I bring up the picnic so much because the bonding and connecting I'd see there each year, would, right before my eyes, bring to life that happier simpler time and place our world seemed to be losing. Among the many magical moments I'd see each year was when my dad and his buddy and namesake cousin Jim would hole up somewhere, perhaps share a shot of Irish whiskey, and laugh and chuckle and reminisce. I would only watch though, it was *their* time not mine . . . as me and Jim's son Jimmy have often discussed, they were our fathers, *not* our buds. As the years went on and the Alzheimer's began to intrude on my dad's brain, the chats did not desist. And if you looked at the face of my uncle Jim as he walked away, the look of love and mirth replaced by love and sadness, you knew a little bit about how those Irish eyes could tear your heart apart . . . .

Time marches on . . . it only goes forward. But that does not mean that which came before us cannot help us or guide us. Only recently has a family picture emerged—and it was taken in Ireland, in 1937 and the man on the far right of a group of men and woman cousins, is without a doubt, Frank, himself—the patriarch of the dark blues. Tommy Owen's oldest son Eugene says he remembers his dad speaking of the visit. For the life of me I can't figure out how he got there . . . in the midst of the abject poverty of the depression, a depression that he and his family felt the worst amongst the New World McGowans, Frank somehow made it over to the "old sod". Perhaps they chipped in to send him . . . perhaps they thought it would help raise him from the throes of *his* depression . . . perhaps it was Sade, remembering from 10 years prior what it had done for her and her father, who suggested it—we will never know. Did it work? . . . did that trip overseas that he took in what would be the last year of his life on this planet, do any good? That too we do not know. But we do know that such a trip some 62 years later did wonders in helping Frank's grandson Jim get over the death of his namesake dad. And we do know that it did wonders in helping his brother's grandson, yours truly, get over certain demons that plagued him.

"The Picture" hangs proudly on a wall in the living room of Sean-Tommy-Owen McGowan . . . up in Derryvilla, a stone's throw away from the barn that sits next the spot where the house from whence Peter came used to sit. *"Their father and mother before them were, in their time, the children each of different parents who in their time were each children of parents . . . "*. indeed. Maura, Sean and Eugene's sister, (and my hostess back in Cavan) wrote a wonderful detailed analysis of the history of my family dating back to the 13th century. Unfortunately in the early 1820's most Irish family trees, especially for those families closer to the North, come to an abrupt end as most churches burned or destroyed records to keep them out of British hands that, at the time, were intent on purging pockets of insurrection. It is figured that *Red Oiney*'s father, or his father's father, drifted up from Glangevlin, the original home of all the Magaurans, (as the McGowans used to be called) to Derryvilla way. And that Magauran name, as Maura noted, traces back as far as that 13th century. They were a clan of warriors . . . a Magauran or two might have marched with Owen Roe as he tried to rid his beloved Ireland of their foreign oppressors. But scholars and teachers were also part of their legacy. I look at the Tommy Owen's 4th child, Margaret, teaching in Dublin . . . Jim and Maura—both teachers, Sean's lovely oldest daughter Ashling, will teach in primary school soon. And across the sea, my sister Sally teaching in the ghetto. This year they enacted a school uniform program in Philly's public schools, and her students seem much better (it is the administration that is driving her crazy!) These kids WANT guidance and direction and it is the likes of my kid sister giving it to them. Patsy's "John Bosco" and the rest, I trust, are running smoothly. Uncle Jim's youngest, Louise, before she moved to Maryland, ended up teaching first grade in a school down in Port Richmond called "Nativity." Now she's a happy capable mom, making babies in near-Abner/Bettyesque fashion.

"and it will continue for a long time . . . . where it will end . . . .". Far more than a name or a nationality is what my family has been handed down. An Esprit or an ideal or a direction is more like it. In reality, a name or nationality is merely a label . . . that which gets chiseled on a tombstone somewhere. What *lives* on is where the import is. Riding home from that airport last March, my brother noted how important my nephew Thomas is. As the only male offspring of my nuclear family, only he can carry on the name. But my cousin Jimmy corrected him, "What's in a name? I look at Louse's kids (they with *vowel* on the end no less!). They are so sharp and cool . . .". As I said, somehow Jimmy *knows* about something going on . . .

Jimmy's birthday, by the way, is May 9th, *not* the 5th . . . mom corrected me.

Bennie, was only 39 or 40 when he died in 1933. He moves from the outside right in the 1904 picture to standing in the center in the '28 one. Perhaps this was done on purpose, perhaps the others realized "Eddie's brother" had spent too long on the fringes.

Bennie was the only one who went off to fight in WWI, and as the word "chemical warfare" again seeps into our national consciousness these days, there was some talk that Bennie's possible exposure to poisonous gas "over there", might have been part of the reason for his lifelong sort of on-the-outside-looking-in status. But Bennie did marry late in his life . . . and I was just recently told by Anne Wilson McGowan, the lovely widow of his nephew John (Moose), that Bennie's wife Laura was deeply in love and committed to him . . . and that when she married again after he died, she ran a very tight ship over a very child*full* union . . . and that Bennie's picture never was removed from her bureau.

The story goes Bennie was a real pushover when it came to forking over the dimes or quarters to the little nieces or nephews "stopping in" at the *B and E* bar he and his brother Eddie had opened down near the river in easternmost Port Richmond—that the little darlings were real glad when they saw it was he who was behind the bar.

October 2, 1893 is the date next the b., next the name of Bernard in the amazingly accurate detailed family tree Judge Latrelle gave me when I got back from Ireland. One hundred and eight years later, October 2nd is now today's date. Yesterday on the feast of St. Theresa of the Little Flower, when I changed the bandage on mom's toe, it looked almost completely healed. That so efficient AND conscientious podiatrist of hers last week told her he wished he'd taken a "before/after" photo.

This Little Bernard was obviously named for Sarah's father. Judge L has put together a whole different, sprawling expansive family tree stemming from the Bernard Sheridan/Mary McManus, then Bernard S/Mary McDonald, parents of Sarah, source. On the inside jacket cover of a 150 year-old Irish history book Anne Wilson McGowan shared with me reads:

Back to Ireland grande
Fond thoughts today would stay
Memory would fain command
My heart for aye : to stay

Mary Sheridan 1889.

Almost surely it was written by Sarah's half-sister Mary who was 23 years old at the time. Sarah had given the book to her daughter Sade . . . Sade had passed it on to Anne. Ironically enough, it was Anne (and Moose's) daughter, Maureen who took the 1904 photo down to the Balche that got this whole trek started. But as I think of it now, I wonder if Mary was maybe Bennie's godmother. Whether she was or she wasn't,

Mary so eloquently expressed the feelings of many Irish émigrés who never did get to go home again.

Sheridan is a big name among writers and actors in Ireland. The union of a mid-18th century Dublin actor and stage manager named Thomas, with a playwright and novelist named Frances Chamberlaine, produced the writer/actor Richard Brinsley Sheridan—a noted playwright, actor and politician in his own right. That Frances secretly learned to read against the wishes of her clergyman father, shows one of those rebellious Sarah-like streaks Dympna noticed in her daughter. And while there is no reason to believe the blood of these Protestant Sheridans of Dublin ever crossed the bloodline of the Bernard Sheridan crew of Creeny Milltown, Cavan, so what. Same goes for Cavan émigré' and Civil War hero, General Phillip Sheridan—even though with his short stature and dark Irish good looks he does resemble my dad a bit . . . and Anne's husband John even more.

It is not quite 80 degrees today, but it is warm and sunny for the first time in a while . . . . in memory of Cougar, on this the feast day of guardian angels, I think I'll take a ride down the Jersey shore and stroll on the beach . . . but now too, it will also be in memory of my grand uncle Bennie.

Unlike his male offspring, **my great-grandfather, Peter** lived a good long life—he was **76 years old when he died on May 19, 1931.**

In all my talk and reverence towards his wife, Sarah, I sometimes think I neglect the monumental import of all that Peter did in making my family's mark in America. Though it seems he was something of a monarch, often times he would have his meals alone—as hard as he worked he probably needed that down time. (As I think of the time when as a child, three of us spilled our dinnertime milk and dad got up and went to *Horn and Hardarts*,

I can sympathize with ol' Pete eschewing THAT dinner table scene!) But about him too were heartwarming stories of the grandkids running off to the store for a pint or whatever, and he too making a big fuss because they got the order right.

But the most memorable thing I've heard about Peter revolves around non-McGowans. Even though he was so deeply committed to his family and to keeping them close together that as each of them married and moved out, a $1,000 gift was part of the deal if they moved no more than a mile away from the Monmouth St. homestead, it was his commitment to *other* Cavan émigrés that touches. For you see after the turn of the century, the presence of a USA-settled "sponsor" to take you in was not only a good idea, it had become a rule. Knowing this fact, Peter would check the list of the incoming ships from Ireland, and if any Cavanites were on it, even ones he'd not pre-arranged to sponsor, off he'd go to the dock-landing, and if no one spoke up to claim these former residents of his native county, Peter would. And so many nights at the big long rectory-like table on Monmouth Street amidst many brothers and sisters and friends (if you were a friend who was around at dinner time, down you set) were fresh-off-the-boat "greenhorns". My Uncle Jim (i.e. Abner, husband of Betty) shook his head saying, "And man some of them were *green!*"

Thus the big house on Monmouth Street became a stopping-off point for many of these. Employment or relatives or close friends would be sought out. Because of Peter, these hungry, were given to eat . . . were homeless and given shelter . . . . I think of the many Irish-American family trees spreading out that would have never found root had it not been for him. I think of all those return voyages that did have to be made because of him. They called the ships that the Irish came over in "coffin ships" because so many died in the voyage. One can only imagine the death rate of a forced return voyage, when along with the scurvy and dysentery, a crushed spirit from a connection not made or a regulation ignored were part of the baggage.

Peter made it very big in America, but in a very big way, never forgot where he came from. That a prominent turn-of-the-century Republican Irish politician named "Sunny" Jim McNichol was in charge of city street work contracts and that whispers of impropriety often followed him, and that Peter's eldest son Owen would become an influential Republican committeeman, makes it seem very probable that Peter, whose masonry company helped build the Broad Street subway, was, on the *sunny* side of big Jim's street. So be it. Peter did damn good work, and he provided good, solid honest employment to many, many men who desperately needed it.

Towards the end though, I doubt if Peter was much involved with actual labor. The story goes that upon his return here from the magical visit back to Erin in 1928, (in fact, I'd suspect there might have been a "while the cat's away" element to the big party held at his house that September Saturday) without his beloved Sarah, Peter just sort of stumbled through those remaining two-and-a-half years of his mortal days. That McGowan "lost without his woman" thing, you know. And when he died, a funeral just as big and just as impressive as was that of Sarah's, graced the ½ mile stretch from Monmouth Street to Nativity. The depression was one-and-a-half years old on that May day when the first-born generation of my father's family became orphans. Because of their dad though, they were still physically close together enough, so that their cooperative huddling together to seek shelter from the storm, had a very corporal element to it.

The world is a much bigger place now; folks no longer stay within a mile of the original homestead. And they should not have to. But on last September 11, this ol' world shrunk a great deal. If we fail to realize that the shelter we seek and supply must extend far beyond the boundaries of neighborhoods or cities or even countries, then the just-begun mayhem will mushroom to God knows where. And as the winds of fate have blown me back here to the very bedroom in which I was brought up, I realize it is the *ideals* that Peter and Sarah carried with them from their beloved Ireland that eventually was the balm that loosed the closed portals of the kingdom in *my* heart . . . and the future holds no exclusivity on the eternal love and gratitude I feel towards them for that.

Sarah Sheridan McGowan was 67 years old when she died on **October 22, 1927**. She was only 17 years old when she made the arduous 2-day journey from up in Cavan to board the "coffin ship" down in the Cove seaport in Cork; she was 23 when she became Peter's bride; 24 when she mothered her first child. We assume Peter had his older brother Francis here when he arrived . . . we know not what awaited Sarah. Many, even most of the female Irish émigrés of that era became domestics over here. There is a good chance she did the same. We have one picture of her from her young womanhood days, her hair pulled back . . . the striking high cheekbones that were her granddaughter Sally's trademark, the eyes, even in a black and white photo, sparkling and steadfast . . . . I made up the good theater of the brash Peter first wooing her on the long voyage over here.

The stories of her service in the neighborhood are many . . . the sight of her in one of those awful high hats, a picnic basket containing food and medicine in tow, walking briskly off to the home of a poor neighbor, was supposedly a pretty common one. She was a midwife and an unofficial nurse. Indeed during the horrible influenza epidemic of 1918, when more Americans died than did in WWI, and where Philadelphia was hit the worst of any American city, and when special pick-ups of the dead lined up outside houses on the sidewalk was part of the daily rhythm of life, alongside a heroic Doctor named Murphy, catering to the sick, was my great grandmother.

The house on Monmouth St. was the control center for this particular burgeoning clan of "Red Oiney" McGowans throughout Port Richmond. And when I hear my uncles speak of McGowan cousins other than the ones I know about, I realize that there were other Red Oineys over here. I also realize our present contact with them is all too distant . . . likewise with the scores of other non-related McGowans that are from Port Richmond. A few centuries back, up in the Glangevlin hills, all our Magauran bloodlines most likely crossed. But the tracing of bloodlines and such is an abstract enterprise . . . its actual significance and import in the day-to-day life of a person or a family, minimal. But in the day-to-day life of the first generation of my family in this country, Monmouth Street was where the entourage headed; and they headed there because of Sarah.

Grandmotherly love and concern and fuss is one thing—a torn-up knee hugged back to health, etc . . . and while Sarah surely provided that, she also provided fun, genuine interest, and an eclectic, electric charm that drew folks to her. I think of Ann Gaffney holding court in those three tiny rooms behind *Favorites*, I think of mom down the shore last weekend peppering a couple of new sets of ears with witty poignant inquiries about everything. I think of people supplying meaning, humor, sparkle and elan to the glorious present moments of theirs and our existence . . . folk who instinctively *know* that it is *in the journey* where there is the wonder, that the destination will take care of itself.

Two nights ago, I just so happened to park my car directly across the street from where my dad grew up. (Because I'd decided to kill the ½ hour before the Wednesday Big Book meeting at my sponsor's house with a very non-vegetarian burger and fries at the *Fat Moma's* store on the corner of Ann and Almond.) So trucking on over to Jamie's I mirrored the walk my dad must have taken hundreds maybe, thousands of times . . . and I wondered how different the walk after the fateful October 1927 day when granny was no longer at the other end of the brief trek. He was in 8th grade at the time . . . near the age I was when I remember uttering the line, "I'm at a weird age . . . too old for little kid stuff anymore, and too young for big kid's stuff." I wonder what it was like for pop to lose the beacon of his grandmother's warmth and wit and wisdom at such a crossroads time of his life. But I take great heart that *now,* in a space and dimension far beyond my limited comprehension, my dad knows that at no time during his journey, did the mother-lode of his dear grandmother's love ever lose its hold on him.

Maybe now you know why those moonlight rosary walks mean so much to me . . . .

On a large tombstone in the New Cathedral Cemetery at 2nd and Luzerne Streets in Philadelphia's Juniata section about a mile up the road from Port Richmond, reads the entry:

James McGowan
born October 24, 1885
died February 2, 1918

And although his parents Sarah and Peter also were placed in this one of the four plots purchased by Peter, their names do not appear on the headstones. This oversight is understandable . . . when Sarah died the children were busy with other pursuits and figured they'd just have hers and Peter's names added when he presently passed on. But by the time Peter died, the die of the depression had already been cast, and paying to have names engraved on a tombstone in a time when getting enough to eat was a daily priority was correctly deemed an unnecessary frivolity.

But it was not the influenza plague of 1918 that got Jim . . . it was plain old tuberculosis. Like so many folk of his era, Jim too spent several years a bed-ridden invalid, more or less waiting to die. The story goes my aunt Betty's father used to go visit and "sit with him", the term they used for the bed side chats with friends gravely ill.

Most of what I hear about Jim is that even before his illness, is that he was a gentle, kind and thoughtful sort. As I realize how close Sarah must have grown to him because of all those years he spent in bed almost totally dependant on her care, and when I look at the *amazing* physical resemblance my dad had to his namesake uncle, I realize it probably was true that dad was Sarah's favorite. Then throw in the fact James is a Sheridan and not a McGowan name. Jim was almost surely named for Sarah's older brother who did make it to America by the way, and who was the patriarch of a huge clan I need to go digging after. But because my dad's Uncle Jim never married and was childless, his siblings, and their offspring did spread his name down through the family tree.

In birth order (and to the best of my recollection . . . .)

Jim's brother Owen named his second son Jim (my dad); my dad named his second son Jim (me). Owen's oldest son Peter named his third born son Jim, my first cousin Jimmy—who named one of his sons Jim.

Jim's brother Frank named his third born son Jim (Abner)—he named his eldest son Jim.

Frank's son Frank named one of his boys Jim.

(I'm sure a Jim or two or three are or four are somewhere in Frank's line, but I surely don't know 'em.)

Jim's sister Mame married a Jim, so that her first born son was a Jim and that that Jim's second born is also a Jim, may not be all because of Jim McG, but who's counting.

In fact I'm not really sure what all this counting of Jimmys has to do with anything really, but it did strike me as pretty neat that I am the third straight 2nd son named Jim . . . in a line directly through my dad to Owen to Peter . . . and with all I've been able to find out about the Jims involved, I am in very good company.

But there is another element to the legacy of my dad's uncle Jim, at least something we are pretty sure that can be traced to him. The following notes written on November 16, 1909 by the recording secretary for the 87th (Port Richmond) AOH is signed by a gentleman named Jim McGowan. Being that, in 1900, Jim's dad and three of his five brothers—those that were over 16 years of age—were among the second group of members joining that 87th brigade of the *Ancient Order of Hibernians* (an Irish society established to insure that the values and traditions of the motherland would be kept alive), it seems very likely that it was my dad's uncle who penned this accurate and enthusiastic account.

In the carefully penned notes, in seemingly the only written account that we have from a member of my grandfather's generation, you can see both the burgeoning patriotism that was surely very strong in these free first-generation *Americans*, as well as the concern and unity they felt for their subjugated brethren across the sea.

Phila Nov. 16 - 1909

Special meeting of Div. 87. A. O. H. held at Co. G. Hibernia Rifles hall. Thompson. bel. Monmouth St on the above date. The business of the meeting was for the burning of the Mortage. which was paid off in full also the receiving of the flag which Div. 87. A. O. H. won from Div. 66. A. O. H. at a contest at Father Flannigans Church. Sharon Hill. Del. County Father. Joseph. McCullar. of Church of Nativity B. V. M made presentation Speech. as Father Flannagan was absent from city on account of Illness. of his brother in Chicago.

Father McCulla gave an eloquent oration on the meaning of the Flag. and the Patriotism which we should pay to it. President. Philip Deighton received the flag in the name of Div. 87. A. O. H. after which we repaired to Hibernia Hall. Thompson & Cambria where the Mortgage was burned Amid a tumult of applause from the members present. after the ceremonies. the members retired to the dining hall where the menue. was most appetizing. Singing & dancing was kept up till the Small. hours of the morning.

I Think Div. 87. Ought to be proud of Itself it certainly has done well in those five years you have paid out sick & Death benefits about. $6000.00 towards charity & fraternal purposes about. $1500.00 } So you See Div. 87 accomplished Something in the past five years and no member was taxed over the fifty cents per Month. So I trust in the five preceding years that we will be more Sucessful. than in the past and that there will Stand on this Site a memorial to Irish men & Sons of Irishmen. that will be a credit to the thirty three Counties of Ireland of which Div. 87. is comp

James. McGovern R. S

November 16, 1909 . . . I look at that date . . . about six-and-a-half years before those 33 counties rose up in violent protest in pursuit of freedom . . . almost exactly 9 years before the Armistice that ended the century's first Great War . . . 30 years before Hitler marched into Poland touching off the century's Second World War . . . and just 2 months short of 92 years before an attack that would touch off a war different than any the world has ever known . . . one so different it might be termed qualitative—one in which men and women welcome death as they aim to kill or destroy any man, woman or child they can—the only qualification for their targets, their proximity to nations and ideals they hate with unbridled passion.

But I wonder if this century that changed the way people live more than any other—changed it so much that one could even term the change qualitative and not quantitative—has taught us anything? Unfortunately it occurs to me that, as much as anything else, the monumental progress we did make these last 90 years taught a considerable number of us, especially a considerable number of the real powers to be, those who teach and sway and even lead the masses, that we ourselves are in control of our own destiny. And from a frozen French battlefield, on Christmas Day 1944, as the second of those great conflicts was drawing to its bloody conclusion, the namesake nephew of that AOH recording secretary named Jim McGowan, my father, could already sense the coming drift.

". . . it strikes me on looking on those two words—peace and hope—that when this war comes to an end we will have the one—"peace"—but it won't be worth a damn without the other. If we are still saddled with the old get-as-much-as-you-can, give-as-little philosophy, the hope is not going to ride with us. Prejudice, Greed, Hatred, Injustice, Pretense and a whole host of others. Either we get rid of them or lose His excellent companionship."

The way things work out. In that note, with penmanship much better, but at least a bit similar to that of his uncle, my dad wrote over the h of that "His", making a small h into a capital one. Maybe

Osama bin Laden did serve a purpose . . . it seems more and more of us are realizing that we *do need* "*H*is excellent companionship."

Jim McGowan—then again, what is in a name? My cousin Jimmy and I have made a pact to have Sarah and Peter's names added below Jim's on that tombstone—and I think somehow this is one resolve that will not dissolve.

* * *

There is one more . . . . but obviously she is in neither the 1928 or the 1904 photo. Little **Catherine** who lived from only **July 3, 1903 until November 10, 1904.**

About the 1904 picture we know all too little. Like when in 1904 it was taken, we also do not know where it was taken. But that is one beaut of an American flag they stand in front of . . . obviously one "lived in" and not just a picture of one.

But there is something else about the picture, about the looks on the faces, and in the light of little Catherine and her struggle for life that was either going on or had just ended the time it was taken, the somewhat somber expression on the faces might be explainable. For in reality, especially considering how fun-loving of a group this was, there is an inherent sadness in many of the faces. On Peter's obviously it is there; there is a definite "keep that stiff upper lip" to the whole bearing of proud erect Owen in the corner; and in Sarah, along with the soft kindness of that strong handsome face, there is an aura of definite weariness. I guessed the picture was taken not long after Catherine's struggle ended. Perhaps there was a motion to scratch the whole picture idea, perhaps Peter or Sarah or maybe even one of the older kids said, "no, let's go through with it . . . it might ease the hurt."

Legend has it that Sarah, wearing her midwife hat, in one instance, lost the mother but saved the baby in a tragic child birthing. Lost babies and parents in those days were hardly extraordinary happenings. But the legend also has it that Sarah who was mothering at the time, gave of her own milk to feed the child. Who knows, a la the closing scene of Steinbeck's great American anthem, *The Grapes of Wrath*, perhaps it was little Catherine's milk that helped keep a poor Port Richmond baby alive.

Indeed Ma Joad's comments towards the end of that great book would serve as a fitting tribute to Sarah and to all the McGowan woman, in-law or otherwise . . . .

". . . . It ain't, Pa. An' that's one more thing a woman knows. Man, he lives in jerks—baby born an' a man dies, an that's a jerk—gets a farm an' loses his farm, an that's a jerk. Woman, it's all one flow, like a stream, little eddies, little waterfalls, but the river, it goes right on. Woman looks at it like that. We ain't gonna die out. People is goin' on—changin a little, maybe, but goin' right on."

I view Steinbeck's words, my mind drifts back to Ireland . . . and to that miraculous Shannon Pot that somehow never runs dry . . . indeed the term "little eddies" reminds me, along with the rain and the bogs, of what Concepta told me helped the Pot grow into the mighty Shannon. The next time a written word would conjure up thoughts for me of that ne'er dry pot, would be up in Vermont when Mike, the Texas preacher, would read from his wonderful book called *The Message*. There, in this modern English version of the New Testament, in the tale of Jesus and the Samaritan woman at the well, were the words,

"Everyone who drinks the water I give will never thirst again. The water I give will be an artesian spring within gushing fountains of endless life."

But as I think now of little Catherine, I recall how the pot was not on our itinerary that day Concepta drove me out to Black Lion in West Cavan . . . . the only reason we went there was because a co-worker friend of Concepta wanted her picture taken at the pot. And as fate would have it, to my, "Goodbye Margaret" when we dropped off this lovely lady, she said "It's funny a lot of people call me Margaret, but my name is Catherine."

Epilogue

90 days in a Life

Tuesday
September 11, 2001

On my way to take my mom out to get a few things at the market, as the day before's hot humid weather gave way to a clear, near perfect day, I quoted a line my dad used to say "this is truly a day that the Lord has made." My little guy query from back then, "but dad doesn't the Lord make EVERY day?" seemed especially appropriate because on this lovely Tuesday morning, as many as ten thousand people are dead as a result of terrorist attacks. The World Trade Center towers are rubble . . . a big chunk of the Pentagon destroyed. Two of the more visible symbols of American wealth and largesse are no more. The home of the American military is not even safe from attack.

The night before my good friend Feudi, the first other person to review this book, had told me that in its present form, I had something, but not a book. "Too much, too unrelated, too unclear"—the main complaints. And even as I knew much cleaning up was desperately needed, I did not know if I had it in me to make the many wholesale changes he deemed I needed to make a "book." Did today's events change anything?

The other epilogue I'd written about one month earlier, seemed insignificant now. But maybe it wasn't . . . .

August 7, 2001 was the one-year anniversary of the last time I got high, and it was not a good one for me . . . self-pity, lust and sloth kept me buried in the covers of my bed. But it was a much worse one for my good qigong friend Julio—for on that day, he took his own life.

The following day, 18 Israelis went down along with a suicide bomber—the camel's back-breaking straw that induced Israel to take over the PLO headquarters in Jerusalem and elsewhere. The "we no longer will retaliate violently for suicide bombing" policy the Jews had spoke of enacting about eight weeks prior, was now a distant memory. The push-shove was now so intense a new Middle East war seemed inevitable.

On Thursday August 9, the real IRA had agreed to decommission their weapons, a "we'll blink first" gesture that would finally get the stalled peace process flowing. But a week later, as the Northern Protestants had failed to bend likewise, the gesture was withdrawn . . . . I pray the Irish, from opposite sides of the fence of Christianity, are not headed down the same thorny path as the Jews and Arabs.

A quote I used in a paper a while back, came from Carolyn Myss's wonderful aforementioned Anatomy of the Spirit.

"Admittedly it is it is frightening to leave the familiar contents of one's life, even though one's life is desperately sad. But change is frightening and waiting for that feeling of safety to come along before one makes a move only results in more internal torment because the only way to acquire that feeling of security is to enter the whirlwind of change and come out the other end, feeling alive again."

My friend Julio was stuck in a job he hated. Irrepressible financial, romantic and existential woes were much the stuff of the contents of his life. Despite his fervent qigong and tai-chi practice, he obviously did not bask in the cool waters of Universal brotherhood that is our destiny. The branches of security he clung to, extended from the poisoned tree of his own 'less-than' psychosis . . . it was from that tree he was hung. "I like Jesus, but not religion," he had once said to me. Coming from South

America, where the Church hierarchy often walked hand-in-hand with repressive dictators, the 'not religion' part was understandable. But his connection with Jesus was not strong enough to ease his pain. He never was able, I suppose, to transfer that yoke.

I'd thought the 'we won't shove back' gesture by the Jews a while back would have been a good time for PLO leader Arafat to respond in kind, with a radical, different "thank you," along with a pronouncement and a course of action to fetter out the radical suicide crowd. His pronouncement to do that ferreting now, was too little, too late. I only hope cooler heads prevail among the IRA as the North Irish exhibit similar feet dragging.

Change, growth . . . acting and being different. The poor tortured rabbi from across the Delaware River in Cherry Hill, NJ last week read a statement about his only daughter, pregnant with what would have been his first grand child who was killed in the bomb blast in Tel Aviv. In it he said he hoped the Israeli government would do whatever necessary to safeguard its citizens . . . . a far cry from "Father forgive them for they know not what they do," or from the English woman who lost her son to an IRA bomb, but whose book about love and not hate, earned her a "keep the peace" award the Irish give out each year.

The post-practice discussion re Julio and his life and death last night shoved back and forth. My contention that his stark rejection that a Higher Power was the source of the qi had hastened his doom was out and out rejected by a Chinese friend. "The suicide rate in China is very low and there this Higher Power thing is almost universally rejected.". But a dear cooler head across the table suggested, "Yes but there they do believe in some form of a universal greater good . . . ". Seems to me, a lot of consternation and struggle revolves around whether or not capital letters are to be used as to the source of our qi, our brotherhood, our everything.

As a recovering addict and alcoholic, I fervently believe in the assessment that the addict or alcoholic, who does not change, will eventually drink or drug again . . . and that, in a lot of cases, to drink or drug again is to die. I also believe in AA's tried and true assessment that eventually the Power necessary to not take that first one must eventually come from a Source much Higher. As I sit here today, despite the fact that I have been a member of Alcoholics Anonymous for nine-and-a-half years now, for the first time since December of 1995, I can say I have been clean and sober for an entire year. Qigong helped me to get that year . . . so did Julio.

And so I will continue to imagine his qi as part of that which I take in when practicing . . . as I did last night in a practice that was very powerful for me. I will continue to pray for him and his family each day and each time I attend mass. And each day I will continue to try to be open and honest and kind to all I meet . . . I will continue to try to stay in the ever-changing, yet consistently loving and benevolent flow of life that sustains me.

Then and now. Last week the world looked on in horror at pictures of little school kids in Belfast scared near-to-death by the pipe-bombs hurled by "the other side." Todays' pictures were much more horrible. The live shots of the collapsing towers, of people jumping from buildings, of the second suicide plane's direct hit will remain with us forever. A "Day in Infamy" part II . . . but in 1941 the enemy had a face, a flag . . . . this one has only an ideal.

Nearly everybody pointed the finger at Osama bin Ladin as the only man with the power, money and connections to orchestrate an attack as sophisticated and deadly as this one. President Bush's promise to GET the killers was appropriate, but how many people really believe he can do it. It seems our insulation is evaporating. How do you GET an enemy as nebulous as hate—blind, indoctrinated, religiously fanatical hate?

Being that it is Tuesday, tonight I'll head over to Mike the Monk's to say the rosary. I expect this week there will be a big turnout. Among the things I pray for, besides all the victims and their families, will be that more and more people will turn to God for guidance and direction. I will offer thanksgiving that my sister Mary Ellen who works in Washington DC called a while ago to tell us that she was okay.

Much more of the arduous task I spoke of many months and many pages ago—that I DO the work to make this book a reality, still awaits.

From the church bells up the street, single solitary dongs have been sounding for almost an hour now. A death knell, I suppose . . . perhaps because of this out-of-character ringing, the birds outside are strangely quiet . . . .

* * *

Four days after the attack on America, after coming home from a very fun AA anniversary/dance at a local church, I wrote the following poem.

For Mom and Dad
On their 56th wedding anniversary

56 years—one heck of a long time
. . . . and yet compared to forever
quick'r than you
ken
spend you a dime

Does Eternity have some special place,
some more c'l'stial manor for a he and a
she
that WERE truly true? . . . for a mom
and a pop
who meant it fer sher when they said,
"til death do us thru"

I hope so, I'll bet so . . . .
(But sure as fer shootin'
I don't hardly know)

Life blabbers on . . . this crazy ol' world
seeming minus a clue . . .

a truly true two . . . now's
as'n'exihib't in a zoo

We clutch on to bods
like they are all that counts
. . . and as the carnaging mounts

we deny with elan'
the connect of the two . . .

but mom still a-round
and dad sadly not . . .
your lives featured not
this new-fangled rot

so thanks for the truth
that you gave unto us . . .

your pureness shall live
. . . ong after we're dust

Walking to my car after the party, I came across a life-sized crucifix. There at its foot, for the first time since the 'attack' did the emotions take me over. Shakes and convulsive tears overcame me—for them and their families, for Him and for how far we have drifted from the ideal He set for us. Perhaps the salvation that will elude us without His intercession, is that of this tawdry, tenuous, temporal world.

Tuesday
October 9, 2001

In a little while my mom will be coming home from an overnight stay at a local hospital, a stay precipitated by some severe chest pains. This is the second of these stays in the last 10 weeks. By last night, though, she seemed well on her way to recovery. She had a lot of company for her brief stay. Me, my sister Sally, my brother Mark and my niece Elizabeth all spent part of their day with her. She will be fine.

At 10:30 AM, I'll be heading over to Resurrection to attend the funeral of a good AA friend—a member of my AA family—who died of an overdose last week. That last time I saw this handsome, fun-loving and very funny Irish-American, when I asked him if he'd like me to take him through the steps, he quoted the "What have I got to lose?" line I'd written in the "Back to Basics—learn the steps," flyer I'd given him.

If you are new in the fellowship . . . if you are having trouble with relapse . . . if your quality of life has not improved . . . if the obsession to get loaded is still your constant companion . . . we suggest you try working the steps with us. All you have to lose is your racy head, your irritability and your own willful discontent.

We both knew he wasn't serious though.

The time I'd seen him before that, it was one week before I had my one year sober . . . and though he was nowhere near as close to me as are many other people in AA, he was the only one to call and congratulate me on that one-year day. He was that nice a guy. The odd thing was, even though he'd been around AA for over 15 years, and even though he'd accumulated more than 10 years sober one time, he'd never worked the steps. And for the last several years, like me, he had had a real difficult time staying sober.

It was an odd series of days for me. As I was last night trying to piece together some writing about them, I got very stuck. So like a true red-blooded American I popped on the tube. There I happened to catch, for the third week in a row, one of this fall's new drama series. The lure of seeing the very attractive former second fiddle from another show as the top banana in this one, worked with me. In last night's episode the groundwork was further laid for the "relationship" that will probably eventually develop between she and a co-worker. That this co-worker happens to be black adds some intrigue and "color" to a tried and true formula from many other shows. The friction between the lead and the live-in "friend" of her post-60-yr-old-forced-into-retirement-ex-cop widowed father, adds another somewhat different element to this show.

Last night's episode featured a wise, warm elderly woman's performing euthanasia on her husband and then suicide on herself being referred to as "the most beautiful romantic thing ever." Also on tap was the brutal mutilating prison murder committed by a fanatically reverent Christian inmate. He'd murdered a female guard because he'd seen her having sex with a different guard in the chapel he'd built. "I could not allow sinning to go on in God's house," he said, "She's safe now, is in heaven, because I held her heart in my hand and she was forgiven."

If you're into a straighter hairdo, you can tune into another gorgeous co-star now being the lead on Tuesday nights. In this one, she's a *Philly* lawyer with a partner who in week one has "in-a-flash" sex with an assistant DA in a court ante-room . . . and in week two she puts up with her cold and mean Irish Catholic mom's "I'll bet you don't even make him say his prayers anymore", as mom charges her own daughter top-dollar babysitting fees.

Last night's rosary walk was a very short one—it was cold and I had not dressed warmly enough. The flood of tears this time though, had nothing to do with joy, they had to do with the enormity of the task ahead.

On the national front, the retaliatory bombing of Afghanistan began in earnest two days ago. Bin Laden promised death to the Americans because God is on his side. Jerry Falwell says we are being punished for the gays, lesbians and our permissive lifestyles. Anyone with half a brain knows that they are both dangerously wrong. But folks with good, functioning *full* brains do not seem to perceive the subtle poison permeating our culture. Marshall McLuhan who told us, "the medium *is* the message," said it all. And every night and every day, in the soaps, dramas and comedies, we are inundated with the message that the squalid excess of the current American way of life is not only perfectly okay, but also that it is hip and cool and desirable. Soon enough, this silly "praying thing" the "Attack on America" precipitated will subside and church folk will return to their proper perches—naïve, insipid little morons like MASH's Father Mulcahy at their best, and deranged fanatical killers at their worst. The indoctrination of the *real* powers to be into the minds of the people will go on undisturbed.

As the name of a *physical* poison called *Anthrax* begins to fill the airwaves, the tragic fact of the matter remains that unless we Americans realize that WE, as a people, also NEED TO CHANGE, then all this praying and chanting of *God Bless America,* will have gone for naught. Indeed, until and unless we realize that it is NOT okay to go on stuffing our appetites, either at the expense of our neighbor across the street or across the ocean, then this awful fear, hate and unrest we are all now feeling, will end up being *our* constant companion.

* * *

The crickets crick outside my window. At Mike the monk's tonight, a few different members mentioned my AA friend Kevin in their intentions. There was also much talk of the fear of the pervading evil that has penetrated our shores.

I'd expect crickets can survive a lot, that it'll take a whole lot to get them to shut up. "Without man, nature would go on in all its violence and beauty . . ." indeed. Tonight's stroll won't include a rosary, but will involve a stop down the local ATM machine because I am outta dough.

This Friday night, on my dad's 88th birthday, the McGowan family picnic meeting will take place here. Because of the "attack" we are being forced to move out of the Naval Depot picnic site that was perfect for us. (Including being nice'n'cheap!) I'm betting though, that come next June, that even thought the good ol' US of A will have maybe absorbed another roundhouse or two, the picnic will go on. And maybe more people will take note of the big flag hanging behind the photos being taken, maybe we'll even make a blow-up of the eloquent piece our grand-uncle Jim probably wrote about it. But I know someone else better be in charge of doing that, cuz I *know, fer sherrr* I'll never get around to it . . . .

Acknowledgements/Afterword

Easter time 2003

In the seeming eternity between the ending of this book and the getting it to publication, a lot happened. First and foremost, I stayed sober. All bets (and writing) are off if that were not the case. There are now four that I know of *Back to Basics* meetings in the Philadelphia area. I am involved with one we got started in January '03 in the Saint Anne's school-next the church where Peter and Sarah were wed in 1883. Very cool indeed.

In February I went down to Towson, Md. to help James Houck celebrate his 97th birthday. Not long after, a clogged intestine landed him in the hospital. But now he is out and slowly recuperating. I suppose good physical health is another benefit of living a life trying to do as God would have us do. On the other end of that pendulum, I was told that the liberal Cardinal Maritni, who was passed over for a post leading to the papacy, is suffering from Alzheimer's. Perhaps one more scalp for the velvet sash of Ratzinger and the boys.

As for the book, when my writing 'ace in the hole' from New York chose to not have her card played, the publication process became much more of a chore than did the writing part. My dear friend Jenn, a *gojus baby* herself I might add (I *better* add!), did yeoman's work in producing an attractive manuscript. My buddies, Mitch and Johnny B, helped a lot in this process. My old U of A writing instructor, Alexandra Grillikis, charged me a fraction of what she could have doing the first real professional edit of the work. Finding out up close and personal why one Penn professor called my punctuation "anarchic", she turned an unorganized hodgepodge of observations into something resembling a book. I was saddened and shocked to find that this wonderful author and teacher and kind and gentle soul, passed away from cancer in February. Her *Yin Fire* book was one of five finalists for a prestigious award that is given out each year for gay and lesbian literature. My debt to her now *is* forever.

I am also indebted to my uncle Jim Flynn, my aunt Betty and uncle Jim, uncle Ed (all McGowans), my aunt Mary and uncle Cy Ciboldi, indeed to all my family for the big and little tidbits of information they shared with me. Down in Port Richmond, among others, the charming—now 87-year-old Annette Boyce is one of several people who offered fond reminders of the old days. Back in the fall/winter of '98, I never really thought my going around to various aunts and uncles would some day turn into this.

As for the publishing process, Michael Washburn an editor from Philadelphia and Dawn Sefarian, one from New York, were kind enough to read one of the earlier manuscripts—and though they both found the book the 'wrong fit' for their respective houses, their encouragement and positive feedback, helped lift my spirits immensely. Bill Thompson, an editor from New York, also offered some timely and worthwhile suggestions. I finally hired *Exlibris* to put the book together for me.

As for the world:

The IRA DID apologize—'for any non-combatants killed in the struggle for freedom' were close to the exact words. The Protestant North Ireland government was so impressed that a bit down the road, they chose to raid Sein Fein offices all over the North, eventually leading to the dissolution of the Catholic-Protestant power sharing general assembly. Several months later, a day or two after President Bush and Prime Minister Blair met to discuss the fate of post-Saddam Iraq, Blair and Birdie Ahern did *not* announce an expected timetable for restoration of the government. Five year later, I wonder how Angela Gaffney's Orange "marching season" border, the one whose life had become livable because of the Good Friday accord, was taking all this in.

Oh yeah, there was another Persian Gulf war—the US and Britain led a coalition unapproved by the UN that overthrew the sadistic dictator Saddam Hussein. But then in a gesture further undermining the power and capability of the supposed worldwide association dedicated to peace and equality, they let it be known the UN would have only marginal influence in setting up the new Iraq. American corporations, including one closely associated with Vice-President Dick Cheney, slobbered at the mouth, waiting for contracts to serve as 'rebuilders of the infrastructure'.

Bush was also pushing through a huge tax cut proposal that even a majority of Americans opposed. Further deference by our *Christian* president to the *haves* of the corporate world—his staunch supporters. And meanwhile on the other side of the aisle, even as the war was kicking up steam, the Democrats staged a filibuster to prevent the voting on the appointment of a conservative judge who might eventually shift the balance so that Roe vs. Wade might be overturned. Two thousand years after Christ, the strongest nation in the world, one our Founding Fathers donned a "Nation Under God", has one political party committed to militaristic domination and the preservation of the holdings of the wealthy, and one most united in preserving the right of a woman to abort her unborn.

Alas even as Bush's righteous judges and *right* hand followers are adamant about protecting the lives of the unborn, their even greater concern for the wealthy and the weapon-makers, relegates how many of these saved embryos to lives sealed in incubators of poverty and non-opportunity? Either implicitly or explicitly, from the bulging coffers of Lockheed Martin and them all, to the slick hands of the lobbyists, to the pockets of the lawmakers—the war machine churns on. As military spending remains the consistent untouchable in both the parties prospected budgets; the trickle down to the really poor is being reduced to drips. But then again perhaps the poor are a necessary part of the process—the flesh and blood raw materials needed to aim the guns and pull the triggers. One wonders how many of the judges, congressmen and senators who cheerleaded this war, will lose sons and daughters in the stifling sands of Iraq.

Then to add to the madness Pope John Paul II issued that Holy Thursday encyclical with pre-Vatican II-like language reiterating the policy that Catholics cannot receive sacraments in non-Catholic churches, and that those 'living in sin' are banned from receiving communion. It seems Rome, in the light of the devastating priestly pedophilia scandals that hit last year, instead of using this opportunity to look at themselves and some of their questionable doctrine, has, instead, gone to a 'let's button down the hatches', reactionary philosophy. The appointment of Irish Bishop Brian Farrell, an archconservative friend of Cardinal Connell as Secretary of the Pontifical Council for Promoting Christian Unity, points strongly towards this further shift to the right. *The Irish Times* went so far as to say,

. . . this appointment has led to the uncharitable suggestion that this was akin to appointing the DUP's Peter Robinson as secretary to a would-be organisation for "Promoting Irish Unity". It is felt that Bishop Farrell's view of Christian unity would not be dissimilar to Robinson's view of Irish unity—both could take place when "the others" became Roman Catholic/British.

In American terms, it might be like naming a governor whose state had an abysmal ecological record, like say, Christie Whitman, as head of the Environmental department.

* * *

It is Holy Saturday here in Philly-town. Mom is 84 now and the diabetes is effecting mostly her eyesight. I was more than a bit worried that she'd be okay taking the train down to DC to visit with my sister Mary Ellen for a few days. But when I got home Thursday night my brother Tony'd left a note saying the trip went very smoothly. Mom had sat next to a black man and talked Sixers all the way down. A younger black fellow 'with those rows in his hair' carried her bag off the train. Seems mom has a couple of new "bus buddies."

I wrote a very brief "to-the point" picnic letter. Attendance has really dropped off since the '00 event. People's lives are so full. We'll be doing Easter dinner again at my brother's country club . . . me and his daughter, and my godchild, Kiera, walked together in the St Patrick's Day parade a month ago . . . she's becoming a real good Irish dancer. I've not written back to Ireland since Christmas. I'm not sure when I'll be able to return in person, but I know for certain that eventually I will.

Jim and Maura Hannigan's lovely daughter Ailbee died on an operating table in the summer of '02; my buddy Whale succumbed to cancer the following fall . . .

Father Mac, from down St. Malachy's, Easter card came yesterday. His own poem is the verse:

The exhaustion of late winter melting into spring
I blame on the endlessness of Lent
Too much purple so many laments that
I am helpless for Holy Week say nothing
of the again endless Alleluias of Easter

The apostle Thomas and his two stories are comfort
We know his mind: undone by Good Friday
He wants no illusions no getting up and down
as though nothing has happened.
At least let me nurse my wounds, embrace
the carrion comfort some feast on lifelong

Yet he rose to the occasion Brought his hurt faith
out for healing: by whose wounds we are healed
His earlier exclamation : let us go and die with him!
Here he is . . . . still among the Eleven . . . waiting . . .
Faith can be like that: going through
the motion in hope of better times.

Christmas 2003

Christmas season '03 brought news of a 'mad cow' in America's Pacific Northwest. A Palestinian suicide bomber killing four in Tel Aviv shattered a period of relative calm in Palestine and Israel. The blast was supposedly in retaliation for an Israeli attack on a Hamas militant that also killed four. Tit for tat near exactly in this skirmish. Five more Americans were killed in ambushes in Iraq. Our national 'danger code' has been moved up a notch as there is fear another major September 11-type attack might be in the offing. It seems our government/military is feasting on our fears.

On May 2, 2004, I'll be part of an "Interfaith walk for Jewish/ Muslim reconciliation." One our way from a mosque to a synagogue, we'll stop at a Catholic church to pray. There's a group conducting fundraising 'house parties' to finance the rebuilding Palestinians *and* Israelis are doing to resurrect Palestinian homes destroyed by Israel. Via a program last fall where a Jew, Muslim and Christian from Jerusalem spoke of the struggle for peace, I learned of a Israeli settlement called "the Oasis of Peace" where 45 mixed Jew and Muslim families choose to live together . . . and of their school where an equal amount of Jewish and Muslim kids come in to learn about the world and each other. A huge interfaith center is being planned for the Fatima site where Mary appeared in 1917. But a fundamentalist Fatima organization is trying feverishly to prevent this desecration of the name of Mary and Catholicism.

I watched the "America is the greatest!" finale of a Kennedy Center award show last night—I thought of the five dead soldiers and all their fallen brethren and of the countless dead and homeless Iraqis that are direct consequences of the war we initiated. I thought of the hundreds of dead Chinese from a natural gas explosion and the explanation that the safety restrictions are lagging behind the *progress* on the vast Sino mainland.

The Yin and Yang on this crazy rock we call earth spinning like a whirling dervish. The friend/sponsee who called me last night, drunk as a lord, was not around for me to take him to the Veterans Administration detox center this morning. He wasn't home yet from the woman's house he'd ventured to after he got off the phone with me.

In about eight weeks, I go back to Ireland for five 'will be very rushed' days. Aer Lingus' incredibly cheap winter sale fare promotion allows only a stay that long.

I'll be flying on Sarah's 145th birthday.

Monday May 3, 2004
Philadelphia, Pa.

In the sunshine of God's Love

To take each moment and live each moment
In peace eternally,
Let there be peace on earth and let
It begin with me.

It was a full-throated crescendo hit by the 400 to 500 people near filling the beautiful St. Augustine's Church at 4th and Vine. Was not the 'some singing, most not' you hear at masses on Sunday morning. But on this late Sunday afternoon, there was something else very different about this congregation. Probably only about 10% of the attendees were Catholic. For this was not Sunday mass being celebrated this day, it was stop two of Philadelphia's version of the *Interfaith Peace Walk for Muslim and Jewish Reconciliation*, and of the congregation, more than 80% was probably Jewish and Muslim. It was very cool.

But it was not this song that moved me most while I sat there. Nor was it the brief, beautiful and poignant welcome by Father

Mestardi, the Augustinian pastor of St Augustine's, nor the refreshments and warm welcome provided by the church's large Filipino community—what it was that had me near quaking with emotion or even vibrations was the chant from the Koran by the Iman of the Al Asqua Mosque where our walk had begun. To *feel* the Spirit is very special. Later walking with some Muslim friends, I was told that is exactly the effect the chanting of the Koran can bring on . . . that it is a lyrical, poetic gift from God, meant to be sung. The things you learn walking three some miles with new friends from different faiths.

Sitting next to me in the pew way up in the front of the Church, was the charming little daughter of the Iman. Way back at our second planning meeting at the mosque, this devout somewhat orthodox child of God wondered what a non-Muslim like me was doing at *her* house of worship. But she surely mellowed as we and her two little buddies chatted a bit—to the extent that now *we* are buds of sorts. She even invited me to the open spot right next to her in that up front pew. Dad really doesn't speak English it turns out, but as we walked along and I asked an older sister to translate the 'tingly good feeling' his Koran chant had given me, his bow and "thank you very much" was as crystal clear as it was sincere. Like the manna falling from the skies sustaining God's children walking through the desert all those centuries ago, the sense of gratitude and open, honest, inquisitive sharing was part and parcel of our little caravan this blessed first Sunday of May, 2004.

Something a bit more concrete than gratitude also was with us as we strolled along. Bright beautiful sunshine. The forecast that had called for rain turned out to be wrong. The clouds gave way just about as we left Al Asqua, and bright sunshine visited upon us actually for the majority of our trip. Indeed the sun burnt, covered only by a muscle shirt, shoulders of a young friend of mine from Alcoholics Anonymous, who was one of the walkers in our eclectic beyond belief group, was testimony of that prevailing sun. His name is Eddie, and when I told him of the 'good vibrations' I'd felt when the Iman had chanted at St. A's he said he felt them too. Just back a week from his latest relapse, he really does seem a lot more open and welcoming than at any of the many times he's come around before. That closed 'no one in invited in' look that was always on his face, somehow seems missing this time. I suggested that maybe this grace that seemed to shake into him this day, might finally be the beginning of his being able to sustain.

"The forecast calls for pain" is a lyric from a song I've heard. On the Internet news headlines, as is near every day now, there are more dead in the torn-apart Iraq we chose to invade 14 months ago. Even as we walked more allegations were coming out re the torture inflicted upon Iraqi prisoners by American soldiers. Palestinian snipers murdered a pregnant woman and her 4 children—the retaliatory air strikes are already taking place. How much more pain and death and hatred are in the forecast with the push-shove diplomacy that seems the prevailing strategy for all the heads of state (and religions) making decisions in the Muslim-Jewish conflict? *Peace on earth and let it begin with me.* Our group is specifically about proving dialogue can take place amongst us.

So now the walk is over. We are city # four, along with Albuquerque, Tucson and New York, who've had peace walks. Spokane, Washington and then a trip 'cross the border to Western Canada are up next. The dream is to coordinate and eventually have all the walks take place on the same day. Already there is a planned brainstorming session as to where to go next with our particular little group. Both Rabbi Lynn Abraham and Iman Abdul Rauf, the Albuquerque, New Mexico clerics who began this reconciliation peace walk movement, and who so lovingly and expertly led us today, strongly suggested some form of community action to keep the juices flowing—that just *talking* about what to do will not sustain us.

Rabbi Lynn actually got the idea for the walk by a group of Buddhist monks who walk miles and miles from city to city purely in the cause for peace. I recall a conversation I had with a Buddhist one time and to my, "but don't you believe Jesus was the Son of God?" query, he replied, "but aren't you and I also sons of God?" I chatted with a Hindu scholar who hopped on board our walk coming from an interfaith forum right in town, telling her how much I admired her Gandhi's statement that "God has no religion." I sat with a big, bearded, very Abraham-looking rabbi and three black Muslim clerics from New Jersey at Congregation Rodeph Shalom at Broad and Green where the powerful closing ceremony and a sorely needed buffet of cheeses, fruits, humus, soft pretzels et al was presented.

My God what a magnificent day!

A bit after 5 PM now—the Monday after. Yesterday's rain waited until today. The games I was supposed to umpire are postponed, thus I'll be able to go say the rosary with my dear Guatemalan friends whose son Diego's first communion mass yesterday morning set the tone for the triumph of the day that was to follow. (The wet hitting my windshield driving there, in fact, was the only I witnessed the entire day.) The second reading at mass was 7: 9-10, 17 from Revelations:

> *"I, John, looked and there before me was a great multitude that no one could count, from every nation, tribe, people and language, standing before the throne in front of the Lamb. They were wearing white robes and were holding palm branches in their hands. And they cried out in a loud voice:*
>
> *"Salvation belongs to our God,*
> *who sits on His throne,*
> *and to the Lamb*
>
> *then one of the elders said:*

For the Lamb at the center of the
throne will be their shepherd
he will lead them to springs of living water
and God will wipe away every tear
from their eyes."

Probably 90% of us followed the directions to wear white yesterday. White—the color of surrender, the color of peace . . .

April 19, 2005
The day they elected a new pope

On this day when Cardinal Ratzinger was elected pope, an author/friend whom I thought might have been helpful in getting this book publicized, cancelled and did not re-schedule the breakfast meeting we'd planned for the next day. Disappointment # *ad nauseum* as far as getting this thing into the public eye.

On the day before the good cardinal became Pope Benedict XVI, his no holds barred sermon included the following:

> *"Having a clear faith, based on the creed of the church, is often labeled today as fundamentalism. Whereas relativism, which is letting oneself, be tossed and 'swept along by every wind of teaching,' looks like the only attitude acceptable to today's standards.*

> *"We are moving toward a dictatorship of relativism which does not recognize anything as for certain and which has as its highest goal one's own ego and one's own desires."*

A commentator on CSN conjectured that the new pope would not mind seeing a smaller Catholic Church, as long as it maintains doctrinal purity. I remembered reading a quote in Mattingly's column by a popular, conservative priest from Washington DC that went something like, "there is a name for those who disagree with the Church's teaching – they're called Protestants." I remember Bob Dylan many, many years ago, bidding adieu to the whole political scene – saying it was too corrupt and far gone to do anything about it – that he was going to take his 'endless tour' to the people.

The people. Last week Father Mac from down at St. Malachy's told me JP II's problems with the Latin American church were about it becoming the 'church of the people' and not of the hierarchy. On Saturday last, I was in Brooklyn experiencing firsthand what the *Iglesia de la Gente* looked like. There in a dirt-poor parish called *Transfiguration,* former and present Latin American refugees treated we *Jesu Caritas Society* followers of the spirituality of a turn-of-the-century Frenchman named Charles de Foucald (who chose to live his life among Muslims in Algeria), retreatants like we were long-lost relatives. 17 separate parish groups meet weekly in family homes praying and living lives in accord with the gospel of Jesus. *The people* surviving, indeed. Carl Sandburg and Ma Joad were right.

* * *

Just like four years ago, late April finds Philly's Seventy-Sixer basketball team getting ready for the playoffs. Allen Iverson after the playoff-spot-clinching game last night spoke of how the team stuck together even during the low points of the season…and how God had made him to play basketball. He had a banner year as he and the new coach, my old St Joe fellow alumna, Jimmy O'Brien, who came home to coach the team this year, hit it off famously. Mom is 86 now and very excited.

She and a bunch of the family will help my cousin Jimmy celebrate his 50th birthday, Kentucky Derby Day, heading on a bus down to the slots and horse races at Delaware Park.

The Interfaith peace walk this year is May 22nd. Father Mac's St M's is the Christian/Catholic stop. They put me in charge of the logistics committee and I haven't done a single logistic thing yet. Yet the walk will go on, I'll get some things done as the deadline approaches and others will pick up the slack. Same for the world, same for the people. On *Judging Amy* tonight I heard of a group of kids called the *straight edges* who came out of the punk rock scene and who do not drink, smoke, do drugs, eat meat or engage in premarital sex. I'm betting nary a single adult had anything to do with their formation.

La gente sobre vivira indeed.

* * *

Oh and finally, the 1904 family picture has ended up in one more place. On a wall as you enter Dublin Airport, in the middle of a genealogy mural, there it sits. Honest.

BVG